H
03/04

FROM THE OUTSIDE IN

PRINCETON STUDIES IN AMERICAN POLITICS:
HISTORICAL, INTERNATIONAL, AND COMPARATIVE
PERSPECTIVES

SERIES EDITORS

IRA KATZNELSON, MARTIN SHEFTER, THEDA SKOCPOL

FROM THE OUTSIDE IN

WORLD WAR II AND THE AMERICAN STATE

Bartholomew H. Sparrow

PRINCETON UNIVERSITY PRESS   PRINCETON, NEW JERSEY

Copyright © 1996 by Princeton University Press
Published by Princeton University Press, 41 William Street,
Princeton, New Jersey 08540
In the United Kingdom: Princeton University Press, Chichester,
West Sussex
All Rights Reserved

Library of Congress Cataloging-in-Publication Data

Sparrow, Bartholomew H., 1959–
From the outside in : World War II and the American state /
Bartholomew H. Sparrow.
p.   cm. — (Princeton studies in American politics)
Includes bibliographical references (p.   ) and index.
ISBN 0-691-04404-X (cl : alk. paper)
1. United States—Politics and government—1933–1945.   2. World
War, 1939–1945—United States.   I. Title.   II. Series.
JK271.S715   1996
320.973′09′044—dc20   95-34357   CIP

This book has been composed in Caledonia

Princeton University Press books are printed
on acid-free paper and meet the guidelines
for permanence and durability of the Committee
on Production Guidelines for Book Longevity
of the Council on Library Resources

Printed in the United States of America by
Princeton Academic Press

10 9 8 7 6 5 4 3 2 1

To my grandparents

Contents

Figures

Tables

Preface

IT IS perhaps ironic to be writing on the international events of the 1940s with the unraveling of the postwar, bipolar world. When a former chairman of the Joint Chiefs of Staff says that he no longer considers the Russians our enemies, a reader might legitimately ask, why an investigation into the nineteen-*forties*—what with the disintegration of the former Soviet Union, the new independence of the Eastern European states, and the uncertain and unsteady unification of Europe? Domestically, the parallels to the 1940s are at least as strained, with the erosion of the party system, the emergence of a service-oriented economy, and the pervasiveness of computer and video technologies. Contemporary American politics, foreign and domestic, bears scant resemblance to that of the 1940s.

What I hope to make clear is that an examination of the major programs and policies of the 1940s contributes invaluably to an understanding of the distinctive and enduring characteristics of postwar American government and society. Consider that the United States in 1940 was just emerging from the Great Depression, with 14 percent unemployment, and was still very much isolationist. By mid-year 1950, however, the Marshall Plan was well under way, NATO had been established, and the U.S. government had entered the Korean War; the United States was ineluctably part of the world. On the domestic front, the economy had begun its sustained growth of the next few decades, the United States had an emerging welfare state, and suburbanization was spreading rapidly; a comparison with the changes of the 1940s makes more recent developments in American politics and society appear incremental, even preordained.

Insofar as the effects of World War II on domestic policy domains have been researched, however, they have been viewed as aberrations in American political development rather than as formative influences on politics and government. Moreover, the features of this institutional development—how politics and government changed as they did in a time of world war—have been understudied. Yet world wars and other severe national crises may exert systematic government-wide shocks able to redirect the paths of political development, and there may be regularities in the institutional change occurring at a time of crisis.

Another reason for this project is to see what leverage could be gained through the use of the "state." While American political culture has been hostile to the concept of the state, and while the actual policies and programs of U.S. national government have differed from those of other advanced industrial states, social scientists, historians, journalists, and others have increasingly used the notion of the state to refer to American government and political authority. This leads to a certain ambivalence on my part: on the one hand, I am aware of the difficulty of using the state as a handle for the intricate and frequently disconnected policies and administrative bodies making up the U.S. government; on the other hand, the use of the state brings a focus and level of analysis to the study of government that goes beyond that typically afforded by separate studies of the presidency, Congress, public administration, political parties, interest groups, or the courts. This project is thus an experiment: only provisionally do I offer a definition of the state (where there are many other possible definitions of the state) and only provisionally do I propose an explanation of the whys and hows of state-building (where there are other models of institutional change). The reader may judge my success.

A further provisional quality of the project comes from the problems of data collection and the ascertainment of the political history of the 1940s. Data on specific budgets and employed personnel were frequently missing (such as the budgets and personnel specifically involved with Navy procurement) or were inconsistently available; still other records, such as the papers of Sen. Walter George (Chairman of the Senate Finance Committee), were either discarded or destroyed. Oral histories were uneven in quality, often highly selective, and frequently contradictory. The experience of another researcher is to the point: "The writer was given access to Chairman Davis' [National War Labor Board] files. These documents proved to be very few after October, 1941 and throughout, there were gaps at important points. This situation was brought to the attention of Dr. George Taylor, then Chairman of the Board. He stated that the important decisions were deliberately undocumented and he refused to discuss these issues on the ground that they were 'too hot to talk about.'" My hope is that future scholarship will be able to fill the silences in the record.

My debts are many. John F. Padgett, my thesis advisor, was part of this project from its inception as a dissertation proposal; he has taught me much. I am also grateful to Charles Lipson and J. Mark Hansen for their comments on and contributions to the manuscript. And I have particular appreciation for the help of David Greenstone, who was warmly encouraging at a time when the project was most uncertain, as a dissertation proposal.

I am doubly indebted to Ira Katznelson. As a member of my dissertation committee, Ira offered helpful criticism and direction despite the fact that he joined the committee late and was also serving as the Dean of the New School's Graduate Faculty in Political and Social Science at the time. His pointed and perceptive comments on the dissertation had much to do with the present framing of my arguments. As an editor of the Princeton Studies in American Politics series—wearing his other hat—Ira helped the organization and clarity of my arguments. I am also grateful to the other Princeton editors, especially Theda Skocpol as a series editor, and to the two external reviewers for their comments and recommendations. Others at Princeton University Press have assisted directly in turning the manuscript into a book. I am especially grateful to Eric Van Tassel for his careful copyediting.

Walter Dean Burnham had the patience to read the entire thesis and offered valuable comments. Edward Berkowitz, Mark Leff, and Jacob Vander Meulen gave detailed responses to several of the chapters, and saved me from numerous mistakes and omissions.

The staffs of the Franklin D. Roosevelt Presidential Library, the University of Chicago's Joseph Regenstein Library, the Harry S. Truman Presidential Library, and The University of Texas's Perry-Castañeda Library were unfailingly generous with their assistance and patience. I especially want to thank Dennis Bilger, Jann Hoag, Irwin Mueller, and Lis Safly at the Truman Library. They and the others at the Truman Library made my visits there at once productive and enjoyable.

The personnel of the Office of Naval History at the Washington Navy Yard, the National Record Center in Suitland, Maryland, and the National Archives in Washington, D.C., were also consistently giving of their time and expertise. Among the staff at the National Archives, I am especially grateful to Rich Boylan, Rich Conn, Bill Sherman, Aloha South, and Barry Zerby. At the Wisconsin State Historical Society archives, I am indebted to Cindy Knight. At The University of Texas at Austin, Suzanne Colwell helped to prepare the manuscript and Carolyn Shaw checked the figures in my tables.

The Harry S. Truman Library Institute twice supported my research: first with a research grant, and then with a generous "Scholar's Award." The Scholar's Award allowed me return to the Truman Library and gave me time in the fall of 1992 to work on the manuscript. The University of Texas's University Research Institute supported my writing and research with a larger grant for the summer of 1992 and with a smaller grant in the spring of 1992. The Papers and Diaries of James V. Forrestal and the Ferdinand Eberstadt Papers, at Princeton University's Seeley Mudd Manuscript Library, are cited by permission of Princeton University Library.

My friends and colleagues have, as always, been a source of ideas, friendly criticism, and support. I would particularly like to thank J. Michael Dennis, Christopher Ansell, Stephen Young, Rebecca Schiff, Blair Gifford, Doug Sun, Zoltan Barany, John Coleman, Rudy de la Garza, Gary Freeman, Andrea Prestridge, and Brian Roberts.

Finally, I am deeply grateful for the support of my parents, brothers and sisters, and grandparents. William R. Huntington and Catherine G. Sparrow made this possible in ways they will never know.

The shortcomings are mine alone.

FROM THE OUTSIDE IN

1

Introduction

> In a true sense, there are no longer nondefense
> expenditures. It is a part of our war effort to
> maintain civilian services which are essential to
> the basic needs of human life.
> —President Franklin D. Roosevelt,
> 6 January 1942

> War does not always give democratic societies
> over to military government, but it must
> invariably and immeasurably increase the
> powers of civilian government; it must almost
> automatically concentrate the direction of all
> men and the control of all things in the hands
> of the government. If that does not lead to
> despotism by sudden violence, it leads men
> gently in that direction by their habits.
> —Alexis de Tocqueville

STATES MAKE WARS; wars make states. The political development of the United States is no exception. The War of Independence brought the United States into being; the Civil War established the politics and government of the United States for much of the nineteenth and early twentieth centuries; and the First World War spurred the development of the twentieth-century American state. But most important for understanding American political development in the latter half of the twentieth century is the Second World War. World War II jolted a moribund national economy out of the Depression, led to the creation of international systems of trade, investment, foreign exchange, and diplomacy, and established the United States as a political, economic, and military superpower.

Far less appreciated, however, have been the effects of the Second World War on domestic programs and, specifically, on the political institutions associated with American exceptionalism: the limited and delayed provision of social services, the politically weak labor movement, the low tax rates and the reliance on income taxation, the absence of strong fiscal policy, and the large defense sector.[1] The *intra*national American state, thought to be the legacy of the New Deal, was systematically affected by the *extra*national factors of World War II and its aftermath; the American state was built from the outside in.

To say that the mid- and late-twentieth-century American state was forged through the crisis of global warfare is, however, to say little by itself. We need to determine that what actually happened during the war years had important and lasting effects on U.S. politics and government; we have to find out the extent to which international crises and world wars more generally affect American political development; and we have to clarify what is meant by the "state"—given the ambiguity of the term—and by "state-building"—how it is that crises transform states.

Many social scientists and historians acknowledge the importance of the Second World War in the establishment of international system after 1945, and many theorists of international relations recognize that wars may reorient the international system; but few social scientists or historians have looked at how the shocks of the Second World War affected the United States internally.[2] The conventional wisdom is that the programs of the New Deal survived the war and continued on in the postwar years, as evidenced by the public ownership of electric utilities (1933), the regulation of the securities industry (1933), the introduction of the social security system (1935), the guarantee of the right of workers to collective bargaining (1935), the provision of unemployment insurance (1938), and the deliberate use of deficit spending for economic stimulation (1938).[3]

[1] For a review of "exceptionalism," see Ira Katznelson, *City Trenches* (Chicago: University of Chicago Press, 1981), 7–17. Also see the essays in Byron E. Shafer, ed., *Is America Different?* (Oxford: Clarendon Press, 1991).

[2] Peter Gourevitch and Stephen Krasner explore the "second image reversed" phenomenon, in which international variables (the third image) affect unit level outcomes (the second image) (Gourevitch, "The Second Image Reversed: The International Sources of Domestic Politics," *International Organization* 32 [1978]: 881–911; Krasner, "Approaches to the State: Alternative Conceptions and Historical Dynamics," *Comparative Politics* 23 [1984]: 223–46). The image-phrasing follows from Kenneth Waltz (*Man, the State and War* [New York: Columbia University Press, 1959]).

For a recent exception, see Gregory Hooks, *Forging the Military-Industrial Complex: World War II's Battle of the Potomac* (Urbana: University of Illinois Press, 1991). Hooks also studies the effect of World War II on national government. Hooks argues that the New Deal was folded into an emergent national security state that placed the Pentagon at the center of national planning.

[3] See, for example, Frank Freidel, "The New Deal: Laying the Ground for Modern America," in Wilbur Cohen, ed., *The Roosevelt New Deal: A Program Assessment Fifty Years After* (Austin: Lyndon Baines Johnson Library, Lyndon B. Johnson School of Public Affairs, 1986), 3–18.

The argument here, however, is that the creation (to borrow Dean Acheson's term) brought about by the Second World War was as much evident in the institutions of domestic government as in international relations.[4] The effect of World War II was to at once delay further reforms of the social security system, cause a small expansion of the budget and staff of the Bureau of Old-Age and Survivors Insurance in relation to other social security programs, and allow for other social provisions to displace federally guaranteed social provisions. Between the rise in employment resulting from the war and the increase in non-government social programs resulting from the wartime policies, social security—the "social insurance" component of government social provisions—became better rooted among employees and employers, and better established as federal policy. Yet the social security program that was becoming better supported and better administered was one that had been directed away from redistribution and was distinctly late in coming.

The war further resulted in greater intervention by the federal government in labor-management relations, beyond anything seen in the 1930s. It brought on large increases in the number of labor-management disputes that were subject to government mediation, caused the government to seize industrial facilities, and resulted in the growth of the agencies regulating labor-management relations. Spurred on by the wartime emergency, the labor boards likewise improved their procedures for handling petitions and settling disputes. The war forced the Roosevelt Administration to seek the cooperation of the AFL and CIO, and top union officials worked closely with the Roosevelt Administration and the Democratic party.[5] The early 1940s marked the transition of American labor from being a social movement to becoming one of many influential interest groups in the latter half of the 1940s and in subsequent decades.

In addition, the events and policies of the 1940s were fundamental to effecting the tax and borrowing policies characteristic of the postwar institutions of U.S. public finance. The war caused a great expansion in income taxation, on both an absolute and a per capita basis, and the Bureau of Internal Revenue significantly increased its budget and staff. Then, with the introduction of current withholding in 1943, the government was able, at the stroke of a pen, to either withhold more money from taxpayers' paychecks or increase their take-home pay (thereby either reducing or increasing consumer spending); the federal income tax became *the* means for raising revenue even while other forms of revenue collection were being rejected.

---

[4] Dean Acheson, *Present at the Creation* (New York: Norton, 1969).

[5] See J. David Greenstone, *Labor in American Politics* (New York: Knopf, 1969), especially 53–56.

With the large expansion in the public debt that accompanied the war, the Roosevelt Administration and the Treasury Department set up a multitude of joint public-private agencies to sell U.S. securities to individual and institutional investors at the local, state, and national levels. Millions of individuals and thousands of financial institutions suddenly started to buy, and would continue to buy, U.S. government securities. The Bureau of Public Debt expanded accordingly in order to handle the increases in sales, redemptions, and resales of government securities. Both the Bureau of Public Debt and the Bureau of Internal Revenue also streamlined their operations in order to better secure the government's financing as a result of the war.

Finally, the events of the 1940s were signally critical in expanding both the quantity and the quality of government-business relations. The government revised its procedures for securing needed matériel and created a variety of agencies for overseeing, coordinating, and expediting procurement. The amount of money spent on matériel soared, as did the volume of contracts and the number of officials administering procurement (i.e., letting contracts, supervising contractors, renegotiating contracts, providing contractor financing, inspecting, monitoring subcontracting, coordinating procurement, etc.). Although the postwar spending on matériel fell off substantially from the wartime levels, the budgets and personnel needed for national defense remained at levels far above their prewar mark. And the new processes and agencies of procurement introduced during the war mostly stayed on, to be integrated first into the National Military Establishment and then into the Department of Defense. World War II affected far more than weaponry and military alliances.[6]

[6] For recent scholarship recognizing the effects of WWII on particular U.S. domestic policies, see Edward D. Berkowitz, *America's Welfare State: From Roosevelt to Reagan* (Baltimore: Johns Hopkins University Press, 1991); Edwin Amenta and Theda Skocpol, "Redefining the New Deal: World War II and the Development of Social Provision in the United States," in Margaret Weir, Ann Shola Orloff, and Theda Skocpol, eds., *The Politics of Social Policy in the United States* (Princeton: Princeton University Press, 1988); Alan Brinkley, "The New Deal and the Idea of the State," in Steve Fraser and Gary Gerstle, eds., *The Rise and Fall of the New Deal Order, 1930–1980* (Princeton: Princeton University Press, 1989); Arthur A. Stein, *The Nation at War* (Baltimore: Johns Hopkins University Press, 1975); and Harold G. Vatter, *The U.S. Economy in World War II* (New York: Columbia University Press, 1985). Also see Walter Millis, *Arms and the State: Civil-Military Elements in National Policy*, with Harvey Mansfield and Harold Stein (New York: Twentieth Century Fund, 1958), 139–42. See Doris Kearns Goodwin for an overview of White House politics and national policy during the Second World War, with special attention to the personal and family lives of Eleanor and Franklin Roosevelt, race relations, and the role of women. (*No Ordinary Time: Franklin and Eleanor Roosevelt: The Home Front in World War II* [New York: Simon & Schuster, 1994]). As Michael Mann observes, however, the military essence of advanced industrial states has been understudied (Michael Mann, *States, War and Capitalism* [London: Basil Blackwell, 1985], 70).

In short, the effect of World War II was not only to transform American government and society, but also to direct the development of U.S. public policies and political institutions in ways that would typify American government for decades to come.

The Second World War as Crisis

Whether periods of non-incremental change are called "critical moments," "punctuated equilibria," or "branching points," the crux of the matter is that some historical periods engender significantly more institutional transformation than others.[7] Change in the state happens not gradually or incrementally, but disjunctively and sporadically. And crises create opportunities for, and make transparent the necessity for, change; it is during crises and major wars that the categories of political identity and the bonds of social networks become subject to severe stress. Alternative paths of political development become possible; factors previously considered fixed for strategic purposes now vary (at least in the short term); and established collectives and everyday government-society relations become unfixed. The decisions and directions taken during critical eras at once guide and constrain future political development.

But crises can take many forms and are present in varying degrees. The study here is of international crises, and of wars especially. For states are penetrated in many policy domains by the actions or even mere presence of other states; they are not simply billiard balls interacting with other states on an outside surface. A state's own constitution and intranational structure may be conditioned by international relations, and particularly by wars.[8] Wars not only shape the "extra-societal or international role" of the state,

[7] See Ira Katznelson, "Rethinking the Silences of Social and Economic Policy," *Political Science Quarterly* 101 No. 2 (1986): 307–25; Krasner, "Approaches to the State"; Stephen Lukes, "Introduction," in Stephen Lukes, ed., *Power* (New York: New York University Press, 1986), 15–16; Peter Gourevitch, *Politics in Hard Times: Comparative Responses to International Economic Crises* (Ithaca: Cornell University Press, 1986); and Michael L. Tushman and Elaine Romanelli, "Organizational Evolution: A Metamorphosis Model of Convergence and Reorientation," in Barry M. Staw and L. L. Cummings, eds., *The Evolution and Adaptation of Organizations* (Greenwich, Conn.: JAI Press, 1990).

[8] Otto Hintze, *The Historical Essays of Otto Hintze*, Felix Gilbert, ed. (Oxford: Oxford University Press, 1975 [1902]), 160. Also see Charles Tilly, *Coercion, Capital, and European States AD 990–1990* (Cambridge, Mass.: Basil Blackwell, 1990); Charles Tilly, ed., *The Formation of National States in Western Europe* (Princeton: Princeton University Press, 1975); Mann, *States, War and Capitalism*; and Gourevitch, *Politics in Hard Times*. Also see Eric Nordlinger, "Taking the State Seriously," in Myron Weiner and Samuel P. Huntington, eds., *Understanding Political Development* (Boston: Little Brown, 1987), 385–86; and Nordlinger, "The Return to the State: Critiques," 884.

then, but may also affect the size and array of societal actors and therefore the relation between government and society.[9]

As a global war and as an international crisis, World War II can be contrasted with the crises that occur within states, such as revolutions, civil wars, and economic depressions, which pit political party against party, region against region, or economic class against class. More specifically, World War II was a *hegemonic* war, to follow the political scientist Robert Gilpin. It manifested direct conflict among the dominant powers in the international system—the United States, Great Britain, France, the Soviet Union, Germany, Japan, and Italy—conflict in which the very "nature and governance" of the international system was at stake. Just as the end of the Punic Wars marked the fall of Rome, and as the end of the Napoleonic Wars marked the beginning of British hegemony, so did the Second World War mark the start of American international dominance.[10]

Since hegemonic wars put the basic features of the international system at stake, they are necessarily total wars, involving entire populations and requiring much if not most of national production and the virtually complete attention of governments. All are devoted to the end of eradicating an opposing system of rule, with few limits on the means or the scope of warfare. For the United States, the Second World War may be contrasted with the limited ambitions and the smaller scales of the Spanish-American, Korean, and Vietnam wars.

The Second World War was also a *democratic* war—at least for the United States, Great Britain, Canada, Australia, New Zealand, and Finland. Democratic wars need the backing of public opinion, since the effects of war pose potential hazards for democratically elected officials: deaths and injuries from military engagements, the stationing of personnel overseas, and large military budgets may cause war to become unpopular and politically unsustainable. Democratic governments therefore have to persuade their citizens of the necessity and importance of war; they have to be justified to a potentially skeptical, even rebellious public.[11] Although the totalitarian governments of Germany, Japan, Italy, and the Soviet Union also depended on public support, nondemocratic governments have more options: Hitler could withstand the opposition of much German public opinion

---

[9] J. P. Nettl, "The State as a Conceptual Variable," *World Politics* 20 (July 1968), 562–66.

[10] See Robert Gilpin, *War and Change in World Politics* (New York: Cambridge University Press, 1981), 199–200. Gilpin also refers to the Peloponnesian War, the Thirty Years' War, and the wars of Louis XIV as hegemonic wars. Hegemony does not necessarily mean complete dominance, of course.

[11] Quincy Wright, *A Study of War* (Chicago: University of Chicago Press, 1964 [1942]). Mann refers to the attitude of democracies to modern warfare as "spectator sport militarism": the technology of killing allowing for a more distant and less participation by actual humans. Modern wars are "popular but appalling" (Mann, *States, War and Capitalism*).

and even that of his own top military leaders; and the Soviet government could withstand the sacrifice of tens of millions of lives for the sake of defeating Germany.[12]

The First and Second World Wars were both hegemonic wars for the United States. Both wars provoked nationwide industrial mobilization, caused the formation of quasi-corporatist government-business-labor partnerships, and brought about large increases in the federal deficits and public indebtedness. They marked permanent increases in the size of government and made for lasting changes in the roles that the federal government would play with respect to labor-management relations, income taxation and public borrowing, and defense spending. After both wars there were similar problems of demobilization, labor unrest, industrial reconversion, and cutbacks in federal spending.

Furthermore, the two wars systematically affected public policies considered characteristic of American exceptionalism. Both wars influenced the fate of proposals for national health insurance: the effect of the First World War was to squelch initiatives towards the public provision of medical insurance, just as the combination of American prosperity and Soviet rivalry obtaining after World War II factored in the success of the private interests that opposed national health insurance and favored the anti-collectivist arguments used against proposals for public health insurance in the late 1940s. The two wars led to government-labor ties that helped suppress labor radicalism and entrenched the positions of more conservative union leaders. The president of the American Federation of Labor during World War I, Samuel Gompers, and the AFL and CIO presidents during World War II used the war to improve their positions both against rival unions and against business management. At the same time, the wars caused the building of government institutions for the purpose of handling labor-management disputes; the wars allowed for the federal government to have a greater impact on labor-management relations in the United States. Nor would the government relinquish the new role it was playing in maintaining industrial peace.

With the big increases in government spending needed to fund the wars, the government had to build new capacity for collecting revenues. One result was the growth of the federal income tax. Another was the unprecedented sale of government securities of various denominations, rates of interest, and maturity periods to individual and corporate investors throughout the country. The combination of the tax and borrowing policies—and their demonstrated efficacy—led to U.S. fiscal policy that would mostly depend on tax and monetary policy, rather than on spending levels or incomes policies.

---

[12] Many aspects of the Second World War defy generalization, of course, such as the extant level of technology, the scope of conflict, and the precise alignment of the major powers.

Finally, the two wars spurred the growth of the defense bureaucracy, accelerated the industrialization of the United States through the military's procurement of matériel, and repositioned the United States in the international system of states.[13] The victory in the Second World War led to a global foreign policy and to characteristically and distinctly high levels of defense spending. Much of what the wars set in place would remain intact for the rest of the twentieth century.

The State, State-Building, and the Resource
Dependence Perspective

But why the state? It could be contended that the 104th Congress, elected in November 1994, represents an attempt to dismantle the federal government. After all, the Contract With America signifies a frontal assault on the U.S. national government. The Contract With America has proposed—among its other provisions—to amend the U.S. Constitution by requiring a balanced federal budget; to impose term limits on members of the House and Senate; and to overturn the present welfare system by prohibiting welfare to mothers under the age of 21, by denying increased support payments for mothers who have additional children while on welfare, and by restricting Aid to Families with Dependent Children to a two-year period only.

Yet the status of the state, and thus the merits of a study of state-building, remain in question. It may be that the decentralization of government simply tranfers the responsibilities of national government to the separate states, and that the fifty states—rather than the national government—will then have to amass the resources necessary to deal with the problems of the day. A smaller national government may therefore result in commensurately larger state and local governments, which in turn aggregate into a national government that is still "big" and "intrusive" relative to individuals and private organizations.

We may also wonder how successful the Republican initiatives will be. For all of the discontent manifested by American voters in the 1992 and 1994 elections, the actual impact of the electorate on legislative action remains in doubt, given the discrepancy between public opinion and congressional action: for example, the budget remains to be balanced; term limits have yet to be imposed on members of Congress; and the existing controls on private weapons may be relaxed rather than reinforced. Despite the angry rhetoric, the manifest popular discontent, and the new members of Congress, politics in Washington, D.C., may still be politics-as-usual. One might

---

[13] Richard Rose observes that the United States's spending on defense is exceptionally large: 6.5 percent of GDP in 1986, in contrast to an OECD mean of 3.0 percent ("Is American Public Policy Exceptional?" in Shafer, *Is America Different?*, 198).

still conclude that presidents, individual members of Congress, and political appointees come and go but that special interests, bureaucracies, and the courts remain the permanent powers in the nation's capital.[14]

Then we may wonder how revolutionary the Contract With America in fact is. The Contract With America specifies the use of the tax system in order to encourage parents to have and adopt children, advocates the repeal of the marriage tax credit, and calls for the creation of tax-exempt personal savings accounts; it thereby pays explicit homage to the government's use of fiscal policy for the furthering of social and economic objectives—consistent with the public finance of the 1940s. The Contract also seeks to raise social security earnings limits, to repeal the 1993 tax increases on social security income, and to introduce tax incentives for private longer-term care insurance for older Americans. Here again, the Contract With America is in accord with the premise of the social security program of the 1940s: that public support for older Americans be based on a logic of individual deserts. Lastly, the Contract With America calls for a stronger national defense. Once more the Contract is consistent with the state-building of the 1940s: U.S. national security being dependent on a potent military, given the fact that Americans cannot be insulated from international threats.

In short, the 104th Congress recognizes the use of the tax system for the achievement of social and economic goals; it acknowledges the role of the government in providing for the elderly; and it supports a strong military establishment. The Contract With America thus seems to be as much supportive of the state-building of the 1940s, reinforcing of national government, as it is anti-state. Furthermore, with the defeat of the balanced budget initiative (as of this writing), the strong likelihood of a tax cut, and the dedication of more resources for national defense, the federal government will continue to have to borrow extensively. An examination of the state-building of the 1940s is most relevant to an understanding of the present.

Although social scientists, historians, and a larger public have in recent years started once more to refer to the American polity as a "state,"[15] there

----

[14] This has been one lesson of American politics for some time, of course. See Grant McConnell, *Private Power and American Democracy* (New York: Knopf, 1966), and Theodore J. Lowi, *The End of Liberalism: Ideology, Policy, and the Crisis of Public Authority* (New York: Norton, 1969).

[15] For earlier work on the state, see Woodrow Wilson, *The State: Elements of Historical and Practical Politics* (Boston: D. C. Heath, 1889); Theodore Woolsey, *Political Science; or, The State, Theoretically and Practically Considered*, 2 vols. (New York: Charles Scribner's Sons, 1877); and James Q. Dealey, *The Development of the State: Its Governmental Organization and Its Activities* (New York: Silver, Burdett, 1909). For more recent work on the state, see Nettl, "The State as a Conceptual Variable"; Stephen D. Krasner, *Defending the National Interest* (Princeton: Princeton University Press, 1978); Peter J. Katzenstein, "Conclusion: Domestic Structures and Strategies of Foreign Economic Policy," in Peter J. Katzenstein, ed., *Between Power and Plenty: Foreign Economic Policies of Advanced Industrial States* (Madison: Univer-

is little consensus on what is meant by the state, especially as applied to the United States.[16] The state has been used in a number of ways, to such an extent that the popularity of the term may lie with its very ambiguity: audiences are able to read what they want into the "state."[17]

The solution here is to define the state in three parts or dimensions: first,

---

sity of Wisconsin Press, 1978); Theda Skocpol, *States and Social Revolutions* (Cambridge: Cambridge University Press, 1979); Eric Nordlinger, *On the Autonomy of the Democratic State* (Cambridge, Mass.: Harvard University Press, 1981); Stephen L. Skowronek, *Building a New American State: The Expansion of National Administrative Capacities, 1877–1920* (Cambridge: Cambridge University Press, 1982); Peter B. Evans, Dietrich Rueschemeyer, and Theda Skocpol, eds., *Bringing the State Back In* (Cambridge: Cambridge University Press, 1985); Edward O. Laumann and David Knoke, *The Organizational State* (Madison: University of Wisconsin Press, 1987); and Gabriel A. Almond, "The Return to the State," *American Political Science Review*, 82 No. 3 (1988): 853–74, together with "Critiques" by Eric A. Nordlinger, Theodore J. Lowi, and Sergio Fabbrini, 875–901.

[16] Eric Nordlinger identifies the state as the sum of personnel in all government positions, federal, state, and local. Louis Galambos equates the state with the federal bureaucracies, and Kenneth Waltz and others conceive of the state as the principal unit of the international system. Theodore Lowi refers to the state as a residual category, "invoked when no other variables suffice"; Stephen Krasner defines the state as "the President and those bureaus relatively insulated from societal pressures"; and Skowronek defines it as at once a coercive power settling class conflict at the macro level, an "integrated organization of institutions, procedures and human talents" at the meso level, and the individuals who attempt to maintain order at the micro level (Nordlinger, *On the Autonomy of the Democratic State*; Louis Galambos, *The New American State: Bureaucracies and Policies since World War II* [Baltimore: Johns Hopkins University Press, 1987]; Nettl, "The State as a Conceptual Variable"; Kenneth Waltz, *Theory of International Politics* [New York: Random House, 1979]; Lowi, "The Return to the State: Critiques," 891; Krasner, *Defending the National Interest*, 62; Skowronek, *Building a New American State*, 11–12).

The state may also be conceptualized as an economic actor and guarantor of the capitalist system. See Ralph Miliband, *The State in Capitalist Society* (New York: Basic Books, 1969); Nicos Poulantzas, *Political Power and Social Classes* (New York: Verso, 1987); Fred Block, "The Ruling Class Does Not Rule: Notes on the Marxist Theory of the State," *Socialist Revolution* 33 (1977): 6–28; Perry Anderson, *Lineages of the Absolutist State* (London: New Left Books, 1974); and James O'Connor, *The Fiscal Crisis of the State* (New York: St. Martin's, 1973).

The state may further be conceptualized as networks. See Laumann and Knoke, *The Organizational State*; and John Higley and Gwen Moore, "Elite Integration in the United States and Australia," *American Political Science Review* 75 No. 3 (1981): 581–97.

[17] For those who speak of a "gargantuan" American leviathan, able to "take and give whatever, whenever, and where ever it wishes," the use of the state bespeaks a centralization and intensification of political authority where the state has the actual or potential ability to manipulate, dominate, or coerce societal actors (Warren Nutter, as cited in Robert Higgs, *Crisis and Leviathan: Critical Episodes in the Growth of American Government* [New York: Oxford University Press, 1987], 4). More benignly, the state may refer to the simple enlargement of governmental goods and services, as in the emergence of the welfare state, able to provide "public programs of social insurance intended to cover risks to a national population from work-injuries, sickness and disability, diminution of earnings in old age, and unemployment" (Theda Skocpol and G. John Ikenberry, "The Political Formation of the American Welfare State in Historical and Comparative Perspective," *Comparative Social Research* 6 [1983], 89).

the bureaucracy; second, the established relations between the government and individuals and organizations; and third, the instruments of policy administration. Each of these three dimensions is arguably consistent with the work of Max Weber on the state: a focus on the bureaucracy echoes Weber's concern with the formal administration of government; an examination of the enduring relations between the government and individuals and organizations includes both public organizations and societal actors in the exercise of a monopoly of legitimate violence over a territory; and an investigation into the instruments of policy administration follows Weber's study of rationalization in organizations of government and commerce. To omit any of these parts of the state—the bureaucracy of budgets and persons, the institutionalized ties between the public and private sectors, or the instruments of rule—would, it seems, miss much of political authority in the United States if one is to take seriously Weber's work on the state.[18]

We may consider the government *bureaucracy* to be part of the state insofar as it is a central administrative and legal order, operating over a territory and in particular jurisdictions. For Weber, the state "possesses an administrative and legal order subject to change by legislation, to which the organized activities of the administrative staff, which are also controlled by regulations, are oriented." Like Weber's administrative order, the bureaucracy is subject to change by legislation, is the outcome of the activities of administrative staffs, and has binding authority over action and territory within its jurisdiction. It is assumed here that the diverse departments and numerous independent agencies of the U.S. federal government may be aggregated into an "administrative order."[19] The bureaucratic state—the tangible manifestation of the administrative order—may be measured by budget dollars (in absolute figures and as a proportion of the federal budget) or by personnel numbers (again, in absolute and relative terms).

A second dimension of the state is the *routinized relations* that the gov-

---

[18] A reading of Nettl's "The State as a Conceptual Variable" illustrates the potential disharmony between the coercive authority of the state and its sectoral autonomy. Nettl defines the state as (1) a collectivity of functions and structures, generalized, depersonalized, and institutionalized; (2) a unit of international relations where the "state is the gate keeper between intrasociety and extrasociety flows of action"; (3) an autonomous collectivity, a distinct sector; and (4) a sociocultural phenomenon of common experiences and expectations (562–66). Note that it would be possible for Nettl's state to exist as an institutionalized collectivity (definition 1), an international unit (definition 2), and a "sociocultural phenomenon" (definition 4) yet *not* have sectoral autonomy (definition 3). For an enduring, legitimately coercive system to constitute a distinct "sociocultural phenomenon" with an international presence, it need not be sectorally autonomous—remaining unpenetrated by private actors; there may be realms of shared power, both formal and informal, that are nonvoluntary and controlling.

[19] Jeffrey Pfeffer and Gerald Salancik, *The External Control of Organizations: A Resource Dependence Perspective* (New York: Harper & Row, 1978), 258–59. Also see Richard Cyert and James G. March, *A Behavioral Theory of the Firm* (Englewood Cliffs, N.J.: Prentice-Hall, 1963).

ernment has with individuals and organizations: the persisting, patterned ties existing between the national government and societal actors. If the state is to be distinguished from other political actors by virtue of its "enduring and manifest existence as a well-established power," as Weber puts it, then a conceptualization of the state as composed of insulated and distant bureaucracies—as is suggested by the notion of an autonomous state and implied by a sole focus on Weber's work on bureaucracy or a constricted view of an "administrative order"—seems dubious.[20] Surely it is not the narrowly autonomous quality of American government that constitutes "well-established power" in the United States or that leads the political scientist Stephen Skowronek to introduce the state as a "sense of organization of coercive power operating beyond our immediate control and intruding into all aspects of our lives."[21]

A crucial tension thus exists between the use of the state as an autonomous actor and Weber's identification of the state as the monopoly of legitimate violence throughout a territory. The "state must be considered more than 'government,'" as Alfred Stepan puts it.[22] For Stepan, the state "is the continuous administrative, legal, bureaucratic and coercive systems that attempt not only to structure relations *between* civil society and public authority in a polity, but also to structure many crucial relationships *within* civil society as well."[23] It comprises the influential and enduring relations spanning public authority and civil society (what Stepan calls "systems"). Although the "relational state" offered here does not include societal actors (i.e., individual citizens and corporate actors) themselves as part of the state, it includes as part of the state those institutionalized ties that these actors have with the government. Such relations might include the financial obliga-

---

[20] Max Weber, *Economy and Society*, ed. Guenther Roth and Claus Wittich (Berkeley: University of California Press, 1978), 903.

[21] Weber, *Economy and Society*, 909; Skowronek, *Building a New American State*, 3. Weber defines the state as a compulsory political association "insofar as its administrative staff successfully upholds the claim to the monopoly of the legitimate use of physical force in the enforcement of its order" (Weber, *Economy and Society*, 54). Krasner's definition of the American state as the "President and those bureaus relatively isolated from societal pressures" is representative of the state-as-autonomous position (*Defending the National Interest*, 62). Indeed, Krasner's definition of a strong state as one that is able to "remake the society and culture in which it exists—to change economic institutions, values, and patterns of interaction among private groups" (56)—could well apply to the United States of the mid-twentieth century.

[22] A focus on government-society relations may be consistent with Michael Mann's "infrastructural power" of the state: the power of the state diffused throughout a territory. To the extent that such infrastructural power is embedded in societal actors exerting monopoly control in particular policy domains and can be measured, then the "relational state" and the "infrastructural power" of the state may be identical (Mann, "The Autonomous Power of the State: Its Origins, Mechanisms and Results," *Archives européennes de sociologie* 25 [1984]: 185–213).

[23] Alfred Stepan, *The State and Society* (Princeton: Princeton University Press, 1978), xii; emphasis in original.

tions of individuals and groups to the government (e.g., income or inheritance taxes), the obligations of the government to societal actors (e.g., government pensions or unemployment compensation), and the regulations the government imposes on societal actors (e.g., rules of commerce or qualifications for citizenship).[24]

This notion of the state as the institutionalized relations between the government and societal actors is consistent with Weber's focus on the state as a "system of order [that] claims binding authority, not only over the members of the state, the citizens, most of whom have obtained membership by birth, but also to a very large extent over all action taking place in the area of its jurisdiction." It is further consistent with Weber's description of the state as "a compulsory association with a territorial basis."[25] But since compulsion may remain unobserved or be unused in daily practice, we need to focus more on how a system of order may arise from the coordination between, or joint policies effected by, the government and ostensibly non-government actors; the cooperation and combination of the government with societal actors may effectively monopolize authority across policy domains. Consider the areas and eras of dominance by the American Medical Association, the American Farm Bureau Federation, the AFL-CIO and Teamsters, the major defense contractors, and other interests and associations. Indeed, the inclusion of government-society ties in a definition of the state may represent a "better way of characterizing state structures as organizational configurations," as Peter Evans, Dietrich Rueschemeyer, and Theda Skocpol advise in their concluding essay in *Bringing the State Back In*.[26]

The institutionalized ties obtaining between the government and private actors may be measured by *extent*—the numbers of contracts or separate relations the government has with the societal actors in any one domain—and by *intensity*—the amount of money (in absolute numbers or in relative amounts) or degree of coercion implicit in each single tie or dyad. To

---

[24] To focus on the potential coercion exercised jointly by governmental and societal actors takes us away from the notion of the United States as a "weak state," as those defining it as an autonomous sector call it. See Krasner, *Defending the National Interest*; John Zysman, "The French State in the International Economy," in Katzenstein, ed., *Between Power and Plenty*; Ira Katznelson and Kenneth Prewitt, "Constitutionalism, Class and the Limits to Choice in American Foreign Policy," in Richard R. Fagen, ed., *Capitalism and the State in U.S.-Latin American Relations* (Stanford: Stanford University Press, 1979); and Peter Katzenstein, "Conclusion: Domestic Structures and Strategies of Foreign Economic Policy."

[25] Weber, *Economy and Society*, 56.

[26] Evans, Rueschemeyer, and Skocpol, "Towards a More Adequate Understanding of the State," in *Bringing the State Back In*, 355, 360. The present study is also consistent with the recommendations of Evans, Rueschemeyer, and Skocpol to disaggregate the state and to focus on the "reorganization episodes" of state structures occurring after major wars at both the national and transnational levels.

recognize that joint public-private ties need not always produce complete or continual policy monopolies does not undermine the importance of studying the common exercise of political power.[27]

The third dimension of the state is the *means* by which the government administers and operates its policies: the instrumental state. State-building occurs when the personalized power of governmental officials is replaced by formalized and specified political authority, consistent with Weber's analysis of the predominance of *zweckrational* behavior in the administration of public and private organizations in the West. The more authority is made permanent through coordination, codification, standardization, slack-reduction, and other administrative means, the more nearly authority approximates Weber's "well-established power."[28]

Changes in the instrumental state may be documented by observing developments in the government's procedures for producing, effecting, standardizing, and otherwise improving administration. Although it is difficult to assess an overall level of efficiency or slack at any point in time, say in 1940, it is possible to witness the introduction of more rationalized administration through legislation, executive orders, departmental directives, and intradepartmental documents. Defining the state in terms of the bureaucracy, the institutional relations between the government and society, and the means of administration allows us to measure and observe discrete changes in the state; we can "de-reify" the state. But if states themselves are obviously incapable of action, what are the bases—or microfoundations—of state action? How can we understand the effect of World War II on the American state through the behavior of sentient individuals? Discussions of the state often leave the processes or mechanisms of state-building either underspecified or unclear.[29] As James March and Johan Olsen comment in

[27] As used here, "state" refers to any or all of these three dimensions; "government" refers to the federal government of elected and appointed federal officials and civil servants; "institution" refers to either the overall definition of the state or any of its three constituent parts or dimensions; and "political development" refers to changes in the state or in the institutions of government.

[28] See Max Weber, "Bureaucracy," in *From Max Weber: Essays in Sociology*, H. H. Gerth and C. Wright Mills, trans. and eds. (New York: Oxford University Press, 1946), 196–244. Weber defines "bureaucratic authority" by the presence of fixed rules and duties, delimited and specified official authority, and regulated qualifications for assuming bureaucratic duties. "Distinctly developed and quantitatively large bureaucracies are: . . . (e) in ever purer forms, the modern European states and, increasingly, all public corporations since the time of princely absolutism; (f) the large modern capitalist enterprise, the more so as it becomes greater and more complicated" (204). Weber did not, however, get to complete his work on the state (Reinhard Bendix, *Max Weber: An Intellectual Portrait* [Berkeley: University of California Press, 1977 (1960)]).

[29] Nordlinger provides a theoretical argument for the possibility of state autonomy—autonomy even when opposed by divergent social preferences (his "Type I"); he does not claim to explain how the state changes. The state for Nordlinger is an independent variable, not a

reference to the construction of an institutional theory of government, "the relevant theoretical work remains to be done. It is interesting to suggest that political institutions and the society are interdependent, but that statement needs to find a richer theoretical expression."[30] Ira Katznelson similarly observes that both the Marxist and Weberian versions of macro-structural research "have yet to develop analytical perspectives subtle or nuanced enough for the purpose of accounting for the impact of organization and policies of states on the limits and content of a given country's social agenda."[31]

The resource dependence perspective, from organization theory, is offered here as a possible model or tool kit of state-building. Coming out of work on organizations as open systems and as contingency-avoiding actors, the resource dependence perspective posits that organizations exist in exposed, uncertain environments.[32] Organizational survival depends on the continued securance of resources within a larger context of interdependent individuals and organizations. Seeking to stabilize their existence, organizations attempt to influence, negotiate with, and manage their external rela-

---

dependent variable. Krasner argues that "the American state often confronts dissident bureaus, a recalcitrant Congress, and powerful private actors" (Krasner, *Defending the National Interest*, 61–66). Since any of these actors may be involved in policymaking, the consequence is that Krasner's mechanisms of institutional change can be known only through a comprehensive study of the juxtaposition of political vectors pertaining to a particular political outcome. For all its probable verisimilitude, such an explanation of institutional change is ungeneralizable as an explanation of state-building.

Skowronek explains state-building as the result of a convergence of tensions provoked by crisis, class conflict, and complexity (i.e., the dislocations of industrialization), mediated by existing institutions and electoral politics. Crises reveal tensions in state capacities and in the social order, which may be patched up and, later, reconstituted. State-building is a political contingency, Skowronek says, the outcome a struggle for political power and institutional position (*Building a New American State*). Skowronek's mechanisms of state-building are complex, frequently implicit, and ill suited to general application. Nor do Louis Galambos and his colleagues in *The New American State* present a theory of institutional change in bureaucracies. Galambos's own view is of a secular trend to specialization and complexity that naturally develops into the big government and entrenched bureaucracies of the present ("By Way of Introduction," in Galambos, ed., *The New American State*, 19).

[30] James G. March and Johan P. Olsen, "The New Institutionalism: Organizational Factors in Political Life," *American Political Science Review* 78 No. 4 (1984): 742.

[31] Katznelson, "Rethinking the Silences of Social and Economic Policy." Terry Moe is explicit about his hope for the theory to come: a positive theory of institutions "has vast *potential* as a theoretic foundation for the study of institutions generally" ("Interests, Institutions, and Positive Theory: The Politics of the NLRB,"in *Studies in American Political Development*, 2 Karen Orren and Stephen Skowronek, eds. [New Haven: Yale University Press, 1987], 298; emphasis added).

[32] Daniel Katz and R. L. Kahn, *The Social Psychology of Organizations* (New York: John Wiley and Sons, 1966); James D. Thompson, *Organizations in Action* (New York: McGraw-Hill, 1967); Pfeffer and Salancik, *External Control*.

tions in ways that protect their budgets and staff. "The underlying premise of the external perspective on organizations," Jeffrey Pfeffer and Gerald Salancik write, "is that organizational activities and outcomes are accounted for by the context in which the organization is embedded"—the environment of specific societal and international actors and particular resources.[33] Organizations respond and adapt to changes in their environment; the more interdependent an organization is, the more interorganizational alterations have to be made in order to reduce uncertainty under changing conditions.[34]

The resource dependence perspective's attention to organizational ecology does not mean, however, that there is an automatic fit, or isomorphism, of organizational structure to environment. On the contrary, it is because organizations are *loosely* coupled with the environment that the processes by which organizations attempt to reduce the uncertainties in their external relations become critical. The specifics of how organizations respond and adjust to their environments depend on the locus and type of uncertainty facing the focal organization. It is the very looseness of the coupling—the inexactness of the fit between organizations and their environments—that makes it possible to generate (as Pfeffer and Salancik do) falsifiable propositions of institutional development, depending on the particular resource environment and the interorganizational field of an organization.

Three features of the resource dependence perspective as presented by Pfeffer and Salancik prevent, however, its direct application to state-building. One of these features is that it lacks microfoundations, or the grounding of organizational action in an adequate explanation of individual behavior. Pfeffer and Salancik do not say if individual executives (who may be symbolic actors, responsive executives, or discretionary decision-makers) necessarily act in the interests of their organizations. Yet because the interests of individual executives may clash with those of an organization, we need to make assumptions about how individual executives behave.

Assumed here is that individual executives constitute a small "privileged group," to follow the work of Mancur Olson on collective action: responsibility for organizational action falls on the individual executive, with the result that any executive (and there may be more than one) has a sufficient

[33] Pfeffer and Salancik, *External Control*, 39. Also see Pfeffer, "A Resource Dependence Perspective on Intercorporate Relations," in Mark Mizruchi and Michael Schwartz, eds., *Intercorporate Relations* (Cambridge: Cambridge University Press, 1987), 25–33 and Lukes, *Power: A Radical View* (New York: Macmillan, 1974), 15–16.

[34] The resource dependence perspective's focus on organizational interdependency may be contrasted with other macrostructural approaches, such as ecological models, which hold that surviving organizations are selected out of a population of organizations according to their suitability to the environment, and closed system analyses of organizational goals, personnel, or procedures. See Pfeffer and Salancik, *External Control*, 6–10; and Pfeffer, "A Resource Dependence Perspective."

stake in the collective outcome of the organization to induce him or her to act in the organization's collective interest.[35] Since organizations are distinguished by their particular resource environments and specific interdependencies, the actions of individual executives will be tailored to an organization and its ecology—to what the organizational environment dictates as necessary for survival.

A second problem is that Pfeffer and Salancik apply their perspective to business firms rather than to government. The authors note that "[n]ot only are organizations constrained by the political, legal and economic environment, but, in fact, law, legitimacy, political outcomes, and the economic climate reflect, in part, actions taken by organizations to modify these environmental components for their interests of survival and growth."[36] Yet not only may the government be altered through the actions of societal organizations (consistent with a pluralist view of government), but government organizations may also be doing the modifying. That is to say that the behavior of government organizations can be understood from the supply side (the government acting upon society to secure resources) as well as from the demand side (the government responding to societal demands).

Following from the fact that Pfeffer and Salancik apply their model only to business is a third problem with the direct application of the resource dependence perspective to state-building: the matter of constructing a model of government amenable to theory-testing. Assumed here is that the bureaucracy, government-society relations, and administrative practices of the state may be viewed as parts of a large and complex federal government; the federal government may be considered as an assemblage or coalition of organizations—departments, bureaus, and agencies—which, fractal-like, are themselves coalitions of organizations, each with its own branches and sub-departments.[37]

[35] There are also iterated plays for organizational executives, to follow Robert Axelrod: executives see their performance in office tied to the performance of the organization as a whole, and thus their logic of collective action goes beyond the one-shot prisoner's dilemma. See Axelrod, *The Evolution of Cooperation* (New York: Basic Books, 1984). Pfeffer's exposition appears to be consistent with Mancur Olson's privileged group: social pressures (Pfeffer's "prestige") combine with private material interest to promote collective action. See Pfeffer, "A Resource Dependence Perspective."

[36] Pfeffer and Salancik, *External Control*, 108. Pfeffer and Salancik treat the government as only one among many possible environmental factors (188–222), and Pfeffer focuses exclusively on business organizations ("A Resource Dependence Perspective").

[37] The consideration of the government as a (complex) organization departs from both the resource dependence perspective and the resource exchange literature, both of which see the government as a constraint on or a resource for private organizations in the control or exchange of resources. (See Richard M. Emerson, "Power-Dependence Relations," *American Sociological Review* 27 [1962]: 31–41), and Emerson, "Exchange Theory, Part II: Exchange Relations and Networks," in J. Berger, M. Zelditch, and B. Anderson, eds., *Sociological Theories in Progress*, 2 (Boston: Houghton Mifflin, 1972]).

State-building can thus be understood as a process of organizational change: change in the bureaucracies of government, change in the relations between government organizations and societal actors, and change in the means of administration. Changes in the institutions of government happen through actions by discrete government personnel, where the president and his advisors (cabinet officers and White House staff both) attempt to minimize political risk and avoid blame in order to stay in office. Government officials—the president and his appointees as well as members of Congress—come to regard their offices as property, as Robert Michels noted, and we may assume that the members of a presidential administration act as a team, working towards their common goal of staying in office.[38]

Executive branch officials and members of Congress therefore focus their attention on the national environment of other governmental actors, business corporations, other non-governmental organizations, and the public of individual voters and taxpayers in order to reduce uncertainty over their supply of resources (i.e., what it takes to get reelected).[39] They also monitor the larger environment of other states, for first and foremost among threats to the government are those that threaten its very existence, whether international (wars as well as trade and international payments disputes) or domestic (economic depressions, civil wars).[40]

Under conditions of hegemonic warfare (which obtain here), the president and Congress depend on a few tangible resources in order to stay in office: the expanded production of matériel, sufficient personnel for staffing the military and the government, an adequate supply of raw materials, the cooperation of the workforce, and the necessary funds. Voters in a democratic state want the war conducted as quickly and painlessly as possible, without labor unrest, without untoward inflation, and with the fewest possible casualties; expediency is everything.

---

[38] David Mayhew, *Congress: The Electoral Connection* (New Haven: Yale University Press, 1974); R. Kent Weaver, "The Politics of Blame Avoidance," *Journal of Public Policy* 6 No. 4 (1986): 371–98; Peter A. Hall, ed., *Governing the Economy* (Oxford: Oxford University Press, 1986). As Pfeffer characterizes the self-protecting and risk-reducing behavior of organizational actors, "To have power because of one's organizational position ties one psychologically as well as materially to that organization. One's prestige and income are affected by the success of that organization and one's ability to maintain one's position in it. Thus we would expect individuals to be interested in furthering the interest of their organizations" (Pfeffer, "A Resource Dependence Perspective," 32).

Thomas Cronin notes, however, that presidential staff may have different motivations and behaviors than cabinet appointees (*The State of the Presidency* [Boston: Little, Brown, 1980]).

[39] Contra Pfeffer's claim that "organizations are the primary social actors" (Pfeffer, "A Resource Dependence Perspective," 26, 40), however, the government's dependence may extend to both organized and unorganized actors.

[40] The present study addresses only the executive and legislative branches; it mostly omits the courts, since judges were not directly involved in wartime resource mobilization.

Investment, productivity, and government revenues all have to exceed what existing institutions can generate. Because the government cannot extract all the resources it needs by fiat without incurring substantial political costs, the government's extraction of resources approximates an *exchange*: to secure additional resources, it has to promise future goods, permit high profits, grant positional goods, or allow legal rights to societal actors.[41] But the government has limited alternatives in this exchange. In the near term, at least, it has to make contracts, ensure the production of necessary goods and services, and collect taxes within an embedded structure circumscribing the availability of resources; resources have to be extracted and goods have to be produced from given populations, with known materials, and through established technologies. Because not all resources are financial (e.g., labor, information), because resource transactions are usually conducted among known actors, and because those transactions may not be directly reciprocal, however, resource exchange may be as much political and social as economic.

As head of state and commander in chief in wartime, the president leads this resource securance. The president has the centralized command necessary for gathering information, planning strategies, coordinating policies, and directing projects. The emergency powers of the president—those granted him under the U.S. Constitution and those deferred to him by Congress—establish his position as wartime leader; the previous balance between the president and Congress (as uneven as it may be) becomes upset. The president becomes the point man for a resource-dependent government, able to initiate regulations, appoint new personnel, establish temporary bodies, and create organizations.[42] The war thus impels the president to mobilize maximum resources for the minimum goal of maintaining his administration's political standing. It is not that the president and his top appointees necessarily work in the national interest, however (though they may); it is rather that the success of the mobilization for war now figures greatly in the politics of the president (and, to a lesser degree, for members of Congress).

The resource dependence perspective's focus on the environment turns our attention to four issues of political development during and after a critical period: first, the direction of state-building (since we have to provide microfoundations) as determined by the legal environment; second, the form that state-building takes, given the institutional creation possible in a crisis period; third, the permanence of state-building, given that the alter-

---

[41] Assumed here is that interests are straightforward across cases: elected leaders wish to stay in office, and individuals, businesses, and labor unions, *ceteris paribus*, seek to maximize governmental concessions and to minimize taxation and regulation when their interests are at stake.

[42] For historical reasons, I refer to U.S. presidents in masculine terms.

ations in national and international environments that accompany total war will determine how organizations of government adjust after the crisis; and fourth, the relative terms of exchange among actors, both governmental and societal, since not all fare equally well during a critical period.

The Direction of State-Building One key environmental factor is legal: both the U.S. Constitution and enacted law set boundary conditions on the command of government policy, where the president's emergency command does not extend uniformly across policy domains. While the president can issue executive orders and direct state-building in most policy domains, a few remain in which Congress retains authority to set policy.[43] Even during wartime, appropriation and revenue bills have to be duly processed through the legislative branch, for instance.[44]

After a war, however, the president's emergency powers are withdrawn, and a more balanced relation between the president and Congress resumes. As a corollary, the criteria for the reelection of federal officials leave their tangible wartime bases and return to their more ambiguous former status. The accretion of legal authority in the hands of the president under emergency conditions thus amounts to a switching mechanism in presidential-congressional relations; after the war, authority switches back.[45] The legal

---

[43] Members of Congress have limited scope for opposing the president, of course, with the nation's fate possibly hanging in the balance.

In resource exchange terms, this is an issue of actor *position* (Emerson, "Power-Dependence Relations"). Although the resource dependence perspective used here borrows from the resource exchange literature, the "resource dependence" label is retained, since the arguments used here are applied to the federal government and its constituent agencies as organizations.

[44] Aaron Wildavsky, for one, bifurcates presidential power with regard to foreign and domestic policymaking ("The Two Presidencies," in Aaron Wildavsky, ed., *Perspectives on the Presidency* [Boston: Little, Brown, 1975]). For prominent works on the presidency that neglect the effects of wars, see Theodore J. Lowi, *The Personal President: Power Invested, Promise Unfulfilled* (Ithaca: Cornell University Press, 1984); George E. Reedy, *The Twilight of the Presidency* (New York: New American Library, 1970); and Jeffrey K. Tulis, *The Rhetorical Presidency* (Princeton: Princeton University Press, 1987). Meanwhile, studies of the president's role as a military leader do not discuss presidential leadership in domestic policy domains (Warren W. Hassler, *The President as Commander in Chief* [Reading, Mass.: Addison-Wesley, 1971]; J. Malcolm Smith and Stephen Jurika, *The President and National Security* [Dubuque, Iowa: Kendall/Hunt, 1971]).

Even prominent textbooks on the presidency that include foreign and domestic policymaking slight the impact of international factors on domestic policy domains (Erwin C. Hargrove and Michael Nelson, *Presidents, Politics, and Policy* [New York: Knopf, 1984]; Richard M. Pious, *The American Presidency* [New York: Basic Books, 1979]; and Benjamin I. Page and Mark P. Petracca, *The American Presidency* [New York: McGraw-Hill, 1983]).

[45] Research on the presidency is unclear about the causes for and the dimensions of presidential power in times of war and crisis. Scholarship on the legal dimensions of presidential power, such as constitutional mandates, precedents from earlier wars, and the extra-constitutional powers formerly assumed by presidents, shows the law to be of scant effect in

environment of the timing and extent of the executive branch's emergency
authority should dictate the direction of state-building.

Hypothesis 1a: In policy domains where the president has extraordinary emergency powers, the president and his executive branch officials are able to direct
the securance of resources.

Hypothesis 1b: Congress will determine the state-building of policy domains
where it retains its legal powers, as in tax policy.

Hypothesis 1c: After the war, when the president loses his exceptional wartime
powers, Congress will regain its central position in policymaking across policy
domains.

The Form of State-Building To say that law constrains how the government operates and determines who directs the state-building does not, however, explain what kind of state will be built. As much as the president may
be the point man for a resource-dependent government, and as much as the
Congress may still make policy in some policy domains, the federal government as a whole becomes more dependent on societal actors: supplies that
were optional or of only moderate importance in time of peace become dire
necessities in wartime; raw materials and manufactured products have to be
secured, funds have to be raised, and soldiers have to be recruited and
trained.

Whether state-building takes the form of bureaucratic expansion or linkages between the government and society (linkages ranging from tacit relations, signaling, and contracting to joint ventures or mergers) depends on
the configuration and distribution of needed resources.[46] Of prime importance is the organization or diffuseness of societal actors. In the case of labor
unions, for example, the government had to accept the presence of unions in

---

limiting or predicting the exercise of presidential power. Clinton Rossiter's finding still holds:
since the courts have placed few limits on presidential behavior when it comes to national
security, the extent of presidential power can be known only *post hoc*. See Arthur M. Schlesinger, Jr., *The Imperial Presidency* (Boston: Houghton Mifflin, 1973); Pious, *The American
Presidency*; Edward S. Corwin, *The President: Office and Powers 1787–1984* (New York: New
York University Press, 1984); and Clinton Rossiter, *The Supreme Court and the Commander in
Chief* (Ithaca: Cornell University Press, 1951).

Yet those who write on the tenure of individual presidents have difficulty constructing theories of the presidency from thick descriptions of individual presidents and the management
styles of various administrations. See James David Barber, *The Presidential Character* (Englewood Cliffs, N.J.: Prentice-Hall, 1977); Erwin C. Hargrove, *Presidential Leadership* (New
York: Macmillan, 1966); Hargrove, *The Power of the Modern President* (Philadelphia: Temple
University Press, 1974); Richard E. Neustadt, *Presidential Power* (New York: Wiley, 1980
[1960]); and Stephen Hess, *Organizing the Presidency* (Washington, D.C.: Brookings Institution, 1976).

[46] Pfeffer and Salancik, *External Control*. "Clienteles" refers to societal actors within a policy domain.

TABLE 1.1
Organization of Policy Domains

Organized Clienteles	Unorganized Clienteles
Labor Regulation	Social Security
Navy Procurement	Income Taxation
Public Debt	

individual plants and industries. It was in its interest to work through existing labor organizations rather than independently with American workers. In contrast, the taxpaying public and the stakeholders in the social security system (contributors and beneficiaries both) presented disunified fronts and thus the government could conduct its resource securance bureaucratically (see Table 1.1).

> **Hypothesis 2a:** In policy domains with large numbers of individual and corporate actors possessing needed resources, the government will expand bureaucratically in order to reach out to the diffuse clienteles.
>
> **Hypothesis 2b:** Where few societal actors possess the resources needed by the government, the government will be able to secure resources by setting up interorganizational bodies connecting it with the clienteles; it will not have to set up its own parallel organizations.

Ratchet Effects To the extent that crisis-induced state-building does not disappear, subside to prewar conditions, or revert to prewar trajectories but, rather, persists independent of the crisis, there is a "ratchet effect." State-building should persist insofar as the war also causes lasting changes in the environments in which the government operates. Should the crisis cause lasting alterations in domestic society, we should then expect corresponding change in the environmentally dependent organizations of government. Likewise, should the crisis cause lasting alterations in the international environment, then the institutions of government will again have to adapt. A change in a state's position in the international order—from being a major power to becoming a lesser power, or vice versa—means a reallocation of resources between military use and civilian consumption, and therefore a freeing up or tying down of government resources.[47]

The state-building born of crisis has an important, related effect: the shift of the political agenda. A pre-crisis policy agenda—call it A—does not be-

---

[47] See Carroll, Delacroix, and Goodstein on the effects of the political environment on populations of organizations, and specifically on innovation and the length of warfare as reasons for the permanent effects of wartime changes on organizations (Glenn R. Carroll, Jacques Delacroix, and Jerry Goodstein, "The Political Environment of Organizations: An Ecological View," in Staw and Cummings, eds., *The Evolution and Adaptation of Organizations*).

come submerged by mobilization for war, only to reemerge after the conflict as an incrementally transformed policy agenda—call it A'. Rather, the pre-crisis agenda is supplemented and even supplanted by the policy agenda of the war—call it W. During the war, then, we should find a combination of the prewar and wartime agendas, AW, with components that are at once similar to and departing from agenda A. With the end of the war, a new agenda emerges, AW'. The differences between A' and AW' may be considerable; no longer may some policy agendas be possible and no longer may it be possible to deny the presence of others.

> **Hypothesis 3a:** The wartime state-building will endure to the extent that alterations in the international and domestic environments force the government to adjust.
>
> **Hypothesis 3b:** Coincident with the crisis of hegemonic war will be lasting shifts in policy agendas.

Relative State-Building The shock of world war also affects the distribution of resources among government organizations and societal actors. Not all change is economic or explicitly contractual, and some clienteles fare better than others in their new relations with the government.[48] The government and societal actors have better or worse positions from which to exchange resources.[49]

Of prime importance are the alternatives available to actors in an exchange.[50] The government can choose from whom to raise money—from wage earners, smokers, consumers, heirs, or buyers of imported goods, for instance—but it has little choice in its purchases of naval vessels and mili-

[48] Gourevitch also makes this point (Gourevitch, *Politics in Hard Times*).

[49] As Steven Lukes asks, "*Cui bono?*" ("Introduction," in Lukes, ed., *Power* [New York: New York University Press, 1986], 14). A second, related distinction in the use of the government as an organizational actor concerns "reciprocity." The resource exchange literature assumes that reciprocity obtains, but the existence and degree of reciprocity in governmental exchange may of course vary widely according to resource and the policy domain. Consider the contrast between the reciprocity of the social security system (OASI taxes in "exchange" for future benefits) and that of taxation: voters may expect something in return for their taxes (an expectation that members of Congress have to heed), yet what they receive in exchange (diffuse public goods) is obviously different from what retirees receive (which may be more or less than what they contributed as workers but is still their selective, private good).

In terms of resource exchange between actors A and B, "organization" involves the formation of coalitions of actor B with other actors so as to form a one-to-one correspondence with A. Assumed here is that Emerson's other two balancing operations—a change in the motivations of B so as to lessen dependence on A, or the conferring of status on B so as to lessen the dependence on A—are of secondary importance (Emerson, "Power-Dependence Relations"; Emerson, "Exchange Relations and Networks").

[50] Emerson, "Power-Dependence Relations"; Emerson, "Exchange Relations and Networks"; Emerson, "Toward a Theory of Value in Social Exchange," in Karen S. Cook, ed., *Social Exchange Theory* (Newbury Park, Calif.: Sage, 1987); Cook, "Exchange and Power in Networks of Interorganizational Relations," *Sociological Quarterly* 18 (1977), 62–82.

TABLE 1.2
Alternatives of Policy Domains

Governmental Alternatives		Clientele Alternatives	
Yes	No	Yes	No
Social Security	Labor Regulation	Social Security	Labor Regulation
Public Debt	Navy Procurement	Public Debt	Income Taxation
Income Taxation			Navy Procurement

tary aircraft: it has to buy from the established shipbuilders and from the existing aircraft manufacturers. At the same time, however, societal actors may have choices of their own. Investors can put their money in real estate, in corporate equities, or under mattresses, just as real or potential stakeholders in the social security system can provide for their retirement by buying life insurance annuities, subscribing to pension plans, or saving on their own. Aircraft manufacturers and shipbuilders, on the other hand, in the face of prohibitions on the production of many civilian goods and the possibility of government reprisal, may have had no choice but to produce what the military needed (see Table 1.2).

Table 1.2 may be represented schematically. Figure 1.1 shows the juxtaposition of the alternatives available to societal actors with those of the government, where the presence of alternatives for an actor (government or societal) increases the amount of resources able to be extracted in an exchange. The best position for societal actors is to have non-government alternatives while the government has no other options for securing the resource in question (as may have been the case for American Telephone and Telegraph and the major oil companies). The worst bargaining position for societal actors is not to have any choices while the government has alternatives (as was the case for taxpayers). (Assumed here is that the bargaining position in the cell where neither the government nor the clientele has alternatives is equivalent to the one where both government and clientele have alternatives.)

Separate from the organization of societal actors and from the alternatives available to either the government or the clienteles of particular policy domains is the uncertainty of resource supply.[51] Without sufficient funds of its own to finance the war, without recourse to slave labor, and without the ability to itself build all the airplanes or ships it needs, for instance, the U.S. government confronts owners of wealth, labor unions, and industrial corporations who, if they so choose, can impede or wreck its designs. The wartime

[51] Arthur L. Stinchcombe, *Information and Organizations* (Berkeley: University of California Press, 1990); Douglass North, *Structure and Change in Economic History* (New York: Norton, 1981).

FIGURE 1.1
The Alternative Sets of Policy Domains

	Societal Actors	
	Alternatives	No Alternatives
Government		
Alternatives	Public Debt Social Security	Income Taxation
No Alternatives	Oil (?) Telecommunications (?)	Navy Procurement Labor Regulation Agriculture (?)

government, for all its emergency powers, has reason to be reluctant to take chances on the supply of irreplaceable resources. The result of this uncertainty—over investors investing, workers working, and manufacturers manufacturing—is that public officials may have to induce societal actors to exchange resources voluntarily.

In contrast, individual taxpayers and social security stakeholders not only have little market power of their own, but may be imprisoned or fined should they not cooperate with the government. A wartime government may thus be vulnerable in its relations with financial investors, organized labor, and military contractors, while at the same time it can be virtually certain of tax revenues, social security contributions, and manpower from the military draft (see Table 1.3).[52]

Once war is over, however, conditions change drastically. The government has a surfeit of resources; its alternative sets matter much less; and it has to pay less attention to the alternatives of societal actors. In the absence of war or crisis, uncertainty still matters for government actors, but it becomes more ambiguous: winning elections now depends on attracting voters in peacetime. Assumed here, then, is that the most important factor in determining the terms of exchange in government-society relations is the *size* of the clientele. The policy domain with the largest number of voters should be in the best position for bargaining with the government, then, and that with the fewest number of voters should be in the worst position.

---

[52] Uncertainty coincides with the organization of societal actors among the cases used here. While this may not be surprising, given the force of the logic of collective action, the two are distinct. Consider, for instance, the drafting of teenagers for serving in an unpopular war (with a probability that they will fail to report, leave the country, or prove unsatisfactory soldiers); there may be little in the way of organized resistance but still uncertainty over the government's supply of soldiers. Or, consider agriculture with the probability that bad weather and the wartime labor market could wreak havoc on the production of food; there may be little organization among farmers but great uncertainty, nonetheless, on the part of the wartime government.

TABLE 1.3
Uncertainty of Policy Domains

Uncertain	Certain
Labor Regulation	Social Security
Public Debt	Income Taxation
Navy Procurement	

Hypothesis 4a: The bargains obtained by societal actors in wartime depends on the correspondence of alternative sets and the uncertainty of resource supply; the best bargains should obtain for clienteles with alternatives and with uncertain supplies of resources (see Tables 1.4, 1.1, and 1.3).

Hypothesis 4b: After the war, the ordinal rank of bargains among societal actors and the government should vary simply according to the size of the clientele.

Cases

The following cases are taken as representative of American state-building: social security and social policy more generally; the regulation of labor-management relations; public finance (income taxation and public borrowing); and military procurement (by the U.S. Department of the Navy). The cases pass several screens: they are important issue areas; they represent domestic policy domains exemplary of American exceptionalism; and they experienced variations in their state-building in the 1940s.

Each case at once represents a substantively important policy domain and is characteristic of exceptional American public policies. Social insurance and public assistance form the basis for the modern American welfare state, where the U.S. has less comprehensive social provisions than other advanced industrialized states and no national health insurance as yet. The regulation of labor-management relations is likewise a crucial issue in the politics of advanced industrial economies, where labor has had a historically weak position in American politics.

Public finance, the third case, not only comprises the means by which government secures its needed funding, but policies of taxation and public borrowing determine who bears the cost of government. Public finance constitutes a primary battleground for competing interests and social classes, where the U.S. government imposes fewer and lower taxes than comparable states, and spends proportionally less of its national income.[53] Fourthly, the political economy of national defense is crucial to the political development

[53] O'Connor, *The Fiscal Crisis of the State*, 2–6.

TABLE 1.4
Terms of Resource Exchange: War

Alternatives	Uncertainty	Sum Ordinal Rank
(1) Navy Procurement/	(1) Navy Procurement/	(1) Navy Procurement/
Public Debt	Public Debt	Public Debt
Social Security	Labor Regulation	Labor Regulation
Labor Regulation	(4) Social Security/	(4) Social Security
(5) Income Taxation	Income Taxation	(5) Income Taxation

Note: Policy domains following a slash have equivalent ordinal rankings. Thus under the column "Uncertainty," "Navy Procurement" ranks on a par with "Public Debt" and "Labor Regulation."

of states. Not only has U.S. defense spending been larger in relation to total government spending than that of other advanced industrial states, but the U.S. government-industry relations begun in the 1940s have been thought to be particularly wasteful and damaging economically (even if necessary).[54]

The third criterion for choosing the cases was that they vary in the amount of state-building experienced during the 1940s. The war had little effect on the size of the Social Security Board (after 1946, the Social Security Administration), and inconsistent effects on the extension and intensity of social provisions. The war had a more direct effect on the regulation of labor-management relations: the powers of the National Labor Relations Board and the United States Conciliation Service were supplemented by the creation of other labor boards, and the federal government acted to settle many more labor-management disputes (so as to prevent and preempt wartime work stoppages) than it had before the war.

Wars being typically expensive, there was a closer identity between the incidence of World War II and state-building in public finance. The Treasury Department and the Congress had to find hundreds of billions of dollars with which to pay for the war, hence the great expansion of federal income taxation and the massive sales of U.S. government securities. The benefits of wartime spending further revealed fiscal policy to be a potent instrument by which the government could influence the economy. The increase in the scale and the changes in the administration of matériel procurement by the Navy Department varied most directly with the external threat of world war, however. Not surprisingly: the executive branch and Congress spared little to ensure that the Navy had sufficient funding, matériel, and manpower.

---

[54] Military contractors could, of course, be wholly or partially nationalized. The grounds for including procurement in the state would still stand, however, since a substantial part of the economy would be captive to governmental requirements for the production of military goods.

In short, the cases represent important policy domains that have been identified with American exceptionalism: a partial welfare state of limited redistribution; politically weak labor unions; low tax rates, low levels of government spending, and an absence of a national employment policy; and high levels of military spending. And the war had varying effects on the institutions of each of the policy domains.[55]

Summary

International factors not only may affect a state's foreign relations and military policy, but may deeply influence the internal aspect of the Janus-faced state. Wars are capable of affecting political development in domestic policy domains remote from international factors. The Second World War and its aftermath had precisely such effects on the American state. Between mid-year 1940 (when the United States began to rearm) and mid-year 1950 (when the United States entered the Korean conflict) there occurred a virtual revolution in U.S. domestic policies—one that put into place many of the institutions of American government characteristic of the postwar decades. Nor were such transformative effects distinctive to World War II: the First World War had an analogous, though lesser, impact—as will be seen later.

If we are to trace the outside-in effects of hegemonic war, however, then we have to make explicit what we mean by the *state* and by *state-building*. The three-part definition of the state proposed here is arguably consistent with a reinterpretation of Weber's writing on the state, and it also facilitates the measurement of institutional change. State-building is explained in organizational terms, through an adaptation of the resource dependence perspective to the U.S. federal government.

In times of hegemonic war the government (i.e., the president, other executive branch officials, and the Congress) has to reach out for resources owned or controlled by societal actors in order to survive. State-building obtains when the government expands its administrative bureaucracies, develops new relations or intensifies its existing ties with individuals and private organizations, and improves its means of administration. But the exact character of state-building in any one policy domain depends on the particular resource environment.

Specifically, attention to the environment of government organizations allows us to determine, first, the *agents* of change, since the direction of

[55] The cases parallel Skowronek's cases of civil service reform, the reform of the army, and business regulation (the railroads): all three are functional tasks of the state, comprise distinct areas of state activity, and represent a cross-section of state activity (Skowronek, *Building a New American State*, 4, 15).

state-building depends on the legal conditions that determine the balance of authority between the president and Congress; secondly, the institutional *form* of change, since the government depends on clienteles that differ in number, organizational coherence, and resources; third, the *persistence* of change, since whether the state-building resulting from a crisis persists depends on the extent to which the changes in national and international environments will, in turn, affect the size and shape of government organizations; and lastly, the *terms of exchange* for governmental and societal actors in crisis and post-crisis periods, depending on the alternative sets available to government organizations and societal actors, and on the uncertainty in the government's supply of needed resources.

The next four chapters study the effects of World War II on each of the cases above, and explore how well the changes happening in the three dimensions of the state follow the hypotheses derived from the resource dependence perspective. Chapter 2 examines the institutional changes of the 1940s in the social security system. Chapter 3 explores the developments in the regulation of labor-management relations occurring as a result of the war and the immediate postwar years. Chapter 4 discusses the changes in public finance with respect to the extension of personal and corporate income taxation, the growth of federal borrowing, and the introduction of fiscal policy. This chapter also allows for a preliminary comparison of relative state-building during the 1940s, since income taxation and the management of the public debt involve distinct government agencies and different clienteles.

Chapter 5 looks at the changes in the administration of matériel procurement by the Navy Department. Although Navy procurement is not a wholly domestic policy domain (military logistics being a natural extension of a state's international existence), military spending has important and obvious impacts on the national economy and political development: it sets the amount and sources of funding for scientific research and development; it controls the markets for top scientists and engineers; it channels industrial specialization; and it indirectly affects the amount of spending available for other programs.

Chapter 6 compares the terms of exchange obtained by government organizations and societal actors in the state-building of the 1940s (consistent with the fourth set of hypotheses), given that the clienteles of the policy domains discussed in the preceding chapters were not equally positioned in their wartime and postwar exchanges with the government.

Chapter 7 concludes the book. It first determines the degree to which the findings from testing the resource dependence perspective held true more generally during the 1940s, by looking at evidence beyond that of the cases.

It then discusses the extent to which the findings of the 1940s were fore-shadowed by the experiences of World War I, between the years 1915 and 1925, given that the First World War, as a hegemonic war, should exert similar effects on the American state. Last, the chapter looks at how three competing explanations of American state-building compare with the re-source dependence perspective as it is developed here.

2

Social Security's Missing Years

Because everyone gets old.
—William F. Green, President, American
Federation of Labor

I agree there is this innate yearning for power
in the heart of each individual. We all want to
be significant as possible during our brief span
of mortal life. We believe we know the answers
and undertake to supply the answers. I believe
that there is another deep-seated instinct
though and that is the law of self-preservation,
so while we yearn to be significant we also
want to be sure that we have not, to use a
vulgar phrase, "stuck our necks out" in the
process.
—Arthur J. Altmeyer, 1944

I have said many times that a successful
administrator ought to be about as interesting
as spinach—cold spinach at that.
—Arthur J. Altmeyer, 1967

As RECENTLY AS 1988, the Democratic National Platform claimed that
"[t]here is no good reason why . . . the greatest and richest nation on earth
should rank first among the industrialized nations . . . in the percentage of
total expenditures devoted to defense but nearly last in the percentage devoted to education and housing."[1] Contra this conventional wisdom, there
may be good reasons for what many identify as a weak American welfare
state.[2] The decade of the 1940s in particular—from the beginning of U.S.

[1] New York *Times*, 19 July 1988, 10.

[2] In contrast to the social provisions in other advanced industrial nations, social security in
the United States did not include a national program of general relief and excluded national
health insurance. Social provisions in the United States came late compared to Great Britain
and Germany. See Katznelson, "Rethinking the Silences of Social and Economic Policy"; Ellis
W. Hawley, "Social Policy and the Liberal State in Twentieth Century America," in Donald T.
Critchlow and Ellis W. Hawley, eds., *Federal Social Policy: The Historical Dimension* (Univer-

rearmament after the German invasion of France to the beginning of the Korean conflict—was crucial in establishing the U.S. social policies of the latter half of the twentieth century.

What in 1940 covered only 6 percent of the 8.5 million people over the age of sixty-five was, by 1950, firmly established as part of American public policy: benefit levels and contributory tax rates had just been increased; Old-Age and Survivors Insurance was being successfully promoted as a federally guaranteed, individualized program of retirement benefits; and employers and the labor unions both fully supported the social security program. Social security would eventually become a national retirement program covering all occupations, and would later expand to include care for the disabled and medical care for the elderly and the poor.

The survival and subsequent success of social security as the linchpin of the American welfare system was hardly a given, however, despite the overwhelming focus on the 1930s by later politicians, social scientists, historians, journalists, and social security administrators.[3] Before the Second World War, the existing social security system had come under attack from all sides. Members of Congress, the labor unions, the public at large, and even officials in the Roosevelt Administration were clamoring for higher, flat-rate social security benefits and for increased coverage. The CIO (among others) charged that the current social security system provided inadequate benefits, limited coverage, overly complicated eligibility requirements, and "payment of benefits 'substantially less than the incoming funds.'"[4] At a time

---

sity Park: Pennsylvania State University Press, 1988); Amenta and Skocpol, "Redefining the New Deal"; Edwin Amenta and Theda Skocpol, "Taking Exception: Explaining the Distinctiveness of American Public Policies in the Last Century," in Francis G. Castles, ed., *The Comparative History of Public Policies* (London: Polity Press, 1989); and G. John Ikenberry and Theda Skocpol, "Expanding Social Benefits: The Role of Social Security," *Political Science Quarterly* 102 No. 3 (1987): 389–416.

[3] See Arthur J. Altmeyer, *The Formative Years of Social Security* (Madison: University of Wisconsin Press, 1966); Gaston V. Rimlinger, *Welfare Policy and Industrialization in Europe, America and Russia* (New York: Wiley, 1971); Martha Derthick, *Policymaking for Social Security* (Washington, D.C.: Brookings Institution, 1979); Edward D. Berkowitz and Kim McQuaid, *Creating the Welfare State*, Second Edition (New York: Praeger, 1990); Skocpol and Ikenberry, "The Political Formation of the American Welfare State"; Jerry R. Cates, *Insuring Inequality: Administrative Leadership in Social Security, 1935–54* (Ann Arbor: University of Michigan Press, 1984); and Mark H. Leff, "Speculating in Social Security Futures: The Perils of Payroll Financing, 1939–1950," in Gerald D. Nash, Noel H. Pugach and Richard F. Tomasson, eds., *Social Security: The First Half Century* (Albuquerque: University of New Mexico Press, 1988).

[4] Derthick, *Policymaking for Social Security*; Berkowitz and McQuaid, *Creating the Welfare State*; Berkowitz, *America's Welfare State*; Berkowitz, ed., *Social Security after Fifty Years* (New York: Greenwood Press, 1987); Skocpol and Ikenberry, "The Political Formation of the American Welfare State"; Jill Quadagno, "Welfare Capitalism and the Social Security Act of 1935," *American Sociological Review* 49 (October 1984): 632–47; Quadagno, *The Transformation of Old Age Security: Class and Politics in the American Welfare State* (Chicago: University of Chicago Press, 1988); Mark H. Leff, "Taxing the 'Forgotten Man': The Politics of Social

when there was no guarantee of the success of the new bureaucracy and the new programs, the direct and indirect effects of the Second World War irreversibly altered American social provisions; the early 1940s were every bit the "Crucial Years" that Arthur J. Altmeyer, Commissioner of the Social Security Administration until 1953, labeled the late 1940s and early 1950s.[5] What, then, explains the resilience of the social security system during the war years in the face of the absence of new social security taxes or increases in benefit levels?

The expectations from the resource dependence perspective are, first, that the Congress should set social security policy during the war, since social security was a social welfare as well as revenue program (even in the emergency of war), and that Congress should continue to set social policy after WWII.

Second, the lack of organization among social security stakeholders should result in the expansion of the social security program, in the form of an extension of existing bureaucracies. The diffusion of actual and potential social security stakeholders (both contributors and beneficiaries) across the United States should cause the government to extend its existing centralized bureaucracies. Growth in the social security system should therefore be manifest in an increase in the number of ties connecting the federal govern-ment with individual employers and employees, rather than through the establishment of new agencies or intermediary bodies.

Third, the war should alter social security policy. With a larger workforce earning income needed by the wartime government, we should expect the government to expand the social security system through an exchange of future benefits for present revenue. We should also expect the state-building of the war years to survive the war, given the larger number of Americans now covered by social security. Not only should the impact of war affect the wealth and demographics of those contributing towards and receiving benefits from the social security program, but the effects of the war on government policy should in turn alter the population of social secu-rity stakeholders. There should also be a change in the agenda of social policy as a result of the crisis period.

The Bureau of Old-Age and Survivors Insurance (BOASI) and the Social Security Board (SSB) are taken to be representative of the social security

---

Security Finance in the New Deal," *Journal of American History* 70 No. 2 (September 1983): 359–81; Leff, "Historical Perspectives on Old-Age Insurance: The State of the Art on the Art of the State," in Berkowitz, ed., *Social Security after Fifty Years*; Hugh Heclo, "General Welfare and Two American Political Traditions," *Political Science Quarterly* 101 No. 2 (1986): 179–96; Ikenberry and Skocpol, "Expanding Social Benefits"; and Daniel Levine, *Poverty and Society: The Growth of the American Welfare State in International Comparison* (New Brunswick, N.J.: Rutgers University Press, 1988).

[5] Altmeyer, *Formative Years*, 169–209.

bureaucracies (a national health insurance program would also have been vested in the SSB).[6] The numbers of social security beneficiaries and individual contributors—those tied directly to the national government through the social security program—are considered as indicators of the extent of the relational state. And the amount in per capita income received by social insurance beneficiaries and the amount paid by employees in social security taxes may be considered as measures of the intensity, or salience, of government-society ties.

Background

There was little legislated change in the social security system in the period between the 1939 amendments to the Social Security Act and the passage of the 1950 social security reforms.[7] The only amendments to the Social Security Act were an expansion of coverage for seamen affiliated with the War Shipping Administration in 1943 and the inclusion of qualified veterans' survivors in 1946. Social security taxes stayed at 1 percent of wages for both employers and employees from 1939 through 1949 (for an effective total rate of 2 percent of employee wages), increased to 1.5 percent each for employers and employees from 1950 through 1953, and then rose to 2 percent each in 1954. The reforms of 1950 also increased social security benefits by an average of 70 percent and expanded social security coverage to 7.5 million additional workers, including regularly employed domestic and farm workers, certain categories of self-employed workers, employees of nonprofit organizations (optional), and those state and local workers not covered by other retirement programs. Employees working in OASI-covered occupations now paid social security taxes on the first $3,600 of personal income (up from $3,000), and social security was extended to Puerto Rico and the U.S. Virgin Islands.

National health insurance was, of course, not to be. The attempts by President Truman and others to establish national medical insurance in the late 1940s would achieve only partial realization with Medicare and, later, Medicaid (see Chapter 7 for a further discussion of public health insurance).

---

[6] Both the SSB and the SSA were part of the Federal Security Agency (FSA), the precursor to the Department of Health, Education and Welfare and, later, the Department of Health and Human Services.

The Social Security Board had its own sources of revenue and could hire and promote as it saw fit; its lawyers and experts were immune from Civil Service guidelines (Derthick, *Policymaking for Social Security*, 27).

[7] See Berkowitz on the events leading up to the 1939 amendments to the Social Security Act and to what I shall argue are parallels to the period just before the entry of the United States into World War II (Edward D. Berkowitz, "The First Advisory Council and the 1939 Amendments," in Berkowitz, ed., *Social Security after Fifty Years*, 55–78).

The President, Congress, and Social Security

Despite the New Deal legislation establishing and amending the social security program, despite the wartime government's desperate need for revenue, and despite the apparent ease and convenience of expanding the social security system, there were no significant new social security programs set up during the 1940s; social security tax rates, benefit levels, and employee group coverage remained virtually unchanged. Yet the absence of new social security legislation was not for lack of effort. Both the Roosevelt and Truman Administrations attempted on several occasions to expand the social security system, but Congress would not cooperate.

Soon after the declarations of war on Japan and Germany, in early 1942, President Roosevelt exhorted Congress to expand the social security system: "Additional . . . [social security] contributions will cover increased disbursements over a long period of time. [They] would result in reserves of several billion dollars for postwar contingencies. The present accumulation of these contributions would absorb excess purchasing power."[8] A few months later, Roosevelt wrote the Chairman of the Senate Finance Committee, Walter George (D., Ga.): "This is one case in which social and fiscal objectives, war and postwar aims are in full accord. Expanded social security, together with other fiscal measures, would set up a bulwark of economic security for the people now and after the war and at the same time would provide anti-inflationary sources for financing the war."[9] But Congress refused to expand the social security system, though it did hold hearings and debates on expanding coverage and revising OASI tax rates.

Social security taxes stayed frozen at the rate of 1 percent each for employers and employees. Senator Arthur Vandenberg (R., Mich.) spoke on behalf of the Vandenberg Amendment to the 1943 revenue bill, which was to freeze social security tax rates at their existing level:

> Nothing would more greatly weaken the Social Security System than to permit its taxing function, in the first great emergency it has ever faced, to be utilized for something more than or different from the social security benefits which the payroll taxes are presumed to buy. In my view the only purpose to be served by increased pay-roll taxes next January is to create a super-surplus not required for the payment of social security and old-age benefits under the 1939 program, but

---

[8] 1942 Annual Budget Message, *The Public Papers and Addresses of Franklin D. Roosevelt*, Samuel I. Rosenman, comp. (New York: Harper & Brothers, 1950), Vol. 10, 17.

[9] Letter of President Roosevelt to Senator Walter George, 3 October 1942, file 71, "Vandenberg Amendment to H.R. 7378," Box 2, Records of the Commissioner of the Social Security Administration, Record Group 47. The President sent an identical letter to Representative Robert Doughton (D., N.C.), Chairman of the House Ways and Means Committee.

solely to create an automatic market for the sale of about $1,000,000,000 more of War Bonds.[10]

Vandenberg argued that the amount in the reserve fund exceeded the formula given Congress by SSB Chairman Altmeyer and Treasury Secretary Henry Morgenthau. The 1939 amendments (which took social security off a full reserve system) established that the contingency reserve should amount to "not more than three times the highest prospective annual benefits in the ensuing 5 years." And Altmeyer had admitted in earlier testimony that the reserve fund was "six times the highest anticipated benefit requirements in the next 5 years."[11] The Senate supported the Vandenberg Amendment by a vote of fifty to thirty-five.

When the President requested another increase in OASI taxes in 1944 (including it in the "Revenue and Borrowing" section of the annual Budget message), Congress again rejected it.[12] The second request was held to be irrelevant to the fiscal soundness of the OASI trust funds, since the trust fund had "8 to 12" times the highest prospective annual expenditure; the tax hike was therefore "wholly unnecessary and unjustifiable."[13] Any increase in social security taxes would amount to a straight tax for the benefit of the Treasury. Vandenberg thought that "the use of the social-security tax trust fund, directly or indirectly, for any purpose on earth except social security purposes [was] a violation of a public trust in the rankest possible degree."[14]

Table 2.1 illustrates the imbalance prevalent throughout the early and mid-1940s between the incoming funds from the social security tax and OASI outlays. Social security outlays came to $88 million in 1941, for instance, while the trust fund had a balance of more than $2.7 billion. By 1945, OASI outlays came to $274 million while the trust fund reserves had risen to more than $7.1 billion.[15] As we see, neither the Roosevelt Administration nor Congress had reason to fear for the solvency of the social security system in the foreseeable future: the government was collecting far more in social security taxes than it was having to pay out in benefits.

[10] *Congressional Record*, 9 October 1942, 8009.

[11] *Congressional Record*, 9 October 1942, 8007. Also see Leff, "Speculating in Social Security Futures."

[12] See "Freezing the Social Security Tax Rate at 1 Percent," Hearings Before the Committee on Ways and Means, House of Representatives, 78th Cong., 2nd sess., 27, 28, and 29 November 1944. See statements by Albert M. Linton, president, Provident Mutual Life Insurance Co., Fred Perkins, and the Ohio Chamber of Commerce.

[13] *Congressional Record*, 5 December 1944, 8839.

[14] *Congressional Record*, 8 December 1944, 9052.

[15] By way of comparison, contributions to the OASI trust fund in 1938 amounted to $360 million, social security outlays came to $10 million, and the OASI balance summed to $1,132 million. The balance in the OASI trust fund came to 20 percent of federal government outlays.

TABLE 2.1
Reserves in OASI Trust Fund (millions of dollars)

Year	Contributions	Outlays	OASI Balance	% USG
1940	325	35	2,031	28
1941	789	88	2,762	40
1942	1,012	131	3,688	33
1943	1,239	166	4,820	30
1944	1,316	209	6,005	32
1945	1,285	274	7,121	40
1946	1,295	378	8,150	47
1947	1,558	466	9,360	39
1948	1,688	556	10,722	51
1949	1,670	667	11,816	46
1950	2,671	961	13,721	52

Sources: OASI figures are from Robert J. Myers, *Social Insurance and Allied Government Programs* (Homewood, Ill.: Irwin, 1965), 37, Table 25. Federal figures are from "Outlays of the Federal Government," Series Y 457–465, U.S. Department of Commerce, Bureau of the Census, *Historical Statistics of the United States,* 1114.

Notes: "Contributions" and "Outlays" both refer to the OASI trust fund. "% USG" refers to the balance in the OASI Trust Fund as a proportion of federal government civilian outlays. These and subsequent agency figures in the tables refer to expenditures as a percentage of government civilian outlays, since the federal government's civilian outlays (and civilian employment) figures provide a more stable baseline than if war expenditures (and personnel) were included.

Yet the very imbalance between OASI assets and OASI obligations points to the bewildering failure of Congress to act on the Roosevelt Administration's repeated requests: a further expansion in the social security system would have guaranteed a large net increase in federal revenues, since most of the government's obligations would not be incurred until contributors retired. In the meantime, the government would receive desperately needed funds and would ease inflationary pressures by limiting consumer spending (given the wartime surge in the money supply). The imposition of higher social security taxes would have fulfilled the Roosevelt Administration's goals of drawing off discretionary income and raising additional revenue.

Despite the force of this argument and despite the fact that Treasury Secretary Morgenthau, Secretary of Labor Frances Perkins, Budget Director Harold Smith, Federal Security Agency head Paul McNutt, and SSB Chairman Altmeyer all agreed to an expanded social security system, Congress would not go along. Neither the President nor those members of Congress favoring higher OASI taxes were able to convince a majority of the

House and Senate of the fact that expanding the social security system was indispensable for fighting inflation and raising revenues. With no such case being made, there would be no social security reform during the war. And when Congress overrode President Roosevelt's veto of the 1943 tax bill in early 1944, it passed an amendment to freeze OASI tax rates. Congress controlled policymaking in social security, as expected.

But the stalemate in social security was more than the result of Congress's recalcitrance; it was also the result of equivocation on the part of President Roosevelt. The President insisted on "no breakdown" or simply a "continuation" of the social security system on numerous occasions (26 May, 11 September, and 14 September 1940, and 3 January 1941), while at other times he advocated a double-decker plan (minimum federal payments plus retirement benefits based on wage contributions), increased benefits, and higher contribution rates (11 September 1940, and 3 January and 6 January 1941). The President later promised, on 30 September 1941, to recommend that Congress expand social security coverage and increase social security payments to the most needy.

But after a conversation with the President on 8 October 1941, the Chairman of the Senate Finance Committee was led to believe "that the President had made some commitments and felt obliged to send some sort of message to the Hill. However, the President said such a message would be general in nature, would not send it for three or four weeks, and the leaders of the Senate Finance and House Ways and Means Committees would have an opportunity to talk with the President before the message was sent." Senator George reported that the President "understood there was to be plenty of other work to keep these two committees busy in the meantime and that he had no intention of sidetracking this work with the Social Security Program."[16] Roosevelt made no recommendations for the expansion of the social security system in the period before the attack on Pearl Harbor.

Once the United States was at war, however, the President requested higher social security taxes in his Budget Message to Congress of 4 January 1942. Raising social security taxes would combat inflationary pressures, provide increased insurance payments for the elderly, prepare for the social security system for the years following the war, and absorb excess cash. Roosevelt further called for extended OASI coverage and for hospitalization benefits. Yet in the State of the Union address delivered to Congress in person and broadcast nationally one day after the message on the budget, the President said nothing about social security or about public insurance for hospitalization. Roosevelt became still less precise about his plans to

---

[16] Memorandum of John L. Sullivan, Assistant Secretary of the Treasury, to the Secretary of the Treasury, 8 October 1941, file "Daily Record, September–December 1941," Box 1, Papers of John L. Sullivan.

expand social provisions as the war went on. In the 1943 Budget Message, for instance, the President advocated "freedom from want" but released no details of his program, and Roosevelt held out the promise of "cradle to the grave" protection in the 1943 State of the Union address but again provided no specifics. Despite the urging of many of his advisers, including Labor Secretary Perkins, and despite his earlier promise to extend the social security program, Roosevelt would not even publicly support the Wagner-Murray-Dingell Bill of 1943, which would have imposed higher social security taxes, extended social security coverage, and established a program of national health care.[17] The Wagner-Murray-Dingell Bill died in committee.

Then, in the 1944 annual Budget and State of the Union addresses, the President requested protection for "nearly all" of the population and asked that Congress implement an "economic bill of rights." The economic bill of rights would guarantee "adequate protection for the economic fears of old age, sickness, accident, and unemployment." In Roosevelt's 1945 annual messages, he once more asked for an economic bill of rights as well as for the extension of social security coverage and protection from medical costs.[18] As for the details of the changes in the social security system, these Roosevelt would "communicate with the Congress . . . at a later date." Dying in Warm Springs, Georgia, on 12 April 1945, he never got the chance.

Roosevelt's handling of the veterans' programs (which rivaled the social security program as well as other social policies) echoed his ambivalent support for an expanded social security program. In 1935, Roosevelt had declared that "[a]ble-bodied veterans should be accorded no treatment different from that accorded other citizens who did not wear a uniform during the World War. . . . There is before this Congress legislation providing old-age benefits and a greater measure of security for all workers against the hazards of unemployment. We are also meeting the . . . need of immediate relief. In all of this the veteran shares."[19] Including veterans' bonuses and benefits in the administration of existing social programs would thus

[17] See letter of Robert F. Wagner to the President, 21 December 1944, expressing his and SSB Chairman Altmeyer's requests that the President devote himself "to the fight," and letter of Philip Murray to the President, 27 September 1943 (file "SSB misc., 1943–1944," OF 1710, Box 4, Roosevelt Papers). Also see "Digest of Social Security Recommendations of National Social Congress Committee, CIO," Submitted to 1942 Convention, Congress of Industrial Organizations, file 011.4, "1943," Box 4, Records of the Executive Director of the Social Security Board (Accession Number 56-A533), Executive Director's Files ("EDF"), Record Group 47.

[18] See David Brody on the reluctance of the President to press for his New Deal programs in the 1940s (David Brody, "The New Deal and World War II," in John Braeman, Robert H. Bremner, and David Brody, eds., The New Deal, Vol. 1: The National Level [Columbus: Ohio State University Press, 1975]).

[19] The Public Papers and Addresses of Franklin D. Roosevelt, Vol. 4, 187 and 189, cited in Davis B. Ross, Preparing for Ulysses: Politics and Veterans during World War II (New York: Columbia University Press, 1969), 19.

have been consistent with Roosevelt's record.[20] But veterans' programs were kept apart. The only overlap between the Social Security Administration and the billions in veterans' programs was the granting of insurance benefits for qualified veterans' survivors in 1946, and the $160 per month credit for wartime service, effective in 1950.[21]

By November 1943 veterans were already receiving government life insurance, guarantees on commercial life insurance premiums, coverage of hospitalization and medical care, pension rights, and reemployment rights. Indicative of the emphasis placed on veterans' programs was the ease with which veterans' survivors could receive OASI benefits under the 1946 bill: benefits were paid to the survivor(s) of any serviceman who died within three years after being discharged, if he had been on active duty between 16 September 1940 and the end of the war and had received an honorable discharge within four years of the end of the war, or if he had been terminated by service-related disability or injury after serving for fewer than ninety days. Never in American history had the returning soldier and his family been treated so well.

In short, the Second World War had little direct effect on social security policies. President Roosevelt limited his appeals for extending the social security system and then, after January 1942, put such appeals in only the most general of terms. Congress, for its part, refused to expand or reform the social security system and kept social policies separate from veterans' programs. After the war, Congress continued to set social policy, but again the policy was mostly one of inaction. Congress passed only minimal amendments in 1946, refused to pass national health insurance, and did not significantly reform the social security program until 1950—five years after the end of the war.

Bills were introduced in 1945 to establish national health insurance and to extend the social security system, but they never left committee. Although Congress did amend the Social Security Act by making veterans' survivors eligible for social security benefits and did pass the Hill-Burton Act for the construction of hospitals,[22] Congress removed newspaper vendors from social insurance coverage, passing the bill over Truman's veto. And when the House of Representatives held its hearings on social security in 1948, the Ways and Means Committee reported out a compromise bill that was subse-

[20] Ross, *Preparing for Ulysses*, 25–29.

[21] Also see Skocpol and Ikenberry ("The Political Formation of the American Welfare State") and Ross (*Preparing for Ulysses*) for a discussion on the relation between social security and veterans' benefits.

[22] On the controversy around and failure of the 1946 proposals to expand the social security system, see "Amendments to Social Security Act," Hearings before the Committee on Ways and Means, House of Representatives, 79th Cong., 2nd sess., February, March, and April 1946.

quently passed on the floor; but the Senate did nothing with the bill.[23] The only positive action taken by the 80th Congress was to increase the social security tax rate to 1.5 percent each for employees and employers, effective January 1950.

In contrast to Congress's inaction, President Truman strongly and continually called for expansions in old-age and health benefits.[24] Upon succeeding Roosevelt as president, Truman almost immediately pressed for an expanded social security program and for national health insurance. He expanded Roosevelt's economic bill of rights into a "21 point" program on 6 September 1945, and on 19 November 1945 he sent a "Special Message to Congress Recommending a Comprehensive Health Program." Truman restated the need for a national health program in the combined Budget message and State of the Union address of 1946, and he spoke of his wish to see social security for veterans: their period of service could be considered "employment." There was no "adequate reason" why the self-employed, agricultural and industrial workers, and the employees of nonprofit organizations should be excluded from old-age security (the expansion of the social security system was later included as part of Truman's "Fair Deal").

The President's support for social programs, even in the face of the weakened state of the postwar presidency, continued over the rest of the decade. In his "First Economic Report" of 8 January 1947, Truman asked for "immediate steps" to adjust social security benefits and extend OASI coverage. He also requested a national health plan that would spread the risk pool for costly medical services.[25] Then, on 19 May 1947, Truman restated his five points on the nation's health in a special message to Congress, and he again exhorted Congress to pass legislation for national health insurance as a "logical extension of the present social security system." The requests for national health insurance, extended social security coverage, and increased federal benefits were repeated in the 1948 State of the Union address; they

[23] Robert J. Donovan, a journalist and chronicler of the Truman presidency, blames this on the antagonism between the President and Senator Harry Byrd (*Tumultuous Years: The Presidency of Harry S Truman, 1949–1953* [New York: Norton, 1982], 126). The bill would have increased wage levels to $3,600 and extended coverage to 11 million more workers (as opposed to Truman's requested 25 million) but would not have lowered the age of women recipients from 65 to 60.

[24] See Richard E. Neustadt on Truman's commitment to New Deal goals ("Congress and the Fair Deal: A Legislative Balance Sheet," in Richard M. Abrams and Lawrence Levine, eds., *The Shaping of Twentieth Century America* [Boston: Little, Brown, 1965]).

[25] President Truman proposed to finance social security out of general revenues—something that the SSB and President Roosevelt had previously been loath to do (*The Public Papers of the Presidents of the United States: Harry S. Truman, 1947* [Washington, D.C.: U.S. GPO], 37).

were also the "long range objectives" of the President's annual Budget message of 14 January 1948.

In his 1949 Budget message Truman once more advocated the extension and liberalization of old-age, survivors', and unemployment insurance and the enactment of health insurance: one-third of American workers were uncovered by the existing programs, and old-age benefits averaged only $25 per month. As for health:

> We must spare no effort to raise the general level of health in this country. In a nation as rich as ours it is a shocking fact that tens of millions lack adequate medical care. We are short of doctors, hospitals, nurses. We must remedy these shortages. Moreover, we need—and we must have without further delay—a system of prepaid medical insurance which will enable every American to afford good medical care.[26]

Finally, with the election of the 81st Congress and the subsequent hearings held on extending OASI coverage and raising social security benefit levels, Truman was able to tell Congress in his 1950 State of the Union address that he hoped it would "complete action" to extend insurance coverage and increase OASI benefits.[27]

Pressure for an expanded social security system came from the fact that the noncontributory half of social security, Old-Age Assistance, was becoming the dominant form of old-age relief (as the SSA, the White House, and the members of the Ways and Means Committee well realized): by the late 1940s, about one-fifth of the elderly were receiving OAA payments, and in some states the proportion was more than half.[28] But OAA was regarded as an undesirable program by many in the Truman Administration and in Congress, so the more desirable Old-Age and Survivors Insurance was retailored in order to meet citizen demands and be able to offer benefits capable of replacing OAA benefits. A "very substantial" increase in social security benefits was needed to head off the Republican-led initiatives towards flat plans or a general pension plan.

The Social Security Administration and Congress thus agreed to expand the OASI program, and officials from the SSA, including Robert Myers (the SSA's chief actuary), served on the Advisory Committee to the Senate Finance Committee for the reform of the social security system. The House passed the proposed reforms to the social security system in the summer of 1950, and President Truman signed H.R. 6000 into law on 28 August: OASI benefits were to be increased by 77 percent, OASI coverage expanded, and

[26] *The Public Papers of the Presidents of the United States: Harry S. Truman, 1949*, 5.

[27] "Social Security Revision," Hearings before the Committee on Finance, United States Senate, 81st Cong., 2nd sess., on H.R. 6000, Parts 1 and 2, January and February 1950.

[28] Leff, "Speculating in Social Security Futures," 268.

restrictions eased on the proportion of received benefits to the amounts paid into the system.[29]

Although the Senate Finance Committee had agreed with many of the recommendations proposed by the Advisory Council on Social Security in 1947, the committee rejected the Council's advice (and the recommendations of the Truman Administration) that social security be financed out of general revenues. The committee chose instead to renew the commitment to the contributory principle, which it saw as financial responsibility (Myers being a strong advocate of the self-financing component of the social security system).

The proposed reforms ignored many of the other recommendations of the Advisory Committee as well.[30] The revised social security program excluded several occupational categories (among them agricultural workers, domestic servants not employed on a regular basis, and most professionals), and the new bill made social security optional for nonprofit employees and for local and state government workers. Not surprisingly, many workers preferred the reality of fuller paychecks in the present to the promise of future benefits upon retirement, even though they would be much better off in the long run by participating in OASI. Nor did the 1950 bill include veterans' programs in an expanded social security program, despite the intentions of the Council of Economic Advisers (under chairman Leon Keyserling). The CEA called for veterans' programs to be committed to the "protection and improvement of the social insurance structure." An integrated program would eliminate the duplication of benefits, would defuse the pressures to liberalize veterans' pensions, and would make veterans' and non-veterans' benefits commensurate.[31]

[29] The House Ways and Means and Senate Finance Committees intended to study proposals for future improvement in the social security laws (*The Public Papers of the Presidents of the United States: Harry S. Truman, 1950*, 601).

[30] See "The Major Differences in the Present Social-Security Law, the Recommendations of the Advisory Council, and H.R. 6000," in "Social Security Revision," Hearings before the Committee on Finance, U.S. Senate, 2–18. Also see Wilbur J. Cohen and Robert J. Myers, "Social Security Act Amendments of 1980: A Summary and Legislative History," reprinted from *Social Security Bulletin*, October 1950, in file "1950 October," 011.1, Box 37, Office of the Commissioner Files, 1949–50.

Berkowitz sees three factors contributing to the success of the 1950 reforms. For one, "Agricultural states had a higher welfare rate among the elderly than did industrial states . . . Extending coverage to the agricultural workers would mean that they could receive social security rather than welfare." Secondly, heightened administrative capacity, with the improved "technology of tax collection," eased the problems in extending social security. Thirdly, the 1950 amendments occupied the "middle of the road" between liberal and conservative alternatives (Edward D. Berkowitz, "Introduction: Social Security Celebrates an Anniversary," in Berkowitz, ed., *Social Security after Fifty Years*, 20–21).

[31] Memorandum of David Christian to Leon H. Keyserling, 16 February 1949, file "Christian Work Assignment," Box 9, Papers of Leon Keyserling. Also see Memorandum of Gerhard

In short, Congress succeeded in blocking, delaying, and diluting the expansions in social provisions requested by the President and proposed by the SSA. The inability of the executive branch to effect more extensive changes in social provisions is thus, as expected, consistent with Congress's control of social and tax policies in both wartime and peacetime, even if President Truman's doomed efforts on behalf of a public health care system and his support for an earlier and more complete expansion of OASI are unexpected.

The Shape of Social Security

The diffuseness of the social security clientele (except for the labor unions and the Townsend movement) leads us to anticipate that the government would not have to establish any new organizations in a crisis period but could expand the existing Social Security Board (SSB) and the Bureau of Old-Age and Survivors Insurance (BOASI) to the extent needed. The Roosevelt Administration would not need to set up new organizations linking up the resource-controlling societal actor with the government. This is, in fact, what happened.

No new social security agencies were established between 1940 and 1945, and the SSB and the BOASI increased barely at all in size. BOASI employment grew from about nine thousand persons in 1940 to twelve thousand persons by 1950, while SSB employment declined over the first half of the decade, from 12,164 persons in 1940 to 10,629 persons in 1945 (see Table 2.2). The proportion of BOASI employees to total federal civilian employees also fell, dropping from about 1 percent of the number of federal civilian employees in 1940 to under a third that level from 1943 through 1945 and remaining at under two-thirds of 1 percent in the immediate postwar years.

Meanwhile, BOASI expenditures rose by $5 million during the war, from $12.4 million in 1940 to $17.5 million in 1945, while overall SSB expenditures increased up to 1943 and then fell back to their 1940 level by 1945 (see Table 2.3). BOASI (and SSB) expenditures shrank as a percentage of federal spending, although BOASI expenditures (like BOASI employment) grew in proportion to total SSB figures. In short, the SSB bureaucracy shrank over the course of the war and that of the BOASI expanded slightly in terms of personnel and budgets, consistent with the absence of legislated increases in social security contributions and coverage.

The government could have become more dependent on societal actors—the social security stakeholders—during the 1940s but chose not

---

Colm and David Christian to Mr. Keyserling, 18 January 1949, file "Christian Work Assignment."

TABLE 2.2

Employment in the Social Security Administration

Fiscal Year	BOASI	SSB/SSA	Fed. Civ.	% USG
1940	8,918	12,164	1,042 (000)	1.1
1941	9,353	12,682	1,437	0.88
1942	9,752	13,297	2,296	0.58
1943	8,734	10,585	3,299	0.32
1944	8,392	10,045	3,332	0.30
1945	9,007	10,629	3,816	0.28
1946	9,494	11,261	2,696	0.42
1947	11,156	12,830	2,111	0.61
1948	11,775	12,889	2,071	0.62
1949	11,726	12,854	2,102	0.55
1950	11,995	11,899	1,961	0.61

Sources: Employment figures are from Social Security Board/Social Security Administration *Annual Reports,* which list employees and budget through FY 1948 (1940 corresponds to the 5th *Annual Report,* 1941 to the 6th, and so on, up to the 13th *Annual Report* of 1948). Figures on federal civilian employees are from "Paid Civilian Employment of the Federal Government," Series Y 308–317, *Historical Statistics,* 1102. The 1948 BOASI figures are from the 1948 Hearings by the House Subcommittee on Appropriations on the Labor-Federal Security Agency Appropriation Bill, House Report No. 724, 80th Cong., 1st sess., Serial Vol. 11121, 639. The BOASI data for 1949 and 1950 are from 1950 Hearings by the House Subcommittee on Appropriations on the Labor-Federal Security Agency Appropriation Bill, House Report No. 892, 81st Cong., 1st sess., Serial Vol. 11299, 568. SSA employment figures for 1949 and 1950 are from the Federal Security Administration *Annual Reports.*

Notes: Figures are for 30 June (the end of the fiscal year). "BOASI" is the employment in the Bureau of Old Age and Survivors' Insurance. "SSB/SSA" is the total number of employees in the Social Security Bureau and, after 1946, the Social Security Administration. "Fed. Civ." is the number of civilian employees in the federal government. "% USG" is the percentage of the total number of federal civilian employees constituted by BOASI employees.

to do so until 1950. With both the Democratic and Republican presidential campaigns of 1948 pledging to increase and expand the social security system, and with letters flooding Congress complaining about the paltry benefit levels of the existing OASI payments, Representative Doughton and his colleagues on the Ways and Means Committee took steps to address the demands of those currently receiving benefits, those due to receive benefits in the near future, and those being left out of the social security system.

The other consequence of the interdependence between the government and individual citizens was that social security stakeholders reduced their dependence on the federal government for protection against sickness and

TABLE 2.3
Social Security Administration Expenditures (thousands of dollars)

Fiscal Year	BOASI	SSB/SSA	USG Outlays	% USG
1940	12,428	18,533	7,256 (000)	0.171
1941	14,305	21,731	7,003	0.205
1942	15,838	21,638	11,132	0.142
1943	17,617	22,518	15,954	0.110
1944	17,120	19.746	19,010	0.090
1945	17,516	18,642	17,765	0.098
1946	20,805	25,973	17,174	0.121
1947	26,724	34,278	24,154	0.110
1948	30,219	35,994	20,972	0.144
1949	37,819	(NA)	25,486	0.148
1950	43,266	(NA)	26,104	0.166

Sources: "Outlays of the Federal Government," Series Y 457–465, Historical Statistics, 1114. 1948–50 BOASI figures are from the 1948 hearings cited in Table 2.2 sources (p. 629), the 1950 hearings cited there (Pt. II, 568), and the 1949 Hearings of the House Appropriations Subcommittee on Labor-Federal Security Agency Appropriations, House Report No. 2247, 80th Cong., 2nd sess., Serial Vol. 1121, Pt. II, 19.

Notes: Expenditures are established obligations. In some years, these amounts match appropriations; in others, because of overtime, changes in salaries, or supplemental appropriations, the amounts differ from actual appropriations. "USG Outlays" is "total" federal spending, including interest on public debt and veterans' compensation, minus spending for the departments of War and Navy (and the Air Force after 1948). Outlays for the years in question are from "unified budget figures." "% USG" represents the BOASI budget as a percentage of the civilian federal budget, from year end. The United States Employment Service was transferred from the Department of Labor to the SSB as of 1 July 1939. As of 1 July 1942 its personnel activities were transferred from the FSA to the SSB; and the USES was transferred from the SSB to the newly created War Manpower Commission, together with $1,816,740 of Bureau appropriations, in November 1942.

old age. Given the slow expansion of social security coverage and the small increases (and the real decreases) in OASI benefit levels, employees began to look elsewhere for financial and medical security. The number of subscriptions to private pension plans increased by 239 percent between 1940 and 1950 (from 4.1 to 9.8 million subscribers: see Table 2.4), employer and employee contribution levels soared, the amount in the pension reserves rose by almost a factor of five, the number of monthly beneficiaries rose by 281 percent, and the amount disbursed increased by 264 percent.[32]

[32] Average annual pension benefits declined from $875 per person in 1940 (because of the small numbers receiving pensions then) to $710 per person in 1945, and then rose to $822 per person by 1950.

Beth Stevens argues that it was not until the mid-1940s that employees began to look to nongovernmental sources of old age security ("Labor Unions, Employee Benefits, and the Privatization of the American Welfare State," Journal of Policy History 2 No. 3 [1990]: 233–60).

TABLE 2.4
Growth of Private Pensions (figures in millions, except monthly beneficiaries)

Fiscal Year	Total No.	Employee Contribs.	Employer Contribs.	Money Reserves	No. of Mo. Benefic.	Amount Disbursed
1940	4.1	$130	$ 180	$ 2,400	160,000	$140
1945	6.4	160	830	5,400	310,000	220
1950	9.8	330	1,750	12,100	450,000	370

Sources: "Private Pension and Deferred Profit-Sharing Plans—Estimated Coverage, Contributions, Reserves, Beneficiaries, and Benefit Payments: 1930 to 1970," Series H 287–304, *Historical Statistics,* 353–354.

Notes: "Total No." is the total number of persons subscribing to private pensions. "Employee Contribs." is the amount contributed annually to private pensions by employees; "Employer Contribs." is the annual amount paid in by employers. "No. of Mo. Benefic." is the number of monthly beneficiaries of private pension plans. "Amount Disbursed" is the amount paid out annually in benefits; it includes refunds to employees and their survivors, and lump-sum payments under deferred profit-sharing plans.

With federal programs being unable to cover medical and hospitalization costs, more and more Americans turned to private health insurance: whereas private plans for insuring against hospitalization costs incurred from ill health covered twelve million persons in 1940 (under 10 percent of the American population), by 1950 private plans insured over 76 million persons—or more than half the population of the United States. About half of all persons insured were covered under Blue Cross/Blue Shield (see Table 2.5).

The recourse to private welfare provisions was especially notable among companies with hourly employees: whereas 8 percent of firms had company-wide pension plans and 36 percent offered employee health insurance in 1940, 23 percent of firms had pension plans and 68 percent offered health insurance by 1946.[33] The unions played a crucial part in the spread of non-government plans. The CIO resolved that it had to "conduct a vigorous

---

[33] National Industrial Conference Board (NICB), "Personnel Activities in American Business," Studies in Personnel Policy (SPP) No. 20 (New York, 1940), p. 24; NICB, "Personnel Activities in American Business (Revised)," SPP No. 86 (New York, 1947), pp. 22–23, Table 8.4, "Welfare Benefits for Hourly Workers in Manufacturing, 1940–1946" (proportion of firms), cited in Sanford Jacoby, *Employing Bureaucracy* (New York: Columbia University Press, 1985), 266.

As Beth Stevens observes, "employer contributions to pension funds quintupled, soaring from $171 million in 1941 to $857 million in 1945" ("Blurring the Boundaries: How the Federal Government Has Influenced Welfare Benefits in the Private Sector," in Weir, Orloff, and Skocpol, eds., *The Politics of Social Policy in the United States,* 131). Stevens sees the rise of private pensions as resulting from public sector action, however, and not from the impact of the labor unions, which she sees as indifferent on this front—at least during the early years of the war (130–42).

TABLE 2.5
Growth of Volunteer Health Plans (Hospitalization)

Fiscal Year	No. Covered	% Insured	Blue Cross/ Blue Shield
1940	12,312 (000)	9.3	6,072 (000)
1941	16,349	12.4	8,469
1942	19,695	15.2	10,295
1943	24,160	18.9	12,696
1944	29,232	22.9	15,828
1945	32,068	24.0	18,961
1946	42,112	29.9	24,342
1947	52,584	36.4	27,646
1948	60,995	41.5	30,619
1949	66,044	44.2	33,576
1950	76,639	50.7	37,645

Sources: "Persons Covered by Private Health Insurance for Hospital and Surgical Benefits: 1939 to 1970," Series B 401–412, Historical Statistics, 82; estimates by the Health Insurance Association of America (HIAA).

Note: "% Insured" is the percentage of the population insured with volunteer hospitalization plans (there was also insurance for surgical benefits). Other plans besides Blue Cross/Blue Shield include group and individual insurance policies and independent plans unaffiliated with Blue Cross/Blue Shield or other insurance companies.

collective bargaining program to bring its members a coordinated program of security and economic benefits . . . adequate sick benefit plans, hospitalization programs, and pension plans."[34] And as AFL President William Green declared in a keynote address to the 1946 AFL convention, the United Mine Workers' innovative health and welfare fund would "now be the objective of organizations affiliated with the American Federation of Labor."[35] Without federal alternatives, the unions turned to their own designs.[36]

There were at least four reasons for the rise of union-based welfare programs. One was that fringe benefits were not considered "wages" under the war-induced wage stabilization plans. Many employers sought to reduce la-

[34] Congress of Industrial Organizations, Convention Proceedings, 1947, p. 237, in "Report on the Growth and Characteristics of Union-Management Health and Welfare Plans," p. 23, 25 June 1948, folder 2, Box 46, Wilbur J. Cohen Papers.

[35] American Federation of Labor, Convention Proceedings, 1946, p. 12, in "Report on the Growth and Characteristics of Union-Management Health and Welfare Plans," p. 20, 25 June 1948, folder 2, Box 46, Cohen Papers.

[36] See Jill Quadagno (The Transformation of Old Age Security, 157–71) on the rise of pensions in the industrial unions.

bor turnover at a time of scarce manpower, and providing health and welfare plans could help. Another reason was that the costs of such plans were counted as legitimate business expenses for employers subject to the high wartime tax rates. A third reason for the surge in union-management welfare plans was that the unions were themselves competing for members (since the National Labor Relations Board had determined that union-management welfare plans were a legitimate subject of collective bargaining); better health and pension plans might bring more members and more union affiliates. Fourth, some union leaders thought that the benefits secured under union-management plans could substitute for wage increases, and many union officials were sensitive to the widespread charges that wage demands by unions were responsible for the inflation of the late 1940s.[37] The first two reasons for the increase in private plans are related directly to the war; and insofar as the war brought about a surge in employment (and thus in union membership: see Chapter 3) the third and fourth reasons for union-promulgated private pension plans are also war-related.

Curiously, the SSA actually helped to establish the industrial health, welfare, and retirement plans negotiated by the labor unions and business management, despite the fact that the success of these non-governmental programs would seem to undermine the prospects for broader-based social provisions. But the SSA cooperated with labor unions and business management to set up private health and retirement programs, beginning with the United Mine Workers in mid-1946.

It was obvious to SSA officials in 1946—as well as to labor leaders and business executives—that federal programs were not going to fill the (serious) gaps in social security coverage any time soon.[38] Social Security Commissioner Altmeyer admitted as much: "The particular character and force of the current pressure for health and welfare plans is in large measure the result of our failure to complete the structure of our basic social insurance system." He continued, "I look upon existing and proposed voluntary employee benefit plans, therefore, as either supplementary to social insurance or temporary substitutes for social insurance. In both roles, they can—if soundly developed—be constructive."[39] The SSA was thereby able to channel the expansion of social insurance programs in ways complementary to its own objectives: "The Social Security Administration takes a friendly view of

[37] "Report on the Growth and Characteristics of Union-Management Health and Welfare Plans," pp. 4–9, 25 June 1948, folder 2, Box 46, Cohen Papers. Also see Stevens, "Blurring the Boundaries."

[38] "Health, Welfare and Retirement Plans in Industry" [Preliminary Draft], p. 2, [ca. 1948], folder 2, Box 46, Cohen Papers.

[39] Arthur J. Altmeyer, "Conference on Union health and Welfare funds," *National Industrial Conference Board*, 23 January 1947, p. 23, in "Report on the Growth and Characteristics of Union-Management Health and Welfare Plans," p. 23.

union-management plans, or any similar arrangements which supplement the protection afforded under the Social Security Act."[40]

While the SSA was helping the labor unions and business management to set up their own social programs, the unorganized—those left out of the 1950 reforms and not members of labor unions, management, or professional associations—were being omitted from the newly established independent programs. A case in point was the American Legion's successful promotion of extensive benefits for war veterans (with one observer describing the American Legion "as the most powerful pressure group of any sort").[41] But no organization, with the exception of the small (and poorly managed) Townsend Clubs, existed to represent the broader constituency of the social security system. The organized benefited at the expense of the unorganized.

In sum, we see the limited expansion of the social security program in 1950, and the spread of non-governmental programs for organized societal actors. In fact, in the case of the union-management health and welfare programs, the government actually collaborated with societal actors. But many Americans were comparatively neglected in the immediate postwar years when it came to the provision of insurance for old age and illness.

The Effects of the War

In the face of the federal government's desperate need for funds, we should expect the President and Congress to extend government-society relations and improve the instruments of government, since social security taxes constituted both a potentially important source of revenue and a consumption-suppressing measure. Yet the war, as noted above, brought about no increase in OASI tax rates and resulted in little expansion in the social security bureaucracy. There was little for the end of the war to ratchet into place.

The size of the BOASI grew by over 1,200 employees between fiscal years 1940 and 1948, and the SSB/SSA staff increased by about 600 employees over the same period. Meanwhile, the percentage of BOASI employees of total SSB/SSA employment increased slightly, and BOASI employment as a percentage of the federal government civilian employment decreased sharply from 1940 to 1945 (1.1 to 0.28 percent) and then rose steadily up to 1950 (to 0.61 percent) (refer to Table 2.2). As noted above, the war years

---

[40] "Report on the Growth and Characteristics of Union-Management Health and Welfare Plans," p. 22, 25 June 1948, folder 2, Box 46, Cohen Papers. Also see Berkowitz, "Growth of the U.S. Social Welfare System in the Post-World War II Era: The UMW, Rehabilitation, and the Federal Government," *Research in Economic History* 5 (1980), 233–47.

[41] Ross, *Preparing for Ulysses*, 11.

brought about declines in real benefits and in social security payments as a percentage of average per capita income.

Likewise, the BOASI budget increased from under $12.5 million in 1940 to over $43 million by fiscal year 1950, and also increased as a percentage of the SSB/SSA budget. With the onset of war, both BOASI employment and expenditures fell sharply as percentages of the federal government totals—spending dropped from 0.21 percent in 1941 to 0.09 percent in 1944, and personnel dropped from 1.1 to 0.3 percent of federal civilian employment over the same years—and then both rose after the war. Expenditures increased to 0.17 percent of federal spending by 1950, and BOASI employment rose to 0.61 percent of federal levels (refer to Tables 2.2 and 2.3).

In contrast to the stasis in the social security bureaucracy was the considerable change in government-society relations. Whereas there were 222,000 OASI beneficiaries and 35 million contributors in 1940, there were 1,300,000 beneficiaries and 46 million contributors by 1945. In just five years' time, six times as many persons were receiving OASI benefits and ten million more persons were paying into the social security system. By 1950, 3.5 million persons were receiving OASI benefits and 48 million individuals were paying social security taxes. The proportion of the workforce covered by the social security system similarly increased from 57.8 percent in 1940 to 68.9 percent by 1945, and remained at about 65 percent for the rest of the decade (see Tables 2.6 and 2.7).

Yet note the contrast between the larger numbers receiving OASI benefits and the greater amounts being disbursed, on the one hand, and the smaller level of real benefits, on the other hand. Real social security benefits declined by more than a third over the 1940s, falling from $51 per month in 1940 to $33 per month in 1948; and OASI benefit levels were halved as a percentage of average personal income, dropping from 36 percent of average per capita income in 1940 to 18 percent in 1949. Even after including the 1950 reforms in OASI benefits, social security stakeholders received real benefits only modestly higher than their level of ten years earlier, going up to $55 per month in 1950 from $51 per month in 1940 (see Table 2.6). Workers were steadily paying much more into the system over the course of the 1940s—about twice as much by the end of the decade—but beneficiaries did not receive their increases until 1950. So while the *extent* of government-society relations grew for social security stakeholders over the 1940s (with more employees and employers contributing, and with more persons receiving social security benefits), the *intensity* of government-society relations rose for those paying OASI taxes, remained level in terms of OASI tax rates and OASI benefit levels (in current dollars), and actually declined in terms of real benefits until the summer of 1950.

There was, however, substantial and unequivocal change in the *means* of

TABLE 2.6
OASI Benefits

Fiscal Year	Total No. of Beneficiaries	Avg. Mo. Benefits	Total Disbursed	% of Income	Benefits/ Month
1940	222 (000)	$22.60	$ 40.6 million	35.9	$51.48
1941	434	22.70	93.9	29.2	48.09
1942	598	23.02	137.0	23.6	43.43
1943	748	23.42	172.8	20.0	41.23
1944	955	23.73	218.1	18.8	41.78
1945	1,288	24.19	287.8	19.2	40.52
1946	1,642	24.55	387.7	20.0	36.81
1947	1,978	24.90	482.5	18.6	33.38
1948	2,315	25.35	575.9	17.3	31.85
1949	2,743	26.00	689.0	18.1	32.87
1950	3,477	43.86	1,050.9	28.0	54.69

Sources: Myers, *Social Insurance and Allied Government Programs,* 134, Table 22. *Social Security Bulletin,* September 1950, 33, Table 11. 1950 figures are from the issue of September 1952.

Notes: Beneficiaries are single retirees receiving monthly OASI payments. "% of Income" equals individual monthly benefits as a percentage of annual per capita income. "Benefits/ Month" are the monthly receipts under OASI in real terms (1958 constant dollars).

administering social security. The rearmament period and the mobilization for war forced the Roosevelt Administration and the SSB to introduce new administrative practices.

• The Bureau of the Budget's Circular of 23 September 1941 suspended standard operations in effect since 1939 (with the reorganization of the Executive Branch). Standard operations could be effectively "traded off" for exertions on behalf of the national defense: "Normal forward progress can be temporarily sacrificed and the emphasis shifted to the primary needs of this emergency period . . . you are instructed to absorb all possible defense activities within the limits of existing funds. In doing this, you should reduce or postpone all activities . . . not vital at this time to the public welfare."[42]

• On 25 May 1942, Chairman Altmeyer acknowledged that the BOASI's Claims and Control Divisions would be decentralized in accordance with the President's order to vacate space in Washington.

• On 31 August 1942, the President issued Executive Order 9235, "Providing for the Effective Utilization of Supplies and Equipment by Government Agencies." Equipment and supplies were to be used as economically as possible.

[42] File 040.01–1, "Circulars 1922–1944," Box 13, EDF.

TABLE 2.7
Social Insurance Coverage

Fiscal Year	Employers Reporting	Workers with Wage Credits	% of Workforce	Avg. Taxes per Worker	% of Total Earnings
1940	2.50 million	35.4 million	57.8	$ 932	92.4
1941	2.65	41.0	62.1	1,021	92.0
1942	2.66	46.4	65.1	1,142	90.9
1943	2.39	47.7	69.1	1,310	89.6
1944	2.47	46.3	70.3	1,392	87.8
1945	2.61	46.4	68.9	1,357	88.0
1946	3.02	48.8	64.8	1,414	87.2
1947	3.25	48.9	64.6	1,602	84.8
1948	3.30	49.0	65.3	1,716	82.3
1949	3.32	46.8	64.0	1,748	81.8
1950	3.35	48.3	64.5	1,812	79.7

Sources: "Old Age, Survivors, Disability, and Health Insurance—Estimated Paid Employ-ment and Coverage Status: 1940 to 1970," Series H 186–196, *Historical Statistics,* 348; "Old-Age, Survivors, Disability, and Health Insurance—Covered Workers, Earnings, and Selected Trust Fund Transactions: 1937 to 1970," *Historical Statistics,* 347; *Social Security Bulletin,* January 1951 and June 1951.

Notes: "Employers Reporting" is the number of employers reporting taxable wages. "Workers with Wage Credits" are employees reporting taxable wages. "% of Workforce" is "Percent of paid employment." "Avg. Taxes per Worker" is the average amount in taxes paid by social security contributors. "% of Total Earnings" refers to the percentage of total earnings liable for social security taxation.

• In November 1942, the Civil Service Commission reported to the President that it had "adjusted its recruiting, examining, and placement methods to meet the war needs of the Government. Recruiting practices [have become] more flexible than ever."[43] The report went on to list its proposals for the BOASI's Basic Train-ing program, its Technical Training of the Executive Staff, and its Training of Clerical Staff.

• On 31 December 1942, the Bureau of the Budget issued Circular No. 408, on the subject "Program to Save Manpower in Government Agencies." The circular's questions about work scheduling, problems, machinery, specific methods, econ-omies undertaken, services rendered to the War Manpower Commission, and other items spurred the creation of the SSB's "work plans."[44]

• On 15 April 1943, the SSB had to pledge that the number of its employees did not exceed the numbers approved by Bureau of the Budget in letters of 24

[43] President Roosevelt to Harry B. Mitchell, President of the U.S. Civil Service Commis-sion, and Frederick M. Davenport, Chairman of the Council of Personnel Administration, 14 January 1942, File 331, "FSA," Box 201, EDF.

[44] File 310, "All Regions," Central Files of the Social Security Board.

March and 31 March 1943. Then, in mid-1945, the BOASI developed a program for maximizing personnel utilization.

After the war, the BOASI reorganized the functions of the Analysis Division, the Personnel Office,[45] and the Training Office.[46] The Social Security Administration's Office of the Commissioner was also reorganized.[47] In addition, the SSA made plans to maximize decentralization and to devolve administrative tasks as much as possible to the field offices. Finally, in late 1949, the SSA began its management improvement programs for reviewing programs, providing for routinized appraisal systems, scheduling, and periodic reporting to the Bureau of the Budget. With the exceptions of legislation relaxing merit standards in wartime and the Administrative Procedures Act of 1946, the White House was able to direct the development of the instrumental state.

The Social Security Administration also possessed significant actuarial and statistical expertise. It provided cost and payout estimates for the social security program, and it determined how industrial plans fit with OASI provisions and with wage-loss benefits of other federal and state programs.[48] As one 1948 report noted, "The Bureau of Research and Statistics has for a number of years compiled and published detailed information on voluntary prepayment medical care organizations. In cooperation with the Office of

[45] Memorandum of Roy L. Wynkoop, Coordinating and Procedure Division, Office of the Executive Director, to W. L. Mitchell, Acting Executive Director, 13 and 14 July 1944, file 321.3, "Jun.–Dec. 1944," Box 86, EDF.

[46] Memorandum of Wynkoop to Mitchell, "Reorganization of Old-Age and Survivors Insurance Training Office," 10 March, file 0321.3, "1945," Box 86, EDF.

[47] Memorandum of Mitchell, Acting Commissioner, to Wilbur, Director Bureau of Accounts and Audits, 18 November 1947, file 321–7.5, Box 88, EDF.
To cite one example, the reorganization of the Office of the Commissioner involved identifying tasks as either developmental or administrative, with the former involving "analysis, appraisal and coordination of programs already in effect, identification and analysis of additional social security needs; development of plans and proposals, presentation of testimony at hearings, and preparation of reports on bills; studying grants-in-aid policies and making recommendations for their improvement; analyzing the economic effects of financing social security providing the public with information concerning their rights and responsibilities under the Act; and the arrangement of proper Agency representation on social security matters with other governmental agencies and in international relations. Under Group 2 [Administrative] is included general supervision of administration, approval of laws plans, grants and operating policies; work planning; direction and supervision of field operations; budget preparation and control of appropriations; merit system standards and consultation; participation in the development of uniform Federal-State relations policies and application of them; and similar administrative activities." "Reorganization of Commissioner's Office," Memorandum of W. L. Mitchell, Deputy Commissioner, to R. G. Wagenet, Director of Employment Security, 2 December 1947, File 321–9 Reorganization, "1946," Box 88, EDF.

[48] "Welfare and Retirement Fund," n.d. [ca. June 1946], folder 3, Box 54, Cohen Papers; and Memorandum of I. S. Falk to Mr. Gerig, Miss Klem, Mrs. Merriam, and Mr. Cohen, 22 July 1946, folder 3, Box 54, Cohen Papers.

the Actuary it has assembled and published certain over-all annual estimates of private insurance coverage and benefits payments."[49]

In short, the war prompted substantial change in the means of administering social security, but minor change in the bureaucratic state, modest expansion in the extent of the government-society relations, and either an increase, no change, or a decline in the intensity of government-society ties. But the indirect effects of the war on societal actors were very much consistent with the expected impact of hegemonic war on state-building. Consider that before the war several large organizations were advocating substantial change in the social policies, among them the Townsend movement, Huey Long's "Share the Wealth" program (until 1935), the CIO (calling for a flat-rate pension plan), and the AFL (calling for a broad-based extension of the social security system). With the onset of the rearmament period and then Pearl Harbor, however, the pressures from organized actors to change the social security system faded away. Paid membership in the Townsend Clubs fell from 762,000 in 1939 to 469,000 in 1941 and to 235,000 by 1945, and Townsend Club membership continued to decline after the war, sliding from 174,000 persons in 1946 to 53,000 in 1949.[50] Similarly, in 1943 the CIO came out in support of expanding the existing social security system (rather than holding out for a new or a more radical system of social provisions), and the AFL also reduced its demands for an expanded social system over the course of the war years. The Second World War affected the organization of and demands by the constituents of the social security system, as expected.

The changes of the war years also caused a transformation in the place of social security on the political agenda, from being an important pending issue for the executive branch and Congress in 1940 and early 1941 to becoming a lesser priority in the mid-1940s. Consider Roosevelt's call for expansion in the social security system during his Fireside Chat of 26 May 1940[51] and his support of the "double-decker" plan in a speech to the Teamsters Union Convention on 11 September 1940.[52] Recall also that both union federations were pressing for substantial changes: the AFL wanted large extensions in the social security system as amended in 1939,[53] and the

---

[49] "Health, Welfare and Retirement Plans in Industry" [Preliminary Draft], n.d. [ca. 1948], folder 2, Box 46, Cohen Papers.

[50] Abraham Holtzman, *The Townsend Movement: A Political Study* (New York: Bookman, 1963), 49.

[51] *The Public Papers and Addresses of Franklin D. Roosevelt*, Vol. 8, 237.

[52] *The Public Papers and Addresses of Franklin D. Roosevelt*, Vol. 8, 410–11. The speech kicked off the 1940 presidential campaign. Wilbur Cohen had also drawn up a double-decker plan in early 1940 for an attack on flat-rate plans. See "A Possible Plan for a Basic Flat Rate Pension With Graduated Insurance Benefits Superimposed Thereon," folder 7, box 45, Cohen Papers.

[53] Letter of William Green to Chairman Altmeyer, 30 July 1940, file "056," Box 60, Central Files of the Social Security Board; also see "Report and Recommendations on Social Security as

CIO opposed the existing dual system of state old-age pensions and federal old-age insurance. The CIO supported a more radical flat-rate system, such as the Townsend plan, given that the dual state-federal system meant a loss of purchasing power for workers. Under the CIO's plan, those over sixty years of age would receive a pension of $60 per month—hence its title, the "60–60 pension plan."[54]

In mid-1941, the Social Security Board responded to these pressures by recommending the broad expansion of "all fields of social security," including the liberalization and simplification of eligibility tests under the old-age assistance program; the introduction of a variable federal grant for old-age assistance and aid for dependent children and the blind; the provision of more federal grants to states (i.e., general relief); the extension of payroll taxation and coverage to farmers, agricultural labor, domestic workers, employees of nonprofit institutions, government employees, businessmen and other non-covered groups; the broadening of the insurance program to cover cash benefits for unemployment due to temporary and permanent disability; and the lowering of the retirement age for women from 65 to 60. The Board also recommended cash benefits for hospital costs, protection of workers in national defense industries, the placing of both collection and distribution functions in one agency, and the raising of payroll taxes to a combined rate of 10 percent by January 1942.[55]

Furthermore, when the Downey Subcommittee of the Senate Finance Committee (Sheriden Downey, D., Calif.) concluded its hearings on old-age pensions, it endorsed by a vote of six to one a program of universal coverage under Title II of the Social Security Act (OASI). Its report called for all qualified persons to receive minimum benefits of $30 a month, regardless of former income or paid-in contributions, and for combined OASI taxes on employers and employees to be raised to 4 percent on 1 January 1943 and to 6 percent on 1 January 1944 (the 1939 amendments to the Social Security Act did not schedule OASI taxes to be raised to 6 percent until 1 January 1949). The report recommended that wives' and widows' insurance benefits

submitted by Executive Council American Federation of Labor," 1940 AFL Convention, attachment to letter of William Green to Secretary of the Treasury Morgenthau, 5 November 1941, file 011.4, "1941," Box 4, EDF.

[54] "Digest of Social Security Recommendations submitted to the 1940 convention, Congress of Industrial Organizations," file 011.4, "1941," Box 4, EDF.

[55] "The 1941 Legislative Program of the Social Security Board," 17 June 1941 (Henry Morgenthau, Diaries, Vol. 409, 217–18); "Memorandum for the Secretary, the current legislative program of the Social Security Board," 10 September 1941 (Diaries, Vol. 409, 45–49); "An Expanded Social Security Program (Revised)," appended to letter of President Roosevelt to "Pa" Watson, 1 April 1941, Official File 1710, "Social Security Board—1941," Roosevelt Papers; "Our Expanded Social Security program," 2 September 1941, file 056, "Sept.–Dec. 1941," Box 20, EDF; and the recommendations in *Annual Report of the Social Security Board for Fiscal Year 1941.*

be increased from one-half to three-quarters of the amount for those receiving primary insurance, that benefit payments start at the age of sixty, that Title I assistance be financed out of general appropriations (rather than from a reserve fund), and that a means test be abolished on public assistance for those above the age of 60. The report also called for disability and unemployment insurance, and for federal cash grants to match the state funding of hospital costs for those receiving assistance.[56] The new program would cost $3 billion.[57]

The President seemed to be in agreement. Roosevelt asked for an increase in unemployment insurance and old-age pensions in a press conference on 30 September 1941, and he asked that more federal aid be channeled to the poorer states (the matching grants being insufficient). He also acknowledged that OASI contributions would have to increase.[58] The new program would increase coverage to the employed and unemployed currently excluded from OASI, consolidate the existing social security programs into a single comprehensive insurance system, increase the amounts of federal grants to low-income states, raise OASI contribution rates, and include military service in the social security system.[59] Commissioner Altmeyer went so far as to clear the proposed amendments with the Bureau of the Budget and the Treasury Department, and Congress was sent a draft of a presidential message on extending social security.[60]

But in a meeting of Senator George, Representative Doughton, Secretary Morgenthau, and other Treasury officials held in early November, the sentiment was that

> the introduction of social security into the [new tax policy] picture would result in a long debate and extended hearings. Mr. Doughton thought it would be impossible to keep out old-age pension debate in the House and Senator George said that he had promised the Townsend people a hearing in December. However, he

[56] "Preliminary Report of the Special Committee to Investigate the Old-Age Pension System," 28 August 1941.

[57] Even the minority report, filed by Senator Theodore Green (D., R.I.), came out in favor of variable state grants, relaxed eligibility conditions, and the extension of coverage to "all gainfully employed persons." Wilbur Cohen had discussed with Green the possibility of putting his dissenting opinion into a bill, "provided it was strategically wise to do so at the time" ("Report of Conference with Senator Green, Wednesday August 27, 2:00 p.m," Wilbur J. Cohen to George Bigge, 28 August 1941, file 011.1, "August 1941," Box 11, EDF). Green's dissenting view mirrored the SSB's subsequent position of 10 September 1941.

[58] Seven Hundred Seventy-first Press Conference [Excerpts], *The Public Papers and Addresses of Franklin D. Roosevelt*, Vol. 9, 402–3.

[59] "Suggested Draft of President's Message on Social Security Expansion," n.d.: Morgenthau, Diaries, Vol. 450, 40–44.

[60] The Treasury Department held meetings on social security, forced savings, and compulsory savings throughout the month of October. See "Daily Record, September–December 1941," Box 2, Sullivan Papers.

thought that old-age insurance rates could be increased this year instead of next without opening the whole problem.[61]

The subject of "new taxes to mop up purchasing power" was raised again one week later, in a meeting with the House Ways and Means Committee. But "[t]he proposals to revise social security raised a great deal of discussion" as well as "[c]onsiderable hostility." The representatives from the Ways and Means Committee were divided between holding an open public hearing on revising social security and conducting a private discussion with the Treasury Secretary in executive session.[62]

By late 1941 the momentum for comprehensive reform had stalled, and what impetus remained for radical change was swept away by the Japanese attack on 7 December.[63] Consider that a 1940 report by the SSB on the "Extension and Expansion of the Social Security Act" had spoken of an "all-inclusive" system that would protect workers and their families from unpredictable wage losses due to "[u]nemployment, sickness, permanent disability, old age, and premature death."[64] But analogous reports by the SSB in 1941 and 1943 made no mention of "sickness" or an "all-inclusive" system, and spoke of a "comprehensive system" instead, to be administered by the SSB.[65] Indicatively, whereas House and Senate members introduced 54 bills on social security, disability payments, unemployment relief, veterans' benefits, and related programs in 1941, only 17 such bills were introduced in 1943.

The discussion of flat-rate pensions would be postponed until the late 1940s and early 1950s, when congressional Republicans sought to impose a (cheaper) flat-rate social security system; the qualifying age for OASI benefits would never be reduced to 60 (although it would eventually be reduced to 62); higher tax rates would not be imposed until 1950, eight years after the first freeze of 1942; and the "blanketing-in" of the uninsured would be only partial. While the OASI reforms of 1950 finally included additional worker groups in the social security system and raised social security benefits, such measures had been pending for some eleven years—since 1939.

[61] Memorandum of John L. Sullivan to the Secretary, 5 November 1941, file "Daily Record, Sept.–December 1941," Box 2, Sullivan Papers.

[62] Memorandum of Blough to the Secretary, 13 November 1941, file "Daily Record, Sept.–December 1941," Box 2, Sullivan Papers.

[63] See "Old-Age Pensions," Hearings for the Committee on Finance, United States Senate, 71st Cong., 1st sess., on S. 1932. Hearings were held on 1, 2, and 15 December 1941.

[64] "Extension and Expansion of the Social Security Act," A Report of the Social Security Board to the Federal Security Administrator for Transmittal to The President and to the Congress of the United States, 12/4/40 and 12/18/40, folders 8–9, Box 38, Cohen Papers.

[65] "Extension and Expansion of the Social Security Act," A Report of the Social Security Board to the Federal Security Administrator for Transmittal to The President and to the Congress of the United States, 1/27/41, 1941 [October], 8/15/41, 1943 [March], and 1943 [April and August], folder 1 (reports dated 1940) and folder 2 (1943), Box 39, Cohen Papers.

Former BOASI director John Corson noted the effect of World War II on delaying changes in social security policy. Before the war, he and fellow BOASI officials were confident of significant reform in the social security system, given that the administration of the social security program had developed "to a point where we could handle the added problems associated with the coverage of the self employed, farm workers, domestic servants, et al. and [that] we were confronted, because of limited coverage, with proposals such as the 'double decker' and Senator Downey's." But suddenly faced with world war and with the prevailing view that the United States "could not have guns and butter too," efforts to reform social security lost their immediacy. In Corson's words, "We in social security, having played on the center of the governmental stage from 1936 thru 1939, found ourselves pushed aside."[66]

In short, the war comprehensively altered social provisions in the United States. The two years preceding the attack on Pearl Harbor—1940 and 1941—presented a special window for the transformation of social provisions in the United States, a window that the mobilization for and entry into the war effectively closed. The high employment induced by the war served to reduce social security payouts and brought about larger-than-expected trust fund revenues, thereby obviating the need for social security tax increases. Recall too that President Roosevelt, the Bureau of the Budget, the Treasury Department, and the Social Security Board had all agreed on a compromise double-decker plan by October 1941.[67] Even the minority report of the Downey Subcommittee advocated increased payments to the states in the form of variable grants, an easing of qualification standards (i.e., one year of residence instead of five), and the extension of Old-Age and Survivors Insurance to agricultural workers and domestic servants. This was the opinion in *dissent*. Reform, compromised reform at that, would not be forthcoming until 1950. Similarly, the improved economic circumstances of wartime—as opposed to the issues of relative importance or squeezing-out effects—helped to prevent the Wagner-Murray-Dingell Bills of 1943 and 1945 from reaching the House or Senate floor. The war halted the momentum for expansion in social security and blocked the chances of bolder relief plans.[68]

---

[66] Letter of John J. Corson to the author, 17 April 1989. Corson had served as head of the BOASI and then, from 1 December 1941 to June 1943, directed the U.S. Employment Service.

[67] The message on expanded coverage was approved by the Bureau of the Budget, the Federal Security Agency, the Treasury Department, and the Social Security Board ("Conferences with the President," 10 October 1941, Harold Smith Papers). Also see Leff, "Speculating in Social Security Futures."

[68] Derthick writes that the Townsend plan "posed no serious threat to the proposals of the Committee on Economic Security and the Social Security Board. . . . The idea of flat, noncontributory grants, which the Townsend movement had popularized, persisted for some years, but

While the expansion of broad-based social provisions languished through-out the 1940s, the veterans' programs expanded dramatically as the number of veterans rose from 4.3 million persons in 1940 to over 19 million veterans in 1950.[69] The comprehensive G.I. Bill of Rights of 1944 provided for terminal leave pay, mustering-out pay, and readjustment allowances totaling $10.2 billion in veterans' payments by 1955. Indeed, 7.8 million veterans in all would take advantage of the education or training provisions of the G.I. Bill.[70] "American life in 1949, even 1959, would probably not have been greatly different from 1939" without the G.I. Bill, as the historian Geoffrey Perrett remarks.[71]

The reemergence of public health care as a topic of national debate represented another shift in the political agenda. Whereas President Roosevelt had soft-pedaled national health care in the 1930s and early 1940s,[72] President Truman revived national health insurance as part of his "21 Points." Addressing Congress in November 1945, Truman proclaimed:

> Millions of our citizens do not now have a full measure of opportunity to achieve and enjoy good health. . . . The people of the United States received a shock when the medical examinations conducted by the Selective Service revealed the widespread physical and mental incapacity among the young people of our nation. We had had prior warnings from eminent medical authorities and from investigating committees. The statistics of the last war had shown the same condition. But the Selective Service System has brought it forcibly to our attention recently—in terms all of us can understand.[73]

With the war over, it was time to establish a national health care program for those unable to afford reasonable medical attention. Health care was

---

lacked mass support after 1940–41. . . . This is the nature of such movements. Spontaneous and unpredictable in their origins, they are also ephemeral" (Derthick, *Policymaking for Social Security*, 193). A contrary argument can be made, however, that the conjunction of the Townsend movement and the pressure from Huey Long was instrumental in forcing the President's hand to appoint the Commission on Economic Security. See statements by Thomas Eliot and Wilbur Cohen, "Social Security: The First Half-Century, A Discussion," 35–40, in Nash, Pugach, and Tomasson, eds., *Social Security*; and Levine, *Poverty and Society*, 242–58.

[69] Vatter, *The U.S. Economy in World War II*, 147.

[70] Ross, *Preparing for Ulysses*, 224, 124. See Ross for a comprehensive treatment of veterans' policies during and after the Second World War.

[71] Perrett, *A Country Made by War*, 439.

[72] The 1943 reports on the "Extension and Expansion of the Social Security Act" did refer to "cradle to the grave" insurance and did recommend that social insurance cover "a considerable part of the expense of hospital and medical services" ("Extension and Expansion of the Social Security Act," 1943 [April and August], folder 2 [1943], Box 39, Cohen Papers).

[73] President Truman's Message to Congress, 19 November 1945. One-third of U.S. draftees were being turned down because of physical or mental illness.

part of the economic security that every citizen deserved, integral to "freedom from want."[74] But the President's initiatives for a national health care program would be opposed by a formidable array of interests, as well as by a majority of Congress (see Chapter 7).

In short, the war transformed the agenda of social policy in the United States. The war effectively eliminated consideration of broad-based relief plans for the elderly; it made the veterans of military service, rather than the elderly poor, the prime beneficiaries of federal aid; and it reintroduced national health care into the political agenda. Less directly, the employment and government spending created by the war altered the balance of power between business and labor and changed party politics. The cartelization permitted in the early 1940s and the lapse of antitrust measures made the war a National Recovery Administration all over again—but this time a successful NRA. After the war, public policy would provide relief for those falling out of a state of employment (veterans, retired people, and the temporarily unemployed)—and not for those needing relief in an economy unable to employ its entire workforce. The Second World War had revealed what full employment was like.[75]

Consistently with the effect of World War II as a critical moment, the war did not simply result in the 1940 and 1941 initiatives (agenda A) emerging later as flat-rate pensions or a double-decker system (A'). Instead, social security issues were displaced and supplemented by veterans' programs, the high postwar employment and income levels, and private programs (agenda AW), and resulted in the elimination of flat-rate pension plans, the reintroduction of national health insurance, and the eventual success of the partial reforms of 1950 and the expansions of social security, disability, and Medicare and Medicaid programs over the next three decades (AW').

Conclusions

There was little change in the social security program during the war and the immediate postwar years, contrary to expectations that the government would increase social security taxes—and thus its obligations to contributors—in exchange for desperately needed funds. The social security bureaucracy grew hardly at all; in fact, its size declined in relation to that of the federal

[74] National health insurance had been on the political agenda before, of course. In 1912, Theodore Roosevelt had national health insurance as a plank in his presidential platform, and in 1935, the Committee for Economic Security (CES) made a recommendation for national health insurance. See Chapter 7.

[75] Chairman Altmeyer, writing in the *Atlanta Constitution*, 8 April 1943, file 062.2, "A. J. Altmeyer," Box 23, EDF.

government. While social security was extended to more workers and retirees, social security tax rates and benefit levels—the intensity of the relational state—remained unchanged (with benefit levels falling in real terms
and in proportion to average per capita incomes). Because of the continued
weakness of the Townsend movement and because of the strength of the
competing veterans' programs of the 1944 G.I. Bill and the 1946 bonus
payments, the organized advocates for reform in the social security system
themselves changed: the AFL and CIO came out in support of the federally
administered social security system (even as they still sought reforms), and
the Townsend movement dissipated.

The history of social security in the 1940s confounds expectations, then,
given the federal government's reliance on U.S. citizens for additional wartime revenues and, after the war, for votes: the social security system was not
expanded in terms of major legislation, and the emergence of other competing benefits (e.g., veterans' programs) would, on balance, prove more costly
to government over the long run (social security being self-financing and
veterans' benefits coming out of general revenues). The modest changes and
even contractions in the bureaucratic and relational states contrast with the
expectation that a resource-dependent government strengthen and enlarge
the social security program in order to secure additional funds.

On other fronts, however, the state-building in social policies during the
1940s is consistent with the resource dependence perspective: Congress
successfully opposed expanding social security in the early 1940s (consistent
with the expectation that Congress set social policy), and Congress continued to set—i.e., obstruct—social policy in the postwar period (Hypothesis
1b, Hypothesis 1c).

The form of state-building in social security was further consistent with
expectations of state-building in a large and diffuse policy domain: expansion in the Social Security Administration occurred through existing organizations, and the size of the BOASI increased moderately in relation to the
SSB/SSA over the war and postwar years (Hypothesis 2a). And the government even engaged in low-level ties with societal actors in order to coordinate the establishment of union and corporate pension and health plans
(and later disability plans), thereby ensuring that the federal and private
policies would reinforce each other, rather than conflict (Hypothesis 2b).
The delay of reforms to the social security system until 1950 cuts both ways:
although this state-building in social security was to be expected for the
postwar period (in a policy domain with a broad-based constituency), the
reforms were distinctly late in coming (in contrast to the logic that federal
officials would be dependent on the number of voters represented by social
security stakeholders).

Without any important legislated changes in social security policy during
the war, the only ratcheting in social security programs was in the expanded

participation in the social security system and the retention of (and continued improvement in) the means of administering OASI (Hypothesis 3a).

The only expansions in the social security system thus turned out to be involuntary: employment grew in industries already covered (thereby resulting in more workers being covered and more employers contributing), and the number of retirees eligible for OASI benefits increased as a matter of course. The simple facts of aging and of larger numbers of employees working in OASI-covered jobs meant that social security could survive to continue to provide old-age benefits.[76] As AFL President William Green put it, "everyone gets old."[77] But with the war's alteration in the social policies demanded by the labor unions, with the dissolution of the Townsend movement, with the war's effects on the numbers of those working in covered industries, with the war's beneficial impact on the OASI trust fund, and with the increased number of those retiring, the OASI program became better entrenched—despite the lack of increased benefits levels or OASI tax rates. In fact, the war caused the redistributive and universal social programs introduced during the late 1930s and early 1940s to be displaced by a minimally redistributive and individually based social security system, by programs for war veterans, and by private retirement pensions and health plans (Hypothesis 3b).

The resource dependence perspective thus has mixed results in explaining the development of social security policy. Not only was there no legislated expansion in social security during the war, but President Truman's outspoken push for national health insurance and his vigorous endorsement of an expanded social security system in the postwar years counter an expectation of presidential prudence in recognizing Congress's powers in a noncrisis period. What state-building occurred in the 1940s was uneven and delayed. On the other hand, Congress controlled social security and national health insurance policies throughout the decade, as expected; we did see the growth and subsequent ratcheting in the extent of the social security program and the means of administering social security policy; and there was an agenda shift between the prewar and the postwar eras. Even without a significant expansion of the social security bureaucracy and without the establishment of more intensive government-society ties with respect to social provisions, the changes in social security are broadly consistent with the effects of hegemonic war as a critical moment.

[76] Jerry Cates notes that the "basic function" of social security, as strategically decided by Chairman Altmeyer and his lieutenants, was to secure the nationally administered OASI system instead of supporting the state-assisted Old-Age Assistance or other, more redistributive welfare policies (*Insuring Inequality*).

[77] Quoted in J. Douglas Brown, *An American Philosophy of Social Security: Evolution and Issues* (Princeton: Princeton University Press, 1972), 83. AFL President William Green was explaining why he supported a fifty-fifty employer-employee contribution to old-age insurance.

Yet insufficient attention has been paid to the Second World War's influence on social policy outcomes. Even those scholars who recognize the impact of the Second World War on the social security system do not systematically address the effects of that war (or of other wars, for that matter) on American social policies. But the American state was, in fact, very much influenced by its participation in a hegemonic war—and this in social security policy, one of the most domestic of policy domains.[78] That the events of the Second World War—and its aftermath—were formative of the social security program and had a detrimental effect on the possibilities for national health insurance merely strengthens arguments about the "outside in" effects of the Second World War on domestic policy domains: extranational factors are likely to have a greater effect in the cases that follow.

[78] Cates, *Insuring Inequality*, 60, 70; Berkowitz and McQuaid, *Creating the Welfare State*, 147–64; Leff, "Speculating in Social Security Futures." Berkowitz and McQuaid acknowledge the transformative effects of the war but emphasize the consolidating and legitimating effects of the war on increasing the role of the federal government in providing for economic security. They mention the G.I. Bill, the 1946 National Mental Health Bill, and the Hill-Burton Act as cases in point. War (the Second World War and the Korean War) enabled businessmen and bureaucrats to cooperate in what was now a positive-sum game, rather than a zero-sum game, of governmental action.

In other writings Berkowitz and Leff both acknowledge the importance of the understudied and indeterminate years of the 1940s (Berkowitz, "The First Advisory Council and the 1939 Amendments," 56–57; Leff, "Historical Perspectives on Old-Age Insurance").

Derthick almost completely omits discussion of the Second World War in her well-known *Policymaking for Social Security* (238–39), and Gaston Rimlinger scarcely mentions World War II in his comparative treatment of social security policies (Rimlinger, *Welfare Policy and Industrialization*, 236). Nor do the historians writing in Wilbur Cohen's *The Roosevelt New Deal* address the Second World War: Clarke Chambers's overview of social security nowhere mentions the crucial role of the Second World War in the development of social security policy; James Patterson explicitly covers the years 1930–45 but finds that the Depression in the United States was like the war in Britain; and Cohen says nothing about the war in his brief "Comment" (Clarke A. Chambers, "Social Security: The Welfare Consensus of the New Deal," James T. Patterson, "Comparative Welfare History: Britain and the United States, 1930–45," and Wilbur J. Cohen, "Comment," in *The Roosevelt New Deal*).

Also see William Graebner's *A History of Retirement* (New Haven: Yale University Press, 1980) for an intellectual and institutional history of retirement policies, for a comparison of the social security program with the railroad pensions and private pension plans, and for a critique of how historians have treated the social security system.

3

The Regulation of Labor-Management Relations

Sidney, I expect you to keep labor in step.
—President Roosevelt to Sidney Hillman

Dear Lew [Schwellenbach]:
  I meant to discuss it with you at the Cabinet
this afternoon but the atomic bomb consumed
so much time that I didn't have a chance.
                                    Sincerely yours,
                                    Jim [Forrestal]

Sherman was wrong. . . . Peace is hell.
—President Harry S. Truman,
    December 1945

EVEN as the National Labor Relations Act (Wagner Act) has been called the "most radical" part of the New Deal, the Second World War played a crucial role in reversing the momentum of the labor movement emerging from the 1930s. Notwithstanding the increase of union membership by over four million persons over the course of the war, the position of labor unions in the American economy was already beginning to slip. By 1942, the rate of union victories in National Labor Relations Board elections (elections on collective representation) was starting to decline, and by 1945, the percentage of union members in nonagricultural establishments had peaked at 35.5 percent.[1] (The absolute number of union members continued to rise, of course, as the industrial economy expanded.)

[1] Michael Goldfield, *The Decline of Organized Labor in the United States* (Chicago: University of Chicago Press, 1987), p. 90, Table 11, and p. 10, Table 1. Those indicating the superior strength of labor immediately after the Second World War include Goldfield, xii–xiv; Arthur Meier Schlesinger, *The Rise of Modern America, 1865–1951* (New York: Macmillan, 1951), 461; Joel Seidman, *American Labor from Defense to Reconversion* (Chicago: University of Chicago Press, 1953), 270; John Morton Blum, *V Was for Victory: Politics and American Culture during World War II* (New York: Harcourt Brace Jovanovich, 1976), 140; David Brody, *Workers in Industrial America* (New York: Oxford University Press, 1980), 174–75; Geoffrey Perrett, *Days of Sadness, Years of Triumph: The American People 1939–1945* (New York: Coward, McCann & Geoghegan, 1973), 103–4; and the recent work of Nelson Lichtenstein, "From Corporatism to Collective Bargaining: Organized Labor and the Eclipse of Social Democracy in the Postwar Era," in Fraser and Gerstle, eds., *The Rise and Fall of the New Deal Order*, and Lichtenstein, "Labor in the Truman Era: Origins of the 'Private Welfare State,'" in Michael J.

What, then, explains the beginning of the decline of organized labor in the United States, given the successes of the 1930s and the high income and low unemployment levels of the war years? The argument here is that the Second World War caused increased government intervention in labor-management relations and resulted in closer ties being formed between the federal government and the unions, and that both occurrences were instrumental in the beginning of the decline of organized labor in the United States.

The expectations from the resource dependence perspective are that the president should, with his wartime powers, be able to set policy on labor-management relations. After the war, with the government less dependent on organized labor and absent the president's emergency authority, Congress should set labor policy.

Second, we should expect the president of the United States, as head of a government dependent on a stable labor supply, to seek the cooperation of the labor unions. With much of the industrial workforce unionized by mid-year 1940, the Roosevelt Administration could work with top union officials without having to reach out to individual rank-and-file members; it should not have to separately organize a skilled workforce, but should be able to secure the cooperation of industrial labor through its ties with union leaders.

We should further expect the new national and international environments resulting from the war to cause alterations in government-labor relations. The combination of the effects of World War II, both direct and indirect, with those of the start of the Cold War should lead to the establishment and retention of new agencies, new relations between the federal government and organized labor, and improved means of administration. Lastly, there should be changes in the political agenda of the regulation of labor-management relations.

The United States Conciliation Service (USCS), the National Labor Relations Board (NLRB), and the various wartime labor boards are taken as representative of the regulation of labor-management relations. The USCS (after 1948, the Federal Mediation and Conciliation Service) negotiates,

---

Lacey, ed., *The Truman Presidency*, Woodrow Wilson International Center for Scholars (New York: Cambridge University Press, 1989).

Among the scholars recognizing the deleterious effects of the war on the strength of the labor movement are Grant McConnell, *Private Power and American Democracy*; James A. Gross, *The Reshaping of the National Labor Relations Board: National Policy in Transition 1937–1947* (Albany: State University of New York Press, 1981); Nelson Lichtenstein, *Labor's War at Home: The CIO in World War II* (Cambridge: Cambridge University Press, 1982); Lichtenstein, "Industrial Democracy, Contract Unionism, and the National War Labor Board," *Labor Law Journal* (August 1982); and Christopher L. Tomlins, *The State and the Unions* (Cambridge: Cambridge University Press, 1985).

mediates, and arbitrates (noncompulsory) settlements between workers and management on strikes, threatened strikes, and disputes arising from wages, working conditions, and other grievances; the NLRB, set up under the provisions of the 1935 Wagner Act, handles complaints by individuals, the unions, or employers on matters such as union representation (determining if a majority of workers want a union and, if so, which union) and unfair labor practices (e.g., firing union organizers, employing spies, suppressing pro-union speech, etc.).[2] (The railroads had separate legislation and their own labor boards.) The number of cases heard by the USCS and the NLRB are taken as indicative of the relational state: the more cases being heard, the greater the role of the government in the regulation of labor-management relations.[3]

Two characteristics of the labor case distinguish it from the social security case. First, instead of looking at two examples of social provisions—Old-Age and Survivors Insurance (primarily) and proposals for national health insurance—this chapter studies several organizations involved in the resolution of labor-management differences: the NLRB, the USCS (and FMCS), the National Defense Mediation Board (March–December 1941), the National War Labor Board (1942–45), and the National Wage Stabilization Board (1946–47).[4] Second, the institutional changes of the war years were only partly changes in financial obligations, unlike the expansion of retirement benefits or the increases in social security tax rates. Government labor agencies had offices, budgets, and salaried employees, to be sure, but more salient changes occurred in the rules for and practices of resolving labor-management prob-

---

[2] Following on the heels of the National Recovery Act's Section 7(a)—the NRA having been found unconstitutional—Congress passed and President Roosevelt signed the National Labor Relations Act in 1935, establishing the rights of workers to bargain collectively and guaranteeing their fair treatment by employers. See Irving Bernstein, *A History of the American Worker*, Vol. 2: *The Turbulent Years, 1933–1941* (Boston: Houghton Mifflin, 1971), for a comprehensive account of organized labor during the 1930s.

[3] To restrict government intervention to cases on just one issue—wages or collective bargaining, say—would, it seems, unnecessarily narrow the study of government-society ties.

[4] The present focus on the NLRB, the USCS/FMCS, the three wartime labor boards, and the fact-finding boards leaves out many other government agencies dealing with labor issues, of course, including the National Mediation Board (for railroads), the Committee on Fair Employment Practices, the War Manpower Commission, the Maritime Commission (Labor Relations Division, Division of Shipyard Labor Relations), the War Shipping Administration (Division of Maritime Labor Relations), the Department of Commerce (Bureau of the Census—Labor Force Project), the War Production Board (Office of Labor Production, War Production Drives Division, Office of Manpower Requirements), the Department of State (Division of International Labor, Social and Health Affairs), the War Department (Labor Branch of Industrial Personnel Division), the Navy Department (District Labor Relations Office), the Federal Security Agency (Bureau of Employment Security), the Federal Works Agency (Division of Labor Relations), and the Office of War Mobilization (Retraining and Reemployment Administration).

lems. State-building in the regulation of labor-management relations was less a matter of union dues, taxes on employees, or wage levels, then, and more a matter of how it was that the federal government intervened in labor-management relations.

Background

With the period of rearmament beginning after June 1940 came increasing labor unrest. The Roosevelt Administration therefore established the National Defense Mediation Board (NDMB) in March of 1941 to supplement the existing USCS and NLRB. The NDMB took up those disputes that the USCS was unable to settle. It mediated between labor and business management, arbitrated cases when the two parties voluntarily submitted to the Board's ruling, and used the moral suasion of "fact-finding" (with the subsequent publicization of Board recommendations). The NDMB's eleven members consisted of four representatives each for business and labor, and three for the public. Although the NDMB had neither subpoena powers nor the authority to issue legally binding settlements, the NDMB nonetheless succeeded in settling 96 of the 118 cases it heard. It collapsed in November 1941, when the representatives from the Congress of Industrial Organizations (CIO) walked out.

The Roosevelt Administration created the National War Labor Board (NWLB) in January 1942 as the successor to the NDMB (Executive Order 9017). The NWLB added a fourth public representative (for a total of twelve) and had the legal authority to arbitrate cases. The NWLB was to control wages, hours, working conditions, and other terms of union agreements according to the Fair Labor Standards Act, the Price Control Act, the Wage Stabilization Act, and other applicable laws. The National War Labor Board had the authority to mandate cooling-off periods, appoint fact-finding boards, and issue final arbitration rulings.[5] The decisions of the Chairman of the National War Labor Board were to be enforced by the Attorney General, backed by the resources of the War and Navy Departments.[6] Although the NWLB was authorized to regulate war contractors (as opposed to all labor disputes as such), "war contractors" came to include practically all industries. On 18 June the NWLB granted unions a "maintenance of membership" clause, such that the status of employees remained the same during

---

[5] Lichtenstein, "Industrial Democracy, Contract Unionism, and the National War Labor Board," 524–31; U.S. Department of Labor, *The Anvil and the Plow: A History of the U.S. Department of Labor* (Washington, D.C.: U.S. GPO, 1963), 130–32.

[6] Employers who refused to comply with the NWLB were liable to have their plants seized, or to have the government cancel their orders or take over the direction of company affairs regarding war contracts, essential materials, transportation, and fuel. Unions refusing to comply were also liable to have their workplaces seized.

the war, whether their industry was previously organized or not (there was a little-heeded fifteen-day escape clause for new workers entering previously unionized plants).

After a series of strikes by the United Mine Workers in mid-1943, Congress passed the War Labor Disputes Act, known popularly as the Smith-Connally Act. The Smith-Connally Act specified a thirty-day cooling-off period between the date of issue of a strike notice and the date when workers could walk out. It also put the National War Labor Board on a statutory basis and provided the president with specific powers for taking over industries (powers that had been previously assumed).

The Truman Administration terminated the NWLB in 1945, and replaced it with the National Wage Stabilization Board in 1946. The NWSB had a six-member tripartite board (instead of twelve) but no binding authority; it lasted until early 1947.

In mid-1947, Congress passed the Labor Management Relations Act (the Taft-Hartley Act) over President Truman's veto. Provisions of the Taft-Hartley Act included:

- a ban on secondary boycotts,
- a prohibition on foremen from joining unions,
- the reintroduction of court injunctions for settling disputes (previously outlawed under the 1932 Norris-LaGuardia Act),
- the bestowal of broad discretionary powers on the Special Counsel of the NLRB (thereby dividing control within the Board),
- restrictions on peaceful picketing and on the dues check-off,
- the provision of presidential powers for establishing boards of inquiry in national emergencies and disputes that affected international commerce,
- the outlawing of the closed shop, and
- the removal of the USCS from the Department of Labor, making it into an independent agency, the Federal Mediation and Conciliation Service.

Despite attempts by the Truman Administration and the 81st Congress to repeal and replace the Taft-Hartley Act after the 1948 elections, the next labor legislation to be passed would not be until 1959, with the Landrum-Griffin Act.

Presidential Regulation of Labor-Management Relations

President Roosevelt, as commander in chief, directed the wartime expansion of government control over labor-management relations. He did so in three ways: by creating labor boards, seizing industries, and regulating the economy.

With the rise in employment beginning after June 1940, labor and management came increasingly into conflict. By the end of February 1941 there were sixteen major work stoppages in progress, involving 20,000 employees working on $60 million worth of defense production: 14,000 men went on strike at four International Harvester plants, 7,500 men went on strike at the Allis-Chalmers plant in Milwaukee, and employees walked off the job at the Ryan Aviation plant in New York, at the Lackawanna works of Bethlehem Steel, and at four International Harvester plants. The strikes were "dramatized by rioting," the NDMB later reported, and "[t]he huge River Rouge plant of the Ford Motor Co. was constantly in danger of being shut down. By the middle of March it was apparent that additional measures had to be taken."[7] The number of work stoppages more than doubled in just three months' time, increasing from 147 stoppages in December 1940 to 316 stoppages in March 1941. In response to the unrest, Roosevelt created the NDMB on 19 March 1941 (E.O. 8716).

Ten days after the attack on Pearl Harbor, on 17 December 1941, the President held a conference for industry and labor in order to prevent work stoppages from disrupting the war effort (since the NDMB had been disbanded).[8] The conference remained deadlocked over the issues of union security and the closed shop until 23 December, when the conferees agreed that there would be no strikes or lockouts, that all disputes were to be settled by peaceful means, and that a war labor board would be set up. The NWLB was established on 12 January 1942. The NWLB, like its predecessor, would receive cases only after all other measures had been exhausted. But "after it takes jurisdiction, the Board shall finally determine the dispute, and for this purpose, may use mediation, voluntary arbitration, or arbitration under rules established by the Board."[9] The NWLB lasted for the duration of the war.

More dramatically, the President used his executive power to seize industries. Roosevelt sent federal troops to break up a United Auto Workers-CIO strike on 9 June 1941 and to take over the North American Aviation plant in Inglewood, California (E.O. 8773). Two months later, on 23 August 1941, Roosevelt seized Federal Shipbuilding and Drydock (E.O. 8868). And when the United Mine Workers went on strike later that year, the President had the Secretary of the Interior, Harold Ickes, take control of the coal mines.[10] The strike was settled on 7 December, the news buried in the middle of Monday's papers.

Less than eighteen months later, John L. Lewis again took the United

[7] United States Bureau of Labor Statistics, "Report of the Work of the National Defense Mediation Board," *Bulletin No. 714*, 1.

[8] The AFL and the CIO were each to have six representatives, the Business Advisory Council twelve.

[9] Executive Order 9017, 12 January 1942.

[10] The UMW was eventually granted a wage increase and closed-shop status when Roosevelt appointed a three-person board with two of the appointees known to favor the miners' position.

Mine Workers out on strike, this time in defiance of the NWLB and in direct violation of the no-strike pledge. President Roosevelt responded with an ultimatum: "The enemy will not wait while strikes and stoppages run their course. Therefore if work at the mines is not resumed by ten o'clock Saturday morning [1 May 1943], I shall use all the power vested in me as President and as Commander-in-Chief of the Army and Navy to protect the national interest and to prevent further interference with the successful prosecution of the war."[11] The President authorized Interior Secretary Ickes to take possession of the coal mines on 1 May (E.O. 9340). The strike was quickly settled. Six months later, in response to a new wave of strikes, the President again ordered Ickes to seize 1,700 coal mines. On 3 November 1943, however—just two days after seizing the coal mines—the government reached an agreement with the UMW.[12] Between them, Presidents Roosevelt and Truman effected a total of seventy-one industrial seizures during the period from 1941 to 1945.[13]

President Roosevelt further regulated labor-management relations by imposing economic controls. In order to discourage absenteeism, a uniform weekly pay scale was set up in October 1942 with double time for the seventh consecutive day of work and time-and-a-half for a workweek of more than 40 hours (E.O. 9240). Two days later the President set up the Office of Economic Stabilization, under the administration of James Byrnes. The President then declared that the only increases in wages allowable as of 8 April 1943 were those under the "Little Steel" agreement (a NWLB decision for Bethlehem Steel, Inland Steel, Jones & Laughlin, et al.). The Little Steel decision applied to all union wage agreements for the rest of the war.

In short, presidential leadership was amply evident in the establishment of labor boards, the seizures of industries, and the regulation of the economy.[14] At least eighteen executive orders related directly to labor regulation

[11] 29 April 1943, in *The Public Papers and Addresses of Franklin D. Roosevelt*, Vol. 11, 184.

[12] The mines would return to private hands on 31 May 1944. See Alinsky on Lewis's brilliant handling of the coal strikes (Saul Alinsky, *John L. Lewis: An Unauthorized Biography* [New York: G. P. Putnam's Sons, 1949], 280–324). Also see Colston E. Warne, "Coal—The First Major Test of the Little Steel Formula," *Yearbook of American Labor*, Vol. 1: *War Labor Policies* (New York: Philosophical Library, 1945).

[13] More than a third of the top 100 corporations had either their entire operations, a subsidiary, or a single plant seized (John R. Blackman, Jr., *Presidential Seizure in Labor Disputes* [Cambridge, Mass.: Harvard University Press, 1967]; Hugh Rockoff, "The Response of the Giant Corporations to Wage and Price Controls in World War II," *Journal of Economic History* 41 No. 1 [March 1981]: 127).

[14] Roosevelt's appointments to the NLRB also affected governmental policy. As the labor historian James Gross points out, the evolution of the NLRB's decisions was very much a product of the board membership. President Roosevelt wanted a more moderate chairman after J. Warren Madden's term expired in late 1940. This was despite Madden's being backed by John L. Lewis, then President of the CIO, and by Senators Wagner and Thomas, who guaranteed the reappointment. Both Roosevelt and Secretary of Labor Perkins wanted a less independent NLRB. The President subsequently appointed the economist Harry Millis as chairman of

in the war and the immediate postwar period through 1946, and all of the industrial seizures by the government from 1940 through 1950 were done through executive order.[15]

An exception to this record of presidential leadership was the passage of the Smith-Connally Act on 25 June 1943, over Roosevelt's veto, in response to the 1943 coal strikes.[16] Another departure from the above record of presidential control was Congress's refusal to pass national service legislation, legislation that would have authorized the federal government to allocate labor manpower to either industrial production or military service. Frustrated with the labor unrest and wanting to get back at organized labor for reneging on the no-strike pledge, Roosevelt pushed Congress to adopt

> a national service law—which for the duration of the war, will prevent strikes, and with certain appropriate exceptions, will make available for war production or for any other essential services every able-bodied adult in this nation. I have received a joint recommendation for this law from the heads of the War Department, the Navy Department, and the Maritime Commission. These are the men who bear responsibility for the procurement of the necessary arms and equipment and for the successful prosecution of the war in the field. They say: When the very life of the Nation is in peril the responsibility for service is common to all men and women. In such a time there can be no discrimination between the men and women who are assigned by the Government to its defense at the battlefront and the men and women assigned to producing the vital materials essential to success-

---

the Board. William H. Leiserson came to the Board in 1939, replacing Donald W. Smith. When Edwin Smith's term expired, Roosevelt stated that a board "wholly different in its membership from the original board will be best." Effective October 1941, Roosevelt replaced Smith, an outspoken supporter of industrial organization, with Labor Department Solicitor Gerard Reilly—Reilly being a critic of the NLRB's alleged CIO bias. The President then replaced William Leiserson (who resigned in 1943) with John Houston, a protégé of Reilly (Gross, *The Reshaping of the National Labor Relations Board*, 226–27, 239).

In 1945 Truman used his presidential office to appoint Paul Herzog, a New York State labor official, to the National Labor Relations Board as a replacement for the resigning Millis. Herzog was "a skilled organization man" who would steer the board down the middle of the road. With Reilly, Herzog, and Huston, the NLRB had a majority that would bend as the reconversion and postwar political climate indicated—away from a liberal interpretation of the Wagner Act. See Moe on the politics of the NLRB from 1950 through 1985 (Terry M. Moe, "Control and Feedback in Economic Regulation: The Case of the NLRB," *American Political Science Review* 79 No. 4 [1985], 1094–1116; and Moe, "Interests, Institutions, and Positive Theory."

[15] Blackman, *Presidential Seizure in Labor Disputes*, "Appendix A."

[16] David Brody writes that Roosevelt opposed the undue harshness of the Smith-Connally Act, because it gave the President "more power over strikes than he wanted (the measure passed over his veto)" (Brody, "The New Deal and World War II"). Yet Roosevelt's relations with organized labor and the text of the veto message point to the President's deep ambivalence (see Chapter 6). On the one hand, Roosevelt the politician was loath to alienate organized labor; on the other hand, Roosevelt was genuinely opposed to wartime strikes and impatient for fuller executive authority with which to deal with disruptive organized labor, as exemplified later in his request for national service legislation.

ful military operation. A prompt enactment of a National Service Law would be merely an expression of the universality of this responsibility.[17]

But both organized labor and business management strongly opposed the legislation, labor vociferously and management more quietly; the bill did not leave committee.[18]

Roosevelt repeated his request for a national service bill in his 1945 State of the Union message: a national service requirement would assure the right number of workers at the right places at the right times; it would show the fighting men that "we are giving them what they are entitled to, which is nothing less than our total effort"; and it would give the Germans and the Japanese an unequivocal answer to their hopes that the United States was becoming half-hearted in its pursuit of the war.[19] Although both Secretary of War Henry Stimson and Navy Secretary James Forrestal strongly supported the bill, Congress again denied the President's request. The absence of a national service requirement and the passage of the Smith-Connally Act thus suggest that the Administration was unable to take complete control over the policies it believed necessary for securing the wartime labor supply.

Once the war ended, the government became less dependent on a secure labor supply. With the different economic environment for both government and business—typified by fears of a postwar depression from the cutbacks in orders for goods and materials—organized labor posed a less formidable threat to elected officials and their appointees. With prices and wages no longer fixed, higher wages could simply be matched by higher prices (and vice versa). Moreover, work stoppages could actually help business (and thus compromise the government's position) by giving companies a chance to retool their production lines for the manufacture of civilian goods.

To the extent that the Truman Administration was able to regulate labor relations by establishing and terminating boards, setting economic policy, and seizing industries, its authority largely coincided with the extension of the President's emergency powers past August 1945. President Truman transferred the NWLB to the Department of Labor on 19 September 1945, terminated the NWLB on 31 December 1945, and set up the NWSB in January 1946 (lasting until February 1947). Truman also appointed factfinding boards in the General Motors and United States Steel disputes, and he set up three more fact-finding boards between mid-December 1945 and

---

[17] 11 January 1944, "State of the Union Address," *The Public Papers and Addresses of Franklin D. Roosevelt*, Vol. 12, 38.

[18] Lichtenstein, *Labor's War at Home*, 182–84; Paul A. C. Koistinen, *The Hammer and the Sword* (New York: Arno Press, 1979), 457; James MacGregor Burns, *Roosevelt: The Soldier of Freedom* (New York: Harcourt Brace Jovanovich, 1970), 432–33.

[19] 6 January 1945, *The Public Papers and Addresses of Franklin D. Roosevelt*, Vol. 13, 496.

mid-January 1946. Secretary of Labor Lewis B. Schwellenbach and the Director of the USCS appointed six more such boards in 1946.[20]

Yet these measures enjoyed mixed success, at best. United States Steel rejected President Truman's offer of 18 January 1946 for an 18.5¢ per hour increase (as was recommended by the fact-finding board and accepted by the United Steel Workers union). The strike went on.[21] Nor were General Motors Corporation and the United Auto Workers any more cooperative in the automobile strike. Despite the President's approval of the fact-finding board's recommendations, labor and management could not agree on a wage increase for another two months. Meanwhile, Truman set up another fact-finding board for the threatened rail strike on 8 March 1946, and on 17 May the President directed the government to seize and operate the railroads. Although eighteen of the twenty railroad unions agreed to arbitration, the two union leaders, Alvaney Johnson and A. F. Whitney, rejected the 16¢ per hour increase recommended by the emergency board.

The President continued to seize private industries after the war, the extraordinary authority coinciding with the extension of the President's emergency powers. Truman ordered three seizures after V-J Day under the authority of the Smith-Connally Act, and he used his powers of seizure on nine more occasions in 1946—including another seizure of the coal mines on 21 May (E.O. 9728).[22] In 1948, the President used the provisions of the Taft-Hartley Act to seize 207 railroads. The President's industrial seizures thus roughly varied with the incidence of war, to vanish almost completely by the late 1940s: there were five seizures in 1941 and twenty-three seizures in 1944, whereas there were only nine seizures in 1946 and just one seizure (of the railroads) in all of 1947, 1948, and 1949.

As for economic regulations, as soon as the war ended President Truman removed wartime controls and called for a return to voluntary collective bargaining (E.O. 9599). He abolished the Office of Economic Stabilization on 20 September 1945 and transferred its responsibility to the Office of War Management and Reconversion (OWMR). On 30 October 1945, Truman established the conditions for wage increases (E.O. 9651). Here, too, the

[20] Arthur F. McClure, *The Truman Administration and the Problems of Postwar Labor, 1945–1948* (Rutherford, N.J.: Fairleigh Dickinson University Press, 1969), 87. Also see Robert H. Ferrell, *Harry S. Truman: A Life* (Columbia, Mo.: University of Missouri Press, 1994), 226–32.

[21] See Barton J. Bernstein on the steel strike ("The Truman Administration and the Politics of Inflation," Ph.D. diss., Harvard University, 1963, 158–77). Bernstein notes President Truman's inability to settle postwar labor problems and to defuse inflation. The White House was flooded by mail opposing the scuttling of the OPA—the most mail it had received since Roosevelt's court-packing plan of 1937 (246).

[22] The CIO's Oil Workers International struck twenty-nine oil companies; employees struck the Capital Transit Co. in Washington, D.C.; and a division of the International Longshoremen's Association struck the Great Lakes Towing Company. See Blackman, *Presidential Seizure in Labor Disputes*, "Appendix A," 275–76.

President was ineffective. He had to reestablish the Office of Economic Stabilization on 21 February 1946 under the impetus of raging inflation, and he lifted wage and salary controls in November 1946. As with the industrial seizures and the establishment and disestablishment of the labor boards, Truman's economic leadership coincided with his war powers (which remained in effect until 31 December 1946). Once the special war powers expired, so did the President's discretionary authority.

Indeed, the President had little success with those postwar labor issues that lay outside his emergency jurisdictions. Truman called for a labor-management conference in Washington on 5 November 1945, given the two parties' "necessity of getting together on their problems. Public opinion will not countenance a refusal on the part of either management or labor to proceed in a peaceful, free, and democratic manner to arrive at just conclusions."[23] Nothing concrete emerged from the conference. As a result, the President told Congress that in the absence of any policy recommendations emerging from the conference "it becomes the duty of Government to act on its own initiative. Therefore, I now suggest to the Congress that well-reasoned and workable legislation be passed at the earliest possible moment to provide adequate means for settling industrial disputes and avoiding industrial strife."[24] A month later, on 3 January 1946, the President repeated his request for legislation on fact-finding boards, and in the State of the Union address, given shortly thereafter, Truman again asked for "[l]egislation to authorize the President to create fact-finding boards for the prevention of stoppages of work in nationwide industries after collective bargaining and conciliation and voluntary arbitration have failed—as recommended by me on December 3, 1945."[25] No legislation was forthcoming.

President Truman proposed additional measures to Congress in response to the national railroad strike of 1946. On 25 May 1946, four days after the railroad unions rejected President Truman's suggested solution, the Presi-

[23] 30 October 1945, *Public Papers of the Presidents of the United States: Harry S. Truman, 1945*, 448.

[24] 3 December 1945, *Public Papers of the Presidents of the United States: Harry S. Truman, 1945*, 519–20. President Truman specifically recommended that the Secretary of Labor certify that a dispute was in fact continuing and that such a strike would vitally affect the public interest. The President would then appoint a fact-finding board within five days (following the precedent set by the Railway Labor Act). During these five days, there could be no disruption of labor, while the Board, composed of three or more "outstanding citizens," would make a thorough investigation of all the facts in the controversy. The board would have the power to issue subpoenas and would make its report within twenty days. The report would be publicized, but neither party would be legally bound to follow its recommendations.

[25] 21 January 1946, *Public Papers of the Presidents of the United States: Harry S. Truman, 1946*, 40. "Government assistance but not government coercion" was necessary for the resolution of labor-management disputes, which Truman thought to be first among the obstacles to national progress.

dent sent Congress a special message urging the passage of temporary legislation for industrial peace (the Temporary Disputes Settlement Bill). The
President requested authorization to issue injunctions or initiate mandatory
proceedings against any union leader, forbidding him from encouraging or
inciting union members to leave or refuse to work; to declare a national
emergency should there be a strike, slowdown, or lockout after the government had taken possession of a plant; to call upon all parties to return to
their jobs; and to draft strikers into the Army. Any worker refusing to return
to work would forfeit his rights granted under the Wagner Act. But the bill
failed to pass in the Senate, despite its passage by an overwhelming margin
in the House. Senator Robert Taft (R., Ohio) thought it ceded too much
power to the executive.[26] On 11 June, Truman vetoed the substitute Case
Bill: it differed too greatly from the legislation he had requested.[27] Truman
also vetoed the Taft-Hartley Bill in 1947, decrying it for its unprecedented
level of intervention by the government in labor-management relations, its
unworkability, and its arbitrariness, only to see the 80th Congress easily
muster the two-thirds vote necessary for the override.

Upon the successful reelection campaign of 1948 and the election of a
Democratic 81st Congress, President Truman used his 1949 State of the
Union address to ask for the repeal of the Taft-Hartley Act. The President
restated his request on 24 February 1949 and asked for the replacement of
the Taft-Hartley Act by a fairer law. Truman called for renewed labor and
business cooperation in his 1950 annual addresses and again asked for the
repeal of the Taft-Hartley Act, but to no avail.[28] The President made three
more public requests for a substitute for the Taft-Hartley Act and for its
replacement by a fairer law (11, 12, and 15 May). Plans for a repeal of the
Taft-Hartley Act foundered with the start of the Korean conflict, however,
just as did the proposed reorganization of the NLRB, initiatives for national
health insurance, the Brannan agricultural plan, and a plan for aiding small
businesses.[29]

---

[26] McClure, *The Truman Administration and the Problems of Postwar Labor, 1945–1948*, 152–54.

[27] The Case Bill would have established a five-person independent conciliation service, would have allowed fact-finding only in disputes involving public utilities, would have deprived supervisory employees of their status as employees, and would have rescinded the Norris-LaGuardia Act's provisions allowing labor injunctions. The Taft-Hartley Act closely resembled the earlier Case Bill.

[28] 4 January 1950, *Public Papers of the Presidents of the United States: Harry S. Truman, 1950*, 7. The President did not mention the Taft-Hartley Act by name (contrary to his claim in the annual Budget message).

[29] Reorganization Plan No. 12 would have transferred all functions of the Board and General Counsel to the Chairman and abolished the office of General Counsel. The Brennan plan would have provided agricultural support for all farmers up to a certain level—thus equalizing support for big and small farmers—and would have encouraged low-cost production. See Ferrell, *Harry S. Truman*, 288–89.

Figure 3.1. Let's Take the Picture. It Looks as if Everybody's Here. From New York *Herald Tribune*, 1946. © New York Herald Tribune, Inc. All rights reserved. Reprinted with permission

The history of the postwar years shows the Truman Administration's experience in regulating labor-management relations to be consistent with expectations of the resource dependence perspective: the President was demonstrably weak in relation to Congress, and the exercise of presidential discretion was restricted to the immediate postwar reconversion period as a result of still-operative presidential war powers.[30] President Truman exerted substantially less authority in the postwar years than either he or President Roosevelt had had in wartime, and Congress blocked what initiatives there were. President Truman was unsuccessful in either amending or replacing the Wagner Act—with neither the Case Bill nor the Taft-Hartley Act meeting the President's criteria—and he was unable to repeal Taft-Hartley.[31]

For all of Truman's proclamation that "[a]s President of the United States, I am the representative of 140 million people and I cannot stand idly by while they are being caused to suffer" because of the striking labor unions, the common lesson of the railroad, General Motors, and U.S. Steel strikes and the history of postwar labor legislation was that the intervention of even the President himself was incapable of resolving labor-management problems.

The Form of Labor-Management Relations

The presence of federated nationwide labor unions allowed the wartime government to act through leading union officials in order to secure needed resources. Rather than establish its own extensive bureaucracy for the direct control of the wartime workforce, the Roosevelt Administration used dispute-settling agencies and the existing labor unions to stabilize its labor supply.

Two bodies created to mediate and resolve labor-management problems, and thereby to avoid a halt in production, were the war labor boards, the NDMB and the NWLB. Both had "tripartite" representation from the business, labor, and public sectors. At the War Labor Conference of December 1941, union officials received a guarantee of "maintenance of membership" in return for the pledge not to go on strike. The maintenance-of-membership clause, granted formally on 25 April 1942, protected existing unions from management as well as from encroachment by other unions (such as John L. Lewis's "District 50" union). The membership clause facilitated the increase

[30] On 31 December 1946, the President issued a proclamation that the period of hostilities of World War II would be terminated as of noon that day: "The proclamation terminates Government powers under some 20 statutes immediately . . . [and] some 33 others at a later date, generally at the end of 6 months from the date of the proclamation. . . . It should be noted that the proclamation does not terminate the states of emergency declared by President Roosevelt on September 8, 1939, and May 27, 1941. Nor does today's action have the effect of terminating the state of war itself" ("Statement by the President," 31 December 1946, *Public Papers of the Presidents of the United States: Harry S. Truman, 1946*).

[31] The responsibility for the failure to repeal the Taft-Hartley Act may lie with the Truman Administration itself, however. See Gerald Pomper, "Labor and Congress: The Repeal of Taft-Hartley," *Labor History* 2 (Fall 1961), 323–43.

in union membership from 10.5 million workers on 7 December 1941 to 14.75 million workers by 15 August 1945 (V-J Day).[32]

Having given the no-strike pledge and having received the promise that unions would not be busted but would in fact be allowed to expand as the industrial economy grew, top officials of AFL- and CIO-affiliated unions cooperated with the Roosevelt Administration to stop wildcat strikes, suppress dissident unions, and defuse local union and shop-floor opposition to government policies.[33] Consider the North American Aviation strike of 1941, where thousands of United Auto Workers members went on strike to protest the 40¢ minimum hourly wage.[34] Federal troops seized the plant by firing tear gas and machine guns at the striking workers, and President Roosevelt, business leaders, top military officials, the radio and press, and UAW and CIO leaders all condemned the strike as a threat to national defense and as being communist-inspired.[35]

Consider also the contrast between the actions of the labor leaders and those of the rank-and-file union members. On 2 May 1943, a thousand delegates representing the 350,000 Michigan UAW members overrode their national officers and voted overwhelmingly to support both the Mine Workers' demands and the UMW strike; only six delegates raised their hands to oppose a resolution backing the coal strike. Four days later, a resolution was adopted that "the fight against John L. Lewis is not the issue in this case" and that "it is evident that the miners' fight, involving as it does the struggle against lowering the living standards, is actually the fight of every working man and woman in America."[36] Similar resolutions were passed in hundreds of local unions in the automobile, rubber, and steel industries, and thousands of CIO members also sent individual messages of encouragement.

At in a 15 May meeting in Cleveland of the CIO Executive Board, President Murray claimed the strike was nothing but part of Lewis's "political vendetta" against "our Commander in Chief."[37] Murray and other CIO ex-

---

[32] Lichtenstein, *Labor's War at Home*, 79–81; Art Preis, *Labor's Giant Step* (New York: Pioneer Press, 1964), 168.

[33] President Roosevelt wrote to William H. Davis, Chairman of the National War Labor Board, on the interpretation of the War Labor Disputes Act: "When a local union refuses to comply, by directing or advising workers not to work under the terms and conditions prescribed by the Board, *action by the responsible national or international officers has thus far, in all but one or two cases, sufficed to bring about compliance*" (Roosevelt to Davis, 16 August 1943, OF 4710, Official Papers of the President, Roosevelt Papers; emphasis added).

[34] The hourly minimum wage was below the Works Progress Administration's minimum wage of 75¢ per hour. UAW wages also came to an average annual wage nearly $200 below the Department of Labor's "minimum health and safety budget."

[35] Preis, *Labor's Giant Step*, 117–20; Perrett, *Days of Sadness*, 178.

[36] Preis, *Labor's Giant Step*, 183–84. Also see Lichtenstein for a UAW example from 1942 (*Labor's War at Home*, 101–3).

[37] Preis, *Labor's Giant Step*, 184.

ecutives condemned the UMW strike and supported the government's position. Later that month, when 30,000 Chrysler and Dodge workers went on strike for four days to protest eleven months' accumulated grievances and unmet demands, UAW leaders publicly chastised their members. And when 50,000 United Rubber Worker union members went on strike for five days in response to a NWLB concession of only a 3¢ increase in wages—this after a year's delay—URW leaders saw fit to openly upbraid the striking workers.

In May 1944, one-quarter of the 13,944 delegates to the United Steelworkers' convention in Cleveland voted against the no-strike pledge, despite the fact that the vote came after extensive debate and followed lengthy speeches by Murray and other union officials emphasizing that "there's a war on."[38] And at the CIO national convention in mid-July, over one-third of delegates voted to rescind the no-strike pledge, despite Murray's protests that strikes would hurt President Roosevelt's chances for reelection and his repeated emphasis that "war, war, war occasioned the no-strike pledge."[39] The union delegates defeated an unconditional affirmation of the no-strike pledge by a vote of 5,232 to 4,988. But Murray and other union officials were able to relegate any proposed changes to the no-strike position to a referendum, delay the date of the vote by ninety days, and get the voting to be done by mail.

The ranking union leaders maintained their public support of Roosevelt and the war effort, even when the President requested and enacted policies hostile to rank-and-file interests (such as the wage freeze). Labor leaders, in turn, received public support for their positions, obtained privileged access to government officials, and received a nominal share in national decision-making. Labor leaders—the William Greens, the Philip Murrays, the Sidney Hillmans—could be statesmen as well as workers' advocates. Unions that did not cooperate, such as the United Mine Workers, were portrayed as unpatriotic, even treasonous.[40]

The success of the government's wartime procedures for settling labor disputes and the fruits of its cooperative strategy with the unions can be seen in the decreasing number of man-days lost to strikes during the war,

---

[38] Preis, *Labor's Giant Step*, 187, 228.

[39] Preis, *Labor's Giant Step*, 234.

[40] The reaction from the government, union officials, business, and the press to the wartime strikes was ferocious (e.g., Dubofsky and Van Tine, *John L. Lewis* [New York: Quadrangle, 1977], 445). The President leveraged this reaction to his advantage. In responding to the 1943 coal miners' strike, for instance, Roosevelt used one of his Fireside Chats to contrast the progress being made in the war and the sacrifices being made by the many against the action of the United Mine Workers, whose national officers refused to cooperate with the fact-finding effort of the NWLB. Roosevelt gave his address *after* Lewis had already negotiated with Ickes to open the mines in two days.

TABLE 3.1
Work Stoppages

Fiscal Year	No. of Stoppages	No. of Workers	% Employed	Man-Days Idle	
				No.	% of Time
1940	2,508	577 (000)	2.3	6,700	0.10
1941	4,288	2,360	8.4	23,000	0.32
1942	2,968	840	2.8	4,180	0.05
1943	3,752	1,980	6.9	13,500	0.15
1944	4,956	2,120	7.0	8,720	0.09
1945	4,750	3,470	12.2	38,000	0.47
1946	4,985	4,600	14.5	116,000	1.43
1947	3,693	2,170	6.5	34,600	0.41
1948	3,419	1,960	5.6	34,100	0.40
1949	3,606	3,030	9.0	50,500	0.59
1950	4,863	2,410	5.1	38,800	0.33

Sources: U.S. Department of Labor, Bureau of Labor Statistics, "1950—Labor Statistics—General," 1 June 1950, Office of the Secretary of Labor, 1950, Box 250, RG 174; 1950 figures from "Work Stoppages, Workers Involved, Man-Days Idle, Major Issues, and Average Duration: 1881 to 1970," *Historical Statistics,* Series D 970–85, 179.

Note: "Stoppages" includes strikes, walkouts, lockouts, etc. "% employed" is the number of striking workers as a percentage of the total workforce. "Man-Days Idle, % of Time" is the time lost to stoppages as a percentage of total worker man-days in the year.

especially when contrasted with the absolute number of work stoppages. Both the number of man-days lost to work stoppages and the percentage of labor time lost to strikes, walkouts, and lockouts fell after 1941, until the end of the war (see Table 3.1). In fact, more man-days were lost to strikes in two months of 1946 than during the entire war period.

In sum, the government was able to establish top-level coordinating groups for securing the wartime labor force. The Roosevelt Administration did not have to establish its own unions or labor organizations in order to provide for a dependable workforce, but could set up intermediary bodies (the NDMB and the NWLB) and also cooperate more informally with the leaders of established labor union leaders.

The Effects of the War

The war caused the expansion of government agencies regulating labor-management relations, enlarged the role of the federal government in labor-management relations, caused an improvement in the administration of labor boards, and brought about the creation of additional bodies for settling

TABLE 3.2
Employment in the Labor Boards

Fiscal Year	Personnel			War Boards	Total Employ.	% USG
	USCS	NLRB	Total			
1940	107	(NA)	(NA)	—	—	—
1941	160	796	956	—	956	0.07
1942	274	889	1,163	(NA)	—	—
1943	385	736	1,111	(NA)	—	—
1944	399	(NA)	(NA)	(NA)	—	—
1945	444	749	1,193	2,613	3,806	0.10
1946	495	990	1,485	939	2,424	0.09
1947	381	720	1,101	—	1,101	0.05
1948	442	(NA)	(NA)	—	—	—
1949	364	(NA)	(NA)	—	—	—
1950	336	(NA)	(NA)	—	—	—

Sources: U.S. Department of Labor, *The Anvil and the Plow: A History of the U.S. Department of Labor* (Washington, D.C.: U.S. GPO, 1963); NLRB *Annual Reports.* NLRB personnel for FY 1946 and FY 1947 are from Emily Clark Brown, "The NLRB—Wagner Act through Taft-Hartley Law," in Warne, ed., *Labor in Postwar America,* 180. Figures for the Federal Mediation and Conciliation service are from the FMCS *Annual Reports.*

Notes: "Personnel" is the sum of Washington and field personnel, for USCS, these are full-time conciliators. Figures for FY 1948 combine the July and August USCS figures and the FMCS data. USCS figures include those of the FMCS, which was made independent of the Department of Labor as of September 1947 (two months into FY 1948). 1945 "War Boards" is the number of full-time personnel employed by the National War Labor Board; 1946 "War Boards" is for the National Wage Stabilization Board. "% USG" is the proportion of the total number of federal civilian employees constituted by labor board personnel.

labor-management disputes. Given the changes in the domestic and international environments, the state-building resulting from the war remained largely intact afterwards across all three dimensions of the state. Nationally, the war reshaped the economy and society as well as government itself; internationally, the beginning of the Cold War created an environment hostile to labor activism.

Not surprisingly, the organizations mediating labor-management relations grew substantially in size over the course of the war. The USCS had 107 employees in 1940 and 444 employees in 1944, and total employment in the regulation of labor-management relations rose from 956 persons in 1941 to 3,806 persons in 1945 (see Table 3.2). (The maintenance-of-membership clause took some of the pressure off the NRLB, and the number of its employees stayed about the same: 796 employees in 1941 and 749 employees in 1945.) Meanwhile, the number of USCS arbitrators (to be distinguished from employees) rose from 192 persons in fiscal 1940 to 463

TABLE 3.3
Expenditures of the Labor Boards (thousands of dollars)

Fiscal Year	Expenditures			% USG	NWLB Budget	Total	
	USCS	NLRB	Total			Boards	%
1940	316	3,184	3,500	0.054	—	—	—
1941	382	2,867	3,249	0.055	—	—	—
1942	832	3,609	3,901	0.039	(NA)	—	—
1943	1,847	3,599	5,446	0.038	4,417	9,863	0.06
1944	2,173	2,463	4,636	0.028	14,437	19,073	0.10
1945	2,214	3,269	5,483	0.039	15,000	20,483	0.12
1946	2,476	4,251	6,727	0.054	10,154	16,880	0.10
1947	2,582	4,437	7,019	0.037	—	—	—
1948	2,680	5,539	8,219	0.052	—	—	—
1949	3,840	8,456	12,296	0.061	—	—	—
1950	2,725	8,595	11,320	0.056	—	—	—

Sources: The Anvil and the Plow; NLRB *Annual Reports,* "Expenditures and Obligations" (except for 1944 and 1945, where figures are from appropriations bills).

Notes: Federal civilian expenditures include veterans' compensation but omit spending by War and Navy departments and interest on the public debt. 1943 budget figures exclude "National Defense" USCS appropriation of $975,635 in a supplement in FY 1943.

persons in fiscal 1941, 1,185 persons in fiscal 1943, and 1,151 persons in fiscal 1945.[41]

The combined expenditures of the USCS and the NLRB similarly increased from $3.5 million in fiscal 1940 to $5.5 million by fiscal 1945, and then rose to $7 million in fiscal 1947 and to $11.3 million in fiscal 1950 (see Table 3.3). The total wartime spending on the regulation of labor as a proportion of the civilian federal budget peaked in fiscal 1945 at 0.12 percent; the labor boards took up 0.054 percent of the federal budget in fiscal 1940 and a virtually identical 0.056 percent in fiscal 1950.

Turning to the extension of government-society relations, the total number of cases handled by the USCS and the NLRB rose from 11,000 cases in fiscal 1940 to 30,000 in fiscal 1945—*excluding* the 20,000 cases heard by the NWLB over its four-year tenure—and to a total of just under 40,000 in fiscal 1950 (see Table 3.4). The federal government was clearly intervening more in labor-management issues though the vehicle of the labor boards.

In terms of the intensity of government-society relations, one indicator of that intensity is the number of disputes being adjudicated in federal courts

[41] *Annual Report of the Secretary of Labor*, 1946, 108, in Leland J. Gordon, "Recent Developments in Conciliation and Arbitration," in Colston E. Warne, ed., *Labor in Postwar America* (Brooklyn: Remsen Press, 1949), 225, Table 1.

TABLE 3.4
Labor Dispute Cases Disposed

Fiscal Year	NLRB Cases	USCS Cases	Total Cases	War Board Cases	Court-Resolved
1940	7,354	3,751	11,105	—	69
1941	8,396	5,599	13,995	—	135
1942	11,741	8,511	20,252	NDMB: 119	87
1943	9,777	17,559	27,336	NWLB: 20,800	96
1944	9,194	24,797	33,991	(Jan. 1942	88
1945	9,092	25,907	34,999	to Aug. 1945)	66
1946	10,892	18,840	29,732	NSW: 17,918	41
1947	14,456	16,711	31,167	—	70
1948	29,151	12,208	41,359	—	52 (22)
1949	32,796	18,822	51,618	—	83 (33)
1950	20,640	16,956	37,596	—	107 (19)

Sources: NLRB, USCS, and FMCS Annual Reports.

Notes: "Cases" are cases closed during the period in question. Figures in parentheses are injunctions issued under the Wagner Act. "Court-resolved" are cases that could not be settled by the labor boards and were referred to the federal courts. Totals do not include these.

(rather than being settled through mediation). Here the number of court settlements was highest in fiscal 1941 (see Table 3.4). (The 1949 and 1950 increases in the number of court cases coincided with new injunction powers of the U.S. government granted under the Taft-Hartley Act.) Perhaps a better indicator of the coercion used to control labor-management relations is the incidence of government seizures. The number of seizures increased as the war went on, peaking in fiscal 1944 and fiscal 1945; there were no industrial seizures in 1940, six seizures in 1942, and twenty-nine in 1945 (see Table 3.5).

The number of strikes disposed by the USCS/FMCS also increased during the war to then tail off in the late 1940s. Similarly, the percentage of strikes being settled more than doubled over the course of World War II, from under one-third of strikes being settled in 1940 to over two-thirds being resolved peaceably in 1945. In short, the indicators of the extent and intensity of government-society relations show clear, if not consistent, ratchet effects.

Although the formal war boards were dissolved after the war, the NLRB and USCS continued to be relied upon by organized labor and management (more than they had been used previously, in fact). Tripartism continued in the form of the ten fact-finding boards set up by President Truman and Labor Secretary Schwellenbach for handling postwar strikes, and organized

TABLE 3.5
Strike Intervention

Calendar Year	No. of Strikes	Average Duration	Strikes Disposed	No. of Seizures
1940	2,508	20.9 days	775	0
1941	4,288	18.3	1,408	5
1942	2,968	11.7	1,586	6
1943	3,752	5.0	1,671	8
1944	4,956	5.6	2,444	23
1945	4,750	9.9	3,207	29
1946	4,985	24.2	3,206	9
1947	3,693	25.6	6,795	0
1948	3,419	21.8	1,296	1
1949	3,606	22.5	1,102	0
1950	4,843	19.2	1,025	2

Sources: Department of Labor and Federal Mediation and Conciliation Service *Annual Reports;* "Work Stoppages, Workers Involved, Man-Days Idle, Major Issues, and Average Duration: 1881–1970," Series D 970–985, *Historical Statistics,* 179; Blackman, *Presidential Seizure in Labor Disputes,* Appendix A.

Notes: "No. of Strikes" is work stoppages, including lockouts; "Duration" is in calendar days, not only working days; "Strikes Disposed" is strikes settled through government intervention. Disposed strikes include threatened strikes as well as actual work stoppages.

labor continued its less formal cooperation and collaboration with the White House. Truman personally led negotiations between unions and management for many of the work stoppages, with his appointment schedule of the late 1940s showing repeated visits by William Green, Philip Murray, and other labor leaders. Labor leaders continued to be of use to elected officials and could be dealt with directly,[42] and Truman's vetoes of the Case Bill and the Taft-Hartley Act helped to keep labor in the Democratic camp even though both Green and Murray disagreed with the President's proposed legislation for dealing with the railway crisis.[43]

Indeed, when we consider Truman's support for the strongly anti-labor Temporary Disputes Settlement Bill, his signing of the Hobbs Anti-

[42] See "Diaries 1945" and "Diaries 1946," Box 16, Eben A. Ayers Diaries, 1944–52, Eben A. Ayers Papers.

[43] Robert J. Donovan, *Conflict and Crisis: The Presidency of Harry S Truman, 1945–1948* (New York: Norton, 1977), 215–16. The vetoes were, of course, partly political strategy on the part of the President: while Truman did not want to antagonize Congress unnecessarily (knowing that the Taft-Hartley veto would be overridden), the labor constituency was too important to neglect. Leon Keyserling, of the President's Council of Economic Advisers, gives Clark Clifford "eighty-five" percent of the credit for persuading Truman to veto the Taft-Hartley Act (Oral History of Leon H. Keyserling, Harry S. Truman Library, 1975, 69).

Racketeering Bill, and the overlap between many of the provisions of the Taft-Hartley Act and earlier statements and proposals by the President (Truman's veto of Taft-Hartley notwithstanding), the continued cooperation of the largest labor unions with the Democratic Administration seems curious.[44] Consider the contrast with the actual or potential recipients of social security provisions and health care who, in the face of a balky Congress, sought privately based alternatives for retirement and medical benefits.

For a fuller explanation we need to look to the national and international environments. Nationally, the split in the labor movement between the AFL and CIO after 1935 (they merged again in 1955) and the opposition between the UMW and both the CIO and the AFL after 1940 were crucial. The division in the union movement limited labor's alternatives and strengthened the hand of the federal government (see Chapter 6).[45] Furthermore, the war strengthened the position of business brought about by the war: business management could resist unionization in the South and curtail unionization elsewhere (witness the Taft-Hartley Act). Internationally, the U.S.-Soviet rivalry enhanced anticommunist sentiment, dis-

[44] One of the President's dramatic successes was his injunction in 1946 ordering Lewis and the United Mine Workers to put an end to the strike. The judge fined Lewis $13 million, reduced upon appeal. See Truman's *Memoirs*, Vols. 1 and 2, and his letters in *Off the Record*, Robert Ferrell, ed. (New York: Penguin, 1980) for documentation of Truman's weak and inconsistent support of organized labor. As Truman wrote his mother and sister, "Big money has too much power and so have big unions—both are riding to a fall because I like neither" (Letter of 23 January 1946, in Ferrell, ed., *Off the Record*, 83).

[45] A brief background to the labor split is as follows. Lewis led a group of industrially based unions out of the AFL in 1935, since the AFL refused to organize by industry rather than by craft or skill. The AFL and the CIO therefore began to compete over union affiliates, over union jurisdiction when industry-based unions clashed with the craft unions, and over favorable decisions from the NLRB, despite repeated attempts at reconciliation and merger (especially in 1937 and 1939). Both the AFL and the CIO also conducted membership raids against each other and supplied strike-breakers in the event of work stoppages by rival unions. A sufficient explanation of the split would also have to include the interpersonal relations (and rivalries) of William F. Green, Philip Murray, John L. Lewis, Bill Hutcheson, and Sidney Hillman, among others. The AFL and CIO would not be reunited until 1955—after a generation of labor leaders had either retired or passed away.

Among the consequences of the divided labor movement were that it encouraged the passage of state laws unfavorable to labor in the late 1930s and early 1940s, and that it put more power in the hands of the federal government and the NLRB in the settlement of jurisdictional and rival union disputes. See Herbert Harris, *Labor's Civil War* (New York: Knopf, 1940); Edwin Young, "The Split in the Labor Movement," in Milton Derber and Edwin Young, eds., *Labor and the New Deal* (Madison: University of Wisconsin Press, 1957); Walter Galenson, *Rival Unionism in the United States* (New York: Russell and Russell, 1966); Galenson, *The CIO Challenge to the AFL*; I. Bernstein, *History of the American Worker*, Vol. 2; Alinsky, *John L. Lewis*; Dubofsky and Van Tine, *John L. Lewis*; Philip Taft, *Organized Labor in American History* (New York: Harper & Row, 1964); and Sam S. Stephansky, "The AFL-CIO Problem of the National Labor Relations Board" (Black Binder), Box 483, Records of the National War Labor Board, Series 75, Record Group 202.

suaded unions from backing third parties, and limited radical strategies: challenges to existing worker-management policies could be labeled as labor radicalism and thus connected with socialism or communism.[46]

As for the building of the instrumental state, the National Labor Relations Board established a Field Division in early 1941 and adopted informal procedures in order to "sift" through cases and thereby expedite action (given the increased caseload resulting from the war mobilization). In 1944, only 7 percent of NLRB cases went as far as a formal board decision.[47] The Board also introduced public hearings for changes in policies or procedures, such as changes affecting run-off elections and supervisors' rights. In 1945, it introduced prehearing elections in situations where there was only one union and where only minor issues were at stake: "The result was a great saving of time in resolution of disputes."[48]

After the war, the NLRB embarked on a number of cost-saving measures.[49] The NLRB also enlarged the scope of the General Counsel under the provisions of the Taft-Hartley Act, abolished the Review Division, and specified that labor organizations file all complaints, requests for litigation, requests for enforcement injunctions, etc., in full compliance of Taft-Hartley. In 1949, the NLRB set up Management Improvement Committees to receive and evaluate suggestions for improvements and savings in services, organization, and procedures.

The USCS, for its part, designated special commissioners in seven key industries as a response to the war emergency. In 1942, it set up a Technical Division to conduct wage studies in order to provide a standard for resolving wage inequalities, and it established circulating panels of three commissioners so that labor and management representatives did not have to travel

---

[46] Norman D. Markowitz, *The Rise and Fall of the People's Century: Henry A. Wallace and American Liberalism, 1941–1948* (New York: Free Press, 1973); Lichtenstein, "Labor in the Truman Era," in Lacey, ed., *The Truman Presidency.*

[47] *National Labor Relations Board Annual Report, 1944,* 8. See NLRB *Annual Reports* for details on improvements in administrative procedures.

[48] Harry A. Millis and Emily Clark Brown, *From the Wagner Act to Taft-Hartley* (Chicago: University of Chicago Press, 1950), 62.

[49] Among such measures were eliminating the need for the Review Section to report to the Trail Examining Division on the updating of representation ("R") cases, by transferring the records on such cases to the Review Section; putting the standard language to be included in the opening and closing sections of "R" cases on mimeograph sheets; transferring the handling of subpoenas to the Field Attorneys, so as to eliminate travel to and from Washington, D.C.; and eliminating biweekly reports on the status of compliance cases in favor of only a final closing report. See Donn Brent, Executive Secretary, NLRB, to Ross Shearer, Bureau of the Budget, 11 September 1946, file "NLRB FY 1941–48 Budget Prep.—general correspondence," Unit 60, Box 11, Estimates Divisions, Records of the Bureau of the Budget ("Budget Records").

to Washington. And in 1943 and 1944, the USCS decentralized by setting up field offices in Chicago, New York, Atlanta, Cleveland, and San Francisco.

After the war, the USCS followed the recommendations of the November 1945 Labor-Management Conference and set up a Labor-Management Advisory Committee. The USCS proceeded to decentralize further, reorganize the Technical Division, establish a Program Division for training new conciliators and offering refresher courses, and set up tripartite procedures in new cases where the involvement of worker and management representatives would be most helpful.

With the passage of the Taft-Hartley Act, the USCS was removed from the Department of Labor and became the Federal Mediation and Conciliation Service. The FMCS conducted studies and reduced the number of top supervisory officials, expanded the field service from eight regions to twelve, eliminated duplicate reporting to the national office, and cut back the duties of the national office to oversight and coordination only.[50]

In sum, the NLRB and the USCS/FMCS improved the efficiency of their administration both during and after World War II. Ratchet effects were thus manifest in the improvements in the means of administering regulations on labor-management relations as well as in the institutions of labor regulation—the labor bureaucracies and government-labor relations—with the exception of seizures and court settlements. Consistent with the Second World War being a critical moment, the war brought about an upheaval in the agenda of labor politics.

Although labor was under attack from Congress in the late 1930s and through most of 1941 (agenda A), the war either delayed legislation or stopped it dead in its tracks. On 3 December 1941 the House of Representatives voted 252 to 136 to pass an anti-labor bill sponsored by Representative Howard W. Smith (D., Va.). The bill would have mandated a cooling-off period, required USCS-supervised secret ballots before strikes, outlawed strikes in defense industries with closed shops, outlawed strikes over jurisdictional disputes and boycotts affecting defense contracts, and denied the protection of the Wagner Act to unions guilty of illegal strikes or to those that elected or appointed officials who were members of the "Communist

---

[50] See *Annual Reports* of the Secretary of Labor and of the Federal Mediation and Conciliation Service. Also see File, "Records Re Budgetary Administration in INCPOT and Independent Agencies Responsible for Labor, Manpower, and Science Programs," FM&CS FY 1949–50 Budget Preparation, Unit 50, Box 10, Series 39.33, Estimates Division, Budget Records; Memorandum of Ross Shearer and Harold Enarson to L. C. Martin, "Completion Report, Project VII-4, Federal Mediation and Conciliation Service, Organizations and Methods," 20 August 1948, file "Federal Mediation and Conciliation Service, general administration," Unit 48, Box 9, Series 39.14a, Budget Records; and Memorandum of F. J. Lawton, Director of the Bureau of the Budget, to Mr. Ching, 11 May 1950, file "FMCS Management Improvement," Unit 49, Box 9, Series 39.14, Budget Records.

party, the Young Communist League, the German-American Bund, or any-one convicted of moral turpitude."[51] After Pearl Harbor, however, the bill died in the Senate. As the historian Joel Seidman observes, the "Pearl Harbor attack . . . necessitated a co-operative rather than a partisan and puni-tive treatment of labor disputes. The nation was at war, and a wholly fresh approach to the problem of industrial peace had to be made."[52]

A comparison of the legislative activity of the 77th and 78th Congresses is indicative. In the 77th Congress (1941–42), according to CIO records, ten bills regulated the internal affairs of unions, five bills and ten riders to other bills attacked the right to strike through outright prohibition or cooling-off periods, ten bills were designed to subject labor activities to the courts by repealing or amending the Norris-LaGuardia Act, and thirteen were to ex-empt certain arenas of union power from collective bargaining proce-dures.[53] In contrast, the 78th Congress (1943–44) considered only four bills requiring union registration with the federal government, only four bills attacking the closed shop, just three bills prohibiting strikes in war produc-tion, only two bills containing anti-racketeering provisions, and only one bill outlawing political contributions; one bill subjecting unions to court injunc-tions, and one bill curtailing collective bargaining rights.[54] The harsher mea-sures delayed by the war would be realized later with the Case Bill, the Hobbs Anti-Racketeering Bill, and the Taft-Hartley Act.[55]

But rather than simply forcing a postponement of restrictions on the gains achieved by organized labor under the Wagner Act (agenda A'), the war caused the labor unions to become quasi-public actors. Top union officials served on government boards, met with the President, and were consulted regularly by members of Congress and federal officials. This new official presence of organized labor is evident in the NLRB and USCS/FMCS per-

---

[51] Seidman, *American Labor from Defense to Reconversion*, 72–73. With some overstate-ment, William Green called the bill "a first move toward totalitarianism," and the CIO called it "a stab in the back for the whole national defense effort" (*CIO News*, 8 December 1941, in Seidman, *American Labor from Defense to Reconversion*, 73).

[52] Seidman, *American Labor from Defense to Reconversion*, 73. Although Steven Fraser speaks of the administration's dependence on the "Tories of Industry," he does not indicate the other half of this: that the government also depended more on organized labor as a result of the war (Fraser, *Labor Will Rule: Sidney Hillman and the Rise of American Labor* [New York: Free Press, 1991], 441).

[53] Letter of Philip Murray to President Truman, 8 June 1946, file "Bills—HR 4908," Box 165, Records of the Secretary of Labor 1945–47, Record Group 174.

[54] "Bills Affecting Labor—78th Congress, 1st Session," file "Labor Legislation 1943," Box 150, Records of the Secretary of Labor 1940–45. The count of bills restrictive of labor excludes three bills addressed solely to wartime conditions.

[55] The Taft-Hartley Act did not so much overturn or undermine the Wagner Act as give the government and business more powers. Taft-Hartley did, however, hurt unionization in small businesses and constrain further organization in general.

sonnel and budget figures, the growing labor-management caseload, and the use of the tripartite procedures.

At the same time, the CIO and AFL leadership became increasingly conservative. Whereas the CIO under Lewis had attacked the existing social security system, pressed aggressively for further unionization, supported an isolationist foreign policy, and opposed the reelection of Roosevelt as U.S. president in 1940, the CIO made a 180-degree turn in just three years' time. By 1943 Murray's CIO supported the existing social security system, repressed labor activism, backed U.S. foreign policy, and sought the reelection of Franklin Roosevelt in 1944 (agenda AW).

After the war, there would be renewed restrictions on labor and at the same time a recognition of the right of collective bargaining in the 1945 Labor-Management Conference and a general acceptance of labor unions in industrial corporations by business management and government. The proportion of cases dealing with unfair labor practices dropped from 64 percent of total NLRB cases in 1940 to 53 percent in 1941, 35 percent in 1943, 25 percent to 1945, and only 10 percent of cases by 1948. Although the proportion of unfair-practice cases climbed back up to 27 percent of the NLRB's cases by 1950, this was still less than half the percentage of 1940.[56] Similarly, the incidence of cases concerning organizational issues dropped from 50 percent of NLRB cases in 1940 to about 16 percent in 1943 and 1944—when the maintenance-of-membership clause was in effect—to 32 percent of NLRB cases in 1946 and then to only 19 percent of NLRB cases by 1950. And with the improving economy and growing acceptance of organized labor, wage issues increased from 30 percent of NLRB cases in 1940 to 43 percent of NLRB cases in 1943, 46 percent of NLRB cases in 1947, and 53 percent of the NLRB cases in 1950 (see Table 3.6).

The CIO, the AFL, and most other unions changed their political agenda, too, by becoming enthusiastic supporters of the Cold War. Every major union leader but Lewis took an oath disavowing communism.[57] The CIO then purged itself of its communist members (the International Brotherhood of Electrical Workers, for one, being notorious for its communist membership). Organized labor became firmly allied with the domestic and foreign policies of the postwar government. In short, the agenda of organized labor changed over the 1940s from one of struggle against management and neutrality towards government to one that accepted a large role for the federal government in regulating labor-management relations and focused increasingly on wages and other benefits rather than further organization (agenda AW').

[56] National Labor Relations Board, *Annual Reports*.

[57] Lewis, while trumpeting his refusal to submit to such "repression," was already bound by such a provision in the United Mine Workers' constitution.

TABLE 3.6
Causes of Work Stoppages

Calendar Year	Total	Wages & Hours		Organizational Issues		Other	
		No.	%	No.	%	No.	%
1940	2,493	753	30.2	1,243	49.9	497	19.9
1941	4,314	1,535	35.6	2,138	49.6	641	14.9
1942	3,036	1,423	46.9	943	31.1	670	22.0
1943	3,734	1,906	51.0	585	15.7	1,243	32.3
1944	4,958	2,146	43.3	808	16.3	2,004	40.4
1945	4,616	1,956	42.4	946	20.5	1,714	37.1
1946	4,990	2,238	44.8	1,617	32.4	1,135	22.7
1947	3,693	1,707	46.2	1,102	29.8	884	23.9
1948	3,419	1,737	50.8	780	22.8	902	26.4
1949	3,606	1,682	46.6	781	21.7	1,143	31.7
1950	4,843	2,559	52.8	919	19.0	1,365	28.2

Sources: "Work Stoppages, Workers Involved, Man-Days Idle, Major Issues, and Average Duration: 1881–1970," Series D 970–985, *Historical Statistics,* 179.

Notes: "Organizational Issues" refers to questions of worker representation. Woytinsky and Associates list identical figures for the wages and hours proportion of work stoppages but give lower figures for organizational issues (*Employment and Wages in the United States* [New York: Twentieth Century Fund, 1953]). In practice, these categories overlap; many wage and hour issues were also ones of organization, for instance. Beth Stevens uses other data to find that "[f]ifty-five percent of the strikes in 1949 and 40 percent of the strikes in the first half of 1950 were over health and welfare issues in labor contracts" (Stevens, "Blurring the Boundaries," 141).

The war thus reversed the momentum of the American labor movement coming out of the Depression and early period of mobilization, and resulted in a two-tier labor system, with entrenched unions serving workers in select crafts and industries, while other workers had only weak and inconsistent possibilities for collective action. Unions would act conservatively, thanks both to their advantaged position in many industries in a booming postwar economy and to the hostile national and international environments. To the extent that labor was successful vis-à-vis capital—as with the 1946 steel strike, where United States Steel was able to pass along higher prices to its consumers—it was in large, oligopolistic industries.[58]

[58] Katznelson also observes that the war years transformed a class-based movement into an interest group—albeit an important and influential one (Ira Katznelson, "Was the Great Society a Lost Opportunity?" in Fraser and Gerstle, eds., *The Rise and Fall of the New Deal Order,* 191–92). Fraser comes to the same conclusion: "Above all, it was the war in Europe that put a period to the era of New Deal reform" (*Labor Will Rule,* 441). See Fraser on Hillman's (futile) efforts, given the larger politics of the war years and the role played by Lewis in the split between the AFL and the CIO.

Conclusions

The evidence of the state-building during and after World War II is consistent with the hypotheses derived from the resource dependence perspective. The exercise of presidential power in the 1940s conforms to the expectation that the president should direct state-building in an organized policy domain in wartime. President Roosevelt and his advisers controlled when boards would be set up and dissolved, directed national economic policies, allocated manpower and materials, and seized industries. The executive branch, through the Bureau of the Budget or the labor boards themselves, built the instrumental state. With the exception of the absence of national service legislation and the partial exception of the Smith-Connally Act, the President was able to direct state-building during the war (Hypothesis 1a).

Conversely, the failure of Truman's fact-finding boards to settle postwar strikes, his inability to satisfactorily amend the Wagner Act, the passage of the Taft-Hartley Act over his veto, and the lack of success in reorganizing the National Labor Relations Board all attest to the loss of presidential authority after the Second World War (Hypothesis 1c). The extent to which the Truman Administration succeeded after 1945 resulted from the extension of war powers to December 1946, thus enabling the President to dissolve the labor boards, direct economic policy, and seize industries in the reconversion period immediately following World War II.

The record indicates the importance of the organization of the industrial workforce. Labor was a partner in the tripartite war boards, and union leaders cooperated with the federal government to subdue and defuse rank-and-file unrest (Hypothesis 2b). Key in these wartime relations and in the postwar cooperation of the unions with the Democratic Administration—Lewis and the UMW excepted—was the immediate environment of organized labor: inter-union rivalry and the anti-strike and anti-labor political climates.

Patriotism may thus have been less important in explaining the quiescence of the labor unions than some contend.[59] That workers could be "cajoled" to stop their wildcat strikes or go back on the job does not necessarily belie the seriousness of their grievances. Rather, the inability of workers to sustain their strikes is consistent with the difficulty of going on strike in the face of widespread opposition from the White House, the military, the press, business management, and the public—not to mention that of local and national union officials. To ascribe the comparative labor-management

[59] See Joshua Freeman, "Delivering the Goods: Industrial Unionism during World War II," *Labor History* 19 (1978): 570–93; and Perrett, *Days of Sadness*. But see Glaberman for debunking the notion that the UAW and other CIO strikes during the war were frivolous (Martin Glaberman, *Wartime Strikes: The Struggle against the No-Strike Pledge in the UAW during World War II* [Detroit: Bewick Editions, 1980]).

peace of the war years to worker patriotism neglects the more tangible bases for cooperation between the labor unions and the wartime government, and underestimates the very real grievances and resentments that workers had against management.

Organized labor's cooperation with the Roosevelt Administration was not preordained. The number of work stoppages taking place in wartime (and the number of workers taking part in them) suggest that the strikes enjoyed widespread support. And other major labor leaders could have publicly supported Lewis: the discrepancy between wage increases and the rising cost of living, poor working and residential conditions, and the President's unfulfilled promises all gave sufficient grounds for worker protests, work stoppages, and the revocation of the no-strike pledge. But neither the CIO nor the AFL supported the UMW strikes or the USW, UAW, or URW wildcat strikes. Instead, wartime work stoppages provoked quick intervention by both top union officials and the U.S. government, and the strikes were not allowed to last or to spread to other unions. They were not to be used by labor officials as bargaining levers.[60]

The no-strike pledge, the presence and actions of the NDMB, the NWLB, the NWSB, the USCS, NLRB, and the Smith-Connally Act all resulted in the government playing a new role in labor-management issues and indicated a turn away from voluntary unionism. This move away from Samuel Gompers's "business" or "voluntary" unionism and towards a quasi-corporatist, government-labor-business condominium is evident in the figures on the personnel and budget used to intervene in labor-management relations, in the continuation of tripartism in the fact-finding boards, and in the later passage of the Taft-Hartley Act. Business revived; both the AFL and the CIO drew back from radical politics; the federal government intervened in labor-management relations to an unprecedented degree; membership in industrial unions soared even as union leaders became distanced from the rank and file; and an increasingly hostile public became fed up with strikes and labor disputes in a time of newfound prosperity (Hypothesis 3a, Hypothesis 3b).[61] The experiences of the war years thus set into place all the ingredients

[60] Jill Quadagno makes the important point that the study of the exceptionalism of American labor demands a look not merely at the other societal factors but at labor itself. She argues that organized labor itself had much to do with its own demise (Quadagno, *The Transformation of Old Age Security*).

[61] The Taft-Hartley Act did not represent such a radical departure from the letter and spirit of the Wagner Act as is commonly thought. By 1947, decisions by the NLRB and the federal courts on such issues as free speech, union elections, collective bargaining, the right to strike, the unionization of foremen and supervisory workers, and representational matters (e.g., craft versus industrial unions, rival unionism, and jurisdictional disputes) had already done much to erode the Wagner Act (Tomlins, *The State and the Unions*, 261–74; Emily Clark Brown, "The NLRB—Wagner Act through Taft-Hartley Law," in Warne, ed., *Labor in Postwar America*, 185–203; Gross, *The Reshaping of the National Labor Relations Board*; McClure, *The Truman Administration and the Problems of Postwar Labor, 1945–1948*; and Seymour S. Scher, "The

for the postwar backlash and the failure of Operation Dixie[62]—the unionization of the South—contra the argument that 1945 and the end of the war marked the turning point for organized labor in the United States.[63] Between the increase in industrialization, the full-employment economy, and the increased role of the government in labor-management relations resulting from the mobilization for war, by 1945 organized labor had already become an accepted partner in pluralist American government.[64]

But the emergence of a stronger state in terms of larger organizations regulating labor-management relations, more intensive and extensive ties of the government to the labor unions, and an improved administration of labor-management regulations did not redound to the benefit of the American labor movement.[65] While more intervention by the government could benefit the unions (as did the Wagner Act's protection of collective bargaining), a more interventionist government could also act against labor interests by imposing more restrictions on union activities, issuing court injunctions, and strengthening the relative power of management. The stronger war-built state turned out to be a two-edged sword for labor. Organized labor grew less committed than it had been in 1937–41, if the rate of union victories in NLRB elections and the percentage of union members in non-agricultural establishments are indicative. The war caused a diminishing shop-level participation by union members, a rejection of class-based action on the part of labor, and an entrenchment of top-down union control.[66] Robert Michels's iron law of oligarchy obtained: organization became oligarchy.

National Labor Relations Board and Congress—A Study of Legislative Control of Regulatory Activity," Ph.D. diss., University of Chicago, 1956).

[62] See Lichtenstein on the unionization drive in the South beginning in 1946 ("From Corporatism to Collective Bargaining," 136; and Lichtenstein, "Labor in the Truman Era," in Lacey, ed., *The Truman Presidency*, 142–45).

[63] See, for example, Amenta and Skocpol, "Redefining the New Deal"; Lichtenstein, "From Corporatism to Collective Bargaining"; and Stephen Paul Cameron, "The Liberal-Labor-Democratic Alliance, 1945–1952: Anti-Communism as a Flawed Unifying Theme," Ph.D. diss., University of Pennsylvania, 1988.

[64] Tomlins, *The State and the Unions*; Glaberman, *Wartime Strikes*; Lichtenstein, *Labor's War at Home*; Gross, *The Reshaping of the National Labor Relations Board*; Paul A. C. Koistinen, "Mobilizing the World War II Economy: Labor and the Industrial-Military Alliance," *Pacific Historical Review* 42 No. 4 (1973): 443–78. Also see David Greenstone on the complacency of the U.S. labor unions (Greenstone, *Labor in American Politics*, 53).

[65] See Tomlins's concluding chapter on this point (Tomlins, *The State and the Unions*, 317–28).

[66] See Lichtenstein on the changing terms of labor-management relations in the early and mid-1940s (Lichtenstein, "From Corporatism to Collective Bargaining"). Moe characterizes business and management in the pre-Taft-Hartley era as having "strong and opposing interests" (Moe, "Interests, Institutions, and Positive Theory," 241).

4

The Revolutions of Public Finance

If we get collection-at-the-source, we will find
that the income tax will be a much better
device than we ever thought possible.
—Milton Friedman, 21 August 1942

My dear Mr. Secretary:
    In consonance with your wishes we sent you
85 crates of assorted property and a large
number guns, tanks, etc., totaling in all some
20 vehicles.
    Owing to conditions beyond our control this
shipment did not leave Sicily until about the
14th of November . . . in any event, we did our
best and trust that if you cannot use this stuff
this time, it may be of value for a subsequent
[war loan] drive.
    Very respectfully,
    G. S. Patton, Jr., Lieut. General
    Commanding Officer, Seventh Army

AT LEAST three revolutions were taking place in U.S. public finance during the 1940s. One was "the permanent shift in the sources of federal revenue": income taxes became the most important source of U.S. government revenues.[1] Whereas individual and corporate income tax receipts constituted 42 percent of government revenues in 1941, income tax receipts (including excess profits taxes) came to 68 percent of federal revenues by 1950.[2] The absolute amount collected in income taxes rose by more than a factor of ten over the same period, from $2.2 billion to $26 billion. Federal revenues from personal and corporate income taxes went from 1 percent of national income in 1939 to 6.5 percent of national income by 1950,[3] and the personal income tax became permanently extended on a mass basis: individual taxpayers (ex-

[1] John F. Witte, *The Politics and Development of the Federal Income Tax* (Madison: University of Wisconsin Press, 1985), 123.

[2] *Annual Report of the Secretary of the Treasury, 1950*, cited in Paul Studenski and Herman E. Krooss, *The Financial History of the United States* (New York: McGraw-Hill, 1952), 450, 473.

[3] Witte, *Federal Income Tax*, 124.

cluding members of the armed forces) filed a total number of 14.6 million tax returns in 1940 and 53 million tax returns in 1950 (with employment rising from 53 to 60 million persons over the same period). By mid-century, virtually all working Americans were paying taxes on their wage incomes.[4]

A second revolution occurred in public borrowing. The 1940s marked a "turning point in the financial history of the United States," with the U.S. public debt rising by more than 500 percent between 1940 and 1950, from $50 billion in 1940 to $255 billion in 1950.[5] Whereas the public debt in the United States equaled about one-fourth of the entire national debt (both public and private) in 1940, the federal debt came to almost two-thirds the national debt in 1945. And by the end of the war, the national debt exceeded national income for the first time ever, with national income standing at $215.2 billion and the national debt at $256.4 billion.

The persistence of the large federal debt after World War II ensured that issues of the debt's size, ownership, terms of maturity, and rates of interest would have a continuing impact on the national economy: the size of the public debt dictated the carrying cost of U.S. public borrowing; the ownership of the debt determined which individual or institutional savers would be affected by the government's policies for managing the debt; the maturity periods of the debt set the timing and rate of debt repayment or refinancing; and the rates of interest on the debt established the baseline for interest rates nationwide.[6] In the words of Marriner Eccles, former Chairman of the Federal Reserve, "public debt has become the dog, and private debt the tail. That is, public debt has become the dominant factor in our economy, and this in turn makes inevitable the conscious control and management of the money market."[7]

A third upheaval in public finance was the fiscal revolution. The U.S. government began to intentionally use public policy for suppressing unemployment, stabilizing price levels, and steadying the rate of economic growth. After the Great Depression and following the wartime economic boom, market mechanisms were no longer assumed to be self-adjusting. No longer could government officials expect voters to tolerate mass unemployment, deflation, or high rates of inflation as the simple vicissitudes of a market economy. Economic recessions and depressions would henceforth be the responsibility of the federal government, particularly that of the president and Congress.[8]

    [4] "Individual Income Tax Returns: 1913 to 1943," Series Y 402–411, and "Individual Income Tax Returns: 1944 to 1970," Series Y 393–401, *Historical Statistics*, 1110.

    [5] Charles Cortez Abbott, *The Federal Debt* (New York: Twentieth Century Fund, 1953), 4–5.

    [6] Abbott, *The Federal Debt*, 197.

    [7] Marriner Eccles, *Beckoning Frontiers* (New York: Knopf, 1951), 345.

    [8] Herbert Stein, *The Fiscal Revolution in America* (Chicago: University of Chicago Press, 1969). Also see Robert Lekachman, *The Age of Keynes* (New York: McGraw-Hill, 1966), 175.

The upheavals in federal taxation, public debt, and fiscal policy constituted state-building in that they made for permanent change in the federal bureaucracy, in the number and quality of government-society ties, and in the instruments of administration. As with the previous two cases, however, these changes demand further explanation. Who directed the state-building? What form did these changes take? Why did they persist after the war? And how did the new relations of public finance match across clienteles, between taxpayers and investors in government securities?

"Public finance" as used here refers to how the government secures its funding. With respect to tax policies, this chapter looks at the changes in the size, policies, and administration of the Bureau of Internal Revenue. The Bureau of Internal Revenue, under a Commissioner of Internal Revenue, assesses and collects taxes for the purposes of providing internal revenue. With respect to the public debt, this chapter studies the developments in the size, policies, and administration of the Bureau of Public Debt.[9] The Bureau of Public Debt, under a Commissioner of the Public Debt, administers the debt by conducting or directing transactions in securities issued by the federal government and those government-owned corporations for which the Treasury Department acts as an agent. The Bureau audits securities and takes custody of retired securities, keeps accounts for registered securities, and drafts interest checks. Its six basic duties are: the issuance, servicing and retiring of savings bonds; the issuance, servicing, and retiring of other Treasury securities; the verification and destruction of unfit currency; the maintenance and audit of public debt accounts, the promotion and sale of savings bonds; and the executive direction and technical analysis of securities markets and the determination of terms and types of new security offerings.

Fiscal policy—being without the tangible bureaucratic and relational components of tax policy and government borrowing—will be taken up in the later discussion of the shift in the political agenda of public finance occurring as a result of the war.[10]

We should expect the Congress, given its constitutional mandate to raise revenue, to be able to set federal income tax policy in wartime. But the

---

[9] Confining analysis to the Bureau of Public Debt and Bureau of Internal Revenue necessarily neglects many of the other agencies connected with the financing of the national government, especially the Federal Reserve System, the Bureau of the Budget, and—within the Treasury Department—the Bureau of Customs, the Bureau of the Mint, the Bureau of Engraving and Printing, and the Bureau of Personnel. The focus on the federal income tax also omits from discussion other sources of tax revenue, such as excise taxes, customs duties, transaction taxes, and inheritance taxes.

[10] The President's Council of Economic Advisers (set up under the Employment Act of 1946) did have its offices and budgets, however: expenditures came to $183,485 in fiscal 1947, $337,000 in 1948, $308,514 in 1949, and $301,521 in 1950; there were 28 employees as of 30 June 1947 (the end of fiscal 1947), 44 in 1948, an average of 38 in 1949, and an average of 37 in 1950 (Edwin G. Nourse, *Economics in the Public Service* [New York: Harcourt Brace, 1953]).

president (and his appointees) should manage nontax financial issues, such as the wartime borrowing policies. In the postwar years, when the president has to relinquish his emergency powers, Congress should continue to determine tax policy and to set public debt policy.

As to the form taken by state-building, the government will have to expand its tax bureaucracy so as to raise the revenues necessary to pay for the war from the population of individuals and profitable businesses. But with relatively small numbers of individuals and organizations possessing significant amounts of assets to invest, the government will use interorganizational agencies to facilitate its borrowing.

The growth in the government's institutions of taxation and debt management should persist after the war as a result of the changes in the national and international environments. The coincidence of new government-society relations occurring within the national economy as a result of the Second World War and the changed international position of the United States should have lasting effects on the taxes of, and investment in the government by, individuals and organizations. Finally, the war's impact as a critical moment should shift the political agendas of public finance.

Because this chapter considers both public debt and taxation as part of public finance, it is possible to conduct an intra-case assessment of relative state-building (before Chapter 6). With the alternatives available to the bond-holding clienteles (investors having more alternatives than taxpayers) and with the greater uncertainties of borrowing (citizens being required to pay their taxes, but investors not being required to buy federal securities), we should expect the investors in government securities to receive more from the government than taxpayers. After the war, the flow of resources between the government and societal groups should reverse itself: government officials now want to grant resources to clienteles, on whom they depend to be reelected. With more bondholders than income taxpayers, the government will have to grant more to its creditors than to taxpayers, even if the large size of the two clienteles should ensure that both benefit in the postwar period.

Background

The most important tax bills of the decade, the Revenue Acts of 1941 and 1942, increased personal tax rates, lowered exemption levels (thereby expanding the tax base), and imposed high excess profits taxes on businesses. The bills nonetheless fell far short of the Administration's requests. When the President subsequently vetoed the Revenue Act of 1943, Franklin Roosevelt became the first president ever to veto a revenue bill.

But Congress did pass the Ruml Plan in 1943 (named after its chief proponent, Beardsley Ruml, then Treasurer of R. H. Macy & Co. and Chairman of the Federal Reserve Bank of New York): taxes on income were to be withheld at source and collected in the same period as income was earned, rather than being collected the following year. This was the "pay-as-you-go" system.

What the U.S. government did not raise through taxes was raised through the sale of securities. Here, the war loan drives provided the bulk of the financing for the war. The eight loan drives succeeded in raising $157 billion in the period from November 1942 through December 1945.[11]

As soon as the war ended, Congress passed and President Truman signed the 1945 Tax Reduction Bill, which reduced individual and corporate income taxes, among its other provisions. In 1946 Congress passed the Employment Act, legislation it had been considering in various forms since August 1944 (it had been known as the Full Employment Act). Section 2 of the Employment Act stated:

> The Congress hereby declares that it is the continuing policy and responsibility of the federal government to use all practicable means consistent with its needs and obligations and other essential consideration of national policy with the assistance and cooperation of industry, agriculture, labor, and state and local governments, to coordinate and utilize all its plans, functions, and resources for the purpose of creating and maintaining, in a manner calculated to foster and promote free competitive enterprise and the general welfare, conditions under which there will be afforded useful employment, for those able, willing, and seeking to work, and *to promote maximum employment, production and purchasing power.*[12]

The Employment Act established the Council of Economic Advisers and called for the Office of the President to make an annual forecast of the national economy.[13]

Between 1947 and 1948, Truman vetoed three bills reducing taxes. The Congress overturned the President's third veto partly because of the chronic

[11] Henry C. Murphy, *National Debt in War and Transition* (New York: McGraw-Hill, 1950), 161.

[12] Stephen Kemp Bailey, *Congress Makes a Law* (New York: Columbia University Press, 1950), 37; emphasis added.

[13] Council of Economic Advisors member John Clark reports that Senator Harry Truman initiated legislation on the Employment Act. Truman, then the chairman of the War Contracts Subcommittee of the Military Affairs Committee of the Senate, ordered a "study of the legislative measure designed to have the government guarantee a 40 billion dollar level of capital investment every year." After receiving favorable reports from the Departments on the study, Truman referred in the committee's report to the right to a job, which was contained in President Roosevelt's economic bill of rights. It fell to Truman's former colleagues in the Senate to introduce a bill (John D. Clark, "Forming National Economic Policies," pp. 4–5, file "Council's Economic Report," Box 3, Papers of John D. Clark).

budgetary surpluses of the late 1940s: the 1947 cash surplus came to $6.6 billion, the 1948 surplus amounted to $8.9 billion, and the 1949 annual surplus stood at exactly $1 billion. In fact, the U.S. public debt fell from $260.1 billion at the end of fiscal 1945 (before V-J Day) to $256.9 billion at the end of fiscal 1950 (five days after the invasion of South Korea on 25 June 1950), or from 142 percent of GNP to 90 percent.

Policymaking in Public Finance

Evidence consistent with a demonstration of presidential leadership in wartime would be if Congress were to approve legislation proposed by the president without extensive delay or significant alteration, and if the president were able to issue executive orders and otherwise make policy on tax and debt policies. Evidence of congressional leadership or decisive influence would be if the president were unable to get his legislation enacted, if he had to veto bills, and if his vetoes were overridden.

Income Taxes With German armies sweeping across Europe in May 1940, President Roosevelt asked Congress for $1.2 billion in revenue for national defense and called for Army and Navy construction to be put on a 24-hour basis. Roosevelt also wanted at least fifty thousand new planes to be produced each year.[14]

Congress had a bill ready by June, which the President signed into law on 25 June 1940. The first Revenue Act of 1940 lowered personal income tax exemptions from $2,500 to $2,000 for joint returns, and from $1,000 to $800 for single returns. Congress increased surtaxes on incomes from $6,000 to $100,000, raised the corporation gift tax to a maximum of 19 percent, and increased income taxes as well as other taxes by a uniform 10 percent.

But with France falling to Germany by the end of June 1940 and with Italy joining the Axis Powers, U.S. government spending on rearmament continued to grow. Monthly expenditures rose from $199 million in July 1940 to $1.4 billion by November 1941, and total spending came to $21.7 billion just in the period between 1 July 1940 to 1 December 1941—and the United States had not yet entered the war. With the imperative need for additional revenue, the President recommended the implementation of an excess profits tax (since the first tax bill had no provision for such a tax): "It is our duty to see that the burden is equitably distributed according to ability to pay so that a few do not gain from the sacrifices of the many." Roosevelt

[14] Studenski and Krooss, *Financial History*, 437; Witte, *Federal Income Tax*, 111; Michael S. Sherry, *The Rise of American Air Power* (New Haven: Yale University Press, 1987), 91.

intended that "not a single war millionaire would be permitted as a result of the war disaster."[15]

Congress passed the Second Revenue Act of 1940 in October. The Second Revenue Act set excess profits taxes at rates between 25 and 50 percent and raised to 24 percent the corporate income tax on businesses earning more than $25,000 per year. It also provided for accelerated amortization rates on corporate investments in war-related plants.[16] The passage of the excess profits tax further allowed for the repeal of the Vinson-Trammell Act (1934), since the uniform excess profits tax made redundant the Vinson-Trammell Act's taxes on aircraft manufacturing and naval construction. (Leaving the Vinson-Trammell Act in place would have penalized those industries most needed for defense.)

In the annual Budget message of January 1941, the President requested still higher taxes, taxes that would not restrict "general consumption as long as unused capacity is available and as long as idle labor can be employed." He recommended $3.5 billion in extra tax revenue, with the additional taxes levied according to the ability to pay.[17] Later, on 31 July, Roosevelt asked Chairman Doughton of the Ways and Means Committee to reduce personal exemptions to $1,500 and $750, to raise excess profits taxes higher than the 1940 level, to levy "a general sales tax or . . . a multiplication of what we have known as nuisance taxes," and to allow low-income returns to be filed at post offices.[18]

Congress passed the third defense tax bill (H.R. 5417) in September 1941. The bill reduced exemptions to $1,500 and $750, raised marginal income tax rates for individuals to between 10 and 77 percent (depending on the tax bracket), and increased corporate tax rates to 31 percent. It also increased excess profits taxes, estate taxes, gift taxes, and excise taxes, and added five million people to the tax rolls.

Although Congress appeared to be cooperating with the Administration (since the bill would raise an estimated $3.5 billion and would finance 60 percent of the war's costs), the President denounced the bill as wholly unsatisfactory: it failed to provide for a sufficient amount of revenue; it did not include a substantial, direct penalty on spending or inducements for additional savings; and it neglected to provide for the collection of the individual

[15] Witte, *Federal Income Tax*, 111; Studenski and Krooss, *Financial History*, 437–38.

[16] Witte, *Federal Income Tax*, 111–12. The Second Revenue Act provided less revenue than the Administration wanted, and it was revised by the Excess Profits Tax Amendment of 2 March 1941.

[17] Letter of President Roosevelt to Representative Robert Doughton, 1 May 1941: Morgenthau, Diaries, Vol. 574, 94.

[18] Letter of President Roosevelt to Representative Doughton, 31 July 1941: Morgenthau, Diaries, Vol. 574, 95–96.

income tax at the source (i.e., tax withholding). The bill did nothing to eliminate privileges and loopholes such as the exemption of interest on state and local securities, the favorable treatment of married couples with separate incomes, and the special depletion allowances for oil wells and mines.[19] Roosevelt signed the bill nonetheless.

The Japanese attack on the American naval base at Pearl Harbor turned a serious situation critical. At the same time, the attack on Pearl Harbor made a complex situation simple: now the whole nation, undeniably and unmistakably, was at war. In the annual message to Congress given shortly thereafter, President Roosevelt requested that the war be financed as much as possible through progressive taxes, "the backbone of the Federal tax system." The President wrote the Chairman of the Ways and Means Committee that "a large amount of purchasing power" had to be absorbed through taxes so as to pay for defense production in cash and to control prices effectively. Inflation, for the President, was "a most inequitable type of taxation."[20]

In a message to Congress of 27 April 1942 on the "Control of the Cost of Living," the President was more specific. He asked for a program of heavy taxation that would keep corporate and personal profits low, eliminate tax loopholes, and limit individual net incomes to under $25,000 a year.[21] Congress responded with the Revenue Act of 1942. The new bill doubled the size of the tax base, instituted a mandatory 5 percent "Victory Tax" on all gross incomes over $624 (partially refundable after the war), and lowered exemptions to $1,200 for joint returns and $600 for individuals. Those in the lowest tax bracket now faced a marginal tax rate of 24 percent, up from the 10 percent marginal tax rate of the Second Revenue Act of 1940. The Revenue Act of 1942 would prove the tax workhorse of the war years.

In the 1943 annual message to Congress, Roosevelt again requested as many taxes as possible in order to finance the war with minimal inflation. In a memorandum sent to the Senate Finance Committee in May 1943, the President advocated a "pay-as-you-go" system, an equitable tax abatement plan, at least partial withholding at source, and a fair and simple bill. The President did not want legislation that would penalize those with moderate incomes, burden those who were little affected by the war, or hurt those whose incomes were decreasing in the early 1940s.[22] After prolonged de-

[19] Memorandum, "The Role of the Treasury Department in Economic Stabilization," 31 October 1942: Morgenthau, Diaries, Vol. 590.

[20] Letter of President Roosevelt to Representative Doughton, 8 November 1941, OF 962, "Governmental Revenue Bills 1941," Official File, Roosevelt Papers.

[21] President Roosevelt, "Message to Congress on the Control of the Cost of Living," 27 April 1942: Morgenthau, Diaries, Vol. 574, 104–5.

[22] "Memorandum to the Senate Finance Committee," 25 May 1943, pp. 3–4: Morgenthau, Diaries, Vol. 636.

bate, Congress approved the current withholding of individual income taxes—the Ruml Plan—"one of the most difficult, controversial, and troublesome bills ever before a tax conference committee."[23] Doughton called it "the biggest outrage ever attempted."[24]

The Ruml Plan had four major elements. First and foremost, the bill provided for the current payment of the individual income tax. All taxpayers had 20 percent of their wages and salaries collected at the source and had to make quarterly payments of surtaxes and estimated liabilities on other types of income.[25] Collection at the source gave flexibility to the government, in that legislated tax increases would immediately put money into federal coffers. Second, it forgave three-fourths of a year's income tax liability in order to prevent the payment of two years' taxes in one year. The 75 percent tax forgiveness represented a compromise between the Treasury Department, which wanted no forgiveness, and Congress, many of whose members considered the levy of the additional 25 percent of personal income tax owed from 1942 or 1943 (whichever was lower) as an additional tax.[26] Third, the bill also prevented some of the windfall gains from tax forgiveness: "An anti-windfall position limits the amount of tax liability canceled for taxpayers whose incomes have increased greatly over the pre-war years."[27] Lastly, the bill gave tax relief for members of the armed forces. Armed forces personnel received a higher base exemption of $1,500 in addition to the personal exemption, and the bill canceled current and previous-year tax liabilities for those servicemen killed in action.

[23] Roland Young, *Congressional Politics in the Second World War* (New York: Da Capo Press, 1972), 136. For the legislative history of the Ruml Plan see Young (130–36); Witte, *Federal Income Tax*, 120–22; and Studenski and Krooss, *Financial History*, 447–49.

The Treasury Department had been calling for current withholding since 1941. Assistant Secretary John L. Sullivan held a closed meeting at his house on the topic immediately after the attack on Pearl Harbor, and Randolph Paul, another Assistant Secretary, sent Morgenthau a five-point memorandum on a "Program in respect to collection at the source" ("Report on the Day's Activities," 11 December 1941, file "Daily Record, Sept.–Dec. 1941," Box 3, Sullivan Papers; Memorandum of Mr. Paul to Secretary Morgenthau, 11 December 1941, file "Daily Record, Sept.–Dec. 1941," Box 3, Sullivan Papers). But the Bureau of Internal Revenue, which would have to administer any pay-as-you-go system, was opposed to withholding and criticized the bill for its nonvoluntary aspect, its additional expense to employers, its effects on the administration of Internal Revenue, and its accounting complexities ("Memorandum for the Secretary," Norman Dean, Acting Commissioner of the Bureau of Internal Revenue, 28 July 1942, file "Daily Record, May–September, 1942," Box 3, Sullivan Papers).

[24] Blum, *V Was for Victory*, 242.

[25] Taxpayers often did not save sufficient income over the course of the year to pay for their taxes the following March.

[26] Roy Blough, *The Federal Taxing Process* (New York: Prentice-Hall, 1952), 247.

[27] Letter of Harold D. Smith (Director, Bureau of the Budget) to M. H. McIntyre, Secretary to the President, 4 June 1943, Official File 407 "Taxes—Income Taxes 1944 June–July," Box 9, Official File, Roosevelt Papers.

The debate over the introduction of a pay-as-you-go income tax delayed deliberations on general revenue legislation and the need for additional taxes. In late August 1943, the President and the Treasury reduced their initial request for revenues of "not less than $16 billion of additional funds by taxation, savings, or both" to $10 billion. Nonetheless, the Administration's proposal

> was immediately opposed by the [House Ways and Means] Committee, and such major issues as compulsory lending, payroll tax increases, and relief for fixed incomes received almost no attention. After hearing the Treasury's presentation on October 4, Chairman Doughton issued a statement referring to the "unbearable increased burdens" it would impose and characterizing some of the recommended excise tax increases as "utterly indefensible."[28]

The tax bill reported by the Ways and Means Committee promised to raise only about $2.1 billion, thus falling far short of Administration goals.[29] Nor did the proposed bill correct the existing inequities in the tax code.

The President consequently vetoed the bill, against the advice of his Treasury Secretary and his Budget Director. He proclaimed that it was "not a tax bill but a tax relief bill providing relief not for the needy but for the greedy." Particularly objectionable to Roosevelt were the "(1) carry-over basis for corporations emerging from bankruptcy reorganization; (2) [the] extension of percentage depletion and excess profits exemption to several non-strategic minerals; and (3) taxing as capital gains the income from increases in the value of timber." The President also opposed the "(4) excess profits tax relief for natural gas companies including pipeline operators; and (5) a carry-over of excess profits credit permitted subsidies for airlines on air mail contracts."[30]

The veto backfired. Senator Alben Barkley (D., Ky.) dramatically resigned his position as Majority Leader upon receiving the President's veto message, although he had been a loyal New Deal supporter up to that time. Roosevelt had to issue an apology, and Barkley was unanimously reelected as Senate Majority Leader. Then, on 25 February 1944, Congress voted by more than a two-to-one margin to override the veto.[31]

The only other significant piece of tax legislation passed during the war was the income tax simplification bill (H.R. 4646). The Treasury Secretary declared in early February 1944 that "fifty million taxpayers are demanding simplification of their income tax returns. They have every right to sim-

[28] "History of the Revenue Act of 1943," 1 March 1944, p. 5: Morgenthau, Diaries, Vol. 705, 31.

[29] R. Young, *Congressional Politics*, 137.

[30] "History of the Revenue Act of 1943," 1 March 1944, p. 9: Morgenthau, Diaries, Vol. 705, 35.

[31] Young, *Congressional Politics*, 137–40.

plification. . . . Some complexity was tolerable in a peacetime income tax applying to five million people. It is intolerable in a wartime income tax applying to ten times that many."[32] Treasury officials, Senator George, and Representative Doughton agreed to confine the bill to simplification only; any attempts to introduce revenue changes or attempts to simplify other than personal income taxes would impede the simplification progress. The resulting tax bill, prepared by the staffs of the Treasury Department and the Joint Committee on Internal Revenue Taxation, imposed a uniform $500 exemption to the federal income tax, allowed claims on dependents over the age of 18, and repealed the victory tax.[33]

In sum, a consideration of the government's income tax policies shows the relative success of the Roosevelt Administration from 1940 through 1942, and the greater role played by Congress in setting tax policies in the subsequent years of the war. Congress's influence, if not its leadership, was manifest in its rejection of a national sales tax or expenditure tax and in the limited taxation provided in the revenue bills of 1942 and 1943. After all, Congress had delayed the implementation of withholding at source in the Revenue Act of 1942, had refused to increase the old-age benefit tax on employers and employees, and had provided far less in tax revenues than the Administration had requested. Indicative of Congress's independence was its prompt repeal of the President's prohibition of salaries over $25,000 in an executive order of October 1942. At another point, the Ways and Means Committee termed "fantastic" a $13 billion tax plan proposed by Fed Chairman Eccles. And on 8 September 1942, the Ways and Means Committee rejected outright a suggested 5 to 10 percent sales tax.[34] The fate of the Revenue Act of 1943 further showed the intransigence of Congress.

The Roosevelt Administration nonetheless succeeded in paying for 46 percent of the war effort with tax revenues, a record that compares favorably to that of Canada and Great Britain: Canada paid 57 percent of its expenditures from 1940 through 1946 out of taxes; Great Britain paid 52 percent. In proportion to prewar taxation (fiscal 1939), the ratio of Canada's wartime peak tax yields to prewar levels was 6.0, and Britain's was 3.4; the United States was 8.8.[35] (Income tax revenues rose by a factor of twelve and the U.S. national income tripled over the same period.)

Although the sequence of tax bills of 1940, 1941, and 1942 might seem to represent an incremental expansion in the tax system, the aggregate effect of the bills was to transform taxation in the United States. Exemption levels were almost halved (corporate excess profit tax rates increased to over

[32] 12 February 1944: Morgenthau, Diaries, Vol. 701.

[33] Letter of Morgenthau to President Roosevelt, 8 March 1944: Morgenthau, Diaries, Vol. 707, 206; Blough, Federal Taxing Process, 248.

[34] Studenski and Krooss, Financial History, 447.

[35] Murphy, National Debt, 255–56.

TABLE 4.1
Changes in Individual and Corporate Income Taxes, 1940–1944

Tax	1940	1941	1942	1943	1944
Individual Income Tax					
Exemptions	$2,000 + $800	$1,500 + $750	$1,200 + $500	°	$1,000 + $500
Depend. Allow.	$400	°	$350	°	$500
Victory Tax	—	—	5%	3%	Repealed
Normal Tax	4%	°	6%	°	3%
Surtax	4–75%	6–77%	13–82%	°	20–91%
Min. Begins	$4,000	0	°	°	°
Max. Begins	$5,000,000	°	$200,000	°	°
Corporate Income Tax					
Normal Tax	14.85–24%	15–24%	°	°	°
Surtax	—	6–7%	10–16%	°	°
Excess Profits	25–50%	35–60%	90%	95%	°

Sources: Annual Report of the Secretary of the Treasury, 1944, 458; Studenski and Krooss, Financial History of the United States, 448, Table 83.

Notes: "Dependent's Allowance" was established at $400 in 1921. "Normal Tax Rate," established at 4% in 1934, applied to net income in excess of certain credits. Surtax minimum rate and minumum level were established at 4% and $4,000, respectively, in 1934; surtax maximum rate and maximum level were set at 75% and $5,000,000, respectively, in 1935. The asterisk (°) represents no change. Figure spans represent the range of marginal tax rates under the tax in question.

90 percent), and tax receipts soared with the reduction of the minimum income threshold and with the lowering of the starting point for the maximum 91 percent marginal tax rate from $5 million in 1940 to $200,000 in 1942.[36] See Table 4.1.

In view of the outcry over the "prohibitive" income and excess profits taxes, the "punitive" excise taxes, and the simultaneous tax relief and additional taxation of the pay-as-you-go system, the absence of new tax programs was remarkable. Although Treasury officials and congressional leaders at various times considered a national sales tax, an expenditure tax, forced savings, expenditure rationing, and compulsory lending, none of these new instruments for collecting taxes or raising revenues were introduced or implemented then; nor were they introduced later, either during the Korean or Vietnam conflicts or since, despite chronic federal deficits and the exponential increase in interest due on the public debt.[37]

The Public Debt With the rearmament that began after mid-1940 and with the subsequent entry of the United States into the war, the Roosevelt Administration and the U.S. government faced the task of raising billions of dollars in order to pay for the war. On the spending side, the White House told Congress how much it needed, and Congress appropriated the necessary funds (ceilings on the permissible amount of national debt being raised routinely). Taxes, by almost all criteria, were the best way for the government to raise revenue: they paid for the war currently and avoided the accumulation of public debt; they minimized the necessity for extensive and costly wartime controls on discretionary income; and they reduced the danger of postwar inflation as a result of accumulated savings.[38] The Roosevelt Administration therefore consistently recommended funding the war as far as practicable through tax revenues: "Heavy wartime taxes do not create the economic sacrifices of war. The burden is already with us whether or not taxes are levied. The function of wartime taxation is to distribute the inevita-

[36] *Annual Report of the Secretary of the Treasury, 1944* ("*Treasury Annual Report*"), 5; Witte, *Federal Income Tax*, 129–30.

[37] For an account of the alternatives that the Roosevelt Administration and Congress were considering in lieu of income taxation for financing the war, see Bartholomew Sparrow, "From the Outside In: The Effects of World War II on the American State," Ph.D. diss., University of Chicago, 1991, 206–11. Also see William L. Crum, John F. Fennelly, and Lawrence E. Seltzer, *Fiscal Planning for Total War* (New York: National Bureau of Economic Research, 1942). Alternative tax programs were also prepared in the event of a Third World War. Plans included a national sales tax and "mandatory investment requirements" (with food and housing expenses exempted from the sales tax). The mandatory bonds for individuals, savings institutions, and nonfinancial corporations would have staggered maturities and would be nonmarketable (Memorandum of Grace T. Gunn to Samuel Cohn, 29 June 1950, file "Fiscal Policy—General 1949–1950," Box 65, Division of Fiscal Analysis, Series 39.3, Budget Records).

[38] Letter of the Treasury Department to James F. Byrnes, Director of Economic Stabilization, Draft VII, 24 October 1942: Morgenthau, Diaries, Vol. 590.

ble burden more equitably. Fair distribution of the burden will be prompted by taxes which help in preventing a damaging rise in the cost of living."[39] Indeed, Secretary Morgenthau went before the Ways and Means Committee in May 1941—in the middle of the rearmament period—and asked that a full two-thirds of government expenditures be raised through taxes.

But given Congress's reluctance to raise taxes, the resultant shortfall between tax revenues and government spending forced the executive branch and the Treasury, in particular, to make up the difference. Most of the money needed to pay for the war thus had to be borrowed. Borrowing's only advantage was that it gave incentives to production: citizens and companies could save their income in the form of government bonds instead of having to pay taxes on their earnings.

One of the Roosevelt Administration's first steps was to approve the Public Debt Act on 19 February 1941.[40] The Public Debt Act made income from federal securities (formerly tax-free) subject to federal taxation, and it allowed the Treasury to introduce three new savings schemes.[41] One was War Savings Stamps for the child or small-scale investor. A second was the conversion of the "D" savings bonds to "E" bonds. The E bonds were offered to individual savers in amounts ranging from $25 to an upper limit of $5,000 and were sold throughout the war and the postwar period. Although the E bonds were non-negotiable, they had a guaranteed redemption after sixty days' ownership. A third innovation was the issue of "F" and "G" bonds. These bonds were offered to institutional buyers and were priced in larger denominations than the E bonds, with a $100,000 ceiling. The F bond was offered at a discount, with interest accruing until maturity; the G bond was priced at par and paid interest quarterly. They had virtually identical interest rates. President Roosevelt opened the savings campaign by buying Defense Savings Stamps for his grandchildren and a $1,000 E bond for his wife, Eleanor.

On 3 July 1941, Secretary Morgenthau announced the introduction of a series of two-year Tax Saving Notes for the payment of taxes by individuals and corporations (effective 1 August 1941). The introduction of the tax notes facilitated the earlier and more timely collection of revenues by offering a convenient means of saving against accrued tax liabilities, since more

[39] "Draft of tax section for Judge Rosenman," 4 September 1942: Morgenthau, Diaries, Vol. 566, 317–18.

[40] The Treasury Department had already been reorganized on 2 April 1940 to include an Office of the Fiscal Service, which consolidated the Commissioner of Accounts and Deposits, the Commissioner of Public Debt, and the Office of the Treasurer. The Public Debt Service was renamed the Bureau of Public Debt on 30 June 1940.

[41] While it is debatable if the Treasury had to increase the return on its bonds, since their income was now subject to federal taxes (thus costing the government more), it is clear that the amounts raised in taxes far exceeded any probable difference from the higher interest rates.

than half of individual taxpayers were paying in one lump sum in March of the following calendar year rather than paying in installments over the course of the year (taxes not being withheld). The tax savings notes were receivable for taxes at par and were redeemable at any time three months after the date of issue. They came in one series of $25, $50, and $100 denominations (A-1943), paying 1.92 percent interest, and in another series of $100, $500, $1,000, $10,000, and $100,000 denominations (B-1943), paying 0.48 percent interest. Series A notes were for the small taxpayer, and purchases by individuals were limited to a $1,200 total. Series B notes had no limits on their purchase. The tax notes and the E, F, and G Series savings bonds were not transferable and could not be used as collateral. On 14 September 1942, the Secretary of the Treasury replaced series B with series C, suitable for investment by corporations and other investors. Series C, unlike its predecessor, did not have to be used to pay taxes, accrued interest on a monthly basis, could be used as collateral, and paid 1.07 percent in annual interest.

In order to encourage the widespread ownership of government securities, the President established the Voluntary Pay-roll Savings Plans on 19 March 1941. Employees in both the public and private sectors could sign up to withhold a proportion of their income for the automatic purchase of U.S. savings bonds. The government amended the sign-up provision later that year, on 27 December 1941, and inaugurated the systematic and regular sale of savings bonds to wage earners. Then, on 16 April 1942, the President established an Interdepartmental Committee for the Voluntary Savings Plan, designed to promote the sale of bonds to civilian employees of the federal government and to the armed forces.

The payroll savings plans were extremely effective. As of 30 June 1942, 108,000 firms and 16 million persons participated in payroll savings plans, deducting from their pay a total of $153 million (or 5.8 percent of their wage income). Sixty-four percent of companies with over 100 workers had payroll savings plans, and 66 percent of the 30 million private-sector employees were exposed to the plans (as of 8 May 1942).[42] Some 33 percent of the 4.4 million government employees (at all levels) were also enrolled in the plans.[43] By 1943, 182,000 firms and 26.8 million employees were participat-

---

[42] Consistent with collective action theory, employee participation in payroll savings plans at the beginning of the war had a strongly inverse relation to the company size: 72 percent of those with under 100 employees, 50.9 percent for those with 300 to 500 employees, and 25 percent of those with 10,000 to 20,000 employees (Memorandum of Mr. Haas to Secretary Morgenthau, "Subject: Operation of Payroll Savings Plans in 4,712 Companies in January," 2 March 1942, Table: Morgenthau, Diaries, Vol. 503, 76).

[43] Participation in the payroll programs ranged widely across federal departments, agencies, and bureaus. As of October 1942, 83 percent of 491,000 Navy Department employees participated, with 12 percent of their wage income being deducted. In contrast, only 48.5 percent of

ing in payroll plans, contributing $415 million (9.0 percent) of their incomes.[44] And 25.1 million persons participated in 1945, deducting a total of $550 million (11.2 percent) from their earnings.[45]

The establishment of the Pay-roll Savings Plans and the imminent introduction of the war loan campaigns demanded new administration, however. The Treasury Department therefore established the Defense Savings Staff in March 1941 (which was renamed the "War Savings Staff" in 1942). Each state had a State Chairman who worked with county and local committees of the War Savings Staff. The War Savings Staffs' primary responsibility was to promote and sell U.S. savings bonds and savings stamps to the mass market, the "hard-to-get" money. The salespeople consisted of local Internal Revenue officials and citizen volunteers.[46]

With the uncertain success of E bond sales to individuals, the Treasury Department asked the regional governors of the Federal Reserve System for their help in selling F and G bonds to institutional investors.[47] "Victory Funds Committees," composed of security dealers, investment bankers, commercial bankers, and representatives from the insurance industry, were therefore set up in each Federal Reserve District in mid-1942.[48] Whereas the War Savings Staffs sought to attract previously uninvested money, the Victory Funds Committees raised money mostly by tapping existing funds.[49]

---

the 13,000 employees of the Public Health Service participated, contributing 5.9 percent of wages ("U.S. Government Pay Roll Savings Plan," file "Daily Record, Oct.–Dec., 1942," Box 4, Sullivan Papers).

[44] *Treasury Annual Report, 1943*, 630. Among private firms with payroll plans in February 1945, for example, 18,400 employees of a total of 21,400 AT&T workers participated, putting 9.5 percent of their incomes into war bonds. But only 4,600 of 11,100 American Tobacco Company employees participated, deducting only 1.3 percent of their wages. See "Top Management Luncheon Meeting," 5 February 1945, file "War Finance Meetings," Box 25, U.S. Savings Bonds Division, Historical Files of the National Director, 1941–1969 ("HF"), General Records of the Secretary of the Treasury, Record Group 56.

[45] *Treasury Annual Report, 1945*, 55. After visiting a naval shipyard, Secretary Morgenthau reported that a "large proportion of the ship builders are on the payroll deduction plan, and are investing 11.3% of their wages; and at the yard which I visited last Thursday, the employees themselves have bought with their own War Bond purchases, every tenth ship they have built" ("Members of Congress," 1 October 1943, 9, OF 962, "Government Revenue Bills 1942–44," Official File, Roosevelt Papers).

[46] *Treasury Annual Report, 1943*, 282.

[47] Morgenthau, Diaries, Vol. 537, 5 June 1942.

[48] Memorandum of Jesse Burkhead to Dr. Pendleton Herring, "Conference with George Buffington," 20 August 1942, file "Treasury Fiscal Policy" Unit 3, Box 41, War Records Section, Series 41.3a, Budget Records.

The district committees had from five to ten members, and the Executive Secretary of each committee was selected by the security dealers of the district, and were paid $7,500 annually. Furthermore, there were regional committees, made up of both commercial and investment bankers, businessmen, and representatives of the smaller insurance companies.

[49] *Treasury Annual Report, 1943*, 282.

Not surprisingly, the sales of the Victory Funds Committees far exceeded those of the War Savings Staffs. Coordinating the actions of the Victory Funds Committees and the War Savings Staffs were the War Finance Committees set up in each of the Federal Reserve Districts.[50]

After the completion of the Second War Loan drive in March 1943, and with the overlapping operations and rivalry between the Victory Funds Committees and the War Savings Staffs, Morgenthau set up the War Finance Division in the Office of the Secretary of the Treasury.[51] The War Finance Division had overall responsibility for the sale of all Treasury securities (as opposed to just the promotion of savings bonds and savings stamps). Its objectives were: "(1) to increase public interest in the war bond program, (2) to siphon off into savings the increased worker earnings resulting from constantly expanding war production, and (3) to provide the people with a reservoir of personal savings for the post-war period."[52] The War Finance Division also oversaw the recruitment and supervision of millions of volunteers across the country, the establishment of bond committees in plants (with representatives from both management and labor), and the personal solicitation of employees and employers.[53]

The main objective of the Roosevelt Administration's innovations in sales organizations and security issues was to conduct the loan drives, the largest single source of funding for the war. Each loan drive lasted from three to six weeks and offered a basket of securities from which investors could choose those securities whose amounts and maturity periods best suited their needs. In the Third War Loan drive, for instance, the Treasury Department offered a basket of securities containing marketable issues of 1-year ⅞ percent certificates of indebtedness, 10-year 2 percent Treasury bonds, and 25-year 2½ percent Treasury bonds. (The omission of bank-eligible bonds of more than ten years' maturity was intended to restrict bank ownership, in order to discourage the expansion of credit from increased bank holdings of government debt; and the absence of short-term maturities available to individuals—the other exception to the range of available options—was because E bonds paid higher rates of interest than either F or G bonds, and were redeemable just sixty days after the day of purchase).[54]

The Treasury preceded each loan campaign with a comprehensive anal-

---

[50] Murphy, *National Debt*, 136–38.

[51] Murphy, *National Debt*, 136–38.

[52] *Treasury Annual Report, 1943*, 282.

[53] Beginning with the Third War Loan drive, in September 1943, the Treasury based security sales on state boundaries, rather than on Federal Reserve districts. Each state (and the District of Columbia, Alaska, Hawaii, and Puerto Rico) had a State Chairman who directed the still-existing War Finance Committees, which had consolidated the representatives from Victory Funds Committees with the War Savings Staffs (*Treasury Annual Report, 1943*, 283).

[54] *Treasury Annual Report, 1944*, 40.

ysis of the funds available to the government and, based on what had been learned from previous drives, recommended the best strategy for the upcoming drive.[55] This analysis set the "quota" for each investor class, served as a check and progress report on the securing of funds, and proved to salesmen (and saleswomen) across the country that the money was actually out there. The base line used to set the amount of each drive's subscription was the expected government deficit for the period to be financed by the loan.[56] The state and regional officials waging the loan campaigns then made up their own quotas according to what different states, counties, companies, and individuals could be reasonably expected to buy. The First War Loan drive began on 30 November 1942.

The war loan campaigns called for an exhaustive effort on the part of the Treasury Department in order to attract the many individual and institutional buyers needed to fund the war. The loan drives had several components. One was the planning of the campaigns, done through the War Finance Division's Publicity and Promotion Division:

> This Division is responsible for securing the cooperation of all publicity sources; for stimulating national advertising by radio, newspapers, magazines, bill boards, and other media; and for the designing of posters, albums, pamphlets, etc., used in promoting the sale of Government securities. This Division has three sections: the Radio Section creates special radio programs, edits radio scripts, and secures cooperation of the radio networks; the Newspaper Section is charged with maintaining a service of news and advertising material to 1,700 daily newspapers and nearly 10,000 weekly newspapers, and also maintains an active news desk to serve the national wire services; and the Magazine Section operates on a basis similar to the Newspaper Section in the national magazine field.[57]

Basic publicity materials for the Sixth War Loan, for example, included sales manuals, a descriptive folder, a campaign book, an official 6th War Loan insignia, and stickers. Advertising was done through major outdoor promotions, radio, newspapers, magazines, posters, window streamers, trolley and bus flags, and matchbook covers.[58]

---

[55] Memorandum of Mr. Haas to Secretary Morgenthau, 6 November 1943. "Subject: A Program for the Fourth War Loan Drive": Morgenthau, Diaries, Vol. 674, 101. The memorandum from Haas, Director of the Technical Staff, reported and analyzed the results of the Third War Loan drive, discussed alternative plans, presented a financing plan for the Fourth War Loan drive, and reviewed policy decisions.

[56] Murphy, *National Debt*, 165.

[57] *Treasury Annual Report*, 1945, 251.

[58] The Treasury Department also promoted its tax programs. In February 1942, Walt Disney released a film that featured Donald Duck preparing his tax return, and in March 1942, the Treasury had Barry Wood's and Danny Kaye's recordings of "I Paid My Income Tax Today" mailed to 872 radio stations. In November of the same year, Morgenthau approved the printing of 52 million copies of the folder "Your New Income Tax." Assistant Secretary Sullivan listed

The war bond campaigns also depended on the cooperation of non-governmental actors (about which more later); the Treasury worked closely with leading bankers, insurance men, company executives, brokers, women's groups, schools, colleges and universities, labor unions, and farmers' associations. Specific organizations working closely with the War Finance Division included the National Federation of Sales Executives, the Industrial Advisory Committee, and The Advertising Council.[59] War heroes, movie stars, popular entertainers, and sports figures agreed to appear at luncheons, war plants, and other rallies. Among the celebrities participating in the campaigns were Abbott and Costello, Fred Astaire, Ingrid Bergman, James Cagney, Bing Crosby, Bette Davis, Alfred Hitchcock, Carole Lombard, Ginger Rogers, Dick Powell, Basil Rathbone, and Barbara Stanwyck.

The tours promoting the war loans featured presentations by war heroes, films, War Bond Symphony concerts, the display of captured enemy matériel, and an Army Air Forces show of an airborne attack, dubbed the "Airmada." Appeals were made to new parents—"A Bond Grows with a Baby" and "Bonds for Babies . . . to give the babies we love a BETTER CHANCE in a BETTER WORLD"—as well as to grandparents. The "Grandmothers' War Bond League" was launched by Mrs. George C. Marshall under the slogan "Grandmothers Bond with the Future—War Bonds."[60]

Bond subscribers could, if they so desired, sponsor equipment used in the war. Prices ranged from $1,165 for a jeep to $5,250 for an amphibious truck and $145,000 for a heavy tank.[61] Fighter planes could be sponsored for $75,000, medium bombers for $175,000, and heavy bombers for $300,000. A 33-foot re-arming boat could be sponsored for $5,000, an amphibious steel tractor for $27,850, a minesweeper for $3,500,000, a submarine for $7,000,000, an aircraft carrier for $71,000,000, and a battleship for $97,000,000.[62] Women were encouraged to "Outfit the Outfit" by buying

---

twenty-five separate measures (including targeted press releases, radio talks, and billboard advertising) that the Treasury was taking "to acquaint the taxpayers with their income tax obligations" (Memorandum of Mr. Sullivan to the Secretary, February 1943, file "Daily Record, Jan.–May, 1943," Box 4, Sullivan Papers).

[59] See Mark H. Leff, "The Politics of Sacrifice on the American Home Front in World War II," *Journal of American History* 77 No. 4 (March 1991), 1296–1318. Leff describes how the advertising industry and The Advertising Council needed the war to revive business, just as the success of the U.S. war effort demanded skilled marketing. For a general overview, see Blum, *V Was for Victory*, 16–21.

[60] Files "Baby Promotions" and "Grandmothers' War Bond League," Boxes 5 and 6, Subject files, Women's Section, War Finance Division ("WFD"), General Records of the Secretary of the Treasury, Record Group 56.

[61] "How to Sponsor War Equipment with War Bonds," p. 10, n.d., file "War Equipment (How to Sponsor) 1944–45," Box 1, Motion Picture and Special Events Section, Sponsored Equipment Campaign, WFD.

[62] "How to Sponsor War Equipment with War Bonds," p. 16.

war bonds to pay for the cost of articles of clothing, barracks equipment, and bedclothes.

The government also propagandized. Slogans used for the Sixth War Loan drive included: "Let's give the Boys a Hand—Buy Another Bond During the Sixth War Loan!"; "There are Two Parts to Every Battle . . . Do *Your* Part—Buy an extra $100 Bond during the Sixth War Loan!"; "Yes, Joe—We've Still got a Big War To Fight—And Here's Why It's Going to Cost More than Ever"; "Here We go to Tokyo"; and "Help Stamp Out this Snake-in-the-Grass" (i.e., the Japanese).[63] Well-known songs were given special lyrics to encourage Americans to invest 10 percent of their earnings in savings bonds. Among the songs made available to the Treasury Department were "Santa Claus Is Coming to Town," "Deep in the Heart of Texas," "The Caissons Go Rolling Along," and "K-K-K-Katy."[64] Also available without a royalty fee was a play, for junior or senior high school production, entitled "Alice in Warland." Twenty-three other play and radio scripts were available. Almost any device or bit of popular culture that could be harnessed to the war was.

An example of the cooperation of private individuals with the war effort and of the popular touch used to sell the war was the Treasury's use of Theodore T. S. Geisel's (Dr. Seuss's) Squander Bug; Geisel, then a U.S. Army captain, donated the Squander Bug to the Treasury (see Figure 4.1). According to the Treasury's press release, "The Squander Bug can be shown feeding greedily on dollar bills, encouraging extravagance, or discouraging thrift, but he should not be pictured as merely an amusing, harmless little animal. He is a rapacious pilferer of pocketbooks, household allowances, and checking accounts. Whatever he consumes means so much less put aside in War Bonds."[65]

The Secretary of the Treasury timed news releases with an eye to their effect on the sale of government bonds. Among Morgenthau's news sources were the reports from the Office of Strategic Services on "The War this Week" and the Office of War Information.[66] The following telephone conversation between Morgenthau and Elmer Davis of the Office of War Information illustrates the Treasury Secretary's concern:

> [Henry Morgenthau, Jr.]: Mr. Davis, on Wednesday and Thursday I'm going to borrow $2 billion dollars.
> [Davis]: Yes.

[63] "Information Program on the 6th War Loan Drive," file "6th War Loan Planning," Box 1, WFD.

[64] File, "War Bond Promotions, War Bond Verses," Box 3, Motion Picture and Special Events Section, WFD.

[65] "Dr. Seuss' Squander Bug," file "Squander Bug," Box 7, Women's Section, WFD.

[66] Morgenthau, Diaries, Vol. 586, 19 November 1942. Blum points out that truth and accuracy were of secondary importance to the wartime government, and that the government used a variety of racist propaganda campaigns to sell the war (Blum, *V Was for Victory*, 21–52).

Figure 4.1. The Squander Bug. "Dr. Seuss' Squander Bug," file "Squander Bug Promotion," Box 7, Women's Section, War Finance Division, General Records of the Secretary of the Treasury, Record Group 56, National Archives

HMJr: If you could persuade various people . . . to hold it [the latent war news] back until Friday morning, it would help me.

D: Latent stuff. . . .

HMJr: Well, something, you know there may have been a ship sunk or something we lost, a transport a month ago or something like that and just got around to announcing it . . .

D: Hold till Friday . . .

HMJr: Yes. . . .

HMJr: So having you here is—is a godsend for me.

D: You don't think bad news would—if any happened to be available, would promote the sale?

HMJr: Well, this is regular financing.

D: I see.

HMJr: This is—I got—and this—I got to go to the banks in this case.

D: Uh-huh.

HMJr: This—this has nothing to do with my War Bonds.

D: Yeah.

HMJr: This—I've got to go and get the banks to subscribe $2 billion dollars in two days, and—oh—I—if something broke, it isn't going to spoil it but I've got troubles enough, you know?

D: Yes, surely.

HMJr: And if [Secretary of the Navy] Frank Knox lost a battle-ship or the War Department a troop-ship or something a month or two ago, and they just thought, "Well, we'll tell the public about it now" . . .

D: Yeah.

HMJr: . . . I don't think it would make a hell of a lot of difference if they waited a day or two. . . .

HMJr: Is my request a fair one?

D: I think it is, absolutely.[67]

The Secretary of the Treasury had to take the condition of the war, market psychology, and the probable effects of existing bond prices all into account when peddling U.S. securities.[68]

Judged by the criteria of attracting sufficient resources without forced loans, mandatory saving, or the inflation experienced in the First World War, the war loan campaigns were an obvious success.[69] Revenues from the eight drives totaled $157 billion, or more money than was collected from all tax sources from 1942 through 1945. The loan drives were able to raise billions of dollars in the space of several weeks and were consistently over-subscribed, by 148 percent of their quotas on average (see Table 4.2). Yet underneath this seeming success lay serious problems: the commercial banks were buying too many government securities, investors were "free riding" on the new security offerings, and the pattern of interest rates being maintained was unrealistically low. The Roosevelt Administration was in fact divided between the Treasury and the Federal Reserve over the issues of how to finance the war, to whom to sell securities, and what rates of return investors should get on their securities. The debates over security owner-ship, free riding, and interest rates converged on the issue of inflation.

[67] Telephone conversation of Morgenthau with Elmer Davis, 6 July 1942: Morgenthau, Diaries, Vol. 547, 35–37.

[68] Statement before the Ways and Means Committee, 10 February 1942: Morgenthau, Diaries, Vol. 495.

[69] Chapter 7 compares the U.S. government's financing of the First and Second World Wars.

TABLE 4.2
War Loan Drives (billions of dollars)

Loan	Goal	Dates	Sales	Oversubscribed	%
First	9.0	Nov. 30 to Dec. 23, 1942	12.9	3.9	144
Second	13.0	April 12 to May 1, 1943	18.6	5.6	136
Third	15.0	Sept. 9 to Oct. 2, 1943	18.9	3.9	126
Fourth	14.0	Jan. 18 to Feb. 15, 1944	16.7	2.7	120
Fifth	16.0	June 12 to July 8, 1944	20.6	4.6	129
Sixth	14.0	Nov. 20 to Dec. 16, 1944	21.6	7.6	154
Seventh	14.0	May 14 to June 30, 1945	26.3	12.3	188
Victory	11.0	Oct. 29 to Dec. 8, 1945	21.1	10.1	192
Total	106.0		156.9	50.9	148

Sources: "Board of Governors of the Federal Reserve System," memorandum to Secretary of the Treasury Fred Vinson, 24 April 1946, Box 128, Vinson Papers (microfilm roll 7). Dates are from Murphy, *National Debt in War and Transition,* 34–52.

Notes: "Dates" are opening and closing dates. "Oversubscribed" is the dollar value of securities sold by the Treasury Department in excess of targets. "%" is the percentage of the target goal oversubscribed in each drive. The percent total is unweighted for the amount raised.

On the one hand, the government had to sell its bonds. The war had to be adequately funded, and the Treasury Department wanted to do so as cheaply as possible. On the other hand, inflation (resulting from the increased purchasing power from higher wartime incomes) meant that the President and Congress, assuming they had their eyes on elections and possible political pratfalls, could not let purchasing power go unrestrained. The difference between the value of goods available for consumption at present prices and the expanded purchasing power generated by the war economy—the "inflationary gap"—had to be bridged.

One way for the Roosevelt Administration to combat inflation was through taxation, which it pursued as far as it was able. Another way was for the President to control wages and prices directly. Roosevelt did just that. He signed the Emergency Price Control Act on 30 January 1942, passed in accordance with the President's request that Congress follow up his executive order establishing the Office of Price Administration, and proceeded to issue the "General Maximum Price Regulation" ("General Max") for overall control on 28 April 1942. Food rationing began in May 1942, starting with sugar. The President then signed the Price Control Act in October 1942, and on 8 April 1943 he issued the "hold the line order," freezing wages and prices (unless increases conformed to existing laws).

The disadvantage of direct wage and price controls was that they did not tackle the source of inflationary pressures: the extra earning power resulting from the government's spending, whereby seven-eighths of national income went into the pay envelopes of those earning less than $5,000 a year.[70] This was the money that the government had to absorb in order to allay inflationary pressures and prevent the worse possibilities of "empty shelves, large-scale black markets, widespread evasion and dealer favoritism, and illegitimate profits."[71] The Roosevelt Administration therefore pursued a mixed strategy that included freezing prices and rents, restricting wage and salary levels, curtailing consumer credit, rationing, imposing higher taxes, and selling U.S. government securities.

In order to limit the inflationary impact of the bond sales, the Roosevelt Administration had decided very early on to raise funds from non-inflationary sources, i.e., to sell as little as possible to commercial banks:

> The question of who owns Government securities is of particular significance . . . because of the desirability of selling new issues to "real savers" rather than to banks. When people purchase government securities out of current savings, the money so spent will not be used by them to bid up prices for goods and services which are limited in available supply by the Defense Program. . . . When Government securities are purchased by commercial banks, [however,] the tendency is for the purchase to result in the creation of new demand deposits, a process which would be a direct stimulus to inflation.[72]

Said differently, the purchase of liquid (transferable) government securities by commercial banks did not take cash from the hands of consumers but, rather, added to the assets of commercial banks and thereby facilitated still more lending.

Although the Roosevelt Administration tinkered with its baskets of securities (in the Seventh War Loan drive, for example, the corporation quota was reduced from $9 to $7 billion, and corporations were no longer offered the 1½ percent bond), the participation of the commercial banks was indispensable to the success of the war loan drives. Secretary Morgenthau took pains to reassure the bankers concerning the Administration's intentions:

> [E]very attempt will be made to borrow as much of the remaining funds required as it is possible to borrow from non-inflationary sources. . . . It is quite obvious that the balance of the financing will have to come from insurance companies, savings banks and other permanent investment funds, and to the extent that these funds are not sufficient, the balance will have to come from the banks. We have no

[70] "Members of Congress," draft of speech by the Treasury Department, 1 October 1943, file "Government Revenue Bills 1942–44," Official File 962, Roosevelt Papers.

[71] Letter of Assistant Secretary Daniel Bell to James F. Byrnes, Director of Economic Stabilization, 24 October 1942, Draft VII: Morgenthau, Diaries, Vol. 590, 166.

[72] "Treasury Fiscal Policy," 2, Unit 3, Box 41, Series 41.3a, War Records Section, Budget Records. Also see Crum, Fennelly, and Seltzer, *Fiscal Planning for Total War*, 335.

way of telling at this time how much the banks will be called upon to take. I believe you can rest assured that it will be a substantial amount.[73]

It was a substantial amount. The holdings of commercial banks rose from $16 billion in 1940 to $17.7 billion in 1941, $25.4 billion in 1942, $48 billion in 1943, $60 billion in 1944, and $72 billion in 1945. Meanwhile, government securities as a percentage of commercial bank assets increased from 37 percent in 1941 to 51 percent in 1943, and to 57 percent by 1945. Not surprisingly, interest income as a proportion of bank profits also increased from 31 percent in 1941 to 46 percent in 1943, and to 47 percent in 1945.[74]

The commercial banks were too important to the financing of the war, despite the Administration's intention to raise money from non-inflationary sources. Morgenthau could do little other than jawbone:

Non-bank investors *have been requested* to refrain from selling securities now owned solely for the purpose of obtaining funds with which to subscribe for the securities offered in the Seventh War Loan Drive. This request is not intended to preclude normal portfolio adjustments.

I *earnestly request* your cooperation in the coming Drive, (1) in declining to make loans for the speculative purchase of Government securities; (2) in declining to accept subscriptions from your customers which appear to be entered for speculative purposes; and (3) in declining to make loans for the purpose of acquiring Drive securities later in your own account. If you have any doubt as to the propriety of accepting a subscription for a marketable issue presented through your bank, please submit the circumstances and all available information to the Federal Reserve Bank of your district.[75]

In short, the Administration depended on the sale of large quantities of U.S. securities to the commercial banks. This participation by the commercial banks was an important reason for the increase in the money supply from $65 billion in 1939 to $165 billion by 1946.

A second reason for the expansion of the money supply (and thus for the

[73] Letter of Secretary of the Treasury Henry Morgenthau, Jr., to Ralph C. Gifford, President, First National Bank, Louisville, Kentucky, 2 June 1942: Morgenthau, Diaries, Vol. 535, 160.

[74] U.S. Board of Governors of the Federal Reserve System, *Banking and Monetary Statistics* (Washington, D.C: U.S. GPO, 1976), Table 6.1, 378–79; Board of Governors of the Federal Reserve System, *Banking and Monetary Statistics* (Washington, D.C: U.S. GPO, 1943), 262–6. Profits from non-governmental securities came to only 6.6 percent of bank profits in 1945, 5.8 percent of profits in 1947, and 5.6 percent of profits in 1949—suggestive of the role that interest income from government securities (as opposed to non-governmental securities) played in bank profits.

[75] Statement of Henry Morgenthau, Jr., 20 March 1945, p. 2: Morgenthau, Diaries, Vol. 830, 98; emphasis added.

inflationary pressures) was the government's cheap money policy. On 8 December 1941, the Monday after Pearl Harbor, the Federal Reserve Board announced, "The System is prepared to use its powers to assure that an ample supply of funds is available at all times for financing the war effort, *and to exert its influence toward maintaining conditions in the United States Government security market that are satisfactory from the standpoint of the Government's requirements.*"[76] As Fed Chairman Eccles told Congress,

> Right after Pearl Harbor a billion and a half issue of the 67–72s [long-term bonds] was pending or was offered to the market on either Friday or Saturday, but had not been issued, that is, they had been subscribed to, and there was $15,000,000 of bills falling due on Monday [8 December]. The Treasury Department did not know and we did not know whether there would be any bids in the market on Monday after the Pearl Harbor incident. The market was very weak, very jittery, and we purchased in the market that Monday and a few days after about $100,000,000 of securities, giving stability and support. Where weakness was shown we purchased to stabilize the market. If we had not I don't know where the market would have gone.[77]

The Treasury and the Fed agreed "to assure a steady and strong market for outstanding securities and to reduce speculative fluctuations in anticipation of possible changes in interest rates during a period of large deficit financing," and to keep down the costs of war financing by holding interest rates to a moderate, steady level.[78] They decided on a ⅜ percent rate on Treasury 90-day bills, a ⅞ percent return for 1-year certificates, and a 2½ percent rate for long-term marketable government bonds.[79] A Treasury report of 1946 explained:

> The present structure of interest rates is one in which short-term rates are substantially lower than long-term rates. This has been the case since the early 1930s. Shortly after the entry of the United States into the war, the Treasury and the Federal Reserve System agreed upon a so-called "pattern" of interest rates on Government securities. The spread between short- and long-term rates in this agreed-upon pattern was considerably less than that which had prevailed during most of the 1930s.[80]

[76] Memorandum of George Haas to Frederick Vinson, Secretary of the Treasury, 25 July 1945, "Background and Analysis of the Federal Reserve Proposals for Increasing Short term Interest Rates," File "Federal Reserve—Interest Rates and Public Debt 1944–45," Box 126, Papers of Frederick Vinson, Secretary of the Treasury, University of Kentucky (microfilm roll 5); emphasis in original.

[77] "2nd War Powers Act, 1942," Hearings on S. 2208, Committee on the Judiciary, House of Representatives, 30 January and 2 February 1942.

[78] Eccles, *Beckoning Frontiers*, 350.

[79] "2nd War Powers Act, 1942."

[80] Memorandum of Haas to Vinson, 25 July 1945, "Background and Analysis of the Federal

This pattern of interest rates remained in effect for the duration of the war, for if interest rates changed or were seen as being unstable, then the debt would be more difficult to finance. Previously issued securities would decrease in value, and purchasers would discount the worth of current issues. The government would get less for its auctioned securities and would have to pay out more in interest. Lower interest rates thus meant cheaper interest payments by the government. But the lower rates also meant an increase in the money supply: investors who might otherwise wait for lower prices (and higher yields) would now have no reason to wait.

The difference in the interest rates for short-term and long-term government securities affected the sale of securities and the money supply, however, since the low rate on T-bills induced investors to sell them and forced the Fed, as the buyer of last resort, to purchase the outstanding bills. According to Eccles, "[w]hat the Reserve System feared might happen did in fact happen. In due course the System came to hold practically all bills outstanding, though the volume of bills was increased enormously from $1.3 billion in 1941 to $17 billion in 1945."[81] On 18 July 1945, for example, Federal Reserve Banks held about $12.8 billion of short-term Treasury bills; only $4.2 billion was held by all other investors. By maintaining low rates and guaranteeing the price levels of its securities, the government was automatically creating excess reserves whenever the Fed had to step in. Purchases of government debt by commercial banks and the Federal Reserve Banks thus increased monetary reserves and added to the money supply. (Purchases of bonds by individuals and institutions would, in contrast, simply withdraw savings from circulation—hence the government's policy to restrict bank purchases.)

Yet the Treasury Department and the Roosevelt Administration had to have that money, so the government sought to induce the voluntary purchase of the war bonds in order to finance the war: hence the interest-rate pattern, the war-loan oversubscriptions, the toleration of free riding, and the large role played by the commercial banks. For all the statements by Treasury Secretary Morgenthau and President Roosevelt on the need to sell government securities as much as possible to non-bank purchasers, they could not afford to live up to their words.[82]

Even the 20 percent oversubscription of the Fourth War Loan drive (the loan drive with the lowest rate of oversubscription) was too close for com-

Reserve Proposals for Increasing Short-term Interest Rates," file "Federal Reserve—Interest Rates and Public Debt 1944–45," Box 126, Vinson Papers.

[81] Eccles, *Beckoning Frontiers*, 359.

[82] John Morton Blum, *From the Morgenthau Diaries*, Vol. 3: *Years of War, 1941–1945* (Boston: Houghton Mifflin, 1967), 26–27; Eccles, *Beckoning Frontiers*, 349; Abbott, *The Federal Debt*, 205; Milton Friedman and Anna Jacobson Schwartz, *A Monetary History of the United States* (New York: National Bureau of Economic Research, 1963), 565–66.

fort. The Fourth War Loan was "unsuccessful," its total sales "disappoint-
ing." One Treasury official thought that the chances of a successful Fifth
War Loan were "slight, unless some miracle comes along."[83] Reasons for the
expected "tough sledding" included:

(3) Beginning today, the Red Cross has a tremendous drive under way. The people
will become fed up on drives very soon, and may be low on money.

(4) In March, tax payments will be heavy, particularly on the larger and medium
individual investors, who fell down badly in the Fourth Loan.

(5) By the time we get ready for the Fifth War Loan, politics will be in full swing.
This will not only dissipate our audience, but will make everything we do open to
argument on political grounds. . . .

(8) Local Civilian Defense Agencies are falling apart, and by the Fifth War Loan
we may be without help from this quarter in many areas. Also, the possibility of
Willkie Club activity (for Dewey or some other candidate) may take up many of
our volunteers and dissipate the efforts of others.

(9) As we get close to what people consider Victory, and as the war goes on, people
are likely to become less eager to give us any real help. This is a possibility we
must consider.[84]

Considering the money raised in the later war loan drives, these fears
appear absurd. Yet such doubts were real enough to Morgenthau and the
others responsible for financing the government, and the Treasury quickly
reversed its tactics.[85] Since the Fourth War Loan represented the height of
"purity" in the effort to exclude commercial banks from participation (the
securities offered in the Fourth containing no bank-eligible securities, except certificates of indebtedness), future loan drives would include medium-
term, bank-eligible securities in their baskets of securities.[86]

In sum, the executive branch had almost total discretion over the management of the public debt. The President and his top financial advisers set the
interest rates on U.S. securities, established the organizations and conditions of bond selling, and introduced new issues (such as the Defense Savings Bonds and Tax Saving Notes). They thereby influenced, and even
determined, who would own the public debt. (Exceptions were Congress's
refusal to tax municipal securities and its unwillingness to raise more tax

[83] Memorandum of Fred Smith to Secretary Morgenthau, 1 March 1944: Morgenthau,
Diaries, Vol. 705, 48.

[84] Memorandum of Fred Smith to Secretary Morgenthau, 1 March 1944, 49–50.

[85] After the Sixth War Loan, for example, a conference of Federal Reserve Bank presidents
agreed "[t]hat unless and until changes are made in the drive procedure, which in the past has
increasingly encouraged padded and speculative subscriptions, 'switching,' and indirect bank
subscriptions, because of the possibilities for profit and ease in attaining quotas, policing will be
relatively ineffectual" ("Suggested Procedure for the Seventh War Loan Drive," n.d., file "7th
War Loan—Planning," Box 1, War Loan Drives—Planning, WFD).

[86] Murphy, National Debt, 147.

revenues—thereby requiring more borrowing on the part of the government.) As Morgenthau never ceased to emphasize—and the President supported him here—any funds not raised through taxes on individuals and business incomes the government would extract only voluntarily. But the contradiction of trying to keep prices, wage demands, and interest rates down and simultaneously selling enough war bonds meant that the Roosevelt Administration could not escape double talk.

Despite Morgenthau's assertion that the first principle of borrowing was that the "necessary funds should be raised in such a manner as to minimize the risk of inflation,"[87] the evidence from the oversubscriptions, the maintenance of the interest-rate pattern, the continued participation by banks, and the resulting expansion of credit suggests that the first principle of borrowing was actually that the necessary funds should be raised in such a manner as to minimize the risk of *failure*.

Taxation and Public Borrowing after the War Despite the labor unrest, food and commodity shortages, and inflation of 1946 and 1947, the postwar period was one of comparative calm. As soon as the war ended, the 79th Congress moved to reduce taxes on individuals and corporations. The new law (H.R. 4309) repealed the excess profits tax as of 1 January 1946, speeded up the payment of refunds from the carry-back of unused excess profits credits from 1946 back to 1944 and 1945, and reduced the standard corporate tax by 2 percent for corporations with incomes over $50,000 and by 2 to 4 percent on corporations with smaller incomes. Reductions in corporate income and excess profits tax liabilities amounted to $3.14 billion in calendar year 1946; the bill reduced total tax liabilities by almost $6 billion in the same year.[88] The bill further gave credits for a spouse and dependents in filing for the normal tax; previously, they had existed solely for the surtax. Married taxpayers and taxpayers with dependents had their taxes reduced by an estimated $782 million, and the 3 percent normal tax was reduced by 5 percent to an effective rate of 2.85 percent. All pay to veterans of active service below the grade of commissioned officers was exempted from income tax: "members of the military or naval forces are, in general, permitted to discharge income tax liabilities with respect to service pay or preservice earned income in 12 equal quarterly payments over a period of three years, without interest."[89] The combined reductions lowered tax liabilities by $2.65 billion.

On 16 June 1947, Truman vetoed the first of three tax reduction bills sent to him:

---

[87] "Raising Funds for Victory," A Report by the Secretary of the Treasury, 17 July 1945 (Washington, D.C: U.S. GPO, 1945).

[88] Letter of Fred Vinson, Secretary of the Treasury, to Harold Smith, Director of the Bureau of the Budget, 7 November 1945, file "Nov. 5–9, 1945," White House Bill File, Truman Papers.

[89] Letter of Vinson to Smith, 7 November 1945.

The bill [H.R. 1] reduces present individual income tax rates by application of percent reductions to the tax brackets as now calculated. It also provides for an additional personal exemption of $500 for a taxpayer of over 64 years of age, and for his spouse if over 65 years of age. Effective January 1, 1948, the bill reduces the present individual tax liability by 30 percent for surtax net incomes (after deductions and exemptions) under $1,000 per year, by between 30 and 20 percent for surtax net incomes of $1,000 to approximately $1,400, and by 20% for surtax net incomes of approximately $1,400 to $136,000. [At higher levels, the percentage tax reduction decreased from 20 percent to 10.5 percent.] . . . Effective January 1, 1947, the present law tax liability is reduced by approximately one-half the percentages which apply after January 1, 1948.[90]

Truman vetoed a second tax reduction bill (H.R. 3950) on 18 July 1947, saying that it was "not consistent with sound fiscal policy." In both veto messages, the President emphasized that because of the inflationary trends there would be no tax reductions; he repeated the message in his First Economic Report (reports mandated by the Employment Act of 1946) and in a May press conference. "As we enter the new year," the President told Congress, "we must surmount one major problem which affects all our goals. That is the problem of inflation." Truman's solution was that tax revenues should exceed government expenses. Congress nonetheless overrode Truman's veto of a third tax reduction bill (H.R. 4790) on 1 April 1948. The new law cut taxes, increased the exemption level to $600, added an exemption for the blind (besides the existing one for the elderly), and permitted income splitting on joint returns. "The cost of the bill was estimated at $6.5 billion, less than the surplus for the past year [fiscal 1948]."[91]

In 1949, Truman restated the need for a balanced budget and for a surplus of revenue over expenditures in order to retire the national debt. He requested new taxes for raising an additional $4 billion, spread among higher taxes on corporate profits, estates, and gifts. But in the Special Message to Congress on the President's "Midyear Economic Report," Truman acknowledged that, in the face of a mild recession, a change in plans was in order:

[W]e cannot immediately correct the tax mistakes of the past or the conditions which led to a lower level of national income and lower Federal revenues. Any tax increase should be judged by the effect which it might have on national income and purchasing power. *Under present economic conditions*, immediate tax increases should be limited to raising estate and gift tax rates and closing the loopholes in their administration. . . . At the same time, the tax on transportation of

[90] Letter of Lawton to Latta [about 7 June 1947], file "June 16–23, 1947," White House Bill File, Truman Papers.

[91] Witte, *Federal Income Tax*, 134; also see Stein, *The Fiscal Revolution*, 208.

goods, which enters directly into such a large number of business costs, should be eliminated. Furthermore, the loss carry-over provisions in the corporate income tax laws should be liberalized in order to give an increased incentive to some business investments which may now be held back because of uncertain profit expectations.[92]

With no legislation forthcoming, the President repeated his message on taxes in late January 1950: excise taxes should be reduced only to the extent that tax loopholes were sealed and corporate income taxes raised. New tax legislation would come only after North Korean troops crossed over the Demilitarized Zone.

The tax record of the Truman years is thus uneven. The Truman Administration was unable to get the tax reforms or tax increases it wanted, and it made only modest progress in reducing the federal debt. Yet even as the President's legislative requests were being rejected, as we should expect, Congress did not demonstrate its independence to the degree that the 78th Congress had when it denied President Roosevelt's requested legislation. The third tax reduction bill *was* milder than the previous two bills, and it combined the most politically attractive characteristics of each. Meanwhile, the President was able to run budget surpluses in 1947, 1948, and 1949, despite the tax cuts, and unemployment came to only 5.9 percent in 1949 and stayed at under 4 percent in 1946, 1947, and 1948.

The history of the management of the public debt in the immediate postwar years is also uneven, with little action and less direction by either the Truman Administration or the Congress. Prominent issues were inflation, the reduction in the public debt, and the conflict between the Federal Reserve and the Treasury.[93] The cost-of-living index, standing at 129 in June 1946, rose to 174.5 in August 1948 and came to 170.2 in June 1950.[94] At the height of the inflationary postwar period, the Treasury increased the discount rate from 1¼ percent to 1½ percent so as to tighten credit and control inflation (effective August 1948), the Fed raised bank reserve requirements (effective September 1948), and Secretary Snyder discontinued Series C Treasury savings notes and substituted a new note, Series D, in line with the increased interest rates on short-term government securities.

Because of the efficiency (and bracket creep) of the personal income tax,

[92] *Public Papers of the Presidents of the United States: Harry S Truman, 1949*, 362; emphasis added.

[93] For a general account of the postwar years up to the mid-1960s, especially the relationship between the Treasury and the Fed, see Stein, *The Fiscal Revolution*, 197–280. Also see Richard H. Timberlake, *Monetary Policy in the United States: An Intellectual and Institutional History* (Chicago: University of Chicago Press, 1978), 309–15.

[94] Studenski and Krooss, *Financial History*, 460–61.

Figure 4.2. The First Budget Surplus in 17 Years. © 1947 The
Washington Post. Reprinted with permission

however, the government was able to raise sufficient amounts of revenue.[95]
Between inflation and the restricted federal budgets, the Treasury succeeded in reducing the national debt from $269.4 billion in 1947 to $252.3
billion in 1948, with more than half of the reduction of the deficit coming
from the liquidation of deposits in war loan accounts. The Treasury's cash
account surpluses of $6.6 billion in calendar 1947 and $8.9 billion in 1948
further helped to reduce the national debt from 119 percent of GNP in
1945 to 90 percent of GNP by 1950.[96]

The postwar years also brought the Treasury Department's conflict with
the Federal Reserve into starker relief. Whereas the Treasury and the Fed
had mostly cooperated at the outset of World War II, by war's end they
were at odds over interest rates, the money supply, and the pricing of securities.[97] As the nation's central bank, the Fed wanted to retain the value of
bank assets and keep inflation under control. It therefore pushed for an

[95] According to the research of the J. Walter Thompson Company, over 21 million families
moved into the group above the $2,000 income level from 1941 to 1949—from 14 million
families in 1941 up to 35 million families in February 1949 (Arno H. Johnson, "Savings Bonds
In Our Economy," 29 March 1950 [no file folder], Box 23, HF).

[96] Abbott, *The Federal Debt*, 208.

[97] Abbott, *The Federal Debt*, 189–91.

increase in short-term interest rates after the war, in order to raise the cost of borrowing money and thereby suppress inflationary pressures. But Morgenthau and his successor as Secretary of the Treasury, Fred Vinson, resisted such an adjustment: their concern was to finance and refinance the debt as cheaply as possible.[98] Even if the premise for the preferential ½ percent rate no longer existed (i.e., to induce banks to buy Treasury bills and Treasury certificates in order to finance the war), the Treasury saw little reason to depart from its successful wartime credit and interest-rate policies. Such action, Treasury officials argued, could be interpreted by investors as indicating that the U.S. government was abandoning low interest rates; in response to an increase in interest rates investors might panic and sell government securities en masse. Raising interest rates would "increase the already large interest charge on the public debt."[99] The Treasury would then face the expensive and difficult task of borrowing money at the higher rates.

The Fed was able to win some battles in its struggle over interest rates, however, even if the Treasury won the war. In April 1946, the Fed was able to unilaterally discontinue the ½ percent guarantees on short-term bills, established in October 1942: "The Government's war program no longer calls for the expansion of bank credit to help finance huge war expenditures. Instead, it calls for action that will stop additions to and bring about reductions in the country's money supply in order to reduce inflationary pressures."[100] The Fed also pushed for a relaxation of certificates of indebtedness and savings bonds, but not until August 1947 did the Treasury agree to raise the rate on certificates from ⅞ of 1 percent to 1⅛ percent; the Treasury allowed a further increase in certificate rates to 1¼ percent one year later, at the height of the postwar inflation (August 1948).

Other small victories for the Federal Reserve were that the Federal Reserve Open Market Committee lowered its support price on bonds in December 1947, to maintain them only at par; that the Fed increased the rediscount rate to 1¼ percent in January 1948, and then to 1½ percent in August 1948; that the Fed abandoned the stabilization policy for government securities on 28 June 1949 (which guaranteed the par values of securities, and thus their rates of return); and that the Board reduced reserve requirements in May 1949 to 22, 18, and 12 percent, depending on the bank (effective December 1949).[101] Yet the average rate of interest on government debt rose to only 2.199 percent in June 1950 (from a 1.995 percent

[98] Henry Morgenthau, Jr., resigned as Secretary of the Treasury on 22 July 1945; Frederick M. Vinson became Secretary of the Treasury on 23 July 1945 and remained in office until 23 June 1946. John W. Snyder was appointed Treasury Secretary on 25 June 1946.
[99] Eccles, *Beckoning Frontiers*, 423.
[100] Statement by the Board of Governors of the Federal Reserve System, 24 April 1946, Box 128, Vinson Papers (microfilm roll 7).
[101] Studenski and Krooss, *Financial History*, 478.

average rate in June 1946), and not until April 1951 did the Fed completely stop supporting Treasury bond prices.

Congress played a surprisingly passive role in this struggle, however, despite its authority to determine how the Federal Reserve and the Treasury Department were to manage the public debt. In June 1946 the Fed asked Congress for further powers to control the expansion of credit so to counteract the postwar inflation. The Fed wanted Congress "(1) to place a maximum amount on the amount of long-term securities held by banks; (2) to set secondary reserves requirements in the form of short-term governments, vault cash, or deposits within the Reserve Banks; and (3) to increase reserve requirements by 100 per cent."[102] Yet Congress saw fit to pass only a Joint Resolution for the continuation of the controls existing in 1947. Not until August 1948 did Congress, in response to the Truman Administration's requests, allow the Fed to regulate consumer credit and increase reserve requirements (by 4 percentage points for demand deposits and by 1½ points for time deposits). But even these measures fell substantially shy of the Truman Administration's requests, and the Fed's additional powers expired on 30 June 1949.[103]

The Douglas Committee hearings of December 1949 (the Subcommittee on Monetary, Credit and Fiscal Policies of the Senate Joint Economic Committee, under Senator Paul H. Douglas [D., Ill.]) brought the increasing differences between the Treasury and the Fed into the public eye. Through the testimony of such persons as Treasury Secretary John Snyder, Fed member Allan Sproul, and Fed Board member and former chairman Eccles (among the most prominent critics of the Treasury's easy money policy), the hearings exposed the public to the debate over monetary policy: they communicated "the fact that there was a deep split between the Federal Reserve and the Treasury, that this was not a contest between the bankers and 'the people,' and that many leaders of business, finance, and agriculture . . . believed that the flexible policy which the Federal Reserve favored was essential to economic stability and prosperity."[104]

For all the educational value of the Douglas Committee hearings, however, Congress did little to settle the conflict between the Treasury and the Fed. Neither did the executive branch. The Treasury and the Council of Economic Advisers dissented vigorously from the Douglas Committee's proposal that "Treasury actions relative to . . . transactions in the public debt shall be made consistent with the policies of the Federal Reserve." The Council of Economic Advisers noted that to change the working relationship between the Treasury and the Fed "would surely evoke the sharpest

---

[102] Studenski and Krooss, *Financial History*, 481.
[103] Studenski and Krooss, *Financial History*, 483.
[104] Stein, *The Fiscal Revolution*, 259.

controversy in the field of debt management where quiet and confidence are supremely important."[105] The Treasury and the Truman Administration agreed to support the prices of long-term government bonds instead, rather than allow the Federal Reserve to control a flexible monetary and credit policy. Interest rates would be raised only within a narrow limit; and the government would not let the value of savings bonds fall below par.

Inertia reigned in both Congress and the White House. The economist Charles C. Abbott reports that

> the record shows an extreme reluctance on the part of the Treasury to abandon wartime policies or to yield any of the powers or prerogatives devolving upon it as a result of the emergency. If the Congress had imposed some general limits on Treasury discretion—narrow or confining limitations would, of course, not have been practicable—or if the Treasury itself had pursued different policies, its enhanced monetary powers would not have remained so large.[106]

With neither the Congress nor the Administration taking significant steps to manage—much less reduce—the public debt, the practices of World War II remained in place in order to handle the $50 billion of federal debt that had to be refinanced annually. As during the war years, in this postwar refinancing—"more than the total refunding operations of all other borrowers during the previous 25 years"—the executive branch determined the timing and strategy for selling government bonds.[107] Also as in the war years, the refunding efforts emphasized payroll savings plans and relied on organized loan drives. The newly created U.S. Savings Bond Division (replacing the War Finance Division on 1 January 1946) launched the "Security Loan" drive in 1948 (April 15–June 30), the "Opportunity Bond Drive" in 1949 (May 16–June 30), and the "Independence Loan Drive" in 1950 (May 15–July 4). There were also Bond-a-Month programs introduced in 1946 and 1948.[108]

In short, the postwar years reveal a lack of command on the part of the Truman Administration in determining U.S. public debt policy. Without emergency powers, the Truman Administration had to relinquish its command of debt management. Yet neither did Congress take up the slack: disputes continued to simmer over interest rates, the lack of a comprehensive program for reducing the federal deficit, and the rapid and panic-inducing increases in postwar prices.[109] Despite the controversy over

[105] Memorandum of The Council of Economic Advisers to the President, 2 February 1950, file "Special Report to President, Debt Management Policy," Box 3, Keyserling Papers.

[106] Abbott, *The Federal Debt*, 50.

[107] Studenski and Krooss, *Financial History*, 476.

[108] File "Fiscal—Savings Bonds—general 1948–52" (folder 3), Box 17, Snyder Papers.

[109] See Chapter 3, and B. Bernstein, "The Truman Administration and the Politics of Inflation."

inflation and interest rates and the rivalry between the Treasury and the Fed, Congress continually rejected the President's requests for tax reform and higher tax rates.[110]

The Truman Administration nonetheless managed to achieve modest budget surpluses for three of the first five postwar years and was eventually able to stop the postwar price increases (given the deflationary impact of retiring the public debt, personal income taxes, and the waning of the demand-pull inflation of postwar consumer spending). And yet the country did suffer the inflation of the postwar years up through 1948 as well as the mild recession of 1949. Even the postwar bond campaigns were smaller and less successful than their wartime predecessors (see below).

The size of the war-induced deficit financing and the importance of decisions on the timing and terms of securities issues intensified the Fed's opposition to Treasury policies. Had there been agreement on a greater reduction in the public debt, then the particulars of the securities being issued, interest rates, and debt refinancing would have been of less significance, and the Treasury Department and the Fed would have had less reason for conflict. But as the financial historians Paul Studenski and Herman Krooss remark, "At no point during this period did the [A]dministration or Congress set any definite annual rate of debt retirement as a goal."[111]

The Organization of Public Finance

Given the increased demands for tax revenues and security sales during and after the war, we may expect an increase in the size of the tax bureaucracy (given the broad-based clientele) and the creation of small agencies for coordinating the government's sale of public debt with (the smaller numbers of) financial institutions, industrial corporations, trade associations, labor unions, and others able to invest in U.S. securities. These expectations are largely borne out.

The budget of the Bureau of Internal Revenue grew from $60 million in 1940 to $147 million in 1945, and the number of the Bureau's employees rose from 22,000 to 50,000 persons over the same period. The budget of the Bureau of Public Debt increased from less than $20 million in 1940 (including transfers to the Federal Reserve for its expenses incurred in selling the debt) to over $73 million in 1945, and the number of Public Debt employees increased from about 2,000 persons in 1940 to almost 12,500 by 1945.

---

[110] President Truman vetoed the first price control bill on 29 June 1946 but then signed the second price control bill—with many reservations—on 25 July 1946.

[111] Studenski and Krooss, *Financial History*, 475.

Although the government raised more money through borrowing than through taxation—the total public debt rising from $43 billion in 1940 to $259 billion in 1945—the budget of the Bureau of Public Debt was still considerably smaller than that of the Bureau of Internal Revenue. After all, funds could be raised from the sale of public debt through far fewer transactions than raising revenues from mass-based income taxation. The Bureau of Internal Revenue, accordingly, had to have a large, extensive organization capable of extracting taxes from individual household incomes.

Surprising, however, was the scope of the volunteer efforts on behalf of the U.S. government. Morgenthau commented that

> in the war loan days the central Treasury staff for savings bonds was only a nucleus. It was the State War Finance Committees, the County Committees, and all of the other local committees which succeeded in organizing millions of volunteers to do the job. It would have been impossible to hire this huge staff. Not only would the cost have been prohibitive, but we couldn't have hired many of the people at any price. And I am sure that the results from a highly centralized effort would not have compared with the achievements of our volunteer organization.[112]

The Payroll Savings Division was able to get corporate chief executive officers to appoint Bond Officers for their companies. The Bond Officer, who was provided with a basic manual and booklet for his co-workers, then appointed Team Captains, who were each responsible for soliciting about twenty fellow workers. In this way, person-to-person solicitation was "broken down to its component parts."[113] As one life insurance company president noted, "Between 1942 and 1945, there were a lot of us . . . who spent a lot more time on savings bonds than we did on our own business."[114]

Virtually all major societal organizations and associations responded to the government's call: "Many investment bankers directed the administration of the Regional Committees, . . . and continued afterwards when the War Finance Committees were organized by the Treasury." Investment bankers sold $147 billion of government securities for the war loan drives, services that were "performed for patriotic reasons by volunteer workers who, with a few exceptions, served without profit or opportunity for personal gain."[115]

[112] John W. Snyder, "Management of the National Debt," 19 March 1947, p. 43 [no file folder], Box 25, HF.

[113] Lawton B. Wolfe, Director of Payroll Savings, "The Primary E Bond Market: Payroll Savings," 18 September 1946 [no file folder], Box 25, HF.

[114] Minutes of the Industrial Committee meeting with Secretary of the Treasury Snyder, 10 December 1947, Washington, D.C., p. 39 [no file folder], Box 25, HF.

[115] Julien H. Collins, President, Investment Bankers Association of America, "Wise Portfolio Management," 19 March 1948, p. 56, in "Proceedings—National Conference on U.S. Savings Bonds," 18, 19, 20 March, Washington, D.C. [no file folder], Box 25, HF.

Business management and labor unions both spent their own money, used their own personnel, and donated their time for the sale of savings bonds. The presidents of the CIO and the AFL made statements on behalf of the Labor Section of the War Finance Division; the AFL and CIO national conventions passed resolutions for the purchase of savings bonds; and top union officials passed directives down to their affiliates to work with local representatives.[116]

The government also created various organizations that were able to reach out to the different saver and investor groups. The National Organizations Section of the War Finance Division, for instance, sold securities to "national labor organizations, civic, fraternal and other national groups, and interstate railroads." There was also an Education Section (for school and college youth), a Women's Section (for women's organizations), an Agricultural Section (for farm organizations), and a Retail Section (for stores and retail associations).[117]

The government was least successful in raising funds from unorganized clienteles. As a report on the Fifth War Loan drive noted, "individuals and unincorporated business groups turned in by far the poorest performance."[118] The Treasury Under Secretary, Daniel Bell, contrasted selling bonds to institutional investors with selling them to individuals:

> The two jobs are entirely different. Getting subscriptions from corporations and insurance companies is relatively easy. There are only a few hundred thousand such companies to reach and they don't need much selling.
>
> But individuals present an entirely different problem. There are 40 million people who will subscribe before this month is over. They have to be reached by six million volunteer salesmen, mostly by personal interview. That is the real work of the drive.[119]

The government nonetheless pursued these least productive sales and pursued them vigorously, as is evidenced by the planning involved in the sale of war bonds, the organization of the war loan campaigns, and the publicity and advertising accompanying the loan drives. Only *eight* people out of every hundred did not know that the Sixth War Loan drive was in progress, for example.[120] But as the historian John Morton Blum observes, the war

---

[116] Joe Swire, Labor Section, "Labor's Part in the Savings Bonds Program," 18 September 1946 [no file folder], Box 25, HF.

[117] *Treasury Annual Report, 1945*, 250–51.

[118] "Sources of Funds for the Sixth War Loan," p. 4, Draft of 22 August 1944, file "6th War Loan Planning," Box 1, WFD.

[119] Daniel Bell, Radio Broadcast over the Blue Network, at 10:15 P.M. EWT, 13 December 1944, file "7th War Loan—Planning," Box 1, War Loan Drives—Planning, WFD.

[120] "Forward to the Seventh War Loan," p. 4, file "7th War Loan—Planning," Box 1, War Loan Drives—Planning, WFD; emphasis added.

bond campaigns were used more for selling the war than the war was used for selling government securities.[121]

The wartime U.S. government, desperate for funding, financed the war by selling and marketing its debt instead of by extracting resources through law and coercion. Curiously, here was a nation of over a hundred million persons, a major world power, leaving to voluntary efforts the provision of the funds with which to fight a total war. We would expect the government to rely on the major financial institutions, and not on the voluntary efforts of millions of individual Americans—the six million local and state-level Defense Savings Staff personnel voluntarily selling U.S. securities,[122] and the 85 million registered owners of U.S. savings bonds.[123]

The Ratchet Effect in Public Finance

The persistence of the change in U.S. public finance after the war years was amply manifest in the indicators of the federal bureaucracy, government-society ties, and the administration of public finance. There was also a shift in the political agenda, consistent with the anticipated effects of hegemonic war on state-building.

Consider that the combined employment of the Bureau of Internal Revenue and the Bureau of Public Debt rose from 24,438 employees in 1940 to 31,060 in 1941, and to 62,222 in 1945. After the war, combined Bureau of Internal Revenue and Bureau of Public Debt employment declined to 58,114 persons in 1949 and then climbed back to 61,221 by 1950 (see Table 4.3). The ratcheting in the size of the postwar government is clearly evident in the personnel totals in the Bureau of Internal Revenue, the Bureau of Public Debt, and the Treasury Department.

The combined budgets similarly expanded from $66 million in 1940 to $212 million in 1945, and then increased to $282 million by 1950. Meanwhile, the Internal Revenue and Public Debt budgets took an increasingly higher proportion of total Treasury funds, from a little over one-third of the Treasury budget in 1940 to over two-thirds in 1945, and to over three-quarters by 1950 (see Table 4.4).[124]

---

[121] Blum, *V Was for Victory*, 16–45.

[122] *Treasury Annual Report, 1945*, 45; Ted R. Gamble, National Director, War Finance Division, "For Clip Sheet (Press)," n.d. file "Victory Loan Planning," Box 1, War Loan Drives—Planning, WFD. The figure of six million persons was used repeatedly by the Treasury, but this figure was not broken down into regions or types of volunteers. Nor was the author able to locate an account of how the number of volunteers rose and fell over the course of the war.

[123] Studenski and Krooss, *Financial History*, 453; Murphy, *National Debt*, 198. The Treasury repeatedly reported the number of bondholders as eighty-five million, citing an unpublished Federal Reserve Board survey of registered owners of bonds.

[124] Prices rose by 33.7 percent over the same period—slightly more than the 28 percent increase in the combined budgets. The price index (100 = 1967) stood at 53.9 in 1945 and at

TABLE 4.3
Finance Employment (Field and Department)

Fiscal Year	Internal Revenue	Public Debt	Finance Total	% USG	Total Treasury
1940	24,417	2,021	26,438	2.5	73,171
1941	28,563	2,497	31,060	2.2	84,984
1942	29,065	(NA)	—	—	68,196
1943	36,338	(NA)	—	—	82,093
1944	46,171	(NA)	—	—	94,292
1945	49,814	12,408	62,222	1.6	97,112
1946	59,693	9,753	69,446	2.6	107,359
1947	52,830	8,848	61,678	2.9	95,294
1948	52,143	7,990	60,133	2.9	86,763
1949	52,266	5,848	58,114	2.8	85,409
1950	55,551	4,670	61,221	3.1	89,065

Sources: Annual Reports of the Secretary of the Treasury.
Notes: Figures cover numbers on payroll. "Internal Revenue" is the Bureau of Internal Revenue (later the Internal Revenue Service). "Public Debt" refers to the Bureau of Public Debt in the Fiscal Division of the Department of the Treasury. "% USG" represents Internal Revenue and Public Debt employment totals as a percentage of non-defense governmental employment. Yearly figures are for the end of the fiscal year (e.g., "1941" equals personnel employed as of 30 June 1941).

Note, though, the different fates that befell the Bureau of Internal Revenue and the Bureau of Public Debt in the postwar years. The budget of the Bureau of Internal Revenue grew from $177 million in 1946 to $230 million in 1950, even as Bureau employment declined slightly, whereas the Public Debt budget declined from $84 million in 1946 to $52 million in 1950, while its employment was halved. There was thus a clear ratcheting of the Bureau of Internal Revenue's budget and employment but less ratcheting for the Bureau of Public Debt (even as the postwar employment and budget figures of the Bureau of Public Debt remained well above their prewar marks).

There was a similarly transparent ratcheting in government-society relations. Whereas 14.6 million individuals filed income tax returns in 1940, 23 million persons filed returns in 1941, 36 million in 1942, 43 million in 1943, 47 million in 1944, and 50 million in 1945—more than four times as many taxpayers as in 1940. Nor did the end of the war produce much change in the extent of income taxation: 53 million individuals filed tax returns in 1946, in comparison to 52 million persons in 1948 and 53 million in 1950. The

72.1 in 1950, for a gain of 34 percent ("Consumer Price Indexes (BLS)—All Items, 1800 to 1970, and by Groups, 1913 to 1970," Series E 135–166, Historical Statistics, 210).

TABLE 4.4
Finance Expenditures (dollars)

Fiscal Year	Internal Revenue	Public Debt	Combined Budgets	% USG	Total Treasury
1940	59,105,855	6,761,884	65,867,739	0.91	177,221,645
1941	66,902,269	7,294,684	74,196,952	1.06	204,623,379
1942	74,161,572	25,051,271	99,212,843	0.89	159,496,664
1943	95,148,549	47,837,684	142,986,233	0.90	224,600,436
1944	130,069,166	86,374,846	216,444,012	1.14	285,181,210
1945	138,437,382	73,303,821	211,741,203	1.19	300,015,968
1946	170,827,886	84,250,000	255,077,886	1.48	342,644,945
1947	200,704,624	65,300,000	266,004,624	1.10	401,292,443
1948	183,731,060	64,913,000	248,644,060	1.18	380,093,119
1949	209,205,715	56,636,128	265,841,843	1.04	395,716,620
1950	230,408,200	52,000,000	282,408,000	1.08	362,371,937

Sources: Department of the Treasury *Annual Reports,* except for federal budget figures, which are from "Outlays of the Federal Government," Series Y 457–465, *Historical Statistics,* 1114.

Notes: The difference between expenditures and budgets was about $3.5 million a year on average; for all but one year, the expenditures came in under budget. "Total Treasury" figures include supplemental emergency budgets. Total 1949 Treasury expenditures are listed as $395,568,810 in the 1950 *Annual Report.*

number of corporations filing taxes fell over the course of the war, however, declining from 517,000 companies in 1940 to 480,000 in 1942, 447,000 in 1944, and 454,000 in 1945. After the war, 526,000 corporations filed tax returns in 1946, 630,000 did so in 1948, and 666,000 did so in 1950.[125]

Consider, too, the amount collected in individual and corporate tax receipts: individual income tax receipts rose from a per capita average of $99 in 1940 to $332 in 1943 and to $341 in 1945; after the war, individual tax receipts dipped to an average of $280 per person in 1949 but still remained at levels well above those of the early 1940s. Meanwhile, corporate tax receipts (including excess profits taxes) rose from $4,533 per company in 1940 to $10,652 each in 1943 and then dropped to $9,935 each in 1945. After the

[125] "Corporate Income Tax Returns: 1909 to 1970," Series Y 381–392, "Individual Income Tax Returns: 1944 to 1970," Series Y 393–401, and "Individual Income Tax Returns: 1913 to 1943," Series Y 402–411, *Historical Statistics,* 1109–10. The number of taxable returns also increased considerably over the course of the war, although it started from a smaller base: 7 million individuals in 1940, 27 million in 1942, and 42 million in 1945. After the war, 38 million of those filing income taxes owed money to the federal government in 1946, and 38 million also paid taxes in both 1948 and 1950. Corporate taxable returns rose as well over the course of the decade, from 221,000 of the 517,000 companies filing in 1940 to 270,000 of the 480,000 filing in 1942 and 303,000 of the 454,000 filing in 1945. After the war, 359,000 corporations owed taxes in 1946, 396,000 did in 1948, and 426,000 did in 1950.

TABLE 4.5
Tax Receipts

Year	Individual (000)	Corporate (000)	Tax per Individual	Tax per Corporation	Corporate Tax/ Individual Tax
1940	$ 1,440,967	$ 2,144,292	$ 99	$ 4,533	1.48
1941	3,815,415	3,744,568	148	7,984	0.98
1942	8,823,041	4,337,728	242	9,814	0.49
1943	14,449,441	4,479,166	332	10,652	0.31
1944	16,216,401	4,353,620	344	10,555	0.24
1945	17,050,378	4,182,705	341	9,935	0.25
1946	16,075,913	8,606,695	304	17,523	0.53
1947	18,076,281	10,981,482	328	19,901	0.61
1948	15,441,529	11,920,260	296	20,060	0.77
1949	14,538,141	9,817,308	280	15,968	0.67
1950	18,374,922	15,929,488	346	25,313	0.87

Sources: "Individual Income Tax Returns: 1944 to 1970," Series Y 393–401; "1913 to 1943," Series Y, 402–411; "Corporate Income Tax Reurns: 1909 to 1970," Series Y 381–392, *Historical Statistics*, 1110, 1109.

Notes: "Individual" figures are total annual federal income taxes paid by individual taxpayers. "Corporate" are income taxes paid by corporations after credits. "Tax Per Individual" is the average tax paid per individual return. "Corporate Tax/Individual Tax" is the ratio of corporate tax receipts to receipts from individual taxpayers.

war, average corporate tax receipts increased to $17,500 in 1946, to $20,100 in 1948, and to $25,300 by 1950 (see Table 4.5).

An equivalent effect occurred with the ownership of savings bonds. Although the Treasury Department reported 85 million registered bond-holders in 1945 and 75 million bondholders in 1950, these figures included repeat registrations.[126] As another indicator of the number of individual bondholders, 2 million employees were on payroll deduction plans in 1940, 27.6 million persons participated in payroll plans in June 1944 (deducting a total of $540 million—or 10.6 percent of their income—from their pay), and 5 million individuals were on payroll savings plans by 1947.

Note the contrast, then: while the numbers of individual taxpayers and bondholders soared during the war years, the number of taxpayers remained about the same between 1945 and 1950, but the number of individuals on payroll plans dropped off after the war to almost prewar levels. Even comparing the 85 million figure for the number of bondholders in 1945 and the 75 million figure for the number of bondholders in 1950, there is still a

[126] W. H. Neal, "Applying Public Relations Techniques to the Savings Bond Program," 29 March 1950, in "Addresses at the U.S. Savings Bonds Independence Drive Conference" [no file folder], Box 24, HF.

significant difference between the *loss* of ten million bondholders in the years from 1945 to 1950 and the *addition* of three million persons on the income tax rolls over the same postwar years.

The postwar histories of the intensity of individual tax payments and the ownership of government securities repeat this pattern of parallel changes during the war and diverging trajectories after the war. In 1945 individual taxpayers paid almost three and one-half times, on average, what they paid in 1940—even with the large extension of the tax base—and after the war, the receipts from individual income taxes remained almost constant on an absolute basis and declined moderately in real terms. Corporate taxes more than doubled over the same period, rising from $4,500 in 1940 to almost $10,000 per tax receipt in 1945, and then to over $25,000 per tax return by 1950. In contrast, the intensity of bond ownership (using the payroll figures) went from about $5,000 per investor in 1940 to a more diffuse $2,300 each by 1945; individuals owned an average of more than $12,000 in government securities by 1947. (The total value of individual holdings of U.S. government securities rose from $9.4 billion in 1940, to $57.6 billion in 1945, and to $66.3 billion in 1950.) If we go by the 85 million and 75 million figures, the average individual investment in U.S. securities came to $688 per bondholder in 1945 and $896 each in 1950, again showing the increasing intensity of postwar bond ownership and the decreasing intensity of postwar tax payments.

The ratchet effect from World War II was further evident in institutional bond holdings. Banks, insurance companies, industrial corporations, and other investors greatly increased their holdings of U.S. government securities during the 1940s. Commercial banks owned $16.1 billion in U.S. securities in 1940 and over five times as much—$84 billion worth—by 1945 (see Table 4.6). After the war, the commercial banks' holdings of government securities came to $65 billion in 1948 and $66 billion in 1950, according to the Treasury's figures (Federal Reserve figures show the commercial banks owning $54 billion in government securities in 1946, $42 billion in 1948, and $41 billion in 1950).[127]

Insurance companies also increased their ownership of U.S. securities during the war, owning $6.5 billion of government securities in 1940 and $22.7 billion in 1945. They, too, mostly retained their stake in government securities after the war, with $25.1 billion invested in 1946, $23.1 billion in 1948, and $20.1 billion in 1950. Industrial corporations similarly increased their holdings of U.S. government securities, which rose from $2.1 billion in 1940 to $21.9 billion in 1945—holdings that they, too, mostly retained after the war (see Table 4.6).

---

[127] U.S. Board of Governors of the Federal Reserve System, *Banking and Monetary Statistics*, Table 6.1, 378–79.

TABLE 4.6
Ownership of the Public Debt (billions of dollars)

Fiscal Year	Total Debt	Individual Holdings	Banks Comm.	Banks Fed.	Insur. Cos.	Industr. Corps.	Misc. Accounts	U.S Gov
1940	47.9	9.4	16.1	2.5	6.5	2.1	4.2	7.
1941	54.7	10.6	19.7	2.2	7.1	2.0	4.7	8.
1942	76.5	17.3	26.0	2.6	9.2	4.9	5.9	10.
1943	139.5	29.6	52.2	7.2	13.1	12.9	10.2	14.
1944	201.1	44.6	68.4	14.9	17.3	19.9	16.9	19.
1945	256.8	57.6	84.2	21.8	22.7	21.9	23.8	24.
1946	268.6	61.7	84.4	23.8	25.1	17.6	26.8	29.
1947	255.2	64.9	70.0	21.9	24.8	13.9	26.8	32.
1948	250.1	64.3	64.6	21.4	23.1	13.5	27.6	35.
1949	250.8	65.7	63.0	19.3	20.8	15.1	28.5	38.
1950	255.2	66.3	65.6	18.3	20.1	18.3	28.8	37.

Source: *Treasury Annual Report, 1950*, 689, Table 113, "Ownership of Governmental Securitie
Note: "Miscellaneous Accounts" includes holdings by mutual savings banks; state, local, and ter
torial governments; savings and loan associations; non-profit organizations; corporate pension tr
funds; and securities dealers and brokers, plus investments of foreign balances and international a
counts in the United States.

With the ongoing need to refinance the public debt, the Treasury Department continued to plan meticulously, organize sales meetings, advertise commercially (with J. Walter Thompson Company and Young and Rubicam), distribute brochures and pamphlets to its sales committees, and employ survey researchers (the University of Michigan's Survey Research Center).[128] "As we did in wartime," said Secretary Vinson, "so must we in peacetime rely for the major part of the Bond promotion and sales operation upon volunteers in the state, county, and city Savings Bonds committees and those who work with them."[129] President Truman hoped that the savings bonds sales committees would "put forth the same sort of effort you did when we were running these Bond Drives in wartime. You are running this Bond Drive for peacetime, and it is just as important to win the peace as it ever was to win the war."[130]

[128] See "Proceedings—National Conference on U.S. Savings Bonds" [no file folder], Box 24, HF.
[129] John Snyder, "Voluntary Support, Mainspring of the Security Loan," 18 March 1948, p. 4, in "Proceedings—National Conference on U.S. Savings Bonds" [no file folder], Box 25, HF.
[130] President Harry S. Truman, 18 March 1948, in "Proceedings—National Conference on U.S. Savings Bonds," p. 35 [no file folder], Box 25, HF.

The Treasury thus maintained its liaisons with major societal organizations, especially the banks, major business corporations, and the unions. The Director of the Savings and Investment Section of the U.S. Savings Bonds Division noted in late 1946 that "[t]he American Bankers Association has gone 'all out' for the Savings Bonds program—they have endorsed it publicly and with letters direct to members. . . . [The] Chairman of the ABA Savings Bonds Committee and . . . [the] Editor of Banking and Secretary of the Committee, *as well as* the Regional and State ABA Chairman have given much time and thought to the continued sales of Savings bonds."[131]

The Treasury continued to work closely with individual business leaders so as to encourage companies to increase their payroll savings plans. Consider that among the persons attending a December 1947 meeting of the Industrial Advisory Committee with the Secretary of the Treasury were chief executive officers, company presidents, and executive vice presidents from General Motors, General Electric Corporation, John Hancock Mutual Life Insurance Company, Bethlehem Steel, General Foods, Shell Oil Company, Swift & Company, Scott Paper Company, Kimberly Clark Corporation, Riggs National Bank, and other companies.[132]

The labor unions again cooperated. The AFL's William Green gave his support "as evidence of the deep interest of millions of workingmen and women in the aim and purpose [of selling savings bonds]." He was "pleased to be associated with those in the Treasury Department" and noted that the Payroll Savings Plan promoted a "most praiseworthy" American objective: it developed the "spirit of the masses of the people to promote . . . a new understanding and a new appraisal of the value of liberty, freedom and democracy. . . . They became more patriotic; they developed that intense solidified patriotic spirit that was reflected in their devotion and service as members of the army of production during the war period."[133]

The CIO was equally enthusiastic. Its Secretary-Treasurer found himself "in a most unusual position [of] . . . being in agreement with a lot of bankers." "[F]rom the first day bonds went on sale to assist this nation in the crisis [WWII] that confronted us . . . [the CIO] has been all-out in its support of bond purchases by our members and by the public generally." Although the CIO representative took management to task for not supporting the payroll plans as it had in wartime and noted that low-wage union mem-

---

[131] Morris M. Townsend, "Banks and the Savings Bonds Program," 18 September 1946 [no file folder], Box 25, HF; emphasis in original.

[132] Minutes of the Industrial Committee meeting with Secretary of the Treasury Snyder, 10 December 1947, Washington, D.C., p. 8 [no file folder], Box 25, HF.

[133] William Green, "Pledge of Support for Payroll Savings," 19 March 1947, p. 42 [no file folder], Box 25, HF. Also see Green, "Now Is the Time to Save," 18 March 1948, p. 16, in "Proceedings—National Conference on U.S. Savings Bonds."

bers could not afford to sacrifice their standard of living in order to buy bonds, the CIO was nonetheless "in earnest support of our Government, our Treasury Department, in trying to get this war paid for and maintain us in such a position that we can make other wars of the kind we have gone through quite impossible."[134]

As it had during the loan drives of the Second World War, the Treasury used "posters, stuffers, payroll and bank pieces" in its campaigns of the late 1940s, as well as radio, motion picture, and television messages.[135] As during the wartime campaigns, the public relations services were provided free: the National Director of the Savings Bonds Division estimated the value of the free publicity at $9.5 million a year for magazines, $6.5 million a year for newspapers, $16 million a year for the radio, and $2 million a year for outdoor advertising. Advertisers further pledged to donate 3,000 large highway posters and 70,000 four-color cards to go on busses and streetcars; and 1,100 magazines were to contribute to the program. The Treasury estimated that the free space and time donated during June and July 1948 would come to $10 million.[136] Among the first Security Loan Volunteers were the cartoonists Rube Goldberg and Ernie Bushmiller (the creator of the comic strip "Nancy").[137]

Indicative of the concerted public-private effort behind the postwar bond campaigns was the planned strategy for the new Bond-a-Month campaign:

> Eleven hundred of the nation's radio stations—and that is . . . practically all of them—have ordered the new Savings Bond transcribed series "Guest Star." These fifteen-minute records, for which the top talent of the nation has been donated, will be keyed during the months of June and July to the easy, automatic bond savings campaign. . . . The "Guest Star" series will be illuminated by such performers as Bing Crosby, Bob Hope, Fibber McGee and Molly, Red Skelton, Burns and Allen and others of equal caliber.
>
> In addition, to take advantage of short and frequent air announcements, a series of short announcements will be sent to radio stations to be used during the June and July period. Short dramatic portrayals of professional men and other self-employed persons, who are prospects for payroll savings, of the Bond-a-Month plan, will be transcribed and sent to hundreds of stations on a request basis.

[134] Harry Read, "Thrift and Security Through Payroll Savings," 19 March 1947, pp. 62–63 [no file folder], Box 25, HF. Also see Philip Murray, "The Best Means of Saving," 18 March 1948, pp. 12–13, in "Proceedings—National Conference on U.S. Savings Bonds."

[135] Leon J. Markham, Director of Sales, U.S. Savings Bonds Division, 29 March 1950, in "Addresses at the U.S. Savings Bonds Independence Drive Conference," [no file folder] Box 24, HF. Also see transcript of the State Chairmen's Conference of the U.S. Savings Bonds Division, 18–19 October 1948 [no file folder], Box 24, HF.

[136] Thomas S. Repplier, "Advertising Support," pp. 31–34, 19 March 1947 [no file folder], Box 25, HF.

[137] "Proceedings—National Conference on U.S. Savings Bonds," p. 33.

Now for the big commercial shows—the shows to which Americans listen in such volume as to have a Jack Benny-Fred Allen feud become everyday, dinner table conversation. No amount of money can buy time on these shows. The advertisers have spent thousands of dollars, and in most cases years, building up large listening audiences. They represent to the advertiser a franchise which is priceless.

Yet during the period, the June-July period, extensive savings bond messages on the new pitch will appear on these network shows.

Well, now, how is this possible? It's possible because The Advertising Council has secured an agreement from virtually all advertisers having commercial network shows to carry a message allocated by The Advertising Council every sixth time the show is on the air. That's where the public-service messages that you hear come from. To give you some idea of the value of this plan, it reaches the staggering total of three hundred million listener-impressions per week—a listener impression being one message heard once by one listener.[138]

The Savings Bonds Division went so far as to deliberately attract school children to its campaigns in order to get to the parents, just as the War Finance Division had done during the Second World War.[139]

But the postwar loan campaigns, for all their hype, were miniature versions of their wartime predecessors. The amounts to be raised in the postwar campaigns were a fraction of those of the war loan drives. Whereas the goal of the two 1945 loan drives was $25 billion, the goal of the E, F, and G bond sales in 1946 was $8 billion.[140] Whereas 47 percent of the population bought bonds in the Seventh Loan Drive of 1945, only 21 percent participated in 1946.[141] Sales of $1,000 E bonds in 1946 came to only two-thirds the amount of 1945, and sales of bonds priced $200 and less came to one-third the previous year's amount. Community and farm sales went from $3.1 billion in 1945 to $2.5 billion in 1946, and payroll sales fell even further, declining from $6.8 billion in 1945 to just $1.7 billion in 1946.[142] Corre-

---

[138] Repplier, "Advertising Support," pp. 30–31.

[139] U.S. Savings Bonds Division, Minutes of the Industrial Advisory Committee meeting with the Secretary of the Treasury Snyder," 10 December 1947, p. 40 [no file folder], Box 25, HF.

[140] Vernon Clark, "Opening Remarks," State Directors Assembly, 18 September 1946, p. 5 [no file folder], Box 25, HF.

[141] "Appraisal of Postwar Bond Selling," September 1946, p. 112 [no file folder], Box 25, HF. The appraisal was based on a national survey of July and August 1946 and was conducted by the Division of Special Surveys, Bureau of Agricultural Economics, U.S. Department of Agriculture.

[142] Division of Research and Statistics, Office of the Secretary of the Treasury, "Analysis of the Savings Bond Program," March 1947, in "Savings Bonds Conference," 19 March 1947 [no file folder], Box 25, HF. The 1946 survey interviewed 2,263 persons; 2,455 persons were interviewed for the Seventh War Loan drive.

spondingly, the U.S. Savings Bonds Division's Washington staff was cut back from 1,700 persons (in the Division's wartime predecessor, the War Finance Division) to 484 persons in 1945, 111 persons in 1946, and fewer than 100 persons by 1947.

In short, there was a decided ratchet effect in both the bureaucratic and relational dimensions of the management of the public debt. The Treasury Department continued to work with the groups it had in wartime and kept its management techniques. The indicators of the bureaucratic and relational state fell from their wartime levels but nonetheless remained far above their prewar levels. There was also the ratcheting in the bureaucracy and the extent and intensity of income taxation, and the observed contrast between the intensity of the ownership of securities (declining during the war and increasing moderately afterwards) and that of the individual tax burden (rising during the war and declining afterwards).

The ratcheted state-building in public finance played out differently with respect to the instrumental state. Major changes included:

• The Revenue Act of 1941 introduced the short form for filing income taxes, by incorporating "Supplement T of the Internal Revenue Code," which provided a table of tax liabilities in Form 1040A for those with gross incomes of $3,000 or less. The Treasury proceeded to print 21 million copies of a pamphlet entitled "How to File Your Income Taxes THE SIMPLE WAY."[143] Congress further simplified tax payment in 1944.

• The withholding of taxes on a current-year basis was introduced, beginning in 1943 with the Ruml Plan.

• The Bureau extended the use of punch-card tabulating machines after 1947, and also installed "several high speed electronic calculators" in collectors' offices. Procedural improvements included the combination of income withholding and Federal Insurance contributions on the same employers' form and the initiation of tax audit exchanges between the state and federal governments. Management savings in 1950 were estimated at 480 man-years.[144]

• The Treasury set up a management studies committee in early 1948 to advise the Commissioner of Internal Revenue on management problems. Then, on 2 August 1949, a Bureau of the Budget report found that the Bureau of Internal Revenue was badly organized (with six different field organizations and a dearth of cooperation between Enforcement and Collections), used outmoded methods and procedures, and was too independent of the other bureaus in the Department.[145] The Treasury Department subsequently brought in outside consultants

---

[143] 16 December 1941: Morgenthau, Diaries, Vol. 473.
[144] *Treasury Annual Report, 1950*, 105–6.
[145] "Summary of Bureau Discussion of the Principal Operating Problems of the Treasury

(Cresap, McCormick & Paget) to evaluate the Bureau's programs and procedures.[146]

• In January 1950, the Internal Revenue Service (the renamed Bureau of Internal Revenue) combined the administration of income tax withholding with the collection of social security taxes.

The administration of the public debt changed at least as much as did that of income taxation. Under Reorganization Plan No. 3, effective on 4 June 1940, the Roosevelt Administration established a Fiscal Service of the Department of the Treasury which included the Bureau of Public Debt. The Bureau of Public Debt established a Chicago office in early 1942, soon after the United States entered the war, in order to handle the processing of U.S. savings bonds. The Chicago office, containing approximately half of the Bureau's employees, conducted virtually all business relating to U.S. savings bonds once the bonds were issued.[147] Other wartime measures included the elimination of tax exemption for U.S. government securities (beginning in 1941), the introduction of nonmarketable securities (the Series E, F, and G savings bonds), and the issuance of tax savings notes.

More changes occurred after the war, when the magnitude of the wartime expansion of the savings bond program caused a backlog of approximately 18 months' work for the Bureau of Public Debt. The Bureau of Public Debt began to decentralize operations in 1947 so as to be able to accommodate its now-expanded functions. It first delegated its overlapping responsibilities with the Federal Reserve Banks wholly to the Federal Reserve, which in turn consolidated operations for the issuance of and interest payments on savings bonds.[148]

Department," file "Management Improvement," Series 39.13a, Estimates Division, Budgetary Administration, Treasury Department Fiscal Years 1941–52, General Subject File, Budget Records.

An internal memo stated that "[i]t is believed that the present organizational structure constitutes a brake on efficient operation. This problem has been under study for a considerable period of time with an early decision unlikely." Furthermore, "[u]nder existing procedures considerably more than half the Bureau's appropriation is utilized in so-called service functions. The present system is generally recognized to be antiquated and costly. The solution lies in the adoption of a mechanized program, the simplification of procedures, a revised approach to the present accounting concepts and methods, and a general reshuffling in responsibility, including the decentralization of fiscal operations" (Memorandum of S. W. Crosby to P. R. Taylor and B. F. Schmid, 15 July 1949, file "Management Improvement," Series 39.13a, Budget Records).

[146] The Treasury Department also contracted with McKinsey & Co. to conduct an overall management improvement study.

[147] The Chicago office did not handle the audit of U.S. savings bonds when they were redeemed through the Federal Reserve Banks prior to release of registration.

[148] See Bureau of Public Debt, "7. Administrative Changes from 1946 On," Attachment 7(b)(1), pp. 1–3, file "Bureau of Public Debt," Box 84, Snyder Papers.

The Treasury then revised procedures for redeeming and reissuing Series A through E, F, and G savings bonds, thereby reducing personnel requirements.[149] Savings in the Bureau of Public Debt "totaled $190,000 in 1947, almost $2 million in 1948, $2.8 million in 1949, and an estimated $2.9 million in 1950."[150] New programs initiated during 1950—as opposed to those resulting from improvements begun in preceding years—resulted in savings of another half-million dollars.[151]

In 1950, the Bureau of Public Debt proceeded to abolish its regional offices in St. Louis and Los Angeles and transferred the issuance of duplicate savings bonds (arising out of claims cases) from the Bureau of Public Debt in Washington to the Federal Reserve Bank of Chicago.

The Savings Bonds Division also used surveys and reports from the state directors and from salespeople to improve the effectiveness of the bond campaigns. The Treasury examined basic sales policies, the role of the national committees, and the amount of information it was providing to the regional committees. Other recommendations for improving the management of the sale of government securities addressed advertising, agricultural sales, the role of the banks, community activities, the school programs, organized labor, and payroll savings.[152]

In short, the war caused an expansion of both central and branch operations for income taxation and for the sale of government securities (consistent with the social security case). But most of the consolidation and refinement of the administration of the Bureau of Internal Revenue and Bureau of Public Debt came afterwards, in the postwar years (and the Bureau of Internal Revenue would not be comprehensively reorganized until 1952). Improvements in the instruments of taxation and borrowing, like the refinements in the regulation of labor-management relations and in the social security system, came both during and after the war.

A look at the change in the bureaucratic and relational dimensions of the state thus reveals substantial change during the Second World War with respect to the budgets and employment figures of the Bureau of Public Debt and the Bureau of Internal Revenue, the numbers of taxpayers and individual owners of securities, and the per capita income tax and ownership of government securities. Far more people owned part of the U.S. govern-

[149] *Treasury Annual Report, 1948*, 87. Also see "Savings Effected on an Annual Basis Through Procedural and Other Changes in the Period of Fiscal Year 1947," in Bureau of Public Debt, "7. Administrative Changes from 1946 On," Attachment 7(b)(1), pp. 1–3.

[150] *Treasury Annual Report, 1949*, 48.

[151] *Treasury Annual Report, 1950*, 92.

[152] "Summary of Opinions and Recommendations Expressed at the July 19–21, 1949, Duluth Conference," attachment, Leon J. Markham, Memorandum to State Directors, 29 July 1949 [no file folder], Box 24, HF.

ment, and far more people owed the U.S. government part of their earnings. The scale of the income tax and public debt bureaucracies reflected these realities. There was also substantial wartime change in the instruments for administering both tax policy and federal borrowing.

As we should expect from national government embedded at once in the international system of states and in domestic society, the ratcheted state-building of the war years was caused by permanent shifts in the government's environment. In terms of the international environment, the reality of the American victory in World War II and the emergence of the United States as a superpower had great influence on government expenditures—and hence on public finance. Whereas international obligations amounted to a total of 24 percent of government spending in 1940 (18 percent for defense and 6 percent for veterans), internationally related commitments amounted to 64 percent of the U.S. government's 1948 budget (32 percent for defense, 14 percent for international aid, and 18 percent for veterans' benefits). Defense spending in 1948 came to more than five times the $1.8 billion budget for the military in 1940—and the 1948 defense budget was at its postwar low of $11.9 billion (down from the $80 billion budget of 1945).[153] As Treasury Secretary Vinson told the House Ways and Means Committee soon after the war,

> Every one of us wants to see an end to the burden of war as soon as possible. But these burdens do not end easily or quickly. . . . Even after completing demobilization, we must meet our obligations to the veterans and to the 85 million bond-holders. . . . Finally, we are determined never again to be caught off guard. The peace must be won. That means occupation of enemy countries to make them powerless and to put them on the road to a peaceful instead of a warlike future. It also means a military establishment large enough to maintain the peace. . . . These facts make it clear, first, that expenditures cannot fall immediately to their eventual postwar level and, second, that when we do reach a postwar plateau it is bound to be far higher than the prewar expenditure level. . . . I regard the modernization of our tax structure as the foundation of our entire program to reach and maintain full employment after the war.[154]

The federal government, given its new responsibilities, had to maintain its principal financial resources, revenues from income taxation and returns from the sale of government securities. Policies of public finance had to adjust to the reality of the bipolar world.[155] As the Council of Economic

[153] The 1940 defense budget exceeded the annual budgets of the 1930s by at least $400 million.

[154] Statement of Secretary Vinson before the Ways and Means Committee of the House of Representatives, 1 October 1945, in "OF 21 (1945)," pp. 1–2, Box 170, Official File, Truman Papers.

[155] See, for example, "Discussion Meeting, Members of Joint Committee on the Economic

Advisers wrote, "The people of the United States have shown strong support for a national policy in international relations. Added to our European Recovery Program, we must now strengthen our forces of military defense through financial outlays so large as to threaten a Treasury deficit in fiscal 1949 or at least the wiping out of the surplus if the tax reduction proposed in this bill were to take effect."[156]

The domestic environment also changed in major ways as a result of the Second World War's effects on the pattern of securities ownership and the role of the federal income tax in public finance and fiscal policy. A comparison of the classes of securities issued between 1940 and 1950 reveals the altered proportions of Treasury debt held in bills, certificates of indebtedness, bank-restricted bonds, Treasury notes, and nonmarketable issues (especially U.S. savings bonds). Whereas there was only $1.3 billion outstanding in T-bills, $26.6 billion in bank-eligible bonds, and $3.2 billion total in nonmarketable issues in 1940, by 1945 the Treasury had $17 billion in T-bills, $70 billion in bank-eligible bonds, and $56 billion total in nonmarketable issues outstanding (see Table 4.7). By 1950, the Treasury had placed $14 billion in T-bills, $53 billion in bank-eligible bonds, and $68 billion in nonmarketable public issues.

The Treasury started to opt for shorter-term securities. After the Eighth War Loan drive, for instance, the Treasury ceased to issue marketable securities of longer than twelve months' maturity. Such policies caused the volume of short-term floating debt to constitute 50 percent of the marketable debt outstanding by 1952. The increased reliance on short-term debt issues not only made the repeated handling and turnover of the debt necessary, but it also pointed to the potentially destabilizing economic effects of financing the public debt in such a fashion. Interest rates became even more important.[157]

Abbott explains the qualitative changes occurring in public indebtedness as a result of the quantitative change in the public debt:

> When the total of federal obligations outstanding exceeds that of all other kinds of debt, . . . when Treasury securities constitute something like half the assets of banks and insurance companies . . . [w]hen [the debt] is made up of various kinds of issues which differ among themselves, not only in their rates of interest and lengths of their maturities, but in other respects, such as marketability, eligibility

---

Report with Business Leaders," 7 April 1948, file "Business Groups," Box 6, Keyserling Papers; The Council of Economic Advisers, "Memorandum to the President," 2 October 1948, file "QR, 3rd Quarter, 1948," Box 2, Keyserling Papers.

[156] Letter of the Council of Economic Advisers to President Truman, 31 March 1948, file "April 2, 1948," Bill Files, Truman Papers.

[157] *Treasury Annual Report, 1950*, 45–50, 201.

for purchase by different classes of buyers, the prerogatives attached to them, and the purposes for which they were issued. . . . [w]hen certain types of issues are continuously offered at fixed prices . . . when all types are immediately convertible into cash, either at fixed or almost fixed prices. . . . [and w]hen the federal government holds a large and growing portion of its own obligations in its own investment accounts as reserves against its own liability . . . the debt ceases to be simply an outlet for the investment funds of persons and financial institutions. . . . It becomes . . . an institution itself. . . . its management acquires a sort of independent significance.[158]

The figures on the ownership of the public debt by individuals, commercial banks, the Federal Reserve Banks, insurance companies, industrial corporations, and the U.S. government document the existence and persistence of this shift (refer to Table 4.6). The new and prominent presence of pension funds, insurance companies, banks, and industrial corporations as owners of government securities meant that they could now, at short notice, affect the market for government securities and thereby influence interest rates.

Individuals were willing to hold on to government bonds after the war, even as their value was being eroded by inflation.[159] E bond redemptions came to only 20 percent of the average amount outstanding in fiscal 1946, 14 percent in 1947, and 11 percent in 1949.[160] Eccles suggests that the retention of assets in the form of government bonds was a result of the experience of the 1930s: fearing deflation, people wanted to save, to keep their savings liquid. As it was, real disposable income in 1949 (after correcting for taxes and prices) was about 50 percent greater than in 1940. The backlog of accumulated individual savings came to about $220 billion at the end of 1949— about three times the 1940 level, and double the real purchasing power.[161] With the reluctance of savers to cash in their E bonds and with the change in the quantity and kinds of assets owned by societal actors, the government was able to keep the institutions used in financing the war, especially given the new demands for federal expenditures.

A second transformation in domestic society, besides the change in the ownership of the public debt, was that the war demonstrated the effectiveness of government spending and income taxation as macroeconomic policy.

---

[158] Abbott, *The Federal Debt*, 4–5.

[159] Blough, *The Federal Taxing Process*, 265.

[160] Murphy, *National Debt*, 225–26.

[161] Eccles, *Beckoning Frontiers*, 415. Milton Friedman and Anna Jacobson Schwartz make the same point (*Monetary History*, 574–85). Also see Thomas B. McCabe, "The Equity Capital Situation," 5 August 1949, file "OF 90, 1949–50," Box 434, Official File, Truman Papers. The Fed was concerned over the sluggish equity market, since individuals were investing in common stocks at far lower rates than in the 1920s.

TABLE 4.7A
Security Classes of the Public Debt, 1940–1945 (millions of dollars)

Class	1940	1941	1942	1943	1944	1945
Interest-Bearing Marketable Issues						
Treasury Bills	1,302	1,603	2,508	11,864	14,734	17,041
Certificates of Indebtedness	—	—	3,096	16,561	28,882	34,136
Treasury Notes	6,383	5,698	6,689	9,168	17,405	23,497
Treasury Bonds						
Bank-Eligible	26,555	30,215	37,202	48,809	58,083	69,693
Bank-Restricted	—	—	882	8,711	21,161	. 36,756
Other	197	196	196	196	196	196
Total	34,436	37,713	50,573	95,310	140,401	181,319
Non-Marketable Issues						
Treasury Notes	—	—	3,015	7,495	9,557	10,136
U.S. Savings Bonds	2,905	4,314	10,188	21,256	34,606	45,586
Other	261	241	308	448	691	505
Total	3,166	4,555	13,510	29,200	44,855	56,226
Total Public Issues	37,602	42,267	64,083	124,509	185,256	237,545

Source: *Treasury Annual Report, 1950*, 493, Table 13.

As the economist Herbert Stein has it, "[t]he war created full employment, deferred the prospect of secular stagnation, provided a respite from the controversies of the New Deal, involved businessmen in the management of government economic policy, and left behind an enormous federal debt, large budgets, and pay-as-you-go taxation. By the end of the war all of the ingredients of the fiscal revolution . . . were present."[162] Indeed, each of the five reasons given by Stein for explaining why tax policy became the preferred instrument of economic stabilization has roots in the experience of the war.

First, the U.S. government successfully used wartime tax policy to fight off the inflationary pressures of the early 1940s. It thereby set the precedent that postwar fiscal policy would be dominated by tax policy. As Secretary Vinson said soon after the war ended, "Taxes should be levied in such a way that they have the least harmful effect on the expansion of business investment and the creation of jobs, because productive employment is the source of our standard of living, of all income, and of the revenue which the Gov-

[162] Stein, *The Fiscal Revolution*, 170.

TABLE 4.7B

Security Classes of the Public Debt, 1946–1950 (millions of dollars)

Class	1946	1947	1948	1949	1950
Interest-Bearing Marketable Issues					
Treasury Bills	17,039	15,775	13,757	11,536	13,533
Certificates of Indebtedness	34,804	25,296	22,588	29,427	18,418
Treasury Notes	18,261	8,142	11,375	3,596	20,404
Treasury Bonds					
Bank-Eligible	65,864	69,686	62,826	60,789	53,159
Bank-Restricted	53,459	49,636	49,636	49,636	49,636
Other	180	166	164	162	160
Total	189,606	168,702	160,346	155,147	155,310
Non-Marketable Issues					
Treasury Notes	6,711	5,560	4,394	4,860	8,472
U.S. Savings Bonds	49,035	51,367	53,274	56,260	57,536
Other	427	2,118	1,838	1,719	1,536
Total	56,173	59,045	59,506	62,839	67,544
Total Public Issues	245,779	227,747	219,852	217,986	222,853

Source: See Table 4.7A.

ernment collects from taxes." Specifically, "Tax policy should be integrated with a fiscal policy designed to prevent inflation and deflation."[163]

Second, the war brought about an expanded government with new veterans' programs, permanently enlarged defense spending, heavy public borrowing, and expanded international obligations that would demand more government resources. Treasury officials and private experts alike recognized that postwar budgets would be greater than the prewar budget. In the words of Budget Director Smith, "The Federal Government will inevitably occupy a larger place in the economy after the war than it did before. Our program for national defense, aid to veterans, and interest in the national debt incurred during the war will all mean large extensions of the Government's activity."[164]

[163] Statement of Secretary Vinson before the Ways and Means Committee of the House of Representatives, 1 October 1945, p. 3, in "OF 21 (1945)," Box 170, Official File, Truman Papers.

[164] Memo of Smith to Rosenman, 23 December 1944, file "Employment [full employment] 1944," Box 71, Bureau of the Budget Fiscal Analysis Division, Series 39.3, Budget Records. Also see Statement of Secretary Vinson before the Ways and Means Committee of the House of Representatives, 1 October 1945, pp. 1–2, in "OF 21 (1945)," Box 170, Official File, Truman Papers.

A third basis for U.S. postwar fiscal policy was that the existing excise taxes, customs revenues, and estate taxes were insufficient to meet the government's funding requirements for the foreseeable future; the (virtually) universal taxation of individual incomes used in wartime had to continue if the U.S. government was to pay for its expanded postwar obligations.

A fourth reason for using income taxation as fiscal policy was the flexibility of the pay-as-you-go system initiated during the war: the withholding of wage incomes allowed for tax legislation to have quick and pervasive effects on macroeconomic outcomes. A reduction in taxes could almost immediately release consumer dollars into the economy, just as an increase in taxes could immediately withdraw income from take-home pay.

Fifth, the revenue-side fiscal policy conducted during the war affected a well-distributed national base of income taxpayers.[165] It reached a vast population of consumers, taxpayers, workers, and citizens. Public works programs, in contrast, would necessarily be tied to particular industrial bases such as highway construction or defense production.

Given the reluctance of Congress to introduce other ways of raising revenue, and given the success of the income tax in raising large amounts of money quickly, it made sense for the government to adjust and refine an existing operating system rather than to introduce new forms of taxation beyond the pay-as-you-go system. With the U.S. government's international obligations in the foreseeable postwar era, especially its commitments to defense and foreign aid, it had to keep the highly effective federal income tax in place. Not until the 1940s did the federal income tax become as inevitable as death.

Accompanying the state-building of the war years and the changes in the United States government's international and national environments were shifts in the political agenda, specifically the acceptance of Keynesian fiscal policy. The political agenda going into the war—the emergency-driven deficit spending by the federal government in the third New Deal of 1937–38 to get the U.S. economy out of the Depression (A)—was unexpectedly and dramatically magnified by the deficit spending of the war years (AW). To continue the trajectory of the third New Deal (with an unemployment rate of 14 percent as late as 1940) would be to predict moderate increases in the public debt, increases directed at relieving unemployment through public works such as the Civilian Conservation Corps and the Works Projects Administration (A').

But the success of the war's expansion of the tax system and the creation of vast amounts of public debt reinforced the record—and thus the expectations—of government responsibility for the national economy: the government provided a gigantic economic stimulus that revealed the benefi-

---

[165] Stein, *The Fiscal Revolution*, 181–83.

cial impact of deficit spending (AW').[166] As Budget Director Harold Smith wrote Sam Rosenman, the President's counsel, "[w]e had full employment during the war. . . . After the war we must maintain full employment."[167]

Keynesianism in the United States would be a limited "commercial Keynesianism," rather than "social Keynesianism," as scholars have noted.[168] The combination of the war's direct effects on the institutions of government with its indirect effects on state-building through changes in employment, business confidence, demography, and consumption directed American fiscal policy away from more comprehensive planning and incomes policies and towards a more limited, conservative public policy. Yet insofar as Keynes advocated government stimulation to the point of raising *effective* demand, it is apparent that there was no actual difference in the United States between social or commercial Keynesianism, given that

[166] Professor E. F. Willett of Smith College, an adviser to Navy Secretary Forrestal, recognized the parallel between the writings of Keynes and the wartime policies of the United States: "Publication in 1936 of Keynes's book 'General Theory of Employment, Interest, and Money,' focused world-wide attention on the new investment-saving theory of the business cycle and the alleged necessity of Government spending to compensate for lack of private spending, instead of relying upon monetary controls to cure depression. Nearly all of the major monetary and economic advisers of the New Deal were followers of Keynes. . . . Among such advisers were Hansen, White, Currie, Cohen, Viner, Reifler, Henderson, Hopkins, Wallace, Eccles, Lubin, and many others. For the first time, theoretical considerations rather than those of immediate expediency seemed to play a major role in fiscal and monetary policy.

"Keynes's theory is still widely held and it seems probable that Government policy with respect to business cycles is likely to be based upon it when need for such policy arises." Willett then reaffirms the position taken here: "The beginning of the defense program in 1939, and its rapid expansion following our ultimate involvement in war, resulted in a tremendous increase in Government expenditures met in substantial part by deficit financing by the Government. Needless to say our war program was accompanied by full employment and a tremendous increase in the national product, and Keynesian economists look upon wartime experience as a definite proof of the validity of the theory that Government expenditure can create full employment and end depression.

"It should be pointed out, however, that while this conclusion is held by Keynesian economists, the actions taken by the Government in financing defense and the war were not undertaken on the basis of any economic theory but were simply the practical path of least resistance followed by the Government as the pressure of conditions dictated. In other words, just as throughout the greater part of the depression, opportunism rather than fundamental theory had dictated monetary and fiscal policy of the government, the same thing continued to be true during the period 1940–1945." "Summary, Monetary and Fiscal Policy and the Business Cycle, 1925–1945," Memorandum to Mr. Forrestal from E. F. Willett, 25 February 1946, file "Willett," SC Subject Files 1942–48, Box 14, Records of the Secretary of the Navy.

[167] Arno Johnson, "Savings Bonds in Our Economy," 29 March 1950, p. 5 [no file folder], Box 23, HF.

[168] Robert M. Collins, *The Business Response to Keynes, 1929–1964*, Contemporary American History Series (New York: Columbia University Press, 1981); Robert Lekachman, *The Age of Keynes*; Margaret Weir and Theda Skocpol, "State Structures and the Possibilities for 'Keynesian' Responses to the Great Depression in Sweden, Britain, and the United States," in Evans, Rueschemeyer, and Skocpol, eds., *Bringing the State Back In*.

Keynes's economics were ultimately concerned with the policy objective of full employment (and highly sensitive to context), rather than with formal economics or specific policy instruments. As it was, the partial or watered-down Keynesian policies of the 1940s, such as tax-based fiscal policy, open-market operations, and the reliance on automatic stabilizing devices such as social security benefits and unemployment insurance—"commercial Keynesianism"—happened to be sufficient for revitalizing the American economy.[169]

Relative Exchange in the Tax and Debt Domains

Taxpayers, without alternatives to levied taxes and with little doubt that they would have to answer for legislated tax increases, should do worse during the war years than investors. Investors had other alternatives besides buying in U.S. government securities and could choose not to invest; the success of the government's solicitation of funds was not assured. The history of the war years bears out the discrepant terms of exchange.

Taxpayers were in fact much worse off during the war years than were investors. Tax liabilities soared. Individuals paid an average $99 each in 1940, and a more-than-triple $341 each by 1945. Meanwhile, investors in government securities received assured returns and some were able to make large profits from the war loan campaigns, given the Fed's support of the government security market and the Roosevelt Administration's commitment not to let the value of government bonds fall below par. "Bankers gradually became aware that it was not only profitable but also safe to invest all available funds in government bonds and to purchase longer term obligations paying higher rates of interest." Accordingly, "member banks could sell low-interest short-term obligations to [the Federal Reserve Banks], and use the reserves obtained as a basis for a five-fold expansion in purchase of longer-term (7–9 year) bonds."[170] As Eccles put it,

[169] Consider the converse: the promulgation of more redistributive, government-centered measures consistent with social Keynesianism (as in the social planning of the National Resources Planning Board, the Fiscal Division of the Department of the Treasury, and the Beveridge Report) received little support. Large-scale social spending programs and imbalanced budgets may have been Keynesian in being proactive policies consistent with full employment; but insofar as such policies undermined investor confidence, they cannot be called Keynesian in the sense of creating effective demand. The deleterious connotations and adverse effects of the "forced savings" and "compulsory savings" labels during the war are to the point. The impact of the Second World War on the American political economy made a chimera of the actual possibility of "social Keynesianism" in the United States. For a discussion of how Keynesian economics at once did and did not apply to U.S. policies during the 1940s see Sparrow, "From the Outside In," 201–25.

[170] Memorandum of J. E. Reeve to Bureau of the Budget Director Smith, 6 March 1946,

[T]he banks took advantage of [the government's support of the interest rates on government securities] by "playing the pattern of rates," and the large investors did likewise in the process of "free riding." The banks played the pattern of rates by selling to the Reserve System (which was the principal buyer) some of the short-term, low-yielding securities as they went to premiums (in line with the pattern of rates) and then purchased the longer-term, higher-yielding securities. This action created high-powered reserve money, out of which the banking system was able to buy six times as many securities from non-bank investors as it sold to the Federal Reserve, and thereby to create a like amount of deposits.[171]

This was the "triple play": the banks (first) sold their newly bought short term securities to the Federal Reserve Banks; each extra dollar of bank reserves in turn created five dollars of bank assets, which the banks (second) used to buy middle-term bonds of 1¾ and 2 percent; and then other investors, with the expanded credit (third), used their proceeds to subscribe to more long-term bank-restricted 2¼ and 2½ percent war bonds.[172] The banks' turnover of government securities was instrumental in the chronic oversubscription of the war loan drives and in the growth of the money supply.

After the close of the successful Second War Loan drive, Eccles pointed out that too much security purchasing was being done by the banks rather than by non-bank investors.[173] A Treasury Department memorandum attested to the sharp increase in bank profits resulting from the shift from short-term to middle-term obligations and from the "unnecessarily large increase in government debt held by banks." Moreover, "the level of profits will remain excessive for some time."[174] Indicative of this is the fact that non-bank investors bought $147 billion in U.S. government securities during the eight loan drives, whereas their actual increase of assets held in the form of government securities came to only $93 billion. Commercial banks, on their part, were allowed only $10 billion in bank-eligible securities,

---

file "Borrowing and Public Debt—Other," Box 50, Division of Fiscal Analysis Series 39.3, Budget Records.

[171] Eccles, *Beckoning Frontiers*, 360. A 1945 conference of Federal Reserve Bank presidents recommended that changes be made in the drive procedure so as not to encourage "padded and speculative subscriptions, 'switching,' and indirect bank subscriptions, because of possibilities for profit and ease in attaining quotas, policing will be relatively ineffectual" ("Suggested Procedure for the Seventh War Loan Drive," file "Seventh War Loan—Planning," Box 1, War Loan Drives—Planning, WFD).

[172] "Appendix A," Memorandum of J. E. Reeve to Bureau of the Budget Director Smith, 6 March 1946, file "Borrowing and Public Debt—Other," Box 50, Division of Fiscal Analysis Series 39.3, Budget Records.

[173] Eccles, *Beckoning Frontiers*, 339.

[174] Memorandum of J. E. Reeve to Budget Director Smith, 6 March 1946, 2, file "Borrowing and Public Debt—Other," Box 50, Division of Fiscal Analysis Series 39.3, Budget Records.

whereas their holdings of U.S. securities increased by $57 billion.[175] The increase in security holdings by nonfinancial investors such as industrial corporations, nonprofit organizations and pension funds suggests the favorable returns to be made from holding (and turning over) U.S. government securities.

A Treasury analysis of the Fifth War Loan drive reported that "[free r]iding was a profitable operation." The analysis found that "[m]any individuals and corporations did it with the cooperation of the commercial banks and they were able to obtain a profit at little cost and practically no risk to themselves."[176] While Murphy writes that speculators were marginal in the investment community and that their marginality factored into the survival and continued toleration of free riding, the economic historian and former Treasury official Henry Murphy also acknowledges that free riding was "a major industry."[177] Another observer remarked that "the Federal Reserve became a slot machine that would always pay off."[178]

Investors were also able to profit from the war loan campaigns by security "switching," whereby companies purchased securities offered in the drives by switching out of already acquired securities. The amount of securities purchased therefore "had no relation to the investor's cash funds, and as a result of the operation, there is often little or no reduction in his liquid balances."[179] The Treasury calculated that for the Fifth War Loan drive, for instance, insurance companies were switching 50 percent of their purchases, savings banks 53 percent, and security dealers and brokers 80 percent. (The corporate average, including state and local governments, was 43 percent.)[180] The asset and profit records of the commercial banks provide circumstantial evidence of the profits to be made from buying and selling U.S. government securities: commercial banks had 27 percent of their assets in U.S. securities in 1941 and made a 31 percent annual profit; banks had 57 percent of their assets invested in U.S. securities in 1945 and made a 47 percent average profit.

Individual investors, on their part, did not have the opportunities that commercial banks and other institutional players had during the war loan drives, but they did have the value of their savings protected by the government's support of security prices. There would be no repetition of the experience of World War I, when, shortly after Armistice Day, the value of

[175] Eccles, *Beckoning Frontiers*, 362.

[176] "An Analysis of the Fifth War Loan Drive," 23 August 1944, p. 7, file "6th War Loan—Planning," Box 1, War Loan Drives—Planning, WFD.

[177] Murphy, *National Debt*, 183–86.

[178] Lester V. Chandler, quoted in Paul J. Strayer, *Fiscal Policy and Politics* (New York: Harper & Brothers, 1958), 41.

[179] "An Analysis of the Fifth War Loan Drive," p. 10. Murphy calls this "quota riding."

[180] "An Analysis of the Fifth War Loan Drive," p. 11.

Liberty Bonds fell from their $100 par value to the low $80s.[181] Both organized and unorganized investors in U.S. securities did better during the war years than did individual and corporate taxpayers.[182]

The evidence from the postwar years does not conform to resource dependence expectations, however. Although bondholders outnumbered income taxpayers by 85 to 50 million (and thus should do better in their new terms of exchange with the government, since they were the larger constituency for federal officials eager for votes), taxpayers did better in their postwar terms of exchange: per capita income taxes declined from $341 in 1945 to $280 in 1949 (cf. Table 4.4).[183] Whereas individuals were paying four times what companies were paying in taxes in 1945, corporations by 1950 were paying 87¢ for every dollar being paid by individuals. (Corporate taxes increased from about $10,000 per corporation in 1945 to about $25,000 each in 1950—consistent with the fact that corporations represented a smaller clientele.)

Even as there was a brief bull market in government securities in the winter and early spring of 1946, with the expectation that there would be a "shortage of 2½ percent bonds, given the end of the loan campaigns,"[184] the bull market was followed by a price retreat. In fact, the Truman Administration succeeded in maintaining the value of its obligations and stabilizing the return on citizens' savings. The Treasury Department was "signally successful in maintaining the price of government obligations at a low yield," report Studenski and Krooss: "even though large amounts of low-interest short-term obligations were being retired and savings bonds with their 2.9 per cent rate were increasing, the computed annual interest charge increased by

[181] The head of the Treasury's War Finance Division told Congress, "[The E, F, and G] bonds were designed to overcome what had happened in World War No. 1. At that time the Treasury raised these funds through the sale of negotiable, market-risk securities, and there were, as you know, millions of people who lost money after World War I through the sale of their Liberty bonds which did not have fixed value and did not have a guaranteed value except only at maturity, and because it was possible to use them as collateral, the price was driven down, and they were sold as low as 82 or 83 dollars on the hundred at that time, but that cannot happen to these bonds" (Ted R. Gamble, National Director, War Finance Division, in "Treasury Department Appropriation Bill for 1947," *Hearings before the Subcommittee of the Committee on Appropriations, House of Representatives*, 79th Cong., 2nd sess., 16 January 1946).

[182] Consistent with the resource dependence perspective's focus on the organization of clienteles, corporate tax payments grew at smaller rates than those of individual taxpayers. Corporations paid $4,533 on average in 1940 and about $10,000 by 1945—only a little more than twice as much. More striking is the decline in the ratio of corporate tax paid to that paid by individuals, from about $1.50 paid by corporations for each dollar paid by individuals in 1940, to 25¢ paid by corporations for each dollar paid by individuals by war's end.

[183] The anomalous figures for 1949 in Table 4.5 (especially the contrast between the 1949 individual and corporate taxation and between the 1949 and 1950 figures) resulted from the combination of the 1949 recession and the 1948 tax cut.

[184] Murphy, *National Debt*, 223–24.

only $230 million and the computed annual interest charge rose from 1.995 to 2.199 per cent between June, 1946, and June, 1950."[185] Meanwhile, without the war loan campaign and without the free riding to be had on new bond issues, life insurance companies and commercial banks invested proportionately less of their assets in government securities; the postwar incomes on interest on securities and the profits of commercial banks fell correspondingly.

In short, expectations for the terms of exchange between individual taxpayers and investors in wartime are borne out and are realized in both the wartime and postwar periods for corporate taxpayers and institutional investors. But we might have expected the more numerous investors in U.S. securities to do better than taxpayers in the postwar years. Even so, it should be noted that bond prices never did fall below par (as they had after WWI)—although they would do so again in the early 1950s.

Conclusions

In Eccles's words, "at no time was there any doubt that the money would be forthcoming to wage war. The promise Morgenthau made to General George C. Marshall was honored in full."[186] With its desperate need for additional funds, the U.S. government had to extract more from its taxpayers—tax revenues that were in large part forthcoming. Income taxes totaled 2 percent of GNP in 1939; they totaled over 15 percent in 1944.[187] In 1940, 7.1 percent of the population paid income taxes; in 1944, 64.1 percent of the population did so.[188]

Congress played a significant role in setting tax policy, consistent with the absence of a wartime switch to presidential command in revenue collection. It passed legislation enabling the federal income tax to become the dominant source of U.S. government revenue and also blocked the Roosevelt Administration's attempts to raise more in taxes (Hypothesis 1b). After the war, Congress was only slightly less balky, passing two tax relief bills which would be vetoed by President Truman, and overriding a third veto.

In contrast, the wartime debt policy was controlled by the Roosevelt Administration (Hypothesis 1a). After the war, Congress held hearings on the government's fiscal and monetary policy but refused to pass legislation endorsed by the President, the Federal Reserve Board, and the Council of Economic Advisers for regulating consumer credit. Congress mostly left the refinancing of the public debt and the determination of interest rate policy

[185] Studenski and Krooss, *Financial History*, 478.
[186] Eccles, *Beckoning Frontiers*, 344.
[187] Witte, *Federal Income Tax*, 124.
[188] Witte, *Federal Income Tax*, 125.

up to the Treasury Department and, to a lesser extent, the Federal Reserve Board. It did not act to settle the conflict between the Treasury and the Fed; neither did the President (Hypothesis 1c).

As to the form of institutional change, the tax and debt bureaucracies expanded greatly over the course of the war, with a much larger expansion in personnel at the Bureau of Public Debt than at the Bureau of Internal Revenue (Hypothesis 2a, Hypothesis 2b). Consistent with resource dependence expectations, the government set up interorganizational agencies to link the Treasury Department with the owners of wealth, and committees were established on the national, state, and local levels for the purpose of selling U.S. securities to financial and commercial corporations, labor unions, and individuals. Yet the changes in the budget and employment of the Bureau of Public Debt (relative to the wartime changes at the Bureau of Internal Revenue) exceeded expectations—a result of the Treasury's insistence on selling as much as possible to individuals (the "hard to get" money) rather than selling exclusively—and more efficiently—to institutional investors and wealthy individuals.

Note, however, the divergent legacies of the Second World War in the tax and debt domains: the size of the Bureau of Internal Revenue and numbers of taxpayers essentially leveled off after the war, whereas the Bureau of Public Debt shrank in size and the numbers of bondholders went down; the intensity of per capita income taxes declined, whereas that of corporate taxpayers and debt owners increased. With the cessation of the war loan campaigns, fewer individuals bought or owned bonds. The Treasury increasingly dealt with financial institutions and other major holders of wealth (and could thereby commensurately reduce its sales and processing staff).

As for the expectation of the permanence of the wartime state-building, the ratcheting in individual and corporate income taxation is consistent with the changes in the domestic and international environments. There was a renewed commitment to the government as a guarantor of American social welfare, whether through direct spending for the relief of the elderly or unemployed or through the adjustment of tax policy to stabilize economic growth. And there was the continued international threat, this time posed by the Soviet Union instead of Germany. Likewise, new populations of businesses and individuals were buying and would continue to buy U.S. government securities. Finally, there was a lasting shift in the political agenda. Not only did the war mark the permanent introduction of proactive government fiscal policy, but decisions about interest rates, the timing of government security sales, and income tax rates would become and would continue to be chronic political issues.

With respect to the relative bargains between the government and institutional and individual taxpayers and between the government and the owners of U.S. securities, taxpayers paid three times as much on average at the end of the war as at the beginning. Owners of the federal debt, in contrast, received guaranteed returns on their money, and some investors, the commercial banks especially, were able to profit considerably from the war loan campaigns (Hypothesis 4a). After the war, taxpayers enjoyed tax cuts, while investors were deprived of the opportunities of the war loan drives and had the purchasing power of their holdings diminished by inflation (Hypothesis 4b).

The resource dependence perspective thus succeeds in accounting for which actors directed state-building in the tax and debt domains in the war and postwar periods, for much of the form of the expanded institutions in public finance, for the persistence of the changes prompted by the war, for the emergence of the American version of Keynesianism, and for the different experiences of the tax and debt clienteles over the course of the 1940s. It does not account for the fact that taxpayers got a better deal than investors in the immediate postwar years, for the indifference of Congress's management of the public debt after the war, or for the ability of the U.S. government to fund the war voluntarily. Not only did six million persons work on behalf of the federal government and the United States without pay, but millions of individuals and investors were willing buy war bonds in the face of investment alternatives. American policymakers used noncoercive means such as mass advertising, door-to-door sales, and the operations of the financial markets to secure needed funds—even in a world at war.

In sum, the Second World War systematically transformed U.S. tax and debt bureaucracies, changed the role of the federal government in the national economy, reconstructed the relations between the government and societal actors—whether banks, insurance companies, nonfinancial corporations, individual investors, or employees—and revised the means of raising revenue. The fact that the United States was a belligerent and then victor in the Second World War had a profound impact on national government, government-society relations, and the administration of public finance.

Yet had President Roosevelt had more time or inclination for financial matters, or had he not estranged Congress by attempting to purge congressional rivals in 1942 or pack the Supreme Court in 1937, there could very well have been stronger and more innovative tax legislation passed in the early 1940s. The possibility existed of a more *dirigiste* American state.

5

The Transformation of Navy Procurement

No break with the traditions of America's past
has been so complete, so drastic, as the one
that has resulted in the growth of the present
military-industrial complex.
  —Fred Cook, *The Warfare State*

Fellow Americans, when your great
grandchildren and mine open their school
books and read about Franklin D. Roosevelt,
they will not read about the New Deal. . . . But
children in public parks will gaze up at his
monument, because under Franklin D.
Roosevelt Columbia became the Gem of the
Ocean, and, in the waters of the Philippines, in
the midst of an election campaign, became the
premier world naval power.
  —Dorothy Thompson, 1944 Radio Address

Licus, you are a gentleman and a procurer.
  —*A Funny Thing Happened on the Way to
    the Forum*

When the European war began in September, 1939, the American merchant fleet comprised approximately 1,150 oceangoing vessels, which totaled something like 10,500,000 deadweight tons. By the time Germany surrendered in May, 1945, we had built in this country about 5,200 large oceangoing vessels, with a total deadweight tonnage of nearly 53,000,000, plus hundreds of smaller types. To say that we built five times as much shipping as we had when the war began is an understatement. Actually, by V-E Day we had turned out just about the equivalent of two-thirds of the entire oceangoing merchant marines of all the nations that afterwards became the United Nations.[1]

The transformation of the U.S. merchant marine—the "fourth arm of defense"—paralleled the changes in the U.S. naval fleet. The total tonnage

[1] Donald M. Nelson, *Arsenal of Democracy: The Story of American War Production* (New York: Harcourt Brace, 1946), 243.

of Navy ships in service increased from 1.9 million tons on 1 July 1940 to 13.5 million tons by 30 June 1945, and the total number of Navy vessels rose from 1,099 to 50,759 over the same period. The U.S. government spent a total of $22 billion in the building and fitting of ships during the war, and $6 billion on Navy aircraft alone; the number of operational aircraft increased from 1,741 in 1940 to 40,912 by 1945. By 1944, the Navy's industrial shore facilities were worth about $12 billion—more than the combined operations of General Motors, United States Steel, and American Telephone and Telegraph. Correspondingly, the total number of personnel working for the Navy (both military and civilian) increased from 203,127 employees to 4,031,097 persons over the course of the war. Here was the war-built state.

The story of American industrial might harnessed for fighting World War II has, however, its dark side. For many scholars, the very success of the wartime mobilization marks the beginning of the "military-industrial complex" of industrial capacity, skilled personnel, and public and private investment becoming tethered to U.S. defense spending.[2] They point to the chronic disclosures of waste and fraud revealed in the Truman Committee hearings dating from 1941 to 1948, the hearings by the House Armed Services Committee in 1959 (the Hébert Committee [Representative Edward Hébert, D., La.]), and the findings of the Packard Commission in 1986.[3]

The historian Richard Polenberg remarks: "If the military-industrial complex reached maturity in the era of the Cold War, it just as surely was born and nurtured in World War II."[4] Another critic, Gordon Adams, writes that "[a]fter World War II, industry pressure and Government decisions led to Federal support for a private defense capacity, in effect subsidizing industry to keep critical personnel in working teams and production facilities open."[5] The economist Robert Higgs agrees:

[2] See Ronald V. Dellums, *Defense Sense: The Search for a Rational Military Policy*, with R. H. Miller and H. Lee Halterman (Cambridge, Mass.: Ballinger, 1983); Seymour Melman, ed., *The War Economy of the United States* (New York: St. Martin's, 1971); James L. Clayton, *The Economic Impact of the Cold War* (New York: Harcourt Brace & World, 1970); Fred J. Cook, *The Warfare State* (New York: Macmillan, 1962); Bruce M. Russett, *What Price Vigilance?* (New Haven: Yale University Press, 1970); Walter Millis, *Arms and the State*, with Harvey Mansfield and Harold Stein (New York: Twentieth Century Fund, 1958); Robert Nisbet, *The Present Age* (New York: Harper & Row, 1988). Over 700 articles and books were written on the military-industrial complex between 1961 and 1970 alone (Clayton, *The Economic Impact of the Cold War*, 3, n.3).

[3] This is not to mention the various reports from other congressional inquiries and commissions, investigative journalists, and whistle-blowers.

[4] Richard Polenberg, *War and Society: The United States, 1941–1945* (Philadelphia: Lippincott, 1972), 237

[5] Gordon Adams, *The Politics of Defense Contracting* (New Brunswick, N.J.: Transaction Books, 1982), 21.

As soon as the Americans ceased firing at the Germans and the Japanese, they turned their silent but still loaded guns toward their former allies, the Soviets . . . it would not do to demobilize. . . . To supply the Cold Warriors with an ever-more-sophisticated arsenal, many of the contractors of World War II—especially the aircraft companies—continued to make the development and manufacture of weapons their main business. The approximately $3 trillion spent on defense goods and services since 1945 has assured them an ample "market."[6]

Higgs cites sources stating that about 80 percent of the government-financed industrial facilities built during WWII passed on to private firms after the war. Higgs finds that the military-industrial complex is related "in some degree" to the extensive purchase of war plants by the federal government's lessees.[7]

This account of the effect of World War II on government-industrial relations is mistaken, however, in the Navy case. Contrary to the conventional belief that military-industrial relations are full of "waste, fraud, and abuse,"[8] the history of Navy procurement in the 1940s reveals a surprising amount of caution and control by the Navy in its ties with civilian contractors. The Second World War did not in fact establish the military-industrial complex, for the reason that Navy-industry relations largely *collapsed* between the end of the war and 1950.

The following analysis of Navy procurement proceeds on three levels. The principal level of analysis is the intra-Navy operational level of procurement conducted under the supervision of the Office of the Under Secretary of the Navy. A second level is the Navy Department's administration of procurement, where it had to coordinate procurement with the Department of War, the Army Air Forces, the independent Air Force (after 1947), and other government organizations. A third and more detailed level of analysis discusses the Navy's procurement of two material supplies in particular: naval destroyers (purchased by the Bureau of Ships) and fighter aircraft (purchased by the Bureau of Aeronautics).[9] As in the previous chapters, however, we want to know who introduced new policies, what organizational form state-building took, and to what extent the changes in the administration of Navy procurement persisted after the Second World War. The resource dependence perspective provides a tool for understanding the industrial mobilization for war, and perhaps for explaining the susceptibility

---

[6] Higgs, *Crisis and Leviathan*, 230.

[7] Higgs, *Crisis and Leviathan*, 232.

[8] Higgs, *Crisis and Leviathan*, 230. Higgs's documentation of military procurement cites figures from World War II and then, significantly, skips to citations of figures from the 1960s.

[9] "Material" is used here as the Navy used the term: identical to "matériel" and in opposition to "personnel."

of military procurement to charges of endemic inefficiency and corporate cupidity.

We should expect executive branch officials to determine the scope and form of change in Navy-industry relations during the war, given the constitutional authority of the president as commander in chief of the armed forces in times of war; we should expect Congress to dictate the administration of Navy procurement in the years between World War II and the Korean War.

Second, we should anticipate that the Navy will create new agencies for administering procurement so as to make necessary the interorganizational linkages with corporate producers.

Third, we should expect the state-building of the war years to endure, given the restructured international system of states and the war-reconfigured national economy. With the war enhancing the position of military contractors as producers and employers in the national economy, the postwar government should maintain the policies and institutions that proved successful in the Second World War. And with the United States becoming a superpower, the Navy Department should retain its war-built bureaucracies, its extended industrial relations, and its new means of procuring material.

The study of Navy procurement contrasts with the preceding policy histories in two important ways. First, there is an obvious extranational dimension to Navy procurement that is less conspicuous in social, labor, and financial policies. Yet insofar as the transformation of military procurement had profound effects on government spending, the American economy, and the overall organization of government (as mentioned earlier), military procurement was very much intranational policy.[10]

A second contrast between the present case and the preceding cases is the exceeding complexity of military procurement. As a Bureau of the Budget report had it, "It is both difficult and dangerous to generalize about 'military material procurement.' The phrase covers a terrific expanse and the problems of material production and procurement are inextricably bound up with the outstanding government policies on size of forces, changes in timing and duration of advanced readiness, assumptions on war reserves versus capacity in being, decisions as to types of weapons, etc." The report concluded, "Even these general distinctions, however, are not adequate for [one hundredth] of the complexity of the actual job."[11]

[10] See Ann Markusen, Peter Hall, Scott Campbell, and Sabina Deitrick, *The Rise of the Gunbelt* (New York: Oxford University Press, 1991).

[11] "Comments on Problems and Possible Action to Improve the Formulation and Execution of Military Material Programs," Draft, 3/17/52, p. 1, file "Military Procurement and Production," Box 21, Records Relating to Budgetary Administration in the National Defense Establishment, FY 49–52, CY 47–52, Series 47.8a, Budget Records.

Navy procurement required numerous discrete activities, including:

> design, development and standardization; item identification and cataloging; selection of contractors and time of contract placement; pricing; contract forms; contract appeals; patents; use of mandatory orders; renegotiation; financing; specifications; scheduling; inspection; packaging; packing and marking; contract termination; surplus property disposal; insurance; auditing; and conservation.[12]

This complexity poses a distinct contrast to the Treasury's securance of funds, for instance, despite the fact that the dollar amounts involved in the collection of taxes and the sale of government securities far exceeded the amount of spending on material procurement by the military (much less the Navy alone). The Navy purchased products that were supplied by few companies, by just one company, or (as was often the case) by no other firms; the Treasury had an array of sources from which it could elicit tax revenues or solicit investment. The Navy's products were, moreover, themselves variable and rarely substitutable: fighter planes could not substitute for torpedo bombers, battleships could not replace landing craft, and destroyers could not replace aircraft carriers.[13] But for the Treasury, one hundred million dollars was (and is) one hundred million dollars.

Consider, second, that the cost of the Navy's material supplies changed over time, whereas the Treasury had a calculable tax base and borrowed money at set rates of interest and set terms of redemption; not only did military contracts have to be altered and renegotiated, but they had to be tailored to specific purchases, given the uncertain production of many material supplies.

Third, the Navy needed ways by which to measure and catalog the vast size and variation in material procurement; the flow of dollars, in contrast, was all of a kind and could be tracked through the existing banking and tax systems.

A fourth difference between military procurement and public finance was that the government itself had to step in to fund the construction of new industrial facilities, given the insufficient industrial capacity in existence at the time. But the Treasury had a variety of available revenue sources—individual earnings, corporate profits, domestic savings, and consumer spending—and thus only had to decide from which sources to raise money.

Fifth, the subcontracting of the prime contractors was a frequent source of uncertainty for both prime contractors and the Navy Department, an

[12] Statement of W. John Kenney, Assistant Secretary of the Navy, for the record of Hearings before the Senate Naval Affairs Committee on S. 2044, 9 May 1946, file "Speech File 1946," Box 6, Papers of W. John Kenney.

[13] "Rarely" because the carrier escorts (CVEs) could fill in for aircraft carriers on convoy duty (CVEs being smaller and cheaper), and destroyer escorts could replace destroyers in protecting allied shipping (the DDEs being slower and less heavily armed).

certainty over reliability and delivery time that was qualitatively more complex than the uncertainty faced by banks or other financial institutions when "subcontracting" their loans to other, smaller creditors by jointly underwriting debt.

Sixth, when the war ended, much of the Navy's contracted-for procurement was suddenly superfluous. The government therefore had to terminate contracts and figure out how to pay for partly completed products. For the Treasury, in contrast, the end of the war simply meant that the government no longer had to fund a growing deficit—and the terms by which U.S. securities could be called in or redeemed were already set in place.

Last, the Navy had to compete for its purchases or coordinate its procurement with other federal agencies; other governmental organizations had their own claims on the raw materials or finished goods needed by the Navy. But the Treasury was the sole government borrower, since there were no other branches of government with which it had to compete or coordinate its activities (with the partial exception of the Fed).

Although it is not possible to discuss all of the dimensions of military procurement, neither is it possible to ignore its sheer complexity.[14] This chapter discusses seven aspects of procurement policies, corresponding to the contrasts between public finance and material procurement spelled out above: (1) the organization and forms of contracting; (2) the negotiation and renegotiation of contracts; (3) the supervision of contracts, including statistical controls; (4) the financing of industrial production; (5) subcontracting; (6) contract termination; and (7) the coordination of procurement with other government agencies and military services.

Because many of these institutional developments involved simultaneous changes in the Navy's own organizations, in the Navy's industrial relations, and in the means by which the Navy secured material supplies (as in the use of lawyers, inspectors, and contract negotiators, for instance), the discussion below combines the study of the instrumental dimension of the state with those of the bureaucratic and relational dimensions of the state.

Background

German armies reached the English Channel on 21 May 1940, and marched into Paris on 12 June. With Denmark and Norway already conquered, the

---

[14] Bernard Baruch, financier and former head of the War Industries Board, testified that Army and Navy procurement presented the most vexing problem of industrial mobilization in WWII (War Policies Commission Hearings, Resolution No. 98, 71st Cong., 2nd sess., Part I, 178, in file "Twenty Years of Planning," Box 114, Ferdinand Eberstadt Papers, Seeley G. Mudd Manuscript Library).

fall of Great Britain seemed just a matter of time. The security of the United States itself appeared in jeopardy.[15]

The Roosevelt Administration and Congress responded with a burst of activity. On 14 June 1940, Congress approved an 11 percent expansion in the U.S. fleet and an increase in the number of airplanes to 4,500, with the authorization for the purchase of an additional 10,000 planes.[16] Congress then passed the Reorganization Act of 1940 on 20 June 1940, which established the Bureau of Ships by merging the Bureau of Construction and Repair and the Bureau of Engineering. Congress created the Office of the Under Secretary of the Navy on the same day. Four days later, President Roosevelt nominated Chicago newspaper publisher Frank Knox, a Republican and former vice presidential candidate, as Secretary of the Navy.[17]

On 28 June 1940 Congress passed the "Speed-up Act," which overturned the rules of Navy contracting set up under the Vinson-Trammell Act of 1934. (The Vinson-Trammell Act limited profits of Navy vessel and aircraft contractors to 10 percent for contracts above $10,000, with all proceeds above that level going to the Treasury, and specified that the government had to produce at least 10 percent of Navy aircraft.) The new legislation allowed for contracts to be negotiated, instead of only being let through advertising: "the Secretary of the Navy is hereby authorized to negotiate contracts for the acquisition, construction, repair, or alteration of complete naval vessels or aircraft, or any portions thereof."[18] The Navy was further

[15] See "Memorandum for the Secretary of the Navy, from the Office of the Chief of Naval Operations," 4 November 1940, file "Navy Department, Nov.–Dec. 1940," Box 79, Personal Secretary Files, Roosevelt Papers.

[16] Two years earlier, on 17 May 1938, Congress had passed the Naval Expansion Act as recommended by President Roosevelt in response to German troops invading Austria. The Naval Expansion Act authorized a 20 percent increase in "under-age" vessels, as provided in the Vinson-Trammell Act, and the production of at least 3,000 aircraft. Other precursors to the declaration of war were a proclamation of a limited national emergency on 8 September 1939 (one week after the European war began), an administrative order establishing an Office of Emergency Management in the Executive Office of the President on 25 May 1940, and the appointment of a (revived) Council of National Defense and a National Defense Advisory Commission on 28 May 1940. The President established himself as chairman of the Commission. On 27 May 1941, President Roosevelt declared the United States to be in an unlimited national emergency.

Much of the following "Background" discussion follows from an internal Truman Administration campaign memorandum ("Memorandum," of H. B. Hinton to Mr. Murphy, 17 September 1948, file "1948 Presidential Campaign, National Defense," Box 34, Papers of George M. Elsey); also see "Chronology of War Events, U.S. Defense Measures and Navy Organization and Policies," in Robert Howe Connery, *The Navy and the Industrial Mobilization in World War II* (Princeton: Princeton University Press, 1951), 464–514.

[17] Congress approved Knox as Secretary of the Navy on 11 July 1940.

[18] 54 Stat. 527.

authorized to modify existing contracts and to buy whatever facilities it needed.

The President proceeded to sign the "Two-Ocean" Navy Bill on 19 July 1940, which appropriated funds for the purchase of an additional 200 war-ships and 15,000 aircraft. The Navy was authorized to increase combat ship tonnage by 70 percent, and appropriations for "Aviation, Navy" were increased fourfold from the level of the preceding year.[19]

But as the historian and former Navy officer Robert Connery tells it, "When Secretary Knox took office he found no central procurement authority—indeed little knowledge and few statistics regarding the expansion program as a whole. There was available no long-range or comprehensive production planning, no inventory of existing stocks, no catalog of machinery. The contracting machinery was primitive, geared to peacetime speeds and a small building program."[20] The Navy lacked an administrative infrastructure adequate for handling the load, notwithstanding all of its financial and legal wherewithal for the expansion of material procurement. One of Knox's first administrative acts as Secretary of the Navy, therefore, was to appoint James V. Forrestal as Under Secretary, on 22 August 1940. Forrestal had specific responsibility for contracting and for tax and legal matters.

Forrestal first tried to conduct the Navy's procurement through existing bureaus and agencies, upon assuming office, but he quickly found that no one in the Material Procurement Section of the Fleet Maintenance Division, the Bureau of Supplies and Accounts, or the Office of the Judge Advocate General was able or willing to supervise procurement.[21] Forrestal therefore ordered the New York lawyer H. Struve Hensel to investigate existing contracting procedures. In July 1941 Forrestal and Knox acted on the recommendations of Hensel's report and established the "Procurement Legal Division" in the Office of the Under Secretary, with Hensel appointed as director. Forrestal then put together a civilian staff for coordinating procurement, culled mostly from his contacts in the New York business and financial worlds.

The Navy could not and did not procure in isolation, of course. At the

---

[19] In September 1940, the President transferred 50 destroyers to Great Britain by executive action. The over-age vessels were exchanged for 99-year leases on naval and air bases in Newfoundland, Bermuda, the Bahamas, Jamaica, and elsewhere. The Lend-Lease Act was signed on 11 March 1941, authorizing the President to sell, lease, lend, or otherwise transfer defense articles to Allied nations. By the end of the war, the U.S. government had lend-leased a total of 5,526 vessels, amounting to 1,052,000 tons.

[20] Connery, *Industrial Mobilization*, 56.

[21] Robert Greenhalgh Albion, *Makers of American Naval Policy 1798–1947*, Rowena Reed, ed. (Annapolis, Md.: Naval Institute Press, 1980), 530–31; Paul Y. Hammond, *Organizing for Defense* (Princeton: Princeton University Press, 1961), 147–49.

same time that the Navy was upgrading its procurement operations, the Roosevelt Administration was modifying contract procedures in general. The President established the Office of Production Management (OPM) in January 1941: the Navy and War Departments had to clear all contracts above $500,000 with the OPM's Division of Purchases (previously, the Navy and War Departments had to clear all contracts in excess of the limit with Commissioner William S. Knudsen of the National Defense Advisory Commission). Congress then granted the President authority over organizational change by Executive Order under the First War Powers Act, on 18 December 1941. The President also reconstituted the Army and Navy Munitions Board on 21 February 1942 to enhance cooperation in procurement; the ANMB included the Under Secretaries of War and Navy, with a civilian chairman. Later that month, the Secretary of the Navy delegated authority to the Procurement Branch of the ANMB to clear the contracts of the newly formed War Production Board.

But the ANMB's Priorities Committee conflicted with the Advisory Commission's jurisdiction on priorities (priorities being all-important with the production bottlenecks, short supplies, and competing demands).[22] The Advisory Commission therefore got the President to sign an executive order that granted full authority over priorities to the newly established Priorities Board.[23] Meanwhile, the Navy decentralized procurement to the material bureaus by authorizing the bureau chiefs to negotiate contracts at their discretion. No longer did the Bureau of Aeronautics and the Bureau of Ships have to route their procurement through the Bureau of Supplies and Accounts, for example.

Yet the Department of the Navy faced internal competition as well as external competition. In response to the attempts by Admiral Ernest King, Chief of Naval Operations, to reorganize the Navy, Knox commissioned outside experts from General Motors and U.S. Steel to survey the Department. The subsequent "Archer-Wolf" report recommended the establishment of both a Fiscal Director and a board of directors. Following these recommendations, Forrestal set up the Office of Fiscal Director in the Secretary of the Navy's Office on 2 December 1944 (Forrestal replacing Knox as Navy Secre-

[22] The Advisory Commission was a seven-member adjunct of the Council of National Defence (a legacy from 1916). The Advisory Commission provided an opportunity for pressure groups to "advise" the President in a manner that did not require congressional approval (Robert Greenhalgh Albion and Robert Howe Connery, *Forrestal and the Navy*, with the collaboration of Jennie Barnes Pope [New York: Columbia University Press, 1962], 71).

[23] Only after the President's mediation did the Commission and the military services reach a compromise: "Orders for items on the ANMB critical list could have preference ratings automatically applied to them by Army and Navy contracting officers, but additions could be made only with the concurrence of the Advisory Commissions Priorities Board" (Connery, *Industrial Mobilization*, 95).

tary when Knox died in office), and creating the "Top Policy Board," linking the civilian secretaries with the principal admirals, for the informal discussion of Navy organization, demobilization, service unification, and war termination.[24] At the end of the war, the Top Policy Group became the "Gates Board."

The recommendations of the Gates Board were the basis for much of the 1946 reorganization of the Navy Department. The Gates Board identified three parts of the naval establishment—the Operating Forces, the Navy Department, and the Shore Establishment—and four executive tasks— "policy control," "naval command," "logistics administration and control," and "business administration." Authority in the Navy Department was to be divided between the Chief of Naval Operations and the Under Secretary and Assistant Secretaries. Since the four tasks of the naval establishment involved different relationships between these two lines of authority, there would be no single pattern of subordination.

Once the war ended, the Secretary of the Navy transferred the Office of Procurement and Material to the Office of the Assistant Secretary's Materials Division. The Materials Division was mandated to "formulate and promulgate policies with regard to procurement, inspection, and disposition of Navy materials and facilities," and was divided into the Procurement Policy Branch, the Production Policy Branch, the Field Operations Branch, and the Materials Control Policy Branch.[25] The Navy's Price Adjustment Board, the Requirements Review Staff and the Board of Contract Appeals also had separate offices.

With the Executive Order of 29 September 1945 (E.O. 9635), the Truman Administration preserved the "war-tested" relations established between the Secretary of the Navy, the Under Secretary, Assistant Secretaries, the Chief of Naval Operations and the Bureau Chiefs. The war-tested solutions were later made into law, "Making certain changes in the organization of the Navy Department, and other purposes" (S. 1252).

Further administrative changes came through the Armed Forces Procurement Act of 19 February 1948 (P.L. 413), which facilitated cross- and single-service procurement, and modernized and standardized procurement methods. The Procurement Act also specified the policies and procedures for the Navy's advertisement of bids and, with certain exceptions, negotiation of contracts. The 1948 Renegotiation Act then reactivated renegotiation procedures in order to prevent excessive profits on contracts "for the procurement of ships, aircraft, aircraft parts, and the construction of facilities or installations outside the continental U.S."

---

[24] Albion, *Makers*, 541–42; Albion and Connery, *Forrestal and the Navy*, 234–35; Ralph A. Bard replaced Forrestal as Under Secretary on 24 June 1944.

[25] *Annual Report of the Secretary of the Navy, 1946* (Washington, D.C: U.S. GPO, 1946).

Even as the Navy continued to reorganize its administration of procurement after the war, however, it virtually ceased its material purchasing. Over two thousand ships were consigned to the "mothball" (reserve) fleet after V-J Day, approximately 6,800 ships were declared surplus, about 3,500 ships were disposed of (including those authorized to be used in atomic testing), and the Navy terminated about 9,800 ship contracts. The Navy disposed of $7.2 billion in surplus property by the end of fiscal 1946, and terminated more than 63,000 prime contracts of all kinds—worth a total of $16 billion—by 1 November 1946.[26]

Dwarfing the other changes in Navy procurement after 1945, however, was the unification issue.[27] The Army and the Army Air Forces (AAF) wanted a unified command under one secretary of defense, with the AAF made independent from the Army proper. The Navy feared that a unified military command would be dominated by the War Department (which coveted the Marine Corps) and the AAF (which disputed the Navy's control over land-based anti-submarine aircraft), since the Army and AAF together received $70 billion of the 1945 defense budget, to the Navy's $28 billion. Then there was the debate on the role of the respective services with regard to nuclear power and the delivery of the atomic bomb.

Shortly before the end of the war, on 19 June 1945, Forrestal asked his friend and former Dillon Read colleague Ferdinand Eberstadt to do a comprehensive study of the effects of unification on overall national security, on what changes were dictated by the war experience, and on the most effective form of postwar organization for the purposes of national security. After much debate in Congress and around Washington on the Eberstadt Report (submitted on 25 September 1945) and the Collins Plan (separately commissioned by the War Department), Congress passed and President Truman signed the National Security Act of 1947. It was mainly based on the Eberstadt Report.

The National Security Act set up a National Military Establishment (NME) under a single Secretary of Defense. The NME was composed of the Joint Chiefs of Staff, the Navy Department, the Department of the Army, a (now separate) Department of the Air Force, and the newly created

---

[26] Memorandum of H. B. Hinton to Mr. Murphy, 17 September 1948, File "1948 Presidential Campaign, 'National Defense,'" 19–20, file 1, Box 34, Elsey Papers.

[27] The unification of the military establishment should be distinguished from the unification of field command (which everyone favored). Proposals for a unified armed forces dated at least since the 1920s. In 1941, Representative Champ Clark (D., Mo.) proposed a consolidated Department of National Defense; in 1943, the War Department made a proposal for unification; and in 1944, Congress convened a special committee to hold hearings on a unified military command: Woodrum's (Rep. Clifton Woodrum, D., Va.) "Committee on Post-War Military Policy." But Chief of Staff General Marshall and others agreed to delay reorganization efforts until after the war.

Central Intelligence Agency, National Security Council, and National Security Resources Board (defunct as of 1952).[28] The Munitions Board replaced the Army and Navy Munitions Board, and was changed to coordinate procurement for the entire NME. The Secretary of Defense and the Joint Chiefs of Staff clarified the missions and roles of the three services at the Key West Conference in March 1948 and at the Newport Conference in August 1948.[29]

After Forrestal realized that his existing powers as Secretary of Defense were insufficient for the job on hand, Congress and the Truman Administration agreed to the 1949 Amendments to the National Security Act. The amendments strengthened the authority of the Secretary of Defense, and made the Army, Navy, and Air Force (and their Secretaries) wholly subordinate to the Secretary of Defense in a new Department of Defense; only the Secretary of Defense would have a position in the cabinet. Ironically, the 1949 amendments were much closer to the original Army plans for unification.

Procuring for the Navy

In theory, strategy drives procurement. The Joint Chiefs of Staff and the Chief of Naval Operations, in conjunction with the Navy bureau chiefs, make the strategic decisions determining material requirements. Procurement, as part of logistics, ensures that the necessary equipment and personnel are delivered to the right place at the right time. Traditionally, the actual purchasing for the Navy was handled by the individual bureaus, while the drafting of contracts was done by both the material bureaus (the Bureau of Ships, the Bureau of Aeronautics, and the Bureau of Ordnance) and the Bureau of Supplies and Accounts (the logistical arm of the Navy).[30] The Bureau of Supplies and Accounts contracted for items used by two or more bureaus, while the Bureau of Aeronautics, the Bureau of Ships, the Bureau of Ordnance, the Bureau of Medicine and Surgery, and the Bureau of Yards and Docks drafted separate contracts for their particular needs. (The Bureau of Ordnance and the Bureau of Yards and Docks could sign their own

[28] The Army Air Forces began its independent existence much earlier, as the Army Air Corps. It was set up as a separate command under the Army Chiefs of Staff in 1942 and was renamed the Army Air Forces.

[29] Congress also passed the Selective Service Act of 1948. This was the first time in history, apart from the few months before Pearl Harbor, that the United States had provided for a peacetime standing army.

[30] The "material" bureaus contrasted with the non-material Bureau of Medicine and Bureau of Personnel (formerly, the Bureau of Navigation). In 1940, the Bureau of Ships and Ordnance was split into the Bureau of Ships and the Bureau of Ordnance.

contracts; the Bureau of Aeronautics had to send its contracts over to the Bureau of Supplies and Accounts.) The war made these practices obsolete.

1. Contracting and Forms of Contracting Before the war, the Navy's contracting was done mostly through competitive bidding and with standardized contracts, where one contract form could be used for potentially thousands of items. With the relatively small amounts of materials being purchased by the Navy in the 1920s and 1930s and with the relatively slow pace of technological change, this bidding arrangement sufficed. The downside to this practice was that the contract forms in use, particularly those of the Bureau of Ships and the Bureau of Ordnance, were cluttered with ambiguous clauses "whose meaning was not clear to anyone."[31]

After June 1940, when the Navy suddenly began to let contracts to hundreds of producers instead of to the known few, however, the Navy's contractors found themselves with few standards by which to determine costs.[32] The fixed-price contract, while it might suffice for shoes and string beans, was no good for untried ships, aircraft prototypes, or new naval bases. Under conditions where demand greatly exceeded supply, the Navy faced uncertainty over the quality or technical performance and reliability of a product, uncertainty over the development time or availability of the product, and uncertainty over the cost of development.[33] Since "[c]ompetition—the prime price control under the Navy's pre-war procurement system—was essentially eliminated," contracts had to be adjustable.[34]

The Navy's first response was to add an escalator clause to the fixed-price contracts. But the escalator clause, used by the Bureau of Ships, simply passed higher costs along to the Navy and encouraged both management and labor to raise their costs. It was "an invitation to trouble." Similarly, the "labor price adjustment clause," used for fixed-price contracts in ship construction, had a number of deleterious effects. It fostered inflation; it pro-

---

[31] Connery, *Industrial Mobilization*, 65.

[32] Connery, *Industrial Mobilization*, 67; Albion and Connery, *Forrestal and the Navy*, 65.

[33] Merton J. Peck and Frederic M. Scherer, *The Weapons Acquisition Process* (Boston: Division of Research, Graduate School of Business Administration, Harvard University, 1962), 19.

[34] Ferdinand Eberstadt, "100 Billion Dollar Navy," Vol. 2, p. 2, Box 114, Eberstadt Papers. Contractors defeated the competitive bid system by submitting identical bids, rotating low bids, tying up patents, and omitting trade discounts when quoting bid prices (Connery, *Industrial Mobilization*, 201–2). In early 1941, however, the Bureau of Aeronautics reported that there was "small likelihood of groups of contractors in the aircraft industry controlling prices. The nature of the product, and the continuation of competition in fact if not in name, tend effectively to prevent this. Previous purchase prices and audited cost records constitute additional safeguards" (Memorandum, "Negotiation, Determination and Review of Costs and Profits under Negotiated Fixed-Price and Cost-Plus-Fixed-Fee Contracts," Chief of Bureau of Aeronautics to the Assistant Secretary of the Navy, 31 May 1941, L4–3(1) Vol. 17, General Correspondence, Bureau of Aeronautics, 1925–42, Record Group 72 ["Aeronautics, 1925–42"]).

tected contractors' profits from the effects of labor disputes (thus, in effect, absolving the contractor from responsibility over its workforce); it led to uneven employment (through the application of industry-wide indexes to specific contracts); it brought on accounting problems; and it raised costs through the provision of a premium in excess of labor costs (should labor costs increase 10 percent, the contractor would receive an additional 10 percent of that 10 percent extra). The labor price adjustment clauses in the Navy (and AAF) contracts for aircraft also contained an index "escape" clause which allowed for the substitution of other indexes. The Navy and Army subsequently began to negotiate the cost-index problem with representatives from the aircraft producers.[35] When the Roosevelt Administration imposed direct price controls in 1942, the need for the escalator clauses disappeared.[36]

A better response to the Navy's uncertain procurement was the negotiated contract. As of mid-1940, the Congress ceded the Army and Navy broad authority for placing contracts by negotiation when buying ships and aircraft, and after Pearl Harbor, Congress abandoned all restrictions on what the Navy could buy and from whom.[37] Then, under the provisions of the First War Powers Act, Roosevelt authorized the Secretaries of the Navy and War to enter into contracts unencumbered by prior restrictions, with the caveats that the cost-plus-percentage-of-cost contracts of the First World War were prohibited and that the fees on cost-plus-fixed-fee contracts could not exceed 7 percent.

But Forrestal realized that lawyers were reviewing the flood of contracts arriving to be signed only after all negotiations had already been completed (rather than during the course of contract negotiations), and that the officials in the Judge Advocate General's office assigned to prepare and appraise contracts knew little about the financial soundness of each contract or about the negotiation process. Forrestal therefore followed the recommendations of Struve Hensel, and established the Procurement Legal Division as an independent office on 10 July 1941. In so doing, Forrestal overrode the objections and counterattacks of the Judge Advocate General's Office and

[35] Memorandum of David Ginsburg to Tax and Finance Committee, 14 December 1940, file "Tax and Finance Committee" No. 56, Box 9, Records of the National Defense Advisory Commission, 1940–41.

[36] The Tryon Conference found that "provisions for automatic price increases based on costs of specific items or OPA ceilings should not be allowed unless the Government controls the actual price of items and not merely the maximum price." In June 1943, the Procurement Policy Board agreed unanimously to eliminate escalator clauses that were tied to OPA ceilings (John Perry Miller, *Pricing of Military Procurements* [New Haven: Yale University Press, 1949], 136).

[37] Miller, *Pricing of Military Procurements*, 87–89. On 25 April 1939, the Navy had been authorized to negotiate contracts in the case of building bases outside the continental U.S.

ignored the House Naval Affairs Committee's refusal to appropriate funds for a full-time legal staff.

The Procurement Legal Division was charged with rendering all legal advice pertaining to "negotiation, preparation, performance of all contracts for the procurement, production or transfer, by the Navy Department of material and facilities (except real estate)," where until the establishment of the Procurement Legal Division legal services (solely responsible to the Under Secretary) had been jointly rendered by the Judge Advocate General and by the contracts divisions in the bureaus (responsible only to the bureau chiefs).[38] Lawyers from the Procurement Legal Division were assigned to each of the technical bureaus, where they would clear the bureaus' contracts and thereby supervise the language, the revision, and the improvement of a contract while the contract was still in draft form. The establishment of the civilian-run Procurement Legal Division meant that the Secretary of the Navy now had the means to monitor and coordinate the procurement process.[39]

Shoring up the legal part of procurement resolved only part of the confusion. The Navy also needed a central office able to collect and coordinate information on the progress of its contracts, and able to iron out common policies among the Navy bureaus and between the Navy and other government organizations.[40] The Office of Procurement and Material (OP&M) was therefore created. It incorporated the Resources Planning Division from the Office of the Chief of Naval Operations, the Division of Reports from the Office of Budgets and Reports, the Machine Tool Section from the Shore Establishment Division, and the oversight of contracts with small businesses; initially, it had four branches.[41] *Planning and Statistics* analyzed and planned for the provision of raw and industrial materials. "To do this, it keeps a current picture of basic war plans and compiles a monthly report [the "Monthly Status Report"] showing actual production of ships, airplanes, guns and ammunition, and estimated future requirements."[42] *Procurement*

[38] Connery, *Industrial Mobilization*, 70–72; James Forrestal, *Memorandum for the Secretary of the Navy*, 4 January 1943, file "Frank Knox, Navy," Box 82, Personal Secretary Files, Roosevelt Papers. For an overview of pre-Forrestal procurement in the Navy Department, see Townsend Hoopes and Douglas Brinkley, *Driven Patriot: The Life and Times of James Forrestal* (New York: Knopf, 1992), 153–61.

[39] Connery, *Industrial Mobilization*, 75. The Procurement Legal Office in the Bureau of Aeronautics, under Stuart Scott, got off to a better start than did the Bureau of Ships, under Patrick Hodgson.

[40] External pressure on the Navy Department to improve operating procedures came from the Office of Production Management. The civilian Office of Production Management, "OPM" (predecessor to the War Production Board), is not to be confused with the Navy's OP&M.

[41] Julius Augustus Furer, *Administration of the Navy Department in World War II* (Washington, D.C.: U.S. Department of the Navy, 1959), 839.

[42] *Annual Report of the Secretary of the Navy, 1942.*

"coordinated the negotiation and awarding of contracts" and revised specifi-cations;[43] it was composed of the Industry Cooperation Division, the Price Adjustment Board, the Finance Section, and the Cost and Audit Branch. *Production* treated production problems such as difficulties in financing new facilities or expediting material bottlenecks; *Resources* took over the functions of the Army and Navy Munitions Board and served as a liaison between the Navy and the War Production Board. Forrestal added a fifth branch in May 1942, *Inspection Administration*, to coordinate the work of Navy inspectors.[44] Like the Procurement Legal Division, the OP&M proved invaluable to the Navy for meeting its material needs, and asserted the civilian control over Navy policies.

With the OP&M absorbing the Material Division from the Office of the Chief of Naval Operations, the OP&M became a target of CNO Admiral King. King opposed the creation of the OP&M, and at several points he attempted to curtail civilian influence (under his broad powers to "stream-line" the Navy Department). King wanted to include material controls un-der the CNO—so as to remove them from the Secretary of the Navy's office.[45] He therefore issued directives to his CNO subordinates in early 1942, giving them control over material and personnel responsibilities. But King had to withdraw his directives for reorganizing Navy procurement af-ter Knox and Forrestal warned the President of the CNO's designs, and on 13 June 1942 Roosevelt ordered King to cancel his plans.[46] The position of the OP&M was solidified and its reputation enhanced when Vice Admiral Samuel Robinson was appointed head. On 18 September 1942 Robinson was appointed a member of the War Production Board's Production Execu-tive Committee.

Navy contracts had four basic forms: the fixed-price contract, the cost-plus-fixed-fee contract (CPFF), the incentive contract, and the maximum price contract. Although the overwhelming majority of contracts were at

[43] Furer, *Administration of the Navy*, 841.

[44] Albion and Connery, *Forrestal and the Navy*, 95. For a fuller treatment of OP&M branches and their appointed officials, see Furer, *Administration of the Navy*, 842–45. Accord-ing to Forrestal, coordination of procurement by the OP&M—the individual bureaus doing the *actual* procurement, of course—had three aspects: internal coordination, coordination with other agencies, and coordination with private producers in the supervision of awarded contracts (Connery, *Industrial Mobilization*, 149).

[45] On 12 March 1942, the President issued an Executive Order which unified naval com-mand, combining the duties of the Commander in Chief, United States Fleet, and the Chief of Naval Operations.

[46] Albion and Connery, *Forrestal and the Navy*, 97–101; Hammond, *Organizing for De-fense*, 139–42; Hoopes and Brinkley, *Driven Patriot*, 173–80. The historian Paul Koistinen, curiously, attributes this incident to the weakness of Navy Under Secretary Forrestal (Paul A. C. Koistinen, *The Military-Industrial Complex* [New York: Praeger, 1980], 637).

TABLE 5.1
Naval Supply Contracts of $10 Million or More

Dates	No.		Value	
	Contracts	% CPFF	All Contracts	% CPFF
1940–41	181	30.4	$ 6,377 million	35.0
Jan.–June 1942	184	35.3	6,932	53.1
July–Dec. 1942	110	33.6	4,997	40.5
Jan.–June 1943	124	25.8	4,082	27.9
July–Dec. 1943	118	31.4	3,787	54.4
Jan.–June 1944	105	30.5	3,383	38.0
July–Dec. 1944	62	17.7	1,654	32.4
Total	884	30.4	31,212	41.5

Source: WPB, Bureau of Program and Statistics, *Cost Plus Supply Contracts in the War Program* (8 March 1945), in Miller, *Pricing of Military Procurements*, 27, Table 1.
Note: Excludes foodstuffs, construction, and production facilities.

first offered on a fixed-price basis, as noted earlier, the exigencies of rearmament and mobilization mandated an increased use of the cost-plus-fixed-fee contracts. Prospective contractors were required to submit cost breakdowns for "labor, material, tooling, jigging, overhead, overtime and other items which affect manufacturing costs," and were then to confer with bureau representatives. The prices quoted by the contractor would be compared to similar articles purchased earlier or elsewhere, and the bureau would then decide if the prices were reasonable.[47]

The longer the war went on, of course, the less the Navy had to rely on CPFF contracts. Table 5.1 shows that of the 181 Navy contracts of $10 million or more in 1940–41, 30 percent were contracted on a CPFF basis. The largest proportion of CPFF contracts was at the beginning of the war, in the first half of 1942, with 35 percent of 184 contracts being awarded on a CPFF basis. But by the latter half of 1944, only 18 percent of contracts were awarded on a CPFF basis. Furthermore, a comparison of the value of the contracts to the number of let contracts shows the CPFF contracts being used for more expensive purchases: the value of CPFF contracts came to 35 percent of the Navy's contracts in 1940–41, 53 percent of the value of Navy contracts in the first half of 1942, and 32.4 percent of the value of Navy contracts in late 1944 (see Table 5.1). As the war went on and as costs became better known through more established production methods and

[47] Memorandum, "Negotiation, Determination and Review of Costs and Profits under Negotiated Fixed-Price and Cost-Plus-Fixed-Fee Contracts," Chief of Bureau of Aeronautics to the Assistant Secretary of the Navy, 31 May 1941, L4–3(1) Vol. 17, Aeronautics, 1925–42.

the realization of economies of scale, the Navy switched its contracts from a cost-plus-fixed-fee basis to a fixed-price basis.[48]

CPFF contracts came under constant fire from members of Congress, many of which thought that CPFF contracts gave producers no incentives to cut costs. But Forrestal defended their use:

> The statement is generally made that cost-plus-a-fixed-fee contracts tend to make a contractor careless of his costs. While this may be true in some cases, I do not believe that it is a statement that can be made categorically. . . . A company with which we have recently been in contact throws interesting light on the general conclusion mentioned above.
>
> Grumman Aircraft Corporation entered into a cost-plus contract with the Navy for 4F4-4 fighters at an estimated cost (including a 6% fee) of $41,340 per plane. The last 575 4F4-4s completed by Grumman had an actual cost of $24,000. Similarly, the estimated cost (including a 6% fee) under a cost-plus-a-fixed-fee contract for torpedo planes was $100,912. Actual cost of the first 326 TBF-1s [torpedo planes] produced was $73,463.82. Thus, Grumman Aircraft Corporation has reduced, in production, the actual cost of these fighters to about 58% of their estimated cost and the actual cost of the torpedo planes came to about 73% of their estimated cost.[49]

Navy attorneys developed a third form of contracting, the incentive contract, which enabled the Navy to estimate probable costs of items by negotiating with the contractor and then allowing a reasonable profit for the contractor on top of the base price. An upper price would also be set substantially above the calculated price, with the incentive that if costs came in below the agreed-upon costs, then profits and profits-as-a-percentage-of-costs increased. Conversely, if costs rose above the threshold price, the dollar profits and percentage profits fell. The Under Secretary commented:

> This kind of contract gives a company a definite incentive to cut its costs. In fact, the heart of the contract is the conviction that American business can perform miracles of low-cost production if it is given a profit incentive for doing so. The Navy Department by giving business this incentive stands to save millions of dollars through lower costs of munitions. You will perceive, however, that the *sine*

---

[48] With the production of aircraft, though, the high rate of obsolescence and continued introduction of new models militated against a more rapid turnover to fixed-price contracts. In the case of the Grumman F6F, however, the Navy used the reverse: a fixed-price (unlimited loss) contract for the prototype, and cost-plus-fixed-fee (limited profit) on production orders ("Confidential Report to Hon. Artemus L. Gates" on *An Investigation of the Financial Condition and Recent Earnings of Aircraft Contractors* by S. J. Ziegler, Captain, USN, and John W. Meader, 14 May 1942, p. 39, file "Contract Terminations," Box 5, Records of the Assistant Secretary for Air, Artemus Gates, Record Group 80 ["Gates Papers"]).

[49] "Renegotiation," Box 42, Papers of James V. Forrestal, Seeley G. Mudd Manuscript Library, Princeton University.

qua non for an incentive contract is a contract price which is based on actual cost experience and which is very close to the current cost line. Without a firm, close contract price, the incentive contract would be open to abuses; the contractor would achieve a saving by merely squeezing the water out of an inflated contract price.[50]

The Navy used the incentive contract for the first time on 18 June 1943, when buying destroyers from Consolidated Steel's shipyard in Orange, Texas.

A fourth type of contract, the maximum price contract, differed from the fixed-price contract in that new prices would be adjusted automatically on the basis of costs incurred in initial production.

In short, time was everything for a Navy severely damaged at Pearl Harbor and faced with a two-ocean war. As the Under Secretary advised the bureaus under the War Production Board's Directive No. 2, "(i) Primary emphasis shall be upon the securing of performance in the *time* required by the war program, [and] (ii) . . . contracts shall be placed so as to conserve, for the more difficult war production problems, the facilities of concerns best able, by reason of engineering, managerial, and physical resources, to handle them."[51] Accordingly, the Navy had the technical bureaus contract their procurement directly, with the assistance of legal advisers, instead of through the Bureau of Supplies and Accounts. The Navy was thereby able to save the time that contracts previously had to spend in the Bureau of Supplies and Accounts, a period ranging from two or three weeks to several months. Further savings in time came from the negotiation of contracts by the bureaus, thereby obviating the time losses from contractors' objections and refusals to sign unsatisfactory contract submissions. With contracts no longer being sent through third parties unfamiliar with the technical aspects of bureau purchases, fewer misunderstandings arose between the Navy and its material suppliers.[52]

The handling of contracts by the Navy thus shows the executive branch's command of procurement policy. The Roosevelt Administration established an Under Secretary, set up the OP&M and the Procurement Legal Division, saw to it that the Secretary and Under Secretary of the Navy (rather than

[50] Letter of James Forrestal to Albert Bradley, Executive Vice President, General Motors Corp., 26 August 1943, in Connery, *Industrial Mobilization*, 218; Miller, *Pricing of Military Procurements*, 144–45.

[51] "Directive No. 2," attached to memorandum from the Under Secretary of the Navy to All Bureaus and Offices of the Navy Department, 4 March 1942, L4–3(1) Vol. 24, Aeronautics, 1925–42; emphasis added.

[52] "Appraisal of Results of Reorganization of Procurement," memorandum of the Chief of the Bureau of Aeronautics to the Subcommittee of the House Committee on Naval Affairs Investigating Naval Personnel, file "1943," L4–3(1) Vol. 35, General Correspondence of the Bureau of Aeronautics, 1943–45, Record Group 72 ("Aeronautics, 1943–45").

the CNO) controlled procurement, and allowed the Navy and Army to negotiate contracts—as they were empowered to do by the Congress. Congress also regulated the use of CPFF contracts.

2. Prices, Negotiated Contracts, and Renegotiation Central to letting contracts was price control. Prices were often extremely difficult to determine, given the unprecedented scale, speed, and complexity of the wartime purchasing. This was especially true when manufacturers had no prior experience producing an item they were selling to the military. Original contract price estimates were, as a consequence, often far higher than actual production prices since economies of scale and improved production techniques typically reduced manufacturing costs.[53] The prices of aircraft engines, three-inch deck guns, and destroyer escorts, for example, dropped steadily over time as prototypes went into production.[54] The Navy's civilian executives therefore undertook specific measures to limit the cost of their contracts by clearing contracts, inspecting cost figures, negotiating more contracts, and renegotiating contracts.

Prices first became an issue in December 1941 when Congress was considering the Price Control Act. The Under Secretaries of the Departments of the Navy and War wrote the chairman of the Senate Banking and Currency Committee and requested broad exemptions from the Price Control Bill's ceilings on military purchases.[55] But the Senate committee refused to overrule the decisions of the Price Administrator, Leon Henderson, and on 19 December 1941 War Secretary Stimson and Navy Secretary Knox appealed to the President. Although Roosevelt refused to overrule Henderson, he expressed faith in the Price Administrator's reasonableness. But the Price Control Act of 30 January 1942 contained no provisions for exempting war materials, and Henderson refused to repeal the existing controls. Only after the Navy and War Departments' repeated complaints did Henderson agree in November 1942 to refrain from further controls on military prices.

Yet the Navy benefited far more than it suffered from the OPA's price controls and the General Max regulations, even as the price controls were withdrawn on military goods—its complaints notwithstanding. Knox reported that the Price Control Act had saved the Navy billions, had ensured

---

[53] "History of Navy Department Renegotiation," Vol. 1, 7(a), p. 2, The History of the Administration of the United States Navy in WWII, Office of Naval History, Washington, D.C., Navy Yard ("Naval Administration").

[54] We may compare this with the financing of the public debt, where the cost of capital stayed constant under the fixed rates of interest set up by the Treasury and as supported by the Federal Reserve Banks. Not uncoincidentally, the Navy's purchase of material occurred at a different time from its receipt. That is, the Navy might pay for a proportion of the product and then, upon the delivery of the good, pay the balance. Rarely could the Navy buy supplies off the shelf. In contrast, the Treasury Department was able to arrange to sell its debt and receive dollars on the spot.

[55] Connery, *Industrial Mobilization*, 227.

"full and uninterrupted production of ships, planes and other Navy material," and had sustained Navy morale.[56] The Navy was also able to use the price controls to its advantage, as when it defeated attempts to amend an OPA agreement on steel castings.[57]

More important than direct price controls, however, were the Navy's indirect controls on contract costs. The Navy established a Negotiation Section in July 1942 and on 13 December 1942 transferred it from the Purchase Division of the Bureau of Supplies and Accounts to the OP&M. The Negotiations Division (renamed) and the Contract Clearing Division of the Procurement Branch monitored contracts for fair pricing and, among other duties, determined whether or not contractors could meet production schedules.

Navy negotiators worked with bureau representatives and with lawyers from the Procurement Legal Division to award contracts by telephone, through letters, and in conferences with the representatives from the contracting firm. As Navy officials gained experience and as procurement records became better tabulated and more centralized, the Navy was able to improve its bargaining position with contracting firms.[58] Navy lawyers, supplied with lists of itemized costs and growing more familiar with drafting particular contracts as time went on, were increasingly able to spot unsubstantiated costs.

Whether the Navy was negotiating a fixed-price or a CPFF contract, responsibility fell to the bureau chiefs for reviewing and reporting on the actual contract. The bureaus had the responsibility to assess the contractor's real costs, the extent of subcontracting, the method of placing subcontracts, the fairness of subcontractor contracts, the duplication of profits between the prime contractors and the sub-contractors, the fairness of the prime contractor's fee or profit, the fairness of increased prices in excess of labor and material price indexes, the record of prior and general contractor profits, the possibility of price-fixing, whether the contractor or any of its officers might receive indirect profits through affiliation with subcontractors, and what procedures were being used to check costs and monitor progress of contracts.[59] With the Navy's new administration of procurement, however, the contracting bureaus no longer had to take on all of these tasks themselves.

---

[56] Senate Banking and Currency Committee, *Hearings*, 78th Cong., 2nd sess., 17 April 1944, 629, in Connery, *Industrial Mobilization*, 236.

[57] Connery, *Industrial Mobilization*, 232–33; Miller, *Pricing of Military Procurements*, 66–82.

[58] Connery, *Industrial Mobilization*, 238–42.

[59] Memorandum, "Negotiation, Determination and Review of Costs and Profits under Negotiated Fixed-Price and Cost-Plus-Fixed-Fee Contracts," Assistant Secretary of the Navy to Chief of Bureau of Aeronautics et al., 15 April 1941, L4–3(1) Vol. 17, Aeronautics, 1925–42.

If negotiated contracts were one way to control costs, another way was to subject contracts to *renegotiation*. Renegotiation became law on 28 April 1942, when the President approved the McKellar amendment to the Sixth Supplemental Defense Appropriation Act of 1942, the "Renegotiation Act of 1942." The Roosevelt Administration and Congress both agreed on the necessity of adapting "our profit economy and system of competitive enterprise to wartime conditions. [Renegotiation] is strictly a war measure, adopted as an alternative to a rigid formula for profit control, as contained in the Vinson-Trammell Act, and in the place of profit control through taxation." The renegotiation law was to encourage efficient war production and to keep the costs of munitions and materials of war under control. It was "not a punitive measure, a revenue measure, nor a regulation measure. It is a pricing statute and as such is an essential part of war production."[60]

Under the provisions of the Renegotiation Act, the Navy had to renegotiate contracts over $100,000, and renegotiation could take place any time up to three years after the end of the war. By taking into account the efficiency of the contractors, the reasonableness of the costs and profits, the amount and source of public and private capital, risk, the nature and extent of contribution to the war effort, the complexity of production, and other factors, Navy officials were able to tailor renegotiation to the contractor and item in question. After determining what they considered a fair profit for any contractor *before taxes*, Navy officials allocated any excessive profit to specific contracts, which usually resulted in the determination of a revised unit price for the product; there could be no one formula for renegotiation.[61]

Congress amended the 1942 Renegotiation Act in the Revenue Act of 1943 (enacted on 25 February 1944). The new law lodged authority with the War Contracts Price Adjustment Board (rather than with the department secretaries), and raised the statutory limit on contracts to be renegotiated from $100,000 to $500,000, in order to expedite settlements.[62] One researcher, citing letters from Forrestal to Representative Carl Vinson, Chairman of the House Naval Affairs Committee, finds that Forrestal himself proposed the legislation on contract renegotiation so that contracts could be

---

[60] "History of Navy Department Renegotiation," Vol. 1, 7(a), p. 41.

[61] Miller, *Pricing of Military Procurements*, 170–74; Connery, *Industrial Mobilization*, 277; John L. Sullivan, "Memorandum of Conference," 6 May 1942, file "Daily Record, May–Sept. 1942," Box 3, Sullivan Papers. Also see "History of Navy Department Renegotiation," pp. 26–28.

[62] Connery, *Industrial Mobilization*, 46. The Chairman of the Navy Price Adjustment Board opposed the proposal "on the ground that it would enable many small concerns to escape with large profits." Industry and Congressmen also opposed the "super-excess-profits tax," the recapture aspect of renegotiation, and the limitations on fixed profits. They saw such provisions as leading to inflation, failing to reduce costs, and not providing for sufficient production incentives.

adjusted according to up-to-date market conditions.[63] The Renegotiation Act, as amended, allowed the Navy and War Departments to set prices by command if they could not be set through negotiation. In addition, Forrestal, Secretary of War Stimson, and other top government officials recommended that Congress extend the Renegotiation Act through 31 December 1945 and for no more than six months afterwards. Competitive conditions had "not been restored to the point where either original pricing or repricing can prevent the realization of excessive profits from the performance of such contracts and subcontracts. It is, therefore, believed that the interests of the Government and of contractors alike require the continuance of renegotiation."[64]

At Grumman, net profits after taxes fell from 4.32 percent of net sales in 1941 to 2.39 percent in 1942; profits at United Aircraft remained at 4.04 percent, and profits at Consolidated fell from 4.6 percent to 3.49 percent.[65] Prices fell as well. The F4U Corsair fighter plane, produced by the Chance-Vought Division of the United Aircraft Corporation, was priced at $69,887 per plane at the end of the first production run of 624 aircraft in June 1943, but at $61,200 each by January 1944. The FM Wildcat, built by the Eastern Aircraft Division of General Motors, cost $41,979 per plane at the end of production of the first 707 planes in August 1943, but cost $32,310 each by December 1943. The price of the F6F Grumman Hellcat dropped from $54,723 per plane at the end of a production run in June 1943 to $43,600 per plane in December 1943.[66] The renegotiation of Navy contracts recovered about $831 million in all between April 1942 and September 1947—over and above the receipts from income and excess profits taxes, and exclusive of the savings offered up voluntarily by contractors who wished to avoid paying large refunds to the Navy at the time of renegotiation. The legislation and administration of renegotiation "made contractors cost-conscious, persuaded them to reduce costs, and consequently, lowered the cost of the War."[67]

In practice, however, it turned out that renegotiators sought to capture profits—and there was a difference between capturing excess profits and

[63] Cecilia Stiles Cornell, "James V. Forrestal and American National Security Policy, 1940–1949," Ph.D. diss., Vanderbilt University, 1987, 68–69.

[64] Letter of Secretary of War, Henry Stimson, Secretary of the Navy, James Forrestal, Acting Secretary of the Treasury, Daniel Bell, Secretary of Commerce, Jesse Jones, and Chairman, U.S. Maritime Commission, Vice Admiral Emory S. Land to Robert L. Doughton, Chairman, Committee on Ways and Means, 2 January 1945, file CD 16–1–12, Box 50, Records of the Secretary of the Navy James Forrestal, 1940–47, Record Group 80 ("Navy Secretary Records").

[65] Attachment to "Memorandum to the Secretary of the Navy," from John Kenney, 9 September 1944, file CD 29–1–38, Box 62, Navy Secretary Records.

[66] "Cost Trend of Principal Naval Aircraft," 2 February 1944, file "Contracts," Box 9, Gates Papers.

[67] Connery, Industrial Mobilization, 289; "History of Navy Department Renegotiation," xiii.

pricing for future delivery—but the responsibility for repricing rested with the original team of officials that made the contract. Because of the difficulty of renegotiation, the Navy set up a Price Revision Division in the OP&M on 11 April 1944 to act as a clearing house. The Price Revision Division saved an estimated $123 million, of which $65.3 million came through price reductions.[68] Only thirteen Navy contracts were exempted from renegotiation.[69] Statutory renegotiation was extended to 30 June 1945, and then to 31 December 1945.

Implementing the Renegotiation Acts was the Price Adjustment Board of the Secretary of the Navy's Office. The Navy put regional boards in Chicago and San Francisco in September and November 1942; the Navy set up a Field Renegotiation Section in late 1943, given the increasing numbers of teams being sent out into the field. (By 31 December 1946 field negotiations had been completed on 2,310 assignments.)[70] The Navy Price Adjustment Board succeeded in lowering total profits on fixed-price contracts from 13.6 percent to 8.8 percent between 1942 to 1945, while profits on cost-plus contracts—the fees—declined from 4.8 to 4.6 percent. Combined contract profits dropped from 12.7 percent to 8.4 percent.[71] Gross recoveries from renegotiation amounted to $2.77 billion, while the Navy Price Adjustment personnel complement never rose above 350 persons. The Navy's expenses in renegotiation as a proportion of total recoveries came to approximately 0.2 percent.[72] Renegotiation reduced prices by a total of nearly $4.75 billion, and by 31 December 1946 statutory renegotiation recovered excess profits of over $10 billion if Navy and War Department figures are combined.[73] The Price Adjustment Board was terminated on 30 September 1947, but the Renegotiation Act of 1948 specified that certain Navy, Air Force, and Army contracts still had to be renegotiated.

Renegotiation was able to succeed because of what some considered its greatest weakness, its absence of a rigid formula for determining excess profits: "there were no established standards for the determination of excessive profits." A fixed formula would be "an attempt to simplify something that is not susceptible of simplification."[74] Navy Assistant Secretary John Kenney commented, "This lack [of a rigid formula] placed the emphasis in determining excessive profits directly upon the human factor. Therefore, the

[68] Connery, *Industrial Mobilization*, 252.

[69] Miller, *Pricing of Military Procurements*, 185.

[70] Connery, *Industrial Mobilization*, 280.

[71] These figures are from a base total of $75.9 billion in sales and $8.0 billion in profits before renegotiation (Statement by Kenneth Rockey, First Chairman of the Navy Price Adjustment Board, to the Special Committee Investigating the National Defense Program, 21 October 1947, file "Speech File 1947," Box 6, Kenney Papers).

[72] "History of Navy Department Renegotiation," Vol. 1, 7(a), xii.

[73] "History of Navy Department Renegotiation," Vol. 1, 7(a), v. The cost of renegotiation was estimated at only 0.37 percent of gross recoveries and 1.23 percent of net recoveries.

[74] "History of Navy Department Renegotiation," 26, 28.

success of the administration of the renegotiation statute chiefly depended on the character, philosophy and ability of the business and professional men who constituted the various price adjustment boards and their administrative staffs."[75]

In short, the Navy was able to use both direct and indirect controls to set pricing policy to the government's advantage through the negotiation and renegotiation of contracts. Congress played an accessory role insofar as it furnished enabling legislation.

3. Contract Supervision and Statistics Fundamental to any successful control of costs by the Navy was the ability to evaluate and supervise its contracts. Negotiation and renegotiation were two ways of doing so. But neither the negotiation nor the renegotiation of contracts could tackle directly the matter of product reliability, the scheduling of contracts, or the quality of the data being used in letting contracts. The complexities of inventories, production bottlenecks, subcontracting, and production quality often made it impossible for the Navy to know its exact supply costs.

One way to monitor contracting was simply to stress to all "Bureaus, Boards, and Offices of the Navy Department" the importance of responsible, feasible and cost-efficient procurement. Forrestal sent out one such blanket appeal in a memorandum of April 1943: "In the interest of adopting a uniform procedure throughout the Bureaus in the treatment of selling expenses, it is recommended that contracting personnel carefully scrutinize cost breakdowns submitted to the Navy Department by contractors with a view to determining the existence of excessive compensation, especially in the form of commissions or contingent fees, for the service of their sales agents or sales engineers."[76] Such exhortations were insufficient by themselves, of course. Better was to supervise the actual production of war material, and this is what the Navy did.

On 27 December 1941, soon after the United States entered the war, the President created the Contracts Clearing Section to ensure that the proper OP&M personnel were being consulted in the awarding of contracts and that the bureaus were converting letters of intent into contracts. (The bureaus were frequently late in converting the letters into legal contracts.)[77] The Contract Clearance Division (renamed) also cooperated with the Cost

---

[75] "History of Navy Department Renegotiation," xi. The report cited, as critical to the success of renegotiation, the care and fairness with which board members exercised their discretionary power. Of the 24,000 assignments, only 450 cases had to be decided unilaterally, and only 130 were appealed to the Tax Court (xii).

[76] "Selling Expense in Navy Contracts," Memorandum from the Secretary of the Navy, 22 April 1943, file "1943," L4–3(1) Vol. 36, Aeronautics, 1943–45.

[77] The "letters of intent" were written contract agreements, introduced to expedite procurement, which omitted definite pricing. During the first four months of 1942, the Navy made commitments valued at $5.3 billion in the form of letters of intent (Miller, *Pricing of Military Procurements*, 123).

Inspection Service and with the Price Adjustment Board in examining cost breakdowns and assisting in contract renegotiation.[78] In 1942, the Contract Clearance Division handled 7,324 requests for contract authority amounting to $24 billion, despite the fact that a restriction of 4 February 1942 limited the Division to clearing contracts over one million dollars.[79]

But the Contract Clearing Division could not itself assess the quality of material products, the accuracy of scheduled delivery times, or the veracity of cost figures. A second, integral part of the Navy's monitoring of contracts was therefore the physical inspection of the operations of material suppliers. Inspection was required for fixed-price contracts in amounts greater than $500,000, and for all CPFF contracts.

Of the seven field inspection groups (in 1940), the most important were the Supervisors of Shipbuilding, the Inspectors of Naval Aircraft, the Inspectors of Naval Material, and the Cost Inspectors. A supervisor of shipbuilding, present at every large private shipyard, commanded a team of officer assistants, technicians, draftsmen, inspectors, and clerks. The supervisor reported directly to the Bureau of Ships. Inspection offices were similarly set up at each major aircraft manufacturing plant. The aircraft inspectors also had sole responsibility over their assigned facility and reported directly to the Bureau of Aeronautics. Each bureau had its own inspectors, and contractors had to inform bureau inspectors within ten days (in writing) of the issue and proposed terms of any subcontracts. The bureau inspectors had to be conscious of both production volume (so as to ensure the delivery of enough aircraft and ships) and quality control (so as to ensure the dependability of ship hulls or aircraft engines). But bureau inspectors also reported on unsatisfactory conditions, such as management incompetence, waste, "widespread loafing," "undue attention to post war plans," "accumulation of excess inventories," "lack of adequate system of cost or price control," and "excessive salaries or wages, or unjustified increases therein."[80]

Whereas the bureau inspectors monitored the production of major contractors, the Inspectors of Naval Material (the largest of the inspection groups) supervised the provision of raw materials, semi-finished goods, and components for procured items. Although the Inspectors of Naval Material reported to the Bureau of Ships for administrative purposes, they effectively served all bureaus, since they also inspected steel production, aluminum and chemical plants, and small industrial plants. There were about six hun-

[78] Contract Clearance was less successful in policing contract quantities (Connery, *Industrial Mobilization*, 209).

[79] Connery, *Industrial Mobilization*, 207.

[80] "Enclosure A," 2–3, Memorandum of Chief, BuAer, to All BAGRs [Bureau of Aeronautics General Representatives], 30 November 1944, file "1943–45," L4–3(1) Vol. 14, Aeronautics, 1943–45.

dred Inspectors of Naval Material in early 1941, and about 17,500 inspectors in 1944—or two-thirds of the total of 28,000 naval inspectors.[81]

The Cost Inspectors worked in cost inspection boards at the plants of all large contractors (the Supervisors of Shipbuilding and Material Inspectors were also on these boards). Contractors had to notify the inspectors of the existence and terms of subcontracting, and the cost inspectors evaluated the contracts with price adjustment or cost incentive features and had final jurisdiction over the reasonableness of contract and subcontract prices.

Whereas inspection in its various forms was essentially a policing function, the supervision needed for expediting contracts and contract scheduling was promotional.[82] Expediting could involve finding available supplies, resolving labor and labor-relations problems, and remedying the production process itself under conditions where plant managers were frequently under multiple demands from various interested parties.[83] The Navy had its own lists and schedules of the priority of vessels, components, and materials, although the War Production Board had formal authority to set priorities and allocations.

Under the emergency conditions of prewar and then wartime mobilization, however, it was increasingly apparent that the inspection of the majority of contractors in 1940 was "uncoordinated" and appeared to "lack unity."[84] In a report commissioned by the Navy Department, Lewis Strauss (a senior partner at investment bankers Kuhn, Loeb) found repeated instances of redundant and poorly organized inspections; the report recommended that inspection be centralized. Despite Forrestal's circulation of the

[81] Connery, *Industrial Mobilization*, 324, 339. In 1940, the country was divided into fifteen material inspection districts (not coinciding with the naval districts).

[82] Connery, *Industrial Mobilization*, 319–20.

[83] Delays in aircraft production for a group of four manufacturers (Boeing, Consolidated, Douglas, and Lockheed) were the result of shortages in aluminum, steel, machine tools, cable, steel screws, forgings, hydraulic fittings, generators and starters, wheels, pumps, neoprene grommets, and glass, among other items. Delays were also caused by incomplete plant construction, design and engineering changes, and labor unrest (Memorandum to Mr. Hopkins, 11 September 1941, attached to letter of Isadore Lubin to Forrestal, Under Secretary of the Navy, 16 September 1941, file "Contractors," Box 5, Gates Papers).

Delays in building destroyers at Federal Shipbuilding and Drydock, Seattle-Tacoma, Consolidated Steel, the Boston, Charleston, Philadelphia and Norfolk Navy Yards, and Bath Iron Works came from labor strikes, shortages of various forgings, presses and lathes, lack of machine tools, late delivery of turbines, and insufficient steel plate (Memorandum "For Admiral Robinson," from Bureau of Ships, 29 September 1941, file "S.P.A.B.," Box 221, Papers of Harry Hopkins).

[84] Much of the material on inspection cited here comes from Furer, *Administration of the Navy*, 870–79. Both Furer and Connery note that one problem of inspection was the lack of skilled personnel for doing what was an unglamorous job. The Navy found that using officers often worked better than civilians, and so mostly relied on uniformed reserve officers for inspection duties.

report among the bureaus and discussion of the report on 21 December 1941, the Navy delayed acting on Strauss's report.[85] Not until 2 May 1942 did Forrestal, following the recommendations of a separate study by management consultants Booz, Frye, Allen and Hamilton, set up an Inspection Administration Office in the OP&M.[86] The bureaus were to retain technical control over specifications and inspection standards, but administrative matters would have to be cleared with the Inspection Administration Office.[87]

The bureaus opposed the centralization as being ineffective, since the Inspection Administration Office, nominally in charge of inspection, was providing weak direction as it was.[88] The Navy was nonetheless able to coordinate inspection under an agreement between a new Director of the Inspection Administration Office and the material bureaus: the bureaus would retain control of their inspection services, and the Inspection Administration Office would command the Inspectors of Naval Material.[89]

The conflict between inspection of costs and materials and inspection for scheduling and expediting material production came to a head with the Navy contracts for landing craft. The Navy had to set up a separate "Material Coordinating Agency" for the sole purpose of expediting production. Yet the bureau inspectors opposed the centralization of inspection in the Mate-

[85] Connery, *Industrial Mobilization*, 128–30.

[86] The "Booz Report" chiefly concerned operations and logistics, not procurement and civilian management. It did stress the need for reorganization and administrative changes in the face of "total war." These unseen and "totally new" conditions demanded "revolutionary operations" by the Navy ("Abstract of Report on Chief of Naval Operations," by Booz-Allen, 1943, file "Organization and functions of the Navy Department—General," Box 1, Series 39.6A, "Navy 1941–48," Budget Records).

Connery reports, "Ultimately, each of the bureaus, the Office of Naval Intelligence, and some divisions of the CNO were covered by these surveys. As a result there were a great many administrative changes. Some bureaus . . . were completely reorganized on a functional basis, and the whole departmental structure was more logically arranged" (113). Immediately after the war, the Navy carried out sixty-eight surveys (at the request of the Bureau of the Budget) at a total cost of $249,254. The surveys concerned such topics as accounting procedures, management and fiscal control, planning, etc.

[87] Eberstadt, "100 Billion Dollar Navy, Vol. 3," Chapter XVIII, 2–5.

[88] Eberstadt, "100 Billion Dollar Navy, Vol. 3," Chapter XVII, 5–9; Connery, *Industrial Mobilization*, 324–25.

[89] See Connery for the organization of inspection (Connery, *Industrial Mobilization*, 325–43).

Coordination also took place between the Inspectors of Naval Materials, the Bureau representatives, and even the War Department. The Inspector of Naval Material, Los Angeles, reported to Assistant Secretary Gates that "[a] close and cordial relationship has been established between BAGR, WD and InsMat, Los Angeles, which has resulted in benefit to both offices as well as to the procurement and inspection of BuAer and AAF material in general" (Memorandum of J. R. Defrees, Inspector of Naval Material, Los Angeles District, to Chief of the Bureau of Aeronautics, Navy Department, 29 April 1944, file "1944," L4–3(1) Vol. 5, Aeronautics, 1943–45).

rial Coordinating Agency. The Material Coordinating Agency was interfering with individual procurement programs by initiating "frequent changes . . . in processing and expediting procedures." The WPB had to step in. It appointed an officer to oversee the production of the destroyer escorts in order to avoid the problems and controversies surrounding the inspection of the landing-craft program.

Once the war was over, Forrestal directed that the boundaries between inspection functions be divided between the Inspection Administration (with direct management control of the Inspectors of Naval Material) and the specialized bureau inspectors (with predominantly technical responsibilities). The Inspection Administration was retitled the "Field Services Division" of the Office of Naval Material.

Besides clearing contracts and inspecting production sites, the Navy also supervised procurement by using the tools of business administration (especially that of "the most convenient tool—the Budget") to remedy an "outstanding condition which may be best described as a lack of integrated, centralized, and coordinated control of the Navy's budgetary system and production program." The Navy established a Fiscal Director (later "Comptroller") on 2 December 1944, responsible to the Secretary of the Navy for formulating, supervising, and coordinating the Navy's budgeting, accounting, and auditing policies. The comptroller's office provided a single central authority able to provide a master pattern of requirements of products or funds, and to record the "availability and consumption of goods and services on which procurement plans can be based."[90] The comptroller's office would, furthermore, "establish such control procedures [such as accounting] . . . as will either force consistency of objectives among the various segments of our business, or failing this . . . serve as a means of telling management, before the money is spent, that the energies of our separate departments are not directed to one common, known objective."[91] The Navy's centralized control of the bureaus would be through the purse.[92]

Common to financial accounting, material inspection, and the supervision of contracts was statistics: the Navy had to have precise information as to what products it did and did not possess. Navy Secretary Knox had set up a statistical unit in the War Material Procurement Section of the CNO as early

[90] Memorandum of M. D. Safanie, Planning and Statistics, OP&M, to the Secretary of the Navy and the Under Secretary of the Navy, "A Budget and Production Control Plan," 16 March 1944, p. 2, file "Appropriations," Box 3, Gates Papers.

[91] Memorandum of M. D. Safanie to the Secretary of the Navy and the Under Secretary of the Navy, "A Budget and Production Control Plan," p. 7.

[92] The Office of the Fiscal Director was the proposal of M. D. Safanie, Planning and Statistics, OP&M, in March 1944. See Memorandum of M. D. Safanie to the Secretary of the Navy and the Under Secretary of the Navy, "A Budget and Production Control Plan for the Navy," file CD 70-1-25, Box 121, Navy Secretary Records.

as 7 August 1940—Knox being aware of the absence of a centralized, up-to-date statistical base—but the Dillon-Belmont report of 7 October 1940 noted that many bureau figures were inaccurate and that other figures were often missing.[93] Following the Dillon-Belmont recommendations, Knox moved the statistical unit to the Secretary's Office in December 1940 and renamed it the "Office of Budget and Records." The distribution of the office's principal product, the monthly "Statistical Summary of Progress," originated from this office.

Statistical controls were further centralized on 5 February 1942, with the establishment of the Planning and Statistics Branch within the OP&M. The Planning and Statistics Branch collected and analyzed the Navy's statistics, and then tabulated, presented, and published its findings. The Branch's main product, the "Monthly Status Report," catalogued the procurement processes and material changes in each of the bureaus.[94] The Planning and Statistics Branch had four, and then six, divisions: Planning, Scheduling and Reporting, Raw Material, Records Control, and, later, Material Control and Inventory Control. At its peak, the Planning and Statistics Branch had a staff of 230 persons.[95]

Another study of the Navy's inventory system (commissioned by Forrestal) recommended the establishment of a central inventory control system for setting standards across products and for prioritizing inventory control in the procurement process.[96] Unbalanced or unnecessary inventory stocks could delay the delivery of vital goods and add to the costs of conducting war. However, not until 14 February 1945—with the Requirements Review Board placed under Assistant Secretary Hensel—did the Planning and Statistics Branch have the support of both the Secretary's Office and the CNO's.[97] At this point Forrestal dissolved the Planning and Statistics Branch, transferred the Scheduling and Reporting Division to the Assistant Secretary's Office, and moved the Finance Group of the Scheduling and Reporting Division to the Office of the Fiscal Director in the Secretary's Office (the Accounting and Control Section remained in OP&M, under the Production Branch). Kenney estimated that despite the late start, the Navy managed to save over $275 million in one year alone by cataloging the inventory of one company's engine parts.[98]

[93] Connery, *Industrial Mobilization*, 130–31.

[94] See Connery, *Industrial Mobilization*, 184–87, on these reports and the comparison with the Army's reports. Donald Belcher, an executive from American Telephone and Telegraph, was named the first director of the Planning and Statistics Branch.

[95] Connery, *Industrial Mobilization*, 183.

[96] J. F. Creamer, A. C. Romer, and C. W. Cederberg, "Navy Inventory Control Problems," 10 May 1944, file CD 70–1–16, Box 120, Navy Secretary Records.

[97] Connery, *Industrial Mobilization*, 195.

[98] "Speech of the Honorable W. John Kenney at a Luncheon of the American Standards

Another set of statistical controls tracked price levels, the Navy Department's costs. The Navy developed an index system divided into 150 class indexes for individual commodities. The 150 commodity classes were combined into 70 subgroups and 26 group indexes, which were, in turn, aggregated into 5 bureau indexes and one overall Navy index (with October 1942 as the common baseline). Although the price machinery was put into place in November 1942, the Navy did not release the first index of prices until October 1944—suggesting the difficulties of indexing and recording the myriad prices and price changes on Navy purchases.

In sum, the Navy monitored its contracts through price indexes, fiscal controls, material, scheduling and cost inspections, and contract clearance. In each instance, it was either Knox or (more often) Forrestal who introduced and implemented new, centralized management practices.

4. Financing Production No matter how much the Navy wanted to buy a given product, however, it was often the case that there were no sellers. In many instances factories did not exist for making the ships, aircraft, ordnance, and other products needed. Not only were the shelves of private industry often bare, but private industry frequently lacked the simple capacity to produce the material supplies to put on the shelves. The U.S. government and the Navy therefore financed production themselves. Of the $25 billion total of new war manufacturing capacity built during the war, the U.S. government financed about $16 billion; the other $9 billion was financed privately.[99]

The Navy financed $3 billion worth of machinery and facilities during the war, while it had private industry actually build the plants and produce the needed material.[100] Table 5.2 shows the number and place of government financing of shipyards producing destroyers (and other ships) during World War II. The government financed over $21 million of the Bethlehem Steel facilities in Quincy, Massachusetts, outside Boston; it financed $18.3 million of the Bethlehem Steel facilities in San Francisco; and it financed $14 million of the Todd-Pacific yard in Tacoma, Washington.

Government financing took four basic forms: the direct financing of a facility, in which case the U.S. government would either operate the facility itself or lease it to a private contractor; tax amortization, for inducing private

---

Association in New York on October 22, 1948," file "Speech 1948," Box 6, Kenney Papers. The Bureau of Ships would save $25 million over the next six years on an inventory of $282 million.

[99] Miller, *Pricing of Military Procurements*, 113.

[100] Peck and Scherer, *The Weapons Acquisition Process*, 164. Despite the general triumph of civilian control in the Navy, Albion and Connery note that "on occasion" Forrestal and OP&M chief Robinson would disapprove an industrial facility, only to find it being built anyway, reclassified as a "command facility" approved by the CNO (Albion and Connery, *Forrestal and the Navy*, 121).

TABLE 5.2
Navy-Financed Shipyards: Destroyer Production (over $5 million)

Name and Location	Facilities	Land	Land Ownership
Bethlehem Steel, Quincy, Mass.	$21,088,000	$ 63,622	Mixed
Bethlehem Steel, San Francisco	18,302,900	1,902,982	Mixed
Bethlehem Steel, San Pedro, Cal.	5,656,565	Leased by Contractor	
Bethlehem Steel, Staten Island, N.Y.	5,939,006	51,094	Mixed
Consolidated Steel Corp., Orange, Tex.	11,272,122	Contractor-Owned	
Federal SB & DD Co., Kearny, N.J.	9,629,347	Contractor-Owned	
Federal SB & DD Co., Newark, N.J.	19,344,625	683,322	U.S. Navy
Gulf Shipbuilding Co., Chickasaw, Ala.	5,541,780	Contractor-Owned	
Newport News SB & DD Co., Newport News, Va.	21,639,832	Contractor-Owned	
Todd-Pacific Shipyard, Tacoma	14,114,132	1,136,615	Mixed

Source: H. Gerrish Smith and L. C. Brown, "Shipyard Statistics," in F. G. Fassett, Jr., ed., *The Shipbuilding Business in the United States of America* (New York: Society of Naval Architects and Marine Engineers, 1948), Vol. 1, 163: Table 76, "Government-Financed Shipyards Costing Five Million Dollars or Over, by Ownership: Privately Owned Shipyards."

Notes: Todd-Pacific Shipyard was formerly Seattle-Tacoma Shipbuilding Corp. The Bethlehem Steel ship-yards in both San Francisco and San Pedro were also repair yards. Federal Shipbuilding and Drydock of Newark was owned by the U.S. Navy; Consolidated Steel Corp. of Orange was jointly owned with the U.S. government; all the other shipyards were privately owned.

investment; cash advances, for providing for construction funds; and capital or credit guarantees, for expanding industrial capacity.

Almost as soon as the United States began to rearm, on 25 June 1940, Congress authorized the Reconstruction Finance Corporation to finance facility construction and expansion. On 22 August 1940 Congress, respond-ing to a request from President Roosevelt, established the Defense Plant Corporation (DPC) as a subsidiary of the RFC. The DPC built facilities making strategic materials and then leased them to contractors for a five-year period. The contractor could either lease the plant at $1 per year if it sold its entire output to the military services, or it could pay rent to the government in amounts sufficient to amortize the entire cost of the plant over its expected lifetime.[101] The total cost of DPC contracts for the Navy between 1 July 1940 and 30 June 1945 came to $608.8 million. The Bureau of Aeronautics received $548.7 million of this total; the Bureau of Ships, $59.4 million.[102]

The National Defense Advisory Commission also sponsored the Emer-gency Plant Facilities Contract Plan for the financing of new facilities during the rearmament period, and in October 1940 Congress agreed to set up the

[101] Miller, *Pricing of Military Procurements*, 117.
[102] Connery, *Industrial Mobilization*, 349.

Emergency Plant Facilities. The Second Revenue Act of 1940 accelerated amortization for contractors acquiring or constructing facilities for national defense to five years at 1⅔ percent per month in lieu of the normal depreciation deduction.[103]

Another way for the Navy to provide working capital for contractors was to progressively pay for the contractor's output—and in the early days of the war, the Navy financed almost any company that could manufacture ships, aircraft, other material, or the components thereof. Contractors had to post bonds for their advance payments at 10 percent of the contract value with no advance or prepayments; 25 percent with partial payment but no advance; 40 percent with a 30 percent advance and no partial payment; and 30 percent for an advance payment of 30 percent and a second 25 percent— two bonds being necessary—for both the partial payment and a performance guarantee. This would, in theory, protect the Navy's advances.[104] Advances—charged at 2½ percent interest—totaled about $2 billion from 1940 through September 1945.[105] Although the Navy was unable to extend advance payments of more than 30 percent of the contract price, this was still advantageous to small manufacturers. Furthermore, product demands on some occasions dictated that the Navy waive the bond payments. While this method ensured that the Navy's advance would be repaid, it offered no guarantee that the Navy's money would be used to produce material—the ultimate purpose of the financing. The Navy therefore developed the "controlled account," whereby funds could be withdrawn by the contractor upon the countersignature of the Navy Inspector. Under the controlled account system, the Navy became its own insurer.[106]

Besides providing direct government funds, amortizing taxes on private investment, and offering cash advances, the Navy offered guaranteed credit. In March 1942 the President granted the Navy Department, the War Department, and the Maritime Commission (charged with constructing the merchant marine fleet) the discretionary authority to make loans, discounts, and advances in order to expedite the prosecution of the war (E.O. 9112). The Federal Reserve Banks were to be the agents of the Navy and War Departments. Shortly after the order, the Federal Reserve Boards established the rates of interest and guarantee-charges under "Regulation V" ("V"

---

[103] See Miller, *Pricing of Military Procurements*, 113–16, more generally.

[104] Cash-advance financing can be divided into three stages: the first lasted from June 1940 until summer 1943, a period when the Navy's desperate need for increased production resulted in few controls over financing risks; the second after mid-1943, when the Navy was able to overhaul its administrative and financing methods so as to screen contractors more carefully; and the third, also beginning after 1943, when the Navy began terminating those loans based on the guaranteed-loan system (Connery, *Industrial Mobilization*, 368).

[105] Miller, *Pricing of Military Procurements*, 119.

[106] Connery, *Industrial Mobilization*, 369.

standing for the twenty-second regulation, following "U" in the alphabet, not for "Victory").

The provision of guaranteed credit was targeted at producers who could not obtain sufficient credit through normal banking procedures but who nonetheless required additional funds. These contractors could take advantage of the "V-loans." The contractor would approach a bank, and the bank would then petition the Federal Reserve Bank for a guaranteed loan. After checking the company's credit and its relationship with the petitioning bank, the Federal Reserve Bank would report its recommendations to the OP&M's Finance Section. The Finance Section would communicate with the relevant bureau and determine the "essentiality of the production," whereupon the Navy would inform the Fed of its decision. According to Robert Connery, "[i]n a high percentage of cases the Finance Section adopted the Federal Reserve Bank's recommendations in toto."[107]

The key to this process was the fact that the Navy included representatives from the Finance Section on its negotiation teams: the presence of Finance Section personnel at the earliest stages of contract negotiation meant that producers could not confront the Navy Department demanding payment or financial support with their strongest lever in hand, the signed contract.[108] The Finance Section received 729 V-loan applications in 1942 alone and authorized 541 of them, amounting to a total of $397.3 million. From the beginning of the program to the end of 1945, the Navy guaranteed 1,794 applications in all, for a total of $2.2 billion.[109] The Navy netted $4.5 million from administering the guaranteed loans.[110]

A Navy contractor could therefore get funding through a loan from the Reconstruction Finance Corporation, accelerated tax amortization, advance payment, or a bank loan under the provisions of Regulation V. That same contractor could also get funded by a loan from the Federal Reserve under Section 13(b) of the War Powers Act, a loan from the Smaller War Plants Corporation, or a combination of the above.[111] Then there were the "T-loans," or termination loans, provided for under the Contract Settlement Act of 1 July 1944. The T-loans were for closing out contracts (and not for production). But the Navy had to issue only 196 T-loans for reconversion

---

[107] Connery, *Industrial Mobilization*, 373.

[108] Connery, *Industrial Mobilization*, 377. Although the Navy was always concerned about defaults by insolvent companies, the Secretary of the Navy did not focus explicitly on avoiding the placement of contracts with firms needing financial assistance until 27 July 1944. A July 1944 report by a group of officers of the New York Trust Company, headed by A. M. Massie, found that "the majority of questionable advances existing today [as opposed to the V-loans] originated in the period from December 1941 to the early part of 1943" (381).

[109] Connery, *Industrial Mobilization*, 387.

[110] The Finance Division, for one, thought the conclusions of the Massie Report to be "inaccurate and misleading" (Letter of Chief, Finance Division, to Lionel Noah, 20 July 1944, in Connery, *Industrial Mobilization*, 381).

[111] Connery, *Industrial Mobilization*, 373.

after 1 September 1944. Connery suggests that contractors, with reconversion financing guaranteed, were thereby assured that they could produce material for the Navy Department up to the last minute.

In sum, contractors had ample sums available for the construction of industrial plants. As with the negotiation and renegotiation of contracts, Congress passed the legislation for the RFC, the DPC, the V-loans, and the T-loans that the executive branch—typically the Navy Department—carried out.

5. Subcontracting The Navy's primary contractors subcontracted much of their production, of course, and subcontracting necessarily involved the Navy insofar as subcontractor performance affected the performance of prime contractors. But subcontracting also affected the distribution of economic growth, since the resurgence of the Depression-stricken national economy was irregular and inconsistent across regions and businesses.

The combination of most defense contracts being let to large manufacturers, the limited availability of strategic materials, and the curtailed production of civilian goods threatened to force thousands of smaller manufacturers out of business. Eberstadt found that "[t]hree large companies—DuPont, Bethlehem Steel, and General Motors—received a very large percentage of the national defense contracts, while the vast majority of the 185,000 United States manufacturers received no prime contracts at all. In December 1940, the National Association of Manufacturers made a survey of 18,000 previously unstudied plants and reported that over 400,000 machines were idle an average of fourteen hours a day."[112]

The Office of Production Management, charged to spread contracts as widely as possible, use industrial capacity to its maximum, and avoid bottlenecks from "labor shortages, housing problems and transportation difficulties," set up the Defense Contract Service in February 1941. The Defense Contract Service had field offices in the Federal Reserve Banks, and it received the endorsement of Secretary Knox: subcontracting was to be done to the greatest extent possible. Knox noted that "the effect of the nine-billion-dollar expansion of the armed services [was beginning] to affect the nation's industrial life," and he sent out directives to the bureaus and various offices of the Navy Department, informing them about the existence and expected cooperation of their agencies with the Defense Contract Service.[113] The Defense Contract Service was to locate unused facilities, and the twelve Federal Reserve Banks, together with their twenty-four branch offices, were to be used as information centers:

In each of these Federal Reserve Banks and branches there will be a District Manager for the Defense Contract Service who will be an industrialist, familiar with the industries centered in that locality. He will have a technical staff of engi-

[112] Eberstadt, "100 Billion Dollar Navy," Vol. 1, 177.
[113] Connery, *Industrial Mobilization*, 119.

neers acquainted with the various industries in that area, men fully conversant with the capabilities and capacities of industrial concerns in their district, and who will be willing and ready to act in an advisory capacity to give "up to the minute" information as to where facilities might be obtained.[114]

Twice in the spring of 1941 the Navy conducted surveys in order to determine where subcontracting was most practical.

In another directive of July 1941, Knox specified that subcontractors were to be used wherever practicable. The bureau chiefs, supervisors of shipbuilding, commandants of Navy yards and stations, and naval inspectors were to appoint a member of their staffs as liaison officer ("Naval Advisor") to the nearest Defense Contract Service for the coordination of subcontracting.[115] Subcontracting was further helped along by the President's directive of 7 October 1941, which permitted the military to negotiate contracts for the acquisition, construction, and repair of naval vessels, aircraft, and machine tools without advertising or competitive bidding. Knox again ordered the Navy to promote increased subcontracting soon after the U.S. entered the war (7 January 1942). Despite these initiatives, the Truman Committee, other members of Congress, and the public decried the Navy's (and the military's) efforts at subcontracting.

Roosevelt abolished the Defense Contract Service on 4 September 1941 (E.O. 8891) and set up the Division of Contract Distribution in the OPM, under Floyd Odlum. The Division of Contract Distribution was to stimulate contracting among a greater number of localities and firms so that small businesses could obtain a fair share of defense orders so as to minimize displacement.[116] But the new Division of Contract Distribution (becoming the "Industry Cooperation Division" of the OP&M in April 1942) was a purely advisory body. The Industry Cooperation Division's primary activity was "procurement development" (constituting about 40 percent of the work done by Naval Advisors): finding manufacturers who qualified for Navy contracts and clearing contracts for those business firms nominated by the WPB

---

[114] James V. Forrestal (Acting), The Secretary of the Navy to All Bureaus and Offices of the Navy Dept., 20 March 1941, L4–3(1) Vol. 16, 25–42, Aeronautics, 1925–42.

[115] Memorandum, "Negotiation, Determination and Review of Costs and Profits under Negotiated Fixed-Price and Cost-Plus-Fixed-Fee Contracts," Chief of Bureau of Aeronautics to the Assistant Secretary of the Navy, 31 May 1941, 184–88, L4–3(1) Vol. 17, Aeronautics, 1925–42.

[116] By 20 February 1942, the Division of Contract Distribution had 115 field offices and had 1,800 employees. The Division held industrial clinics, surveyed the machine tool industry, assisted small businesses to get loans, and investigated distressed communities, among other activities ("Brief Summary of Attached Report by Floyd B. Odlum," attachment to letter of Floyd B. Odlum to the President, 20 February 1942, file "Contracts," Box 137, Hopkins Papers). The liaison to Odlum's office was to be in the Office of the Under Secretary, where the liaison officer could work with Forrestal.

for subcontracting.[117] At its peak, the Industry Cooperation Division employed about 175 field officers.[118]

But the Navy's subcontracting (and contracting) was, fundamentally, the responsibility of the individual material bureaus, who were charged with procuring material as expediently as possible. It was not the Navy's intention "to 'farm out' where the 'farming' would render idle either tools . . . or employees."[119] The OPM released statistics in late July 1941—before Pearl Harbor—"showing that almost three-fourths of Army and Navy material contracts in terms of dollar value, had gone to 56 companies. Six giant corporations held 3 billion dollars worth or almost one-third of all contracts. Bethlehem Steel held almost one-tenth. The other five great corporations were New York Shipbuilding, General Motors, Curtiss-Wright, Newport News Shipbuilding, and DuPont."[120] As the received wisdom had it, "The only way a small business man whose peacetime line of production had been prohibited [because of the war] could stay in business was to obtain a war contract directly from a government agency or by a subcontract from some large manufacturer who already held a prime contract."[121]

With industrial concentration worsening, Congress passed the Small Business Act (P.L. 603), which established the Smaller War Plants Division for the purpose of helping small businesses get government contracts. The Navy cooperated by jointly reviewing the WPB's recommendations with the Smaller War Plants Division (later, the "Smaller War Plants Corporation"), and by selecting for placement definite quantities of those items that the WPB deemed appropriate for small business.[122] The Division's Naval Advisors worked with WPB officials and Smaller War Plants Corporation's field officers to suggest and screen qualified manufacturers.

Subcontracting could break production bottlenecks. Eberstadt reports that "in the New York area, the Industry Cooperation Division working through the Supervisors of Shipbuilding nominated approximately six hundred small plants which became adjuncts to the Navy Yard in the shipbuild-

---

[117] When the War Production Board (the successor to the OPM) reorganized into regional offices in thirteen cities, so did the Industrial Cooperation Division. The offices of the Division were eventually extended throughout the United States, with fifty-five offices nationwide (Eberstadt, "100 Billion Dollar Navy," Vol. 2, Chapter XI, 6).

[118] Eberstadt, "100 Billion Dollar Navy," Vol. 2, Chapter XI, 6–7. Forty-six of the field officers were production engineers, and fifty-one were either business owners or business executives.

[119] Eberstadt, "100 billion Dollar Navy," Vol. 1, 177.

[120] Connery, *Industrial Mobilization*, 119. Also see *Economic Concentration and World War II*, Report of the Smaller War Plants Corporation to the Special Committee to Study the Problems of American Small Business, United States Senate (Washington, D.C.: U.S. GPO, 1946).

[121] Eberstadt, "100 Billion Dollar Navy," Vol. 2, Chapter XI, 1.

[122] Eberstadt, "100 Billion Dollar Navy," Vol. 2, Chapter XI, 8.

ing and ship repair programs."[123] And the installation of a nationwide tele-
type network connected all division field offices and enabled products
to be brought quickly from other regions of the country to relieve
bottlenecks.[124]

Often, however, the Smaller War Plants Corporation recommended ill-
equipped, ill-informed, or inexperienced firms—firms unable to fulfill their
subcontracts because they lacked the technology, did not appreciate the
exact nature of the work, or did not possess sufficient "know-how." Few
small businesses were actually suitable for subcontracting. A SWPC representative commented on this point: "Of the 371 . . . contracts let since
March 16, . . . very few have been let of the type which might be suitably
placed in 'smaller war plants.' There have been a few very small contracts let
for relatively simple items, but in such cases the sums involved have been so
small that prospective manufacturers have not been suggested by the
Smaller War Plants Corporation."[125] The Bureau of Aeronautics, for its part,
had "reasons to believe that prime contractors subcontract with those manufacturers from which they expect to obtain the best prices and services."[126]
Not surprisingly, the large manufacturers were often reluctant to share the
best business they had had in years, and the small manufacturers had little
capital, lacked knowledge of the complex procurement process, and had
little of the requisite expertise.[127]

The Navy (and the Army Air Forces) nonetheless managed to effect a
significant amount of subcontracting (see Table 5.3). Forrestal himself reported that 40 to 50 percent of shipbuilding work was subcontracted, and by
war's end both SWPC chairman Maury Maverick and Congress praised the
Industry Cooperation Division for its assistance and efficiency.[128] Yet the

[123] Eberstadt, "100 Billion Dollar Navy," Vol. 2, Chapter XI, 13. See Eberstadt, pp. 14–16,
for programs for utilizing facilities in the machine tool industry. The Navy's Industrial Cooperation Division was able to match "idle machines" with the demand for subcontractors so that by
December 1942 6,200 firms—about 70 percent of the 8,939 companies reporting that critical
tools were lying idle—had received work.

[124] Eberstadt, "100 Billion Dollar Navy," Vol. 2, Chapter XI, 13–14.

[125] Memorandum of Lieutenant A. Eno, USN, to Admiral E. M. Pace, Jr., USN, 14 June
1943, file "1943," L4–3(1) Vol. 35, Aeronautics, 1943–45.

[126] Memorandum, "Negotiation, Determination and Review of Costs and Profits under Negotiated Fixed-Price and Cost-Plus-Fixed-Fee Contracts," Chief of Bureau of Aeronautics to
the Assistant Secretary of the Navy, 31 May 1941, L4–3(1) Vol. 17, Aeronautics, 1925–42.

[127] Eberstadt, "100 Billion Dollar Navy," Vol. 1, 179.

[128] Eberstadt, "100 Billion Dollar Navy," Vol. 2, Chapter XI, 27. "It has been estimated that
one-half of all money spent on Navy procurement was for the purchase of subcontracted material" (Chapter XI, 51). Subcontractors on destroyers, for example, included manufacturers of
turbines, boilers, reduction gears, shaft forgings, propellers, pumps, air compressors, high pressure valves, turbo and diesel generators, cable and wire, and gyro compasses. Companies receiving subcontracts included Ingersoll-Rand, General Electric, Westinghouse, Anaconda,
Bendix, Sperry, Allis-Chalmers, and Bethlehem Steel.

TABLE 5.3

Subcontracting among Aircraft Companies, 1941–1942 (percentages)

Contractor	September 1941 Subcontracting	October 1942 Subcontracting	October 1942 Final Subcontracting
Brewster Aeronautical Corp.	33	37	(NA)
Consolidated Vultee	20	20	30
G.M./Eastern	(NA)	30	39
Grumman Engineering	30	50	60
Vought-Sikorsky	30	40	50
Douglas (El Segundo)	12	11	15
Curtiss-Wright	10	34	47

Sources: 1941 figures are from "Naval Contract Distribution Subcontracting and Farming Out. Report of Latest Date," 1 September 1941, L4–3(1), Vol. 19, Aeronautics, 1925–42. 1942 figures are from "Report 15 October 1942 Production Analysis Section, Aircraft Division, WPB," file "1943," Aeronautics, 1943–45.

Notes: "Final Subcontracting" represents total subcontracting, inclusive of subcontracting done beyond that initially contracted. The 1942 figure for Brewster (only) is as of 20 December 1941 (Brewster figures are form "Report of Naval Contract Distribution Division, week ending December 20, 1941," in "100 Billion Dollar Navy," Vol. 1, p. 205, Box 114, Eberstadt Papers). Douglas, El Segundo, had 9 prime vendors that distributed the major subcontracting, resulting in actual percentage subcontracting much higher than that shown.

Navy's subcontracting was hardly a triumph. According to Eberstadt, "perhaps the attempt to stimulate subcontracting should not have been attempted from Washington, D.C. Had subcontracting been treated as a regional problem to be handled through local committees, it is possible that great progress might have been made."[129] A report from Atlanta corroborated Eberstadt's conclusion: "If the various bureaus of the Navy, instead of sending their own men into the field to seek out additional facilities for the performance of Navy contracts had been ordered to rely on ICD field organizations, we are certain that the Navy's procurement program would have been accelerated and at a greatly reduced cost." Many competent facilities were overlooked because the Navy bureaus maintained their own files.[130]

Indeed, it made more sense for a bureau to buy from a large firm, with previous manufacturing experience, than from a small, inexperienced contractor:

The instinctive reluctance of procurement officers to trust manufacturers whose technical know-how, engineering skill, and managerial abilities are unknown

[129] Eberstadt, "100 Billion Dollar Navy," Vol. 1, 212.
[130] Eberstadt, "100 Billion Dollar Navy," Vol. 2, Chapter XI, 19–20.

quantities must be overcome. This excessive caution is the normal result of years of inadequate appropriations and ample sources of supply, and perhaps, supplies justifiable reasons for not gambling with the unknown. The necessity for utilizing every additional machine is no longer based on a social or economic objective, but has become a necessity of military survival.[131]

A trade-off had to be made between spreading contracts around and obtaining as soon as possible—and with the least risk possible—the aircraft, ships, and weapons necessary to fight the war. But the aggregate effect of such purchases was that the bureaus concentrated their procurement on certain businesses and ignored others.[132] Consider the third and fourth points of a reply to the chief of the Bureau of Ordnance:

> 3. It is most disturbing to the officers of my Bureau, while being told by practically every Officer coming from the fleet what a fine job the Bureau is doing both in the way of development of new weapons, and in production, to have inferences cast that we are falling down on the job because we cannot provide for the large number of small business concerns now facing ruin because of the forced stoppage of their commercial concerns.
>
> 4. I submit that it is the function of this Bureau to provide the ships and planes of the Navy, the Merchant Marine, and the Marine Corps, and the navies and merchant ships of allied nations, with arms and ammunition and *not* to "spread the work" for the sole purpose of spreading it.[133]

Efforts to influence risk-averse Navy officials came up short, for all of the advertising by the Division of Contract Distribution and despite the recommendations and assistance of the SWPC. The bureaus were first and foremost concerned with expedient material production, not funding.[134] If the Navy could find reliable suppliers under the uncertain conditions of the 1940s, it had little to gain—and much to lose—by giving in to political pressure to let more contracts to small businesses or to distribute tax dollars more equitably.

In sum, while Congress and even the Navy's civilian executives, Knox especially, worked to encourage subcontracting and the spreading of con-

---

[131] Captain A. C. Fisher to Under Secretary Forrestal, 7 February 1942, in Furer, *Administration of the Navy*, 849.

[132] This could be construed as a prisoner's dilemma: the aggregate outcome of rational bureau action (purchasing from established firms and minimizing the resource-supply risk) defeated the Navy's and the U.S. government's collective good of maximum subcontracting and, thus, maximizing industrial production. See Blum on the suspension of antitrust regulations (*V Was for Victory*, 122–40).

[133] Eberstadt, "100 Billion Dollar Navy," Vol. 1, 208; emphasis in original.

[134] Eberstadt, "100 Billion Dollar Navy," Vol. 1, 203.

tracts, the predominant reality of the war years was that the bureaus retained the actual control of procurement.

6. Contract Termination Well before the end of the war, on 28 September 1943, Forrestal set up an "Administration of Contract Termination" in the Office of Production and Material in order "to ensure uniformity of procedure within the Department." He added the Industrial Readjustment Branch to the OP&M on 24 November 1943 so as to plan for the termination of contracts and the disposition of surplus property, and to act as a liaison between the Navy and other agencies. Rather than set up a new integrated organization for contract termination or use the existing procurement machinery, however, the Under Secretary opted to include a "Contract Termination Division" within the Inspection Administration of the Naval Inspection Service.[135] The Contract Termination Division became the Navy's central unit for policy on contract termination, housed within the Industrial Readjustment Branch of the OP&M.

The Director of War Mobilization recommended uniform termination procedures on 1 January 1944: each bureau had to establish a review board for the purpose of going over, within six months' time, the termination of contracts in excess of one million dollars in value. In mid-1944 Congress then passed the Contract Settlement Act (P.L. 395), which delegated to the executive branch the responsibility for carrying out the policies and procedures established by the Congress with respect to the termination of contracts and the disposition of property. But as a matter of practice, the authority and discretion that Congress had conferred on the Secretary of the Navy accrued to the individual bureau chiefs. All bureau directives for "deprocurement" then had to be cleared with the Assistant Chief of Procurement and Material for Industrial Readjustment.[136] In the Bureau of Aeronautics, for example, decisions on contract termination rested with the Planning Division of the CNO Office for Air (after advice from the Joint Chiefs of Staff). The Bureau of Aeronautics established a Contract Termination Division in June 1944; the Bureau of Ships, on 19 June 1944.

Termination was initiated by the Navy Department and not by the contractors, despite the fact that many contractors wanted to retool for civilian production as soon as possible.[137] The contracting officer was responsible

---

[135] Eberstadt, "100 Billion Dollar Navy," Vol. 3, Chapter XVII, 27.

[136] "Contract Settlement Act of 1944," Memorandum of the Secretary of the Navy to All Bureaus, Boards, and Offices of the Navy Department, et al., 20 July 1944, L4–3(1) Vol. 8, Aeronautics, 1943–45.

[137] There is a separate story of the reconversion debate about when companies could begin producing consumer goods, given the anticipated demand for consumer durables. In essence, the military wanted to delay reconversion so that it would be assured of its material, while small businesses and firms with which the government was cutting back business wanted reconver-

for sending out termination notices after a careful study of each case, and for determining the amount to be paid in the prime contractor's termination claim. Although the contracting officer was not bound by formula, he had to be mindful that "not only will speed in reaching an agreement facilitate the prosecution of the war, but after the cessation of hostilities speed is essential to quick reconversion and hence the maintenance of the national economy. At the same time, as an officer of the Government it is his responsibility to protect the interests of the United States." The contracting officer was to receive the recommendations of the Cost Inspection Service and the Field Accounting Representatives, among others, prior to negotiating a final settlement. (All termination claims had to be itemized, and subcontractors were to be treated separately from prime contractors.)[138]

The Navy Inspection Service issued 110,627 termination notices between V-J Day and 16 January 1946, and canceled contracts on 2,000 Grumman F8Fs, 1,876 Eastern FM-3s, 600 Ryan FRs, 1,200 Vought F4U-4s, 2,500 Goodyear FG-4s, 13 North American FJs, and 809 Grumman F7Fs.[139] All but the Grumman contracts and 1,000 of the Goodyear contracts were complete cancellations.[140] Only four destroyer contracts had to be canceled (DDs 720, 721, 768, and 769). (The Navy began to dispose of all but 23 of the 136 privately operated industrial facilities sponsored by the Bureau of Aeronautics within twenty-four hours after the announcement of the surrender of Japan.)[141]

---

sion as soon as possible. Big business, mostly engaged in war production, wanted reconversion only on equal footing with actual or potential competitors—no matter that war contracts had fallen off or stopped. See Nelson, *Arsenal of Democracy*; Barton J. Bernstein, "The Debate on Industrial Reconversion," *American Journal of Economics and Sociology* 26 No. 2 (April 1967): 159–72; and Koistinen, *The Hammer and the Sword*.

[138] Field Accounting Representatives were charged with the following when contracts were jointly made with the Army and the Navy: reviewing the accounting of all prime contracts or subcontracts; determining the inventory levels in relation to the contractors' statements; reviewing the contractors' charges to the government; discussing the results of his review with the company (if necessary); reporting his findings on the termination of the prime contract; and maintaining liaison with the Price Adjustment Board ("Navy Contract Termination Directive No. 3," Memorandum to the Commanding General, Army Service Forces, et al., 18 March 1944, file "1944," L4–3[1] Vol. 3, Aeronautics, 1943–45).

[139] "Bureau of Aeronautics Contract Termination Directive No. 1," 3 April 1944, 29–30, file "1944," L4–3(1) Vol. 3, Aeronautics, 1943–45.

[140] Memorandum, W. A. Kesmodel, USNR, New Contracts Funds Section, Fiscal Division, to Contracts Branch, Procurement Division, 29 August 1945, file "Vol. 8 '1945,'" L4–3(1), Aeronautics, 1943–45. As of 1 October 1945, contracts were left outstanding on 20 FRs, 472 F8Fs, 451 F4U-4s, 7 F2Gs, 30 FD-1s, 30 FJ-1s, and 300 F7Fs ("Continuing Airframe Programs 1 October 1945 Status Of," file "Status of Naval Aircraft," Box 36, Gates Papers).

[141] Statement of the Assistant Secretary of the Navy for Air, John L. Sullivan, before the House Naval Affairs Committee, 20 September 1945, file "Statements and Addresses, 1945–47," Box 13, Sullivan Papers.

The civilian administrators of the Navy Department, together with administrators in the independent wartime agencies, established and operated a deprocurement program capable of handling hundreds of thousands of canceled orders.

7. Interorganizational Procurement That the Navy was not the only governmental agency making material purchases had important consequences. Inefficiencies damaging to the government could come from uncoordinated purchasing (losing economies of scale), from the lack of standardization (hurting inter-bureau and inter-service product substitution), and from contractors playing one purchasing officer off another (resulting in higher prices).[142] Coordination to avert such possibilities took three basic forms: single procurement, whereby one service purchased the material requirements of both; joint procurement, whereby the procurement of an item was assigned to a joint body; and collaborative purchasing, whereby purchasing officers were located together but the services nonetheless maintained separate procurement organizations (e.g., in the case of textile purchasing officers for the Army and the Navy in New York City).

Most food and much ordnance, aeronautics, electronics, and construction was purchased singly. The Navy purchased $3 billion worth of goods for the Army from 1941 through 1944;[143] the Army purchased about $6.3 billion worth of material for the Navy.[144]

Joint procurement eliminated duplicate contracts and procurement organizations and, at the same time, furnished each service with the direct knowledge of and influence on the purchases in question (in contrast to single-service purchasing). During the Second World War, the services jointly purchased lumber, tractors, and other products. Pursuant to the directive of the Under Secretary of War and the Secretary of the Navy of 23 November 1944, the government established joint purchasing agencies in textiles and petroleum, and set up a board for the joint purchase of medical supplies. But little or no combined procurement occurred before the end of the war in other products used by each service, such as ordnance, building construction, small boats, and marine engines.

The Roosevelt Administration first attempted to coordinate service procurement through the use of the Army and Navy Munitions Board. Although the ANMB had been set up in 1922 under the joint chairmanships of the Assistant Secretaries of War and the Navy, the ANMB was only a planning agency until 1938, at which point it began to stockpile tin, magnesium, tungsten, chrome, and other strategic materials. But the National Defense

[142] Miller, *Pricing of Military Procurements*, 62.

[143] *Unification of the War and Navy Departments*, Chapter IV, "Procurement and Logistics," n.d. 114–15, file "National Defense, Armed Forces Unification," Box 82, Elsey Papers.

[144] "Procurement of Material," 114, file "Forrestal Report, Volume II," September 1945, Box 153, Hopkins Papers.

Advisory Commission made little use of the ANMB, and by the end of 1940 the services were able to fill only a small percentage of their material orders—apparently because of the NDAC's insufficient authority.[145] With the backlog and confusion in procurement bringing on attacks from Congress and the press, the President set up the Office of Production Management on 20 December 1940. Roosevelt characteristically split the OPM into three parts and divided authority between Knudsen and Hillman.[146]

But the OPM had many of the problems of the NDAC. A compounding of order backlogs, material shortages, charges of insufficient contract distribution to small businesses, and statistical problems put the OPM under severe pressure and spurred the President to replace the Priorities Board of the OPM, on 28 August 1941, with the newly created Supply, Priorities and Allocation Board.[147] Then, when the United States entered the war, Franklin Roosevelt replaced the ineffective SPAB with the newly created War Production Board, under Sears Roebuck vice president Donald Nelson.

Although Nelson had the nominal authority to control all procurement, he heeded the advice of Bernard Baruch (Wall Street financier and head of the War Industries Board during WWI) and Under Secretary Forrestal not to set up a "Ministry of Supply" in the WPB. Nelson let the Navy and War Departments do their own procurement. Nelson and Knox proceeded to issue a joint proclamation that the WPB would cooperate with the "Navy, Marine Corps and Coast Guard in the formulation and review of supply programs, and in the light of needs as expressed by such agencies, determine the resources that will be applied to war production and to the civilian economy consistent with war necessity." But the Navy "has and will continue to have primary responsibility as to strategic plans, research, design, development of naval war materials, [and] the purchase and acquisition thereof for war use." The Navy—and no other government organization—was to "[d]etermine war needs and compile requirements for supplies, new facilities, transportation, and communication as to quantity, types, and time and translate these into requirements for resources, including raw materials, tools, and labor, and keep the War Production Board continually informed of these requirements."[148]

Nelson did place WPB officials in both the Navy and War Departments so

[145] Connery, *Industrial Mobilization*, 99.

[146] The three divisions were Production, Purchases, and Priorities. Members of the OPM were the War and Navy Secretaries, Sidney Hillman, and William Knudsen.

[147] Donald Nelson was Executive Director. Other Board Members were Knudsen, Hillman, Vice President Wallace, Knox, Stimson, Henderson, and Hopkins. One reason for the establishment of the SPAB (E.O. 6875) was for expediting increased foreign obligations, specifically the Lend-Lease program.

[148] Memorandum from Chairman, War Production Board, and Secretary of the Navy to All Officers and Employees of: All Bureaus and Offices, Navy Department et al., 22 April 1942, "Exhibit Number 1-D, OP&M Planning and Statistics," Vol. 3(b), Naval Administration.

as to facilitate "the formulation and review of supply programs, and in the lights of needs as expressed by such agencies, determine the resources that will be applied to war production and to the civilian economy consistent with war necessity . . . increase production of the materials . . . [e]xpedite the production of raw materials, machine tools and industrial supplies [and] . . . [d]istribute the available supply of materials and equipment by priorities, allocations and otherwise."[149] The WPB also set up the Aeronautics Production Board (with representatives from Army, Navy, and WPB) for the purpose of directing, scheduling, and expediting military aircraft production.

Unfortunately, when the Roosevelt Administration attempted in 1942 to link the military departments with the business community and to coordinate material matters between the services by putting the ANMB under the command of the WPB, the Bureau of Supplies and Accounts and the Bureau of Ships largely ignored the ANMB.[150] Notwithstanding Eberstadt's presence as chairman of the ANMB, one report called WPB control through the ANMB "after the fact" and the efforts of the WPB's Procurement Policy Board "feeble."[151]

Procurement could also be coordinated by way of process rather than content. Here, the Navy shared much of its standardization of contracts, contract financing, contract monitoring, and termination of contracts with the War Department and other federal agencies. The coordination in contract termination was probably most successful in the case of the Joint Contract Termination Board of the Office of War Mobilization (later the Office of Contract Settlement)—a situation where there were no prior established organizations to interfere with contract termination.[152]

The "best coordination achieved" was that between the Army Air Forces and the Bureau of Aeronautics.[153] The Bureau of Aeronautics and the AAF voluntarily worked through the Aeronautical Board to achieve substantial

[149] Memoranda of Agreement, Donald Nelson and Robert Patterson, 12 March 1942, and Donald Nelson and James Forrestal, 22 April 1942, in Connery, *Industrial Mobilization*, 142. The Navy's WPB representative was Frank Fulsom. (Each individual branch of the OP&M— the Planning and Statistics Branch, the Production Branch, and the Resources Branch—had its own WPB liaison.)

[150] In reporting on the Navy procurement program in 1941, Eberstadt himself recommended that the ANMB be revived as a coordinating agency for production requirements between the Army, the Navy, and the Supplies and Production Advisory Board (SPAB) and the OPM ("Recommendations", 7, Eberstadt Report on the Army and Navy Munitions Board, 26 November 1941, "Office of Production & Material," Appendix I, Naval Administration).

[151] "Procurement of Material," 110, file "Forrestal Report, Volume II," September 1945, Box 153, Hopkins Papers.

[152] See Herman Miles Somers, *Presidential Agency: OWMR, the Office of War Mobilization and Reconversion* (Cambridge, Mass.: Harvard University Press, 1950).

[153] "Memorandum for the Secretary of the Navy" from Captain Lewis L. Strauss, 23 January 1945, file CD 28–1–5, Box 62, Forrestal General Correspondence, Navy Secretary Records.

coordination in the development, design, and standardization of engines, airframes, and other aviation equipment and component parts.[154] With at least some items (e.g., Pratt and Whitney aircraft engines) the Navy bought the entire output for both services.

Despite this coordination, "there was a definite need for more comprehensive and effective coordination in the procurement field," concluded one Army-Navy study.[155] The Bureau of the Budget also found progress being made "at a rather slow pace": the services needed to aggressively pursue coordination and integration under unified command; they had to make a fundamental commitment to the vigorous pursuit of "further economy and efficiency."[156] Indeed, all the aspects of procurement considered here— contracting, renegotiation, supervision and inspection, financing, subcontracting, contract termination, and coordination—were implicated in the issue of the unification of the armed forces.

Near the end of the war, Budget Director Smith broke down the functions of the armed services into four areas: first, strategic planning; second, organization and operations in accordance with strategic plans; third, training, organizing, equipping, and transporting forces consistent with strategic plans; and fourth, the execution of strategic plans.[157] While the Joint Chiefs of Staff coordinated the services with regard to the first and fourth points, Smith observed that "after the war the situation will be different. The nation then must limit its allocation to the armed forces of money, material, and manpower; and distribution between the Services of these limited resources in peacetime is a problem of quite different character from distribution . . . in time of war."[158] Greater coordination among the services would facilitate

[154] "Procurement of Material," 112, file "Forrestal Report, Volume II," September 1945, Box 153, Hopkins Papers.

[155] "Procurement of Material," 115–16.

[156] "Progress Report on Joint Army-Navy Procurement Project," Memorandum for the Under Secretary of War, 4 July 1945, file "Coordination of Procurement between the War Department and Navy Department, Report and Bureau of the Budget Comments," Box 82, Series 39.32, Budget Records. Also see V. deP. Goubeau, "Final Report on Coordination of Procurement Between the War and Navy Departments, March–August 1945," file CD 28–1–13, Box 62, Forrestal General Correspondence, Navy Secretary Records. This report, finished months later, noted, "It may well be that the results of our efforts up to this point will be swept away in the next twelve months as Termination and Demobilization take over the stage, unless the policies and practices developed during the second stage are crystallized and given permanence" (23). It further observed that "The current program of coordination of Army and Navy procurement stands at a crossroads" (23–24).

[157] The Bureau of the Budget was instrumental in the unification process, and it remained an interested party throughout the unification debate. Also see Furer on the role of the Bureau of the Budget (*Administration of the Navy*, 474–86).

[158] "National Defense Organization," Statement by Harold D. Smith, Director, U.S. Bureau of the Budget, 18 May 1944, file "Proposals for unification of the armed services," Unit 3, Box 1, Series 39.6a, Budget Records.

the determination of procurement requirements, the operation of supply programs, the construction and utilization of facilities, personnel activities and policies, and such miscellaneous services as medicine, transportation, intelligence, internal security, and administrative services. For the United States "to make the maximum use of peacetime resources, there must be the kind of basic strategic planning which will determine the proper assignment of tasks between the Services and the appropriate strength and organization of each Service."[159]

The JCS Special Committee for Reorganization of National Defense released a report in April 1945 recommending the unification of the armed services under a single cabinet department, with the creation of a separately administered air force equal in stature to the existing War and Navy Departments. A single cabinet department would centralize military authority and eliminate overlaps and duplication; it would make the effective wartime practice the postwar reality as well; and it would give the Air Force equal standing in Congress, in the determination of policy and command, in funding opportunities, and in the development of "equipment and doctrine peculiar to the air arm." The Joint Chiefs' report held that the United States should have a structure of military forces equal to its position as "a decisive factor in the maintenance of world peace and security."[160]

Under the JCS plan, procurement would be headed by an Under Secretary of Defense, whose responsibilities would include stockpiling of strategic and critical materials; balancing requirements against resources and allocating materials, facilities, and industrial manpower between components; overseeing industrial mobilization and demobilization; standardizing war munitions; procuring and disposing of war munitions; developing of standard policies, methods, procedures, and forms for procurement; assigning responsibility for procurement of items of supplies and equipment; standardizing policies, procedures, and forms for business administration; and expediting efficiency in administrative, budgetary, financial, and legal matters.[161] The Army's own study, the Collins Plan, essentially shared this position.

But CNO Admiral King condemned the JCS study:

> Our procurement difficulties can not be solved by consolidation, superficial or otherwise . . . maximum efficiency will be realized by following whatever system is best suited to the procurement of the type of material required. It is generally

[159] Smith, "National Defense Organization."

[160] Joint Chiefs of Staff, "Reorganization of National Defense," 9 October 1945, 98–100, JCS 749/25, SC Subject Files 1942–1948, Box 5, General Records of the Department of the Navy, Record Group 80 ("General Navy Records").

[161] "Report of the Joint Chiefs of Staff Special Committee for Reorganization of National Defense," April 1945, 24–29, file "Postwar Military Organization, JCS Report 1948," Box 92, Elsey Papers.

agreed that standardized items common to both services can and should be purchased by central purchasing, but that specialized equipment must be obtained by the user, the latter on the sound theory that the duty to engineer should carry with it the right to procure. Another system that has been used to good advantage is that commonly known as "cross-procurement," under which one service buys material for both. On this point, I note that the [JCS] Special Committee recognized the impracticability of a central procurement agency for all materials. Thus, it would appear, one of the main advantages claimed for consolidation, namely, more economical procurement, is not susceptible of accomplishment under the organization proposed.[162]

The Navy also opposed the creation of a "supercommander"—a single military official serving under a single civilian head—wished to retain control of its carrier- and land-based naval aircraft, and wanted to keep the Marine Corps. The Navy feared that it would be "not merged, but submerged" by the other two services.[163] After all, the President of the United States was an Army man, who as vice president had written an article in *Collier's* entitled "The Armed Forces *Must* Be United."[164]

The Navy counterattacked with the Eberstadt Report, submitted on 28 September 1945.[165] The Eberstadt Report rejected the creation of an overall chief of staff and a single unified department and instead advocated the creation of a small, centralized administration to coordinate the armed services. "Procurement of material has always been considered in the Navy Department a service function subordinate to the organization which it serves, that is, the Fleet and the operating shore establishments. Operational needs determine procurement. The economies of procurement should not be the basis for determination of the weapons with which the man in the field will fight."[166] The report also proposed that a National

---

[162] "Memorandum by the Chief of Naval Operations," 15 October 1945, 113, JCS 749/27, SC Subject Files 1942–1948, Box 5, General Navy Records.

[163] There was also the "mystery" of the Navy—that the landlocked public and other military men might not understand the complexities of naval warfare. Albion and Connery cite Secretary of War Stimson's attribution of Army-Navy troubles to the "peculiar psychology of the Navy Department, which frequently seemed to retire from the realm of logic into the dim religious world in which Neptune was God, Mahan his prophet, and the United States Navy the only true church" (Henry Stimson, cited in Albion and Connery, *Forrestal and the Navy*, 262).

[164] For the best accounts of the unification controversy and the Navy, see Paolo Coletta, *The United States Navy and Defense Unification, 1947–1953* (Newark: University of Delaware Press, 1981), and Hoopes and Brinkley, *Driven Patriot*.

[165] On the role of Ferdinand Eberstadt in the unification of the armed forces and his friendship with Forrestal, see Jeffrey M. Dorwart, *Eberstadt and Forrestal: A National Security Partnership, 1909–1949* (College Station: Texas A&M University Press, 1991), 108–47.

[166] Statement of W. John Kenney, Assistant Secretary of the Navy, Hearings before the Senate Naval Affairs Committee on S. 2044, 9 May 1946, file "Speech file 1946," Box 6, Kenney Papers.

Security Council replace the wartime and postwar meetings of representatives from the State, War, and Navy Departments.

The debate in Congress begun in late 1945 continued in the spring of 1946, specifically over the Thomas Bill (Elbert Thomas, D., Utah), which derived from the Collins Plan.[167] Forrestal, with the public relations help of Navy aviators Rear Admirals Arthur W. Radford and Forrest P. Sherman, eventually got John McCloy, Assistant Secretary of War, Robert Lovett, Assistant Secretary for Air, and others in the War Department to agree to move ahead on unification, and in early 1947 the Navy Secretary and the Secretary of War, Robert Patterson, narrowed their differences enough to come up with the foundation for the bill. The Navy would have authority "[t]o develop weapons, tactics, techniques, organization and equipment of naval combat and service elements, coordinating with the Army and the Air Force in all aspects of joint concern, including those which pertain to amphibious operations." The Navy would retain the Marine Corps and its air arm in a "federated" defense organization.[168] On 17 September 1947 Forrestal was

[167] The role of aircraft was critical in the debates, especially the Navy's insistence on land-based aircraft for reconnaissance and anti-submarine work (Hoopes and Brinkley, *Driven Patriot*, 365–83). Four of the leading protagonists happened to be aviators: Generals Joseph McNarney and Lauris Norstad of the Army Air Forces, and Admirals Arthur Radford and Forrest Sherman of the Navy (Albion and Connery, *Forrestal and the Navy*, 256, 276). For additional Navy views opposing unification, see testimony by Navy officials in *Hearings before the Committee on Military Affairs*, United States Senate, 79th Cong., 1st sess., on S. 84 and S. 1482, October–December 1945.

Former Secretary of War Stimson drew the contrast between the favorable attitude of Secretary Knox and his successor Forrestal, suggesting that the unsuccessful 1945 and 1946 hearings were the result of this change in personnel (Henry L. Stimson and McGeorge Bundy, *On Active Service in Peace and War* [New York: Harper & Brothers, 1948], 518–19). This position contradicts the attitudes of most of the Navy's admirals and officers and many civilians, however, and Forrestal's known persuasive abilities. It is also inconsistent with Forrestal's own desire for "a much more effective coordination of procurement than existed during World War II . . . There is obvious need for a strong agency with full power to determine policies, to set procedures and to resolve conflicts in the procurement and related logistics field" ("Procurement of Material," 118, file "Forrestal Report, Volume II," September 1945, Box 153, Hopkins Papers).

[168] James Forrestal, Secretary of the Navy, and Robert Patterson, Secretary of War, to the President, 16 January 1947, and enclosed draft of "Executive Order, Functions of the Armed Forces," file "National Defense," SC Subject file 1942–1948, Box 7, General Navy Records; memorandum, "Unification of the War and Navy Departments," 30 January 1947, file "Unification, Unification Bill," Box 17, Papers of Clark Clifford; Albion and Connery, *Forrestal and the Navy*, 265–86.

The Navy thereby managed to sidestep another threat from the Army and the Air Force. The Navy wanted *function* to determine the service roles, with weapons and equipment assigned accordingly, whereas the Army and Air Force wanted the *weapon* to determine organization: the Navy to be restricted to ships, the Air Force to have command of airplanes and missiles, and the Army to control land forces (Secretary John L. Sullivan to Distribution List, 12 November 1948, in Coletta, *Defense Unification*, 63–64).

Everything Unified, Everybody Happy

Figure 5.1. Everything Unified, Everybody Happy. © 1947 The Washington Post.
Reprinted with permission

sworn in as the Secretary of the National Military Establishment, effective
the next day.

Under the 1947 National Security Act, the Munitions Board became responsible for coordinating procurement; planning for the military aspect of
industrial mobilization; recommending the assignment of procurement responsibilities among the several services and planning for the standardization of specifications;[169] preparing for the estimates of potential production,

---

[169] An example of efforts to increase standardization is the replacement of the Army-Navy
Joint Specifications Board by the Munitions Board Standards Agency. The Standards Agency's
objectives were: "a) To attain the maximum possible degree of standardization consistent with
the practical aspects of performance and production; b) To implement the standardization with
a single series of military specifications and standards; c) Drafting directives for the Munitions
Board Procurement Policy Council for promulgation by the members of the Council within
their own Departments through normal command channels; d) Studying the areas and the

procurement, and personnel for use in logistics; determining the relative priorities of the various segments of the military procurement program; recommending whether to regroup, combine, or dissolve existing inter-service agencies operating in the fields of procurement, production, and distribution; maintaining liaisons with other departments for the proper correlation of military requirements with the civilian economy; and assembling and reviewing material and personnel requirements presented by the Joint Chiefs of Staff.[170] The Munitions Board also had nine industry advisory committees (which, as of November 1948, had met a total of nine times in eight months).[171] Because the Munition Board's responsibilities for military-civilian relations and mobilization overlapped with those of the National Security Resources Board, Forrestal postponed making any changes in the Munitions Board.

The National Security Resources Board, founded under the 1947 National Security Act, was to be the civilian counterpart to the Munitions Board: the Munitions Board would handle military procurement, while the NSRB would direct industrial mobilization so as to reconcile "the conflicting and competitive interests of the claimants in a time of emergency." The NSRB would be a skeletal War Industries Board or War Production Board, poised for the next war.[172] The NSRB's foremost duty was "to study and develop, in cooperation with industry, labor and other government departments and agencies, including the armed services, the most effective mobilization techniques and methods—industrial as well as administrative—applicable under alternative types of modern warfare."[173]

On 24 November 1947, Forrestal granted the chairman of the Munitions

---

extent to which joint Army-Navy-Air force equipment standards is practicable; e) Interpretation of policies and development of procedures for Department of Defense standardization operations; f) Establishment of procedures which will assure coordination of Department of Defense standardization activities with those of other agencies of the government and with applicable industrial associations; and g) Recommendation of over-all policies to the Procurement Policy Council" ("Munitions Board Standards Agency," 18 October 1949, file "FY 51—General II," Box 50, Records Relating to the Budgetary Administration of the National Military Establishment, Series 47.8a, Budget Records ["NME Records"]).

[170] "Eberstadt Report: Munitions Board," Chapter VIII, file CD 12–1–26, Box 65, Records of the Office of the Secretary of Defense, Record Group 330 ("Defense Records").

[171] "National Security Organization Report," 15 November 1948, file CD 12–1–26, Box 65, Defense Records. The shipbuilding committee met once, the aircraft committee twice. The Munitions Board head, Thomas Hargrave, served only part-time (four days out of every two weeks at his regular job as the Chief Executive Officer of Eastman Kodak).

[172] Letter from J. D. Small, Administrator, Civilian Production Administration, to President Truman, 5 December 1946, file "National Military Establishment, Security Resources Board," Box 11, Clifford Papers.

[173] "Proposal for Establishment of a Permanent Peacetime National Security Resources Board," n.d., file "National Military Establishment, Security Resources Board," Box 11, Clifford Papers.

Board final authority for NME-wide procurement policies and appointed a Deputy Chairman for the Munitions Board.[174] But Forrestal did not want the Munitions Board to take over procurement: "[a]ctual procurement should be left with the services. Any central contract-making board would dangerously complicate and delay the urgent business of procurement—the business of getting the contracts let at a high rate of speed and getting the necessary production follow-up."[175] The subsequent delays and bottlenecks in procurement occurring as a result of the board's weak powers enabled the separate services to continue to stymie the efforts of the deputy chairman. A stronger charter, approved by Forrestal on 9 June 1948, helped little.[176]

As the first Secretary of Defense, Forrestal became even more over-worked (and he had always worked extremely hard). The military historian Steven Rearden reports that Forrestal became increasingly frustrated by his inadequate authority as Defense Secretary; no longer could he deny the fact that the unification he had worked so hard to create was insufficient to the task of administering the nation's defense. Forrestal and the Office of the Secretary of Defense were "increasingly outgunned and beleaguered," their administrative resources manifestly inadequate for the tasks at hand.[177] Perhaps in response to the realization that the defense establishment had to be still more centralized, Forrestal believed that he had betrayed and lost many of his Navy friends.[178] His discouragement with the existing situation was apparent in a memo written to the President in February 1948[179] and in the

[174] Steven L. Rearden, *History of the Office of the Secretary of Defense*, Vol. 1: *The Formative Years 1947–1950*, Alfred Goldberg, general ed. (Washington, D.C.: Historical Office of the Office of the Secretary of Defense, 1984), 92. Also see Memorandum of James Forrestal to Mr. Hill, Mr. Hargrave, 25 November 1947, file "Defense Department, Report to the President," Box 14, Confidential File, White House Central Files, Truman Papers.

[175] Statement of James Forrestal to "Special Committee to Investigate the National Defense Program," 22 October 1947. As Walter Millis described it, "[t]he Munitions Board and the Research and Development Board, while useful, tended to develop into service 'log-rolling' agencies" (Millis, *Arms and the State*, 184).

[176] See Rearden, *The Formative Years*, 92–94. The charter granted the Munitions Board powers and duties of (1) maintaining procurement and production estimates; (6) formulating overall policies and procedures for translating department requirements into manpower, raw materials, facilities, etc.; (8) assigning procurement responsibilities among departments; (9) determining, with the JCS, the relative priorities of the military procurement programs; (11) developing standards and policies for procedures, contract types and forms, scheduling, inspection, price policies, renegotiation, and contract termination; and (21) making recommendations "to appropriate authorities on requirements for development, administration or implementation of plans, programs, or activities which are within the cognizance of the Board" ("Directive, Munitions Board," 9 June 1943, pp. 2–5, attachment to memorandum of W. F. Schaub to Mr. McCandless, 15 June 1948, file "Military Procurement—General Records," Box 23, NME Records).

[177] Hoopes and Brinkley, *Driven Patriot*, 361.

[178] Rearden, *The Formative Years*, 38–39.

[179] See "Report to the President from the Secretary of Defense," 28 February 1948, file

establishment of a commission to study possible revisions in the National Security Act (under the direction of Eberstadt).

After the release of the commission's report and the endorsement of President Truman, the Senate passed Title IV of the National Security Act (after holding hearings on revising the National Security Act in late June and in July of 1949); it became law on 10 August 1949 (H.R. 5632).[180] The Secretary of Defense now had unqualified "direction, authority, and control" over the entire National Military Establishment (to be renamed the Department of Defense). The heads of the military services lost their cabinet status and thus their right to make recommendations and reports directly to the President and the Budget Director. One of the new three assistant secretaries was to be the "Comptroller" of the Department of Defense for budgetary and accounting purposes. The Secretary also received greater control over the Munitions Board and the Research and Development Board: "[s]ubject to the authority possessed and granted by the secretary, the chairman of each board acquired the power of decision over all matters falling within each board's jurisdiction."[181]

Louis Johnson replaced Forrestal as Secretary of Defense in March 1949, and proceeded to reorganize the Munitions Board's committees and staff functions into four divisions: military programs, industrial programs, military supply, and facilities. Title IV specified that the Munitions Board "regroup, combine or dissolve 'existing interservice agencies operating in the fields of procurement, production, and distribution' when this would promote 'efficiency and economy,' rather than limiting its duty to recommendations for such changes." Congress also directed the board to assign procurement responsibilities—again as opposed to merely recommending such assignments.[182]

The Munitions Board and the Office of the Secretary of Defense could directly control the forms contracts would take, the financing of production, the supervision of contracts, the negotiation and renegotiation of contracts, subcontracting, the termination of contracts, or the coordination of policies—subject, of course, to the supervision of Congress. "No longer could there be any legal basis for the services to question the power and authority of the Secretary of Defense."[183]

"Defense Department Report to the President," Box 14, CF. The report was a personal, almost "semi-annual" report (five months after Forrestal took office) of the comprehensive status of the military establishment's organization, its major problems, its progress towards solving the problems, and the problems outstanding.

[180] Harry S. Truman, "To the Congress of the United States," 5 March 1949, "OF 1285 (1947-March 1949)," Box 1593, Official File, Truman Papers.

[181] Rearden, *The Formative Years*, 54.

[182] Rearden, *The Formative Years*, 94.

[183] Rearden, *The Formative Years*, 55.

But the Munitions Board's problems, including the recruitment and retention of personnel and the size of its domain, remained. It was not until 27
April 1951 that President Truman directed that procuring agencies had to
receive the concurrence and approval of the Munitions Board and the
Comptroller "before committing funds for the execution of proposed procurement and production plans,"[184] and not until 29 July 1952 did the Munitions Board chairman acquire full power.[185]

The Board was also hampered by insufficient funds for the stockpiling of
material, and the Munitions Board chairmen were reluctant to override the
preferences of their Board members despite their statutory authority to do
so. As a result, the Munitions Board "was perhaps least effective" on current
procurement and supply decisions, Rearden reports.[186] Among the reasons
for the Board's ineffectiveness were that "(3) The [military] departments
have insisted that the Munitions Board be a policy making body with no
operating authority. (4) There has been a succession of part-time and unin-
formed chairmen and acting chairmen in the Munitions Board [and] . . . (5)
The Board members have often been pleaders for their departments and
not Department of Defense-wide in viewpoint."[187]

There is, in fact, reason to believe that procurement procedures *deteriorated* in the immediate postwar years:

> it can be generally stated that the facilities which the secretaries of the Army,
> Navy, and Air have equipped themselves with to manage their procurement and
> production programs do not compare favorably in size or in quality with the simi-
> lar organizations which were assembled to handle the job during World War
> II. . . . In the Navy Department, [however,] there has been some rebirth of the
> Office of Naval Material and re-creation of a review board and of a procedure
> approximating the requirements of World War II. . . .
>
> The basic criticism about the Munitions Board's leadership is that it is slow,
> faulty, and wavering. The Munitions Board has operated in an atmosphere of
> service resistance and without full authority for checking and following up on
> many of its actions which would seem desirable. . . .
>
> There should be a clearer statement of responsibility placed upon the Chair-
> man of the Munitions Board or some other appropriate Defense Department
> official for the management job within the Department so far as procurement,

---

[184] "Comments on Problems and Possible Action to Improve the Formulation and Execution of Military Material Programs," Draft, 3/17/52, 3, file "Military Procurement and Production," Box 21, NME Records.

[185] Rearden, *The Formative Years*, 94. Consider that in a four-year program for making
order of the service equipment inventories, the Munitions Board "approved 877,000 item descriptions or about 35 percent of the approximately 2.5 million in the inventory" (96).

[186] Rearden, *The Formative Years*, 96.

[187] Memorandum of Ray Ward to Elmer Staats, 31 January 1952, file "Munitions Board,"
NME Records.

production planning, and scheduling are concerned. Just as the Comptroller can establish policies, etc., for the financial system within the Department, I think that the Chairman of the Munitions Board should have an equally clear statutory authority for acting, on behalf of the Secretary, to assure that each department has internal systems in operation for the establishment of requirements, determination of procurement policies, establishment of stock levels, maintenance of inventory control systems, review of procurement and production operations, and other steps which go to make for a clean and crisp procurement and production operation.[188]

The report noted that the Secretary of Defense had not used his existing powers under the 1949 amendments to centrally manage the procurement process. A "definite conflict" still existed "between the notion of assigning sufficient responsibility to a procurement service" and "having coordinated purchasing programs for items which are themselves necessary parts of the larger items or components."[189]

The Navy bureaus thus continued to control both major and everyday procurement, despite the controversy and administrative changes of unification. Procurement for the most expensive bureau purchases (e.g., ships, submarines, base construction) still lay in the hands of the respective bureaus. As of 1949, 30.7 percent of military contracts were by a single service, 6 percent were "collaborative," 4.7 percent were "joint," and 39.3 percent (mostly aircraft) were coordinated among the services.[190] And where procurement did directly affect the services, the Navy was mostly able to get its way.

In short, the Navy was still able to direct its own procurement in the unified Department of Defense of 1949. Despite the efforts of the Congress and the Truman Administration to coordinate the procurement of the armed forces in a unified defense establishment, the record revealed scant success at coordinated procurement—a situation that Robert McNamara would attempt to correct in the 1960s.

The seven sections above show the Navy Department's considerable authority in making contracts, negotiating and renegotiating contracts, imposing supervisory pricing, inventory, and statistical controls, subcontracting, financing production, terminating contracts, and coordinating procurement. The executive branch—the Secretary of the Navy and the Under Secretary in particular—took charge of the administration of procurement. The Navy Department and the Roosevelt Administration established the Procurement Legal Division, the Office of Procurement and Material (with all of its

[188] Memorandum of Ray Ward to Elmer Staats, 31 January 1952, 6, 8.
[189] Memorandum of Ray Ward to Elmer Staats, 31 January 1952, 11.
[190] "Munitions Board Presentation on Industrial Mobilization Readiness," 16 May 1949, file CD 19–2–27, Box 91, Defense Records.

branches), the Office of Production Management, the War Production Board, and other wartime agencies. The military services had authority to require production and inspect facilities.[191]

With Title VIII of the Revenue Act of 1943, the Congress ceded to the Secretaries of the Navy and War the authority to set what they considered fair procurement prices in the event that negotiations with contractors failed. As noted with respect to the financing of plant construction, the inspection of contracts and contractors, and the supervision of contract renegotiation, Congress typically played little role in determining the specifics of military procurement. Congress let the Navy, the military in general, and the executive branch do the day-to-day supervision of procurement.

But the Navy and the Roosevelt Administration by no means had a free hand in administering procurement. Congress may have allowed the Navy Department to manage procurement, but its powers of investigation and legislation had important influence on procurement policies. Congress specified that cost-plus-percentage-of-cost contracts be abolished, formalized the renegotiation of contracts, encouraged the subcontracting that did take place, and exerted efforts on behalf of the inter-service coordination of procurement. Improvements in the administration of procurement and in contracting methods in large part resulted from a Congress anxious about war profiteering and concerned with spreading military contracts to small business.[192]

Investigations by the House Naval Affairs Committee, the Senate Naval Affairs Committee, and the Truman Committee (the Senate Special Committee to Investigate the National Defense Effort) constituted a further check on Navy procurement.[193] Albion and Connery describe Forrestal's chagrin at being called on the carpet by the House Appropriations Committee and the Truman Committee.[194] Even the mere possibility or threat of congressional action had an effect.

Nonetheless, Congress usually disposed what the Navy and the Roosevelt Administration proposed.[195] The example of price controls illustrates the Navy's success. With the Office of Price Administration authorized to set prices, Under Secretary Forrestal and War Under Secretary Patterson

[191] Miller, *Pricing of Military Procurements*, 106–7.

[192] See Jacob Vander Meulen, *The Politics of Aircraft* (Lawrence: University of Kansas Press, 1991), for an account of Congress's and the public's hostility to military contractors and aircraft producers during the 1920s and 1930s.

[193] Congress merged the Naval Affairs and Military Affairs Committees into the Armed Services Committee on 2 August 1946, effective 2 January 1947.

[194] Albion and Connery, *Forrestal and the Navy*, 146–48.

[195] Albion says that "[n]o armed service could expect better support than the United States Navy received from Congress during World War II." The Navy's Judge Advocate General remarked that "Congress had not passed a single act to which the Navy took exception" (Albion, *Makers*, 448).

feared that the military services would be hampered in their purchases of scarce supplies. Although Henderson excluded ships, tanks, planes, guns, and ammunition from the OPA's price controls (since he was not so much concerned about "tanks, cannons, armored vessels, [and] bombers" as he was about commodities and materials such as "metals, chemicals, fats and oils, fuel, machinery, lumber and building materials"), this still left many military supplies under the OPA's jurisdiction. The Navy and War Departments duly protested. Henderson reassured the Senate Banking and Currency Committee, however, saying that "we cannot let price considerations prevent our getting needed equipment . . . the Price Administrator, like everyone else, is going to gear his program to the needs of the Army and the Navy."[196] The OPA would not obstruct military procurement.[197]

The ability of the Navy to resist the establishment of a comprehensive, uniform procurement authority for the military services constitutes another example of the Navy being able to get its way. The Kilgore amendment to section 113 of the postwar Unification Bill (Senator Harley M. Kilgore, D., W. Va.) would have given the Secretary of National Defense the "authority and control over procurement and standardization of all supplies and material" and would have made the Secretary's offices responsible for the details of procurement belonging to the individual departments. The amendment's provision for the Munitions Board to "procure for the three departments all supplies and equipment of every kind" would have thereby established a single procurement authority that would eliminate the specialized systems of the individual services.[198] Forrestal responded that "the Navy has consistently opposed the establishment of a centralized procurement organization"; the commercial phase of logistics—procurement—should remain in the Munitions Board and not be centralized. Bureau procurement would be only partly centralized.

Later, with the "Armed Services Procurement Act of 1947" of 19 February 1948, Congress allowed the Navy and other Departments to let contracts by negotiation "in those exceptional cases where the national defense or sound business judgment dictates the use of negotiation rather than the rigid limitations of formal advertising, bid and award procedures." Although

---

[196] Letter of Leon Henderson to Senator Prentiss M. Brown of the Senate Banking and Currency Committee, 11 December 1941, in Miller, *Pricing of Military Procurements*, 67; italics omitted.

[197] The services also defeated an attempt to include section (f) of the McKellar amendment in the Renegotiation Act of 1942, which would have "provided a graduated scale of maximum profit percentages ranging from 10 per cent on the first $100,000 of the contract price to 2 per cent on everything over $50,000,000." The Navy Department supported the eventual bill (Miller, *Pricing of Military Procurements*, 172–74).

[198] Letter of Forrestal to Senator Chan Gurney, 19 May 1947, file "National Defense—Armed Forces Unification (folder 4)," Box 82, Elsey Papers.

the bill provided for "the establishment of uniform rules and practices for the various agencies concerned in the exercise of their procurement functions," the Procurement Act of 1947 was essentially what the Navy had forwarded to Congress.[199]

Central to the Navy's ability to either block legislation opposing its interests or shape legislation to its own advantage in the face of congressional investigations and debates was the Navy's cultivated relations with Congress. The Navy kept assiduous contact with the House and Senate, and as the administration of procurement became more complex over the course of the early 1940s, it assigned specialized officials to work with individual members of Congress. The Navy had a Budget Officer, a Legislative Counsel, two officers attached to the Naval Affairs Committee, personnel assigned to the Truman Committee, and representatives sent to other members of Congress as needed. Forrestal himself was a master at cultivating relations with Congress; his candor, facility for dealing one-on-one, expertise, work habits, and persuasive talents earned him wide respect on Capitol Hill.[200] The Navy was also fortunate to have Carl Vinson as Chairman of the House Naval Affairs Committee; Vinson was knowledgeable, senior (he had served on the committee for thirty years), and devoted to the Navy.[201]

The contrast could not be greater, then, between Congress's ready and virtually unlimited provision of funds during the war—when the money for the Navy's strategic requirements was spent almost without protest—and its subsequent cooperation with the Truman Administration in paring the postwar military budgets to levels well below those requested by the Navy (see "The Legacies of the Second World War," below). Whereas billions of dollars in appropriations waltzed through the House and Senate during the war, as soon as the war ended Congress passed two major rescission bills totaling $20.4 billion. Congress then cut back the Navy's own considered reductions for fiscal 1947 from $6.3 billion to $3.9 billion. Only Forrestal's personal intervention succeeded in raising the budget back to $4.2 billion—or less than one-tenth the Navy's budget of $45 billion in fiscal 1945. Budget cuts slashed the size of the fleet, the construction of new ships and airplanes, the personnel ranks, research and development, planning, fleet maintenance, shore maintenance, and naval bases.[202]

---

[199] Marx Leva, Special Assistant to the Secretary of Defense, to Elmer Staats, Assistant Director of the Bureau of the Budget, 11 February 1948, file "Armed Services Procurement Act of 1947," Bill File February 19–25, 1948, Truman Papers; Miller, *Pricing of Military Procurements*, 144–45.

[200] Felix Larkin, General Counsel of the Department of Defense, 1947–51, comments that Forrestal "had a *tremendous* amount of currency in Congress" because of his straightforwardness and honesty (Oral History, 1985, Truman Library; emphasis in original).

[201] Albion, *Makers*, 456. Also see Hoopes and Brinkley, *Driven Patriot*.

[202] Albion, *Makers*, 467.

Under the Republican 80th Congress and the new Chairman of the House Appropriations Committee, John Taber (R., N.Y.), Congress reduced the Bureau of the Budget's $3.513 billion submission for fiscal 1948 to $3.135 billion. The Senate's bill and a supplemental appropriations bill brought the fiscal 1948 budget up to $3.638 billion. Once again, though, the Bureau of the Budget's figures came in well below what the Navy (and Army) thought sufficient.[203]

The Truman Administration and the Congress set the postwar Navy budgets at just under four billion dollars annually from fiscal 1947 through fiscal 1951. For the fiscal 1949 budget, for instance, Congress cut the $3.9 billion budget sent along by the Truman Administration to a compromise House-Senate figure of $3.75 billion.[204] Final budget appropriations remained little changed from the amount submitted by the White House (with the exception of the 1948 allotment for aircraft). The history of the postwar budgets thus suggests an opposite lesson from that of the other aspects of procurement: the Navy had little control over the spigots funding its purchasing.[205]

In sum, the Navy had almost full discretion with regard to the amount and the details of procurement during the Second World War. Although Congress frequently played a part in setting legislation on contract settlement, renegotiation, industrial financing, and other laws, the Navy was usually able to either pre-approve proposed legislation, amend bills as they were being drafted, extract vital concessions in pending bills, or include key clauses in legislation affecting its interests. Even after the war, with all the fighting in Congress and between the services over military unification, the legislation on renegotiation and procurement practice accorded with Navy interests. The Navy bureaus continued to control the essentials of material procurement, despite the creation of a Munitions Board and the two-stage unification of the military. The postwar budgets were another matter.

The Altered Form of Navy-Industrial Relations

The dependence of the U.S. government and the Navy Department on resources controlled by societal actors should result in the creation of inter-

[203] *The Forrestal Diaries*, edited by Walter Millis, with the collaboration of E. S. Duffield (New York: Viking Press, 1951), 20 December 1946, 236.

[204] Albion, *Makers*, 469.

[205] Hoopes and Brinkley suggest that had Forrestal been healthier emotionally, and hence more forceful, things might have gone differently for the postwar budgets. As it was, Forrestal's lack of self-confidence and deep-seated ambivalence were overmatched by the resolution shown by the Truman Administration and the Congress, intent on limiting defense spending (Hoopes and Brinkley, *Driven Patriot*, 377–78, 417–21).

organizational bodies for securing the necessary wartime resources. And the creation of the Office of Production Management, the Supplies and Priorities Allocation Board, the War Production Board, the Office of War Mobilization and Reconversion—established sequentially—manifests the expected government-societal linkages. These agencies facilitated procurement in a number of ways and themselves contained representatives from both the government and the private sector. Yet they—the OPM, the SPAB, the WPB, and the OWMR—did not in fact administer procurement. Rather, Navy procurement was handled at the departmental and bureau level, as noted above. There was nothing analogous to the War Finance Committees, where Treasury officials worked hand-in-hand with business and financial leaders for selling bonds.

Instead of forming organizations that connected the Navy and the government to private suppliers, the Roosevelt Administration created controls, mechanisms, and organizations internal to the Navy Department. The Navy commissioned Naval Reserve Officers, employed dollar-a-year men, and recruited lawyers, investment bankers, publishers, and industrial executives as Navy civilian employees. Even the committees of lawyers, accountants, and businessmen set up to negotiate, renegotiate, or terminate contracts were always divided into sides—the Navy representatives versus the contractors—convened for the negotiations at hand. Yet none of these organizations did the actual buying for the Department of the Navy; they facilitated the coordination and prioritization of procurement instead.[206]

If the Congress left procurement to the Navy, the Navy left the design and production of its needed material to private industry. Rather than producing goods itself (manufacturing its own ships and planes) or extracting those resources it needed from societal actors by fiat (requisitioning plants or nationalizing production), the Navy secured the vast portion of its supplies through voluntary transactions, by contract. Businesses were helped by the President's suspension of antitrust restraints on 20 May 1942 and by Congress's revocation of antitrust regulations on 11 June 1942. John Perry Miller, a Navy lieutenant during the war and a historian of military procurement, writes that "every effort was made to conclude contracts on a *voluntary* basis. Particular effort was made to devise policies and procedures which would not alienate business and care was taken to select personnel to administer these policies who would impress business as being reasonable and understanding."[207]

But the Navy and its bureaus did not have to rely on voluntary relations.

---

[206] That the Director of the WPD possessed the statutory power to administer military procurement does not substantially change matters: Roosevelt (and his advisers) chose Nelson as director knowing of his conciliatory abilities; he was not chosen to be a procurement "czar."

[207] Miller, *Pricing of Military Procurements*, 102; emphasis added.

For one, the Navy could appropriate private facilities. When the producer of over one-quarter the steam turbines used in the Navy's destroyer program threatened to halt production, for example, OP&M head Robinson countered with a threat to take over the entire organization. The manufacturer continued production.[208] A second option was for the Navy to produce the material it needed in its own naval shipyards, as it had done in the years before and during the First World War and throughout the interwar period. But the Navy produced relatively few ships in its yards in the early 1940s; it began the war with eight shipyards and ended it with eight.[209] There was also the Naval Air Factory, used for building aircraft during WWI and in the interwar period (the use of the Naval Air Factory also fulfilled the Vinson-Trammell Act's stipulation that 10 percent of Navy material be produced by the government). But the NAF produced only flying boats and trainers during the war, not fighter aircraft, torpedo bombers, scouts, or other aircraft.[210] Again, the Navy did not use the opportunities presented by World War II to build additional facilities for the manufacture of naval aircraft.

The Navy relied on its external ties to industrial producers (even as much

[208] Connery, *Industrial Mobilization*, 235.

[209] The Navy built many ships at its own ways during the Second World War. Under the 1934 Vinson-Trammell Act, the Navy had to produce 50 percent of its ships in its own yards, and a portion of its aircraft in government-owned factories. The First War Powers Act of 18 December 1941 made the Vinson-Trammell restrictions inoperative. Of the Navy's eight shipyards, it used six to produce destroyers at one time or another, and 54 of the 297 destroyers delivered between 1940 and 1945 (18 percent) were built in Navy yards (Paul H. Silverstone, *U.S. Warships of World War II* [Garden City, N.Y.: Doubleday, 1965]). Of those shipyards producing destroyers, the Navy owned one outright: Federal Shipbuilding and Drydock Co., of Newark, N.J. (contracts on 11 destroyers, 9 completed), where the Navy invested $19,344,625 in facilities and $683,322 in land (H. Gerrish Smith and L. C. Brown, "Shipyard Statistics," in F. G. Fassett, Jr., ed., *The Shipbuilding Business in the United States of America* [New York: Society of Naval Architects and Marine Engineers, 1948], Vol. 1, 164: Table 76, "Government-Financed Shipyards Costing Five Million Dollars or Over, by Ownership: Shipyards Owned Outright by United States Navy"). The U.S. government and private industry jointly owned another shipyard: Consolidated Steel Corporation, of Orange, Texas (38 destroyers produced). The Navy invested $11,272,122 in facilities, and Consolidated Steel owned the land ("Shipyard Statistics," Table 76, "Joint Ownership—Government and Private"). Eleven private shipyards produced destroyers for the Navy.

[210] William F. Trimble, "The Naval Aircraft Factory, the American Aviation Industry, and Government Competition, 1919–1928," *Business History Review* 60 No. 2 (1986). The Navy declined to expand its own production of aircraft. When Chairman Lea of the House Committee on Interstate and Foreign Commerce referred a House Resolution "Providing for the creation of a Federal Aircraft Facility" to the Secretary of the Navy for his opinion, Knox commented that there was no need for the facility. The aircraft contractors had facilities "adequate" to their requirements and were operated "in technical coordination with military projects." Knox cited the existing facilities in naval research, experiment, testing, and cost-analysis that were then available—despite the backlog of orders resulting from bottlenecks and production problems (Letter of Frank Knox to Representative Clarence Lea, 18 March 1942, file "Legislation 1941–44," Box 17, Gates Papers.)

of this production was being financed by the government) for two main-reasons. One reason was the desperate need for resources at the beginning of the war. As Donald Nelson put it,

> We were short of everything in those days—of materials, of finished munitions, of machinery, of plants—but, most of all, and most dangerous of all, we were short of time. Singapore had fallen, and the whole of the Far East had been overrun. There was grave reason to fear that Australia might be cut off and Alaska invaded. Powerful German armies still maintained themselves deep in Russia. Egypt and the Suez Canal were still threatened.[211]

OP&M head Hensel observed that "in the early phases of the war, all emphasis was placed on getting the materials of war in as large quantities and as rapidly as possible. Everything else, including price, had to be subordinated."[212] The dire conditions of war forced the Navy to allocate as much of the production of material as possible to societal actors. With the seller's market persisting well into the war, the Navy had to induce those contractors who had the skills, materials, and personnel necessary for wartime production to exchange with the Navy; it could not afford to alienate private producers through coercion.[213]

Hensel admitted that this meant erring on the side of the contractor:

> we have two alternatives, (1) to contract with these contractors at prices which are acceptable to them, or (2) to use mandatory methods of procurement. Mandatory methods . . . have generally proved to be an unsatisfactory substitute for voluntary procurement.
>
> While competition is largely lacking, our general problem is not the unconscionable war profiteer. The difficulty rather has been the inability on the part of either the contractor or the Government closely to estimate performance costs. Nearly all war procurement involves uncertainties and contingencies. Contractors have maintained that they cannot afford to bear the risk of contingencies which are outside their control. Volume is so great that a loss on a single contract may completely wipe out a contractor's capital investment. That argument has a lot of force. We are therefore *driven* to resolve doubts in favor of the contractor. Contingencies for which additional dollars are provided in the price may result in excessive profits if the contingencies do not materialize.[214]

Given the Navy's dependence on societal production, Knox, Forrestal, Hensel, Kenney, and the other civilian executives in the Department of the Navy had to subordinate everything to the all-out production of material

---

[211] Nelson, *Arsenal of Democracy*, 368.

[212] "History of Navy Department Renegotiation," Vol. 1, 7(a), p. 52, Naval Administration; emphasis added.

[213] Millis, *Arms and the State*, 51–52.

[214] "History of Navy Department Renegotiation," Vol. 1, 7(a), p. 52; emphasis added.

supplies. If the Navy critically depended on expertise, technologies, equipment, and manpower that it did not itself have, then the stick of coercion—seizure, nationalization, and requisitioning—had to be used carefully and infrequently lest the Navy endanger its needed material supplies.[215]

Forrestal spoke of the Navy's approach:

> There is no one panacea for the problem that is created by the vast procurement program upon which the Government is now launched . . . it is my opinion that we must limit earnings or recapture profits up to that point beyond which further penalty would destroy the incentive for efficient operation of industry. And we must remember that the efficient and economical and prosperous management is the one that usually, when all is said and done, will produce the weapons that we need, with the greatest speed.[216]

Cost was not the problem. In fact, the House Naval Affairs Committee determined that the costs of producing destroyers in private yards were on a par with those in the Navy yards and in some cases cheaper.[217] Nor was the "preservation of the know-how" the issue—that is, ensuring that production be sufficiently distributed in the private sector in order to guarantee a nucleus of competent producers from which production could expand in an emergency.[218] While the Navy would shut down shipbuilding in its own yards after the war so as to preserve know-how—it continued to do repair and conversion work—such arguments did not apply in the early 1940s. What mattered was the securing of material resources for a Navy and U.S. government at war.

A second reason for the reliance on external contracting was the Navy's own self-interest: by contracting for supplies instead of producing them internally, the Navy was able to reduce its exposure to the volatility of material procurement.[219] Consider that military producers were experiencing annual increases in revenues on the order of 100, 500, and 900 percent between the years 1940 and 1943, and annual losses on the order of 50, 75, and 90 percent of their annual revenues at the end of the war (see Table 5.4). Few

---

[215] See Blum, *V Was for Victory*, 121–24.

[216] House Committee on Naval Affairs, *Hearings, Sundry Naval Legislation, 1942*, p. 2493, *Hearings on Profit Limitations*, 20 March 1942, in Albion and Connery, *Forrestal and the Navy*, 112.

[217] "Investigations of the Progress of the War Effort," Pursuant to H. R. 30, 11 December 1944, Report of the Committee on Naval Affairs, House of Representatives, 78th Cong., 2nd sess. (Washington, D.C: U.S. GPO, 1944), 201–4.

[218] Harvard University, Graduate School of Business Administration, *The Use and Disposition of Ships and Shipyards at the End of World War II*. A Report Prepared for the United States Navy Department and the United States Maritime Commission, No. 48 (Washington, D.C.: U.S. GPO, 1945), 203–14.

[219] See Harvard University, Graduate School of Business Administration, *The Use and Disposition of Ships and Shipyards*.

TABLE 5.4
Percentage Annual Changes in Contractor Revenues

Years	Bath	N.Y.	CR	TD	B.St	G.M.	B.A.	C.V.	GR	U.A.	Avg.
1940–41	124	119	470	134	60	26	172	927	147	142	232.1
1941–42	86	80	37	124	57	(7.6)	118	218	557	69	133.8
1942–43	55	14	(22)	50	26	69	113	162	95	41	60.3
1943–44	(11)	(11)	—	57	(8.2)	12	(48)	20	16	1.3	2.91
1944–45	(21)	(32)	—	(8.1)	(24)	(27)	(98)	(33)	(27)	(35)	(33.9)
1945–46	(81.5)	(52)	—	(44)	(41)	(37)	—	(98)	(84)	(75)	(64.1)
1946–47	(30)	(48)	—	(34)	31	94	—	246	(36)	73	37.0
1947–48	84	(26)	—	15	27	23	—	139	69	0.1	41.4
1948–49	25	4.1	—	(29)	(3.4)	21	—	73	46	9.1	18.2
1949–50	8.2	39	—	(44)	14	32	—	30	71	19	21.2

Source: Moody's Manual of Investments, 1941–51.

Notes: Bath = Bath Iron Works (destroyers); N.Y. = New York Shipbuilding (Navy and merchant ships); CR = Cramp Shipbuilding (naval cruisers); TD = Todd Shipyard; B.St. = Bethlehem Steel (Federal Shipbuilding and Drydock); G.M. = General Motors (aircraft production under license from Grumman); B.A. = Brewster Aeronautical (Navy torpedo bombers and fighter planes); C.V. = Consolidated Vultee (Army Air Forces and non-fighter planes); GR = Grumman Aircraft Engineering Corporation (Navy fighters and other planes); U.A. = United Aircraft (military and civilian aircraft). Average is unweighted for sales volume.

companies wanted to construct new plants, hire additional labor, or pay for more capital equipment in the face of the volatility of war-related business. The aircraft industry is exemplary: by 1943 it was almost *two hundred* times—19,320.9 percent—larger than its 1936–39 average.

The acceptance of a military contract meant exposure to considerable risk, should the contract turn out not to cover production costs—a very likely possibility given the historical record. One shipyard with $44,000 in assets received contracts worth $14.8 million; it had $13,000 in working capital at the time.[220] In another instance, an aircraft manufacturer with a net worth of little over $800,000 received a $140.6 million contract for manufacturing Corsairs (Chance-Vought F4Us); the manufacturer, Brewster Aeronautical, received an $8,000,000 fixed fee.[221] Not surprisingly, and indicative of the perversity of accepting military contracts, the automobile and aluminum industries shied away from working on military contracts during the mobilization period before Pearl Harbor.[222] (Recall, too, that private funds paid for only $9 billion of the $25 billion invested in the construction of military facilities during the war.)

Not only did corporate revenues vary greatly from year to year, then, but revenues also varied widely among producers, with specialized military producers (Bath Iron Works, Brewster, Grumman, and Consolidated Vultee) faring worse than diversified firms (General Motors, Bethlehem Steel, and, among aircraft manufacturers, United Aircraft). Because the Navy would not have been a diversified producer, it was in its interest to contract out.

An executive with Bethlehem Steel explained his company's relations with the Navy in precisely these terms:

During World War II, Bethlehem was called upon to perform the largest and most complex shipbuilding assignment ever undertaken by one organization. This program consisted of 1,127 seagoing naval vessels and merchant vessels of 40 types, and included over 30 designs developed by Bethlehem.

Bethlehem delivered approximately one-third of all the major combatant vessels (cruisers and larger) that were built in the entire country by all the private and naval shipyards combined.

If destroyers are included, Bethlehem's output was about one-fourth.

In addition, Bethlehem also repaired or converted more than 37,000 vessels. This war effort was made possible only because we had at Quincy a peacetime organization capable not only of expanding itself to 32,000 men but to supply key

[220] Connery, *Industrial Mobilization*, 368.

[221] "Investigation of the Progress of the War Effort," Report of Committee on Naval Affairs, 173.

[222] I. F. Stone, *The War Years 1939–1945*, A Non-Conformist History of Our Times (Boston: Little, Brown, 1988), 60–64, 78–87.

personnel to 7 other building yards in the Bethlehem operations engaged in the construction of naval and merchant ships, and to supply technical assistance to 6 more yards engaged solely on ship repair work.

Today, the Navy Department alone expects Bethlehem to be prepared to undertake an M-day [Mobilization-Day] program of naval vessel construction in 8 yards, 3 more than were so engaged last time. Furthermore, it expects the output to be vastly greater and quicker than the recordbreaking performance in World War II.[223]

Not only did the Navy use its contractors as a cushion during the war, but it expected them to be able to perform economic miracles in the mobilization for future wars.[224]

Given its reliance on contracts instead of on its own production, the Navy was willing to grease the wheels of private producers. The Industrial Incentive Division, created on 19 May 1942 under a directive from the Secretary of the Navy, was "to increase and maintain production of vital Navy Material by heightening the morale of employees in factories and shipyards." Its operation was one of "selling—selling the idea of working to win" to the shipbuilding and aircraft industries and to others engaged in critical procurement, as well as to those actively desiring assistance from the Division or the field District Industrial Incentive Officers (DIIOs).

The Industrial Incentive Division adapted the proven techniques of "advertising, merchandising, sales promotion and showmanship." Techniques included bringing in war heroes, movies, and posters, having labor and managers board vessels and witness training exercises, and granting awards of various kinds.[225] The Navy made the DIIOs available around the clock for the provision of program incentives as well as for public relations campaigns attacking such undesirable employee behavior as absenteeism, personnel turnover, loafing, and carelessness.

In sum, the Navy's relations with the societal actors on which it depended were at a low level of "interorganizational activities"—contracting with suppliers and providing auxiliary assistance—rather than merging or nationalizing material production.[226] At pains to maximize contractual relations and to

---

[223] "Testimony of Daniel D. Strohmeier, Vice President, Bethlehem Steel Co.," 29 March 1954, in "Award of Noncompetitive Negotiated Contract by the Navy Department to Build Destroyers at Bethlehem Yard, Quincy, Mass., February 1954," *Hearings before the Subcommittee on Defense Activities of the Committee of the Armed Services House of Representatives*, 83rd Cong., 2nd sess., on H.R. 125 (Washington, D.C: U.S. GPO, 1954), 48–49.

[224] This is consistent with Williamson's arguments that under volatile market conditions, companies transact rather than integrate production (Oliver E. Williamson, *Markets and Hierarchies: Analysis and Antitrust Implications* [New York: Free Press, 1975]).

[225] "History of the Industrial Incentive Division," attachment to memorandum of H. Struve Hensel, Assistant Secretary of the Navy, to Chief, Material Division, 7 February 1946, file CD 70–1–15, Box 120, Navy Secretary Records.

[226] Compulsory pricing was rarely invoked.

minimize requisitioning, the Navy made sure that private producers had the land and financing available. Procurement stayed at arm's length. This reliance on transactions rather than hierarchical authority, to follow the economist Oliver Williamson,[227] may not surprise in view of the place of laissez-faire government in American political culture; it is more surprising in the context of hegemonic war.

The Legacies of the Second World War

With the resurgence of the nation's economy and industry—fueled by military spending—and in the new bipolar postwar world, we should expect considerable ratcheting in the extent and administration of Navy procurement. Such ratcheting was well evident in the 1940s: most of the Navy's organizational changes lasted into and beyond the Korean War, and the Navy spent consistently more after World War II than it did before rearmament. Yet postwar Navy procurement did not match up with the seriousness of the Soviet threat according to many experts.

The number of civilian personnel in the Navy establishment rose from a total of 113,711 persons in 1940 (combining department and field employment), to a total of 693,944 employees in 1945, and then dropped to a total of 290,703 persons by 1950; the Navy's civilian employment of 1950 was nonetheless almost triple that of 1940 (see Table 5.5). Meanwhile, total paid civilian employment in the military (excluding military personnel) rose from a quarter of a million in fiscal 1940 to three-quarters of a million in fiscal 1950.[228]

The budget of the Navy Department rose correspondingly, from less than $1 billion in 1940 to more than $50 billion in 1945; it then declined to just under $6 billion in 1950—still six times the level of 1940. The relative and absolute levels of military expenditures underwent a similar ratcheting. Total spending on major military products rose from $1.6 billion in fiscal 1940 to $23 billion in fiscal 1942 and to $80 billion by 1945. After the war, material procurement fell from $42 billion in 1946 to $11 billion in 1948 and $12 billion in 1950.[229] In proportion to national income, spending on material rose from 1.5 percent in 1940 to 15 percent in 1942 and to 38 percent in 1945. After the war, the proportion dropped from 20 percent in 1946 to 4 percent in both 1948 and 1950.

[227] Williamson, *Markets and Hierarchies*.

[228] Naval historians Albion and Connery list slightly different figures for civilian employment in the Navy Department. See *Forrestal and the Navy*, 62.

[229] *Annual Reports* of the Secretary of the Navy; Peck and Scherer, *The Weapons Acquisition Process*, Table 5.1, 100. "Major procurement" includes aircraft, ships, tanks, ordnance, ammunition, and electronics; it excludes fuel, clothing, food, ordinary hardware, office equipment, and salaries.

TABLE 5.5
Navy and Defense Employment

Fiscal Year	Navy Civilian Personnel Department	Field	Total Defense Personnel
1940	4,342	109,369	256,025
1941	9,300	200,837	556,073
1942	18,035	399,321	1,291,093
1943	19,555	587,016	2,200,064
1944	19,826	652,343	2,246,454
1945	19,804	674,140	2,634,575
1946	16,333	400,000	1,416,225
1947	13,612	292,728	859,142
1948	12,684	290,762	870,962
1949	309,336 (total)		879,875
1950	290,703 (total)		753,149

Sources: Annual Reports of the Secretary of the Navy, 1945–50; "Paid Civilian Employment of the Federal Government: 1916 to 1970," Series Y 308–317, Historical Statistics, 1102.

The numbers of contractors with whom the Navy did business and the amount of business the Navy transacted with its contractors varied for shipbuilders and aircraft manufacturers. Six companies launched a total of 20 destroyers in 1940, whereas eight shipyards launched a total of 74 vessels in 1945. Of the Navy's destroyer contracts let between 1 January 1941 and 30 April 1943, 28 percent of the Navy's business was with Federal Shipbuilding and Drydock, 21 percent with Bethlehem Steel, 16 percent with Bath Iron Works, 6 percent with Seattle-Tacoma, and 6 percent with Consolidated Steel. The balance of destroyer contracts, 22 percent, went to Navy shipyards: 12 percent to the Boston Yard, 8 percent to the Charleston Yard, 2 percent to the Philadelphia Yard, 1 percent to the Norfolk Yard, and less than 1 percent to the Puget Sound Yard in Bremerton, Washington.[230] But the Navy discontinued its purchase of destroyers shortly after the war ended. Private yards received limited conversion work (upgrading electronics, converting to anti-submarine destroyer escorts and minesweepers, refurbishing for foreign sales, and the like), with the exception of two 1948 destroyer contracts apiece for Bath Iron Works and Bethlehem Steel (Quincy, Mass.); the destroyers were not launched until the early 1950s.

The Navy's procurement of aircraft evidenced a different pattern: the

---

[230] Figures adapted from "Table III—Comparative average costs of combatant naval vessels constructed by private and navy yards," "Investigations of the Progress of the War Effort," 215. Percentages are rounded.

ABLE 5.6

roduction of Destroyers and Fighter Aicraft

iscal ear	Total Ships	Destroyers		Fighter Aircraft	
		Launched	No. of Shipyards	Acceptances	Producers
940	21	20	6	64 (June–Dec. 1940)	2
941	20	16	6	372	2
942	94	81	11	1,616	3
943	158	130	11	6,375	5
944	99	76	8	14,770	5
945	95	74	8	13,117 (est.)	6
946	14	15	6	(NA)	(NA)
947	4	1	1	653	3
948	0	0	0	610	3
949	0	0	0	438	3
950	1	0	0	636 (est.)	4

Sources: Smith and Brown, "Shipyard Statistics," in Fassett, *The Shipbuilding Business;* Silverstone, *U.S. arships of World War II;* "Navy Airplane Acceptances and Working Schedule for 1944," Navy OP&M, nfidential File "Navy 1944–45," Personal Secretary Files, Roosevelt Papers; "Current Aircraft Acceptance hedule," attachment of memorandum from W. H. Mautz, Office of the Secretary of Defense, to Mr. Forres-, 18 February 1949, file CD 19-1-11, Records of the Munitions Board, National Military Establishment, cord Group 330.

Notes: "Total Ships" includes destroyers, cruisers, battleships, and aircraft carriers. Figures do not include bmarines, aircraft carrier escorts, destroyer escorts, or minor craft and support vessels. "No. of Shipyards" cludes active shipyards producing delivered boats, and different shipyards of the same producer, e.g., Beth- em Steel shipyards in San Francisco, San Pedro, and Staten Island treated separately, and U.S. Navy yards Charleston, Boston, and Puget Sound counted separately. "Shipyards" and "Producers" list launched (or livered) ships and plane acceptances (or deliveries), not items under contract or still under construction. e use of different sources explain the anomaly that in 1946 more destroyers were launched than the total mber of ships produced.

amount of purchasing increased over the course of the war and continued in the late 1940s (whereas the purchase of destroyers ceased). The Navy accepted 64 planes from two manufacturers in the last half of 1940, and an estimated total of 13,117 fighters from six manufacturers in 1945; it received delivery on an estimated number of 636 airplanes from a total of four producers in 1950 (see Table 5.6). The Navy's purchases from 1941 to 1943 broke down as follows: Grumman contracted for 37 percent of the Navy's fighter aircraft; Vought, 25 percent; General Motor's Eastern Aircraft, 16 percent; Goodyear, 13 percent; Brewster Aeronautical, 8 percent; and Ryan Aeronautical, 1 percent.[231] By 1950, the Navy was buying fighter aircraft (both turbopropeller and jet-propelled) from Douglas, Grumman, Chance-Vought, and McDonnell.

[231] "Bureau of Aeronautics Analysis of Naval Production Airframe Contracts," 1 January 1941–31 December 1943, Box 3, Gates Papers.

In short, the Roosevelt Administration and the Department of the Navy effected a transformation in the administration and scope of material procurement between the years 1940 and 1945. The Second World War accelerated and redirected procurement under the new conditions of modern warfare: ships, planes, and submarines could easily cross continents, and the technologies of anti-submarine warfare, atomic weaponry, and avionics induced a quick turnover of equipment and high rates of obsolescence.[232] Furthermore, whereas ships had been of the highest strategic value for and of the greatest importance to the Navy up through the 1930s, the Second World War speeded the development of aircraft, missiles, electronics, submarines, and atomic weapons; the blue-water fleet would remain vital to American interests, but jet aircraft, electronics and avionics, nuclear power and atomic weapons, amphibious warfare, and forward bases now rivaled the traditional focus on armor and ordnance.

The volume of Navy procurement remained at far higher levels after the war than before—at least for aircraft procurement (refer to Table 5.6) and total defense employment (refer to Table 5.5)—because of the United States' new international obligations, which demanded a much higher level of military readiness and greater presence overseas than in the years before 1940. The lack of preparedness so painfully evident in late December 1941 and 1942 could not be repeated.[233]

The resolve to maintain a preponderant military power was manifest in the postwar directives and legislation on reforming the various aspects of military procurement—directives and legislation that for the most part legitimated or updated the practices developed in wartime. The President recognized the wartime reorganization of the Navy with his executive order of 29 September 1945, which divided the Navy into three basic functions: military affairs, administration, and business and industrial matters. Truman's order also put the Material Division of the Navy (formerly the OP&M) under a separate Assistant Secretary, and in December 1945 For-

---

[232] But from the first days of manned flight "aeronautics was always racing against obsolescence" (Vander Meulen, *The Politics of Aircraft*, 4).

[233] The Cold War had its origins well before the end of World War II, of course. Suspicion and friction came to characterize relations between the United States and the Soviet Union as a result of conflict over the opening up of a second front against Nazi Germany, the quantity and timing of lend-leased goods, and the Polish government, among other issues. See John Lewis Gaddis, *The United States and the Origins of the Cold War 1941–1947* (New York: Columbia University Press, 1972); Walter Isaacson and Evan Thomas, *The Wise Men* (New York: Simon & Schuster, 1986); and Melvyn P. Leffler, *A Preponderance of Power: National Security, the Truman Administration, and the Cold War* (Stanford: Stanford University Press, 1992). Also see "General Conclusions as to Russia's Postwar Foreign Policy," in "Capabilities and Intentions of the USSR . . . ," Office of Strategic Services, 5 January 1945, "SC Subject Files, 1942–1948," Box 12, General Navy Records; and "Strategic Concept and Plan for the Employment of the United States Armed Forces," 9 October 1945, Joint Chiefs of Staff, SC Subject File, 1942–1948, Box 11, General Navy Records.

restal assigned inventory control to the Material Division (inventory control had previously been assigned to the CNO's Office). The Procurement Legal Office became the Office of the General Counsel.

Two years later, on 3 February 1947, Assistant Secretary Kenney told Congress that the emergency powers present during World War II had to be written into peacetime legislation: certain "war-born techniques . . . have now been so thoroughly tested, and have so thoroughly proved their merit, that their continued use in peacetime is a compelling necessity."[234] In March 1948 Congress approved a bill that gave the Office of Naval Material legal status to "effectuate policies of procurement, contracting, and production throughout the Naval Establishment, and plans therefor."[235] Again, this simply codified and continued the Navy's wartime powers. If the United States was committed to being a global actor, it needed the wherewithal to play its part. And critical to the success of any global strategy was procurement.

Consider the contrast, then, between the reorganization and continued refinement of procurement and the fate of the postwar military budgets. To a surprising degree, the United States allowed its military capacities to erode in the immediate postwar years: the amount appropriated in 1947, $4.148 billion, would be only a little more than the $3.638 billion authorized for fiscal 1948, the $3.749 billion of fiscal 1949, and the $3.524 billion of fiscal 1950.[236] But the Truman Administration's first priority was to balance the budget. Budget Director James Webb explained the administration's intent:

> In looking toward this objective, we face two hard facts—one, that our 1947 expenditures will exceed considerably our 1947 receipts, and two, that receipts for 1948 will, by latest estimates, be lower than those for 1947. Thus, to achieve a balanced budget for 1948, expenditures for that year must be cut sharply below the 1947 level. Under these circumstances, it might be expected that 1948 programs of the armed services would be reduced well below the lowest level contemplated for 1947. However, in recognition of their obligations under existing world conditions, the 1948 budget does not contemplate any material reduction in the over-all strengths of the armed services below those which formed the basis for action by the Congress in the respective appropriations acts for the fiscal year

[234] W. John Kenney, "Statement in Support of H.R. 1366—H.R. 1382, A Bill to Facilitate Procurement of Supplies and Services by the War and Navy Departments and for Other Purposes," 3 February 1947, "Speech File 1947," Box 6, Kenney Papers.

[235] Furer, *Administration of the Navy*, 845.

[236] Total budgets were larger, as they included contract authority of $1.021 billion in fiscal 1949 and $234 million for liquidating contracts, and of $659 million in contract authority with $790 million to liquidate contract authority granted in previous years for fiscal 1950 (Memorandum from Chief of the General Planning Group to Distribution List, 14 March 1950, File "Legislative and Congressional Action," Box 2, Papers of Secretary of the Navy Francis Matthews, Record Group 428).

1947. Thus in effect the budget for the fiscal year 1948 for the Navy is based on a strength of 425,000 enlisted men and 46,000 officers.[237]

Navy officials thought that the Truman Administration's numbers were grossly deficient, however. Navy Secretary John Sullivan complained that the American military had been "pared down to a shadow" of its former strength, thanks to forces "inimical to our government and our way of life." The Navy had been reduced to a "one-shot" force: "if war comes, the fleet would be capable of only 'one shot' and then have to withdraw from action and 'wait for new planes to be built and new groups to be trained.'"[238]

The Navy had only 10,900 active aircraft, rather than the 14,500 active aircraft considered necessary by the Joint Chiefs of Staff.[239] And it had only one pilot per pilot seat, rather than the necessary one and one-half pilots per seat—much less the optimal two pilots per seat.[240] According to a study cited by the Air Coordinating Committee, "the present volume of aircraft production in this country is *totally inadequate* for national security."[241] Secretary Sullivan complained that the appropriations for 1948 "do not truly represent the cost of the Navy currently being maintained. The Navy is consuming equipment purchased with [war] funds. . . . [It is] 'living off the shelf' and, to a disquieting degree, depleting inventory with only partial replacement. . . . Suffice it to say that we are maintaining approximately a five billion dollar Navy on appropriations of only $3.7 billion."[242]

[237] Letter of the Director of the Bureau of the Budget to the Secretary of the Navy, 10 January 1947, file "Budget Preparation Annual Estimates—FY 1948 Gen. Correspondence," Series 39.6a, Records of the Estimates Division, Budget Records.

[238] New York *Herald Tribune*, 28 October 1947, and Washington *Post*, 3 December 1947, file "Press Clippings, August–December, 1947," Box 17, Sullivan Papers.

[239] In testifying to the Subcommittee of the Senate Appropriations Committee, Navy Under Secretary Kenney said that the budget was curtailing the finance of "the services of the professional, scientific, and administrative personnel *essential* to the proper administration in Washington of the several billions of dollars provided under other titles in the Bill for the operation and maintenance of the fleet and supporting shore establishment." In particular, the budget would affect the Industrial Mobilization Program—planning "joint action by the Military Establishment and industry"—the Office of Naval Material, which reviews procurement policy and contract placement, and the Office of General Counsel, which furnishes legal assistance needed by the Bureaus and the Navy Department for the supervision of contracting (Statement of W. J. Kenney, H.R. 6772, 11 June 1948, file "Speech '48," Box 6, Kenney Papers; emphasis added).

[240] Statement by the Secretary of the Navy John L. Sullivan Before the Deficiency Subcommittee of the Senate Appropriations Committee on 27 April 1948, file "Statements and Addresses, 1948–49," Box 14, Sullivan Papers.

[241] Nicholas Ludington, John Meader, and John Cecil, "Report on the Present Condition of the U.S. Aircraft Industry," 10 April 1947, SC subject files 1942–1948, Ludington files, Box 6, General Navy Records, 22; emphasis added.

[242] "Statement of Honorable John L. Sullivan, Secretary of the Navy, Before the Navy Department Subcommittee of the House Appropriations Committee," 14 February 1948, file "Statements and Addresses, 1948–49," Box 14, Sullivan Papers.

An exception came in September 1948, when Budget Director Webb responded to the rapidly deteriorating "present international situation" (i.e., the Berlin airlift) by recommending legislation for special emergency powers, for the government organization of mobilization plans, and for preparedness by governmental agencies servicing such mobilization.[243] The President's Air Policy Commission further recommended a total of $428 million for aircraft procurement by the Navy in fiscal 1948, $691 million in fiscal 1949, and $956 million in 1950.[244] Congress then approved almost one billion dollars beyond the amount requested by the Truman Administration in 1948 for the procurement of aircraft; the Navy received $338 million in 1948 for procurement of piloted and pilotless aircraft, and $738 million in fiscal 1949.[245]

But later that fall Vice Admiral Radford noted that despite the supplemental appropriations, the "Navy is currently 'living off the shelf' at the rate of about one hundred billion dollars per year. This shelf is getting very bare." The current levels of personnel, aircraft, and pilot training were inadequate, and there were not enough destroyers.[246] And by March 1950, the Chairman of the General Board complained to the Secretary of the Navy

[243] Memorandum for the President from James Webb, Budget Director, 16 September 1948, file "Bureau of the Budget, Budget—Military," Box 150, Personal Secretary File, Truman Papers. The reason for Webb's note that "it is extremely difficult to take positive and open steps towards the development of an immediate organization or the securing of emergency powers" was doubtless the pending 1948 elections.

[244] "Commission Aircraft Procurement Recommendations," attachment of memorandum from R.J.H. Conn, Commander, USN, to Brigadier General A. A. Kessler, Chairman, Aircraft Committee, Munitions Board, 10 February 1948, file "Aircraft Procurement," Box 24, NME Records. See Coletta, *Defense Unification*, 55–59.

[245] Expenditures for Construction of Aircraft, Navy Department *Annual Reports*, Fiscal Years 1949 and 1950.

The October 1945 report of the Air Coordinating Committee recommended a *minimum* volume of aircraft production necessary to national security. In 1946, production of military aircraft came to only 44 percent of the minimum level called for (Ludington, Meader, and Cecil, "Report on the Present Condition of the U.S. Aircraft Industry," 10 April 1947, 19).

[246] "Plans and Policy Statement by Vice Admiral Radford," 21 October 1948, file "1950 Policy Statements by Navy Officials," Box 8, Records re. Budgetary Administration in the Navy FY 1949–52, CY 1947–52," Series 47.5a, Bureau of the Budget Division of Estimates, Budget Records.

The Secretary of the Navy also told Secretary of Defense Forrestal that more carrier groups and anti-submarine patrol squadrons were necessary for a sufficient defense (Memo of the Secretary of the Navy to the Secretary of Defense, 29 November 1948, file CD 19–2–8, Box 92, Defense Records). Chairman Vinson of the House Committee on Armed Services said of the proposed 1949–50 appropriations bill, "This budget is the beginning point in the effort to destroy naval air strength. It inserts a knife into the very vitals of naval power. It puts out the eyes of the fleet, sharply reduces its striking power, reduces its protection against submarine attack, and jeopardizes the ability of the American Navy to control the high seas (*Congressional Record*, 95, 4582–83, 13 April 1949, in Elias Huzar, *The Purse and the Sword: Control of the Army by Congress through Military Appropriations, 1933–1950* [Ithaca: Cornell University Press, 1950], 193–94).

that senior officers believed that "the Shore Establishment is disproportionately large in relation to the Operating Forces" and that the "strength
and efficiency of the Operating Forces must be paramount in any budget
considerations and that all other elements of the Naval Establishment must
be subordinate thereto."[247]

Despite the hardening of relations between the United States and the
Soviet Union in 1946, 1947, and 1948, and despite the obsolescing of the
Navy's material supplies, the Bureau of the Budget, the Truman Administration, and Congress all sacrificed military readiness for economy.[248] Exem-
plifying the Truman Administration's rejection of the military's concerns and
epitomizing the Navy's frustration in the immediate postwar years was Defense Secretary Johnson's cancellation of the 65,000-ton supercarrier in
1949. Even though the planning for the flush-deck, state-of-the-art carrier
had been started in October 1945, had cleared approval by the Joint Chiefs
of Staff on three separate occasions (both before and at the Key West conference in March 1948, and in discussion on the Aircraft Procurement Act
of 1948), and had already had its keel laid, the President refused to overrule
his Secretary of Defense. Yet the supercarrier would have allowed the Navy
to fulfill precisely the roles granted it at Key West: "the suppression of enemy sea commerce, the destruction of enemy naval forces and the bases
from which they operate, the control of vital sea areas and the protection of
sea lanes vital to the existence of the United States."[249]

But to explain the ratchet effect on the organization and form of Navy
procurement, we also have to consider the intranational environment. Neither Congress nor the Roosevelt and Truman Administrations could seriously consider public-private linkages between the Navy and its corporate

[247] Memorandum from H. W. Hill, Chairman of the General Board to Secretary of the
Navy, 13 March 1950, file "1947," Box 1, Classified Correspondence of Secretary of the Navy
Francis P. Matthews, 1949–50, Matthews Papers.

[248] For a thorough treatment of the Navy's situation, the unification debates, and the difficulties of Forrestal's position as Secretary of Defense, see Coletta, *Defense Unification*, 169–
203. Coletta has the best single treatment of the Navy's embattled position in the immediate
postwar years and brings out the service, strategic, and personal rivalries prevalent in the new
era of atomic warfare. Also see Hoopes and Brinkley, *Driven Patriot*; Millis, *Arms and the
State*, 197–229; Albion and Connery, *Forrestal and the Navy*, 226–86; and Samuel P. Huntington, *The Common Defense* (New York: Columbia University Press, 1961), 42–43.

[249] "Committee Report on S. 2400" Army-Navy-Air Force Register, 1 January 1949, p. 7, file
"National Military Establishment 1948–49," Box 11, Sullivan Papers. This is not to mention
Congress's rejection of universal military training in 1945, 1947, and 1948—again to the defeat
of the Navy and the Joint Chiefs of Staff. Compulsory military training was regarded as necessary for the provision of a citizens' reserve for a small professional standing army ("Memorandum on Postwar Military Training," Draft #2, n.d., file "Notes on Cabinet Meetings, 1945
August," Box 1, Papers of Matthew J. Connelly). Also see Statement by Secretary of the Navy
John L. Sullivan Before the Senate Armed Services Committee, 25 March 1948, file "Statements and Addresses, 1948–49," Box 14, Sullivan Papers.

suppliers equivalent to those in the labor and public debt cases, given the politics of the 1940s after the Depression of the 1930s and the alleged profiteering of World War I: hence the Vinson-Trammell Act's restrictions on profits from ship and aircraft sales, the Nye Committee hearings of 1935 and 1936 (which condemned the corporate profits made during the First World War), and the 170 bills that Congress introduced between 1918 and April 1942 for the purpose of restricting or eliminating profits from military contracts and for equalizing the economic burdens of war.[250]

The Navy's careful supervision of procurement during and after the Second World War thus had a basis other than its desire to win the war as expediently as possible: congressional concern over war profiteering and the desire on the part of both the Navy and Congress to avoid embarrassment and scandal. Indeed, one of the first acts of Congress after the war was to prohibit "the payment directly or indirectly by or on behalf of a subcontractor in any tier under a Government cost-plus-fixed fee or cost-reimbursable prime contract of any fee, commission, compensation, gift or gratuity to the prime contractor or to any higher tier subcontractor or to any officer, partner, employee or agent . . . as an inducement or acknowledgment for the award of a subcontract or order" (P.L. 319).

Consistent with the ratcheted state-building in Navy procurement were wholesale shifts in the political agenda of national security. Large annual military expenditures and the presence of a standing army in peacetime became accepted components of the postwar world, as was the presence of a large defense plant; it was expected that the U.S. government sponsor scientific research and technological development; and the United States was now inextricably linked to foreign affairs through its own commitments to international aid, participation in the United Nations, and membership in multilateral institutions such as the International Bank for Reconstruction and Development, the International Monetary Fund, and the General Agreement on Tariffs and Trade.

The Military-Industrial Complex

If the ratcheting induced by the war included the extension of government-society relations as well as the expansion of the administration of procurement, did the closer military-industrial relations brought on by the war

[250] See Connery, *Industrial Mobilization*, 266; Vander Meulen, *The Politics of Aircraft*, 140–43. Baruch's proposal was for "Taking the Profit out of War: Suggested Policies to Provide, Without Change in Our Constitution, for Industrial Mobilization, Elimination of Profiteering and Equalization of the Burden of War," Submitted to Joint Congressional Commission to PR 98, 71st Cong. (file "War Profits, 1934–44," OF 1642, Official File, Roosevelt Papers). Also see Cornell, "James V. Forrestal and American National Security Policy," 68.

represent the first manifestation of the military-industrial complex? In other words, did the effects of the war on the scale and organization of Navy contractors have a reciprocal effect on the government (i.e., Navy procurement reflective of the demands from a revitalized industrial sector)? If so, this would be consistent with an ecological account of the history of military procurement: that the effects of World War II on industry and technological development in the United States at large would, in turn, affect U.S. government practices.

Yet the war's effects on Navy contractors were surprisingly limited in the immediate postwar period. The state-building of the 1940s did not mark the beginning of a military-industrial complex if we take, first, collaborative government-business relations, second, the high profits from military sales, and third, the close personal ties among military officials and corporate officials as representative characteristics. Each of these three indicators of a military-industrial complex—political, economic, and social—provides little evidence of a military-industrial complex in the period between 1945 and 1950.

By one account, the military is "a most conformist and pliable aspect of the power system, quite drably bureaucratic, and it serves the purposes of capitalists and politicians without much reticence."[251] Political leaders conduct procurement policy on behalf of economic interests, rather than letting procurement serve strategy. Accordingly, there should be little conflict among politicians, the Navy, and military contractors in their common pursuit of economic interests.

Yet the Congress attacked the relations between the military and industrial producers both in legislation and in its committee hearings. Two congressional committees expressly examined military procurement: the Truman Committee (Senate Special Committee to Investigate the National Defense Effort), and the Vinson Committee (House Naval Affairs Committee).[252] The Truman Committee, created in 1941 with the mandate to investigate how U.S. taxpayers' money was being spent on the war effort, heard 1,798 witnesses, published material totaling almost six hundred linear feet, worked to distribute contracts to more small businesses (not very successfully), and restricted excess profits (more successfully).[253] Yet the Truman Committee directly implicated the Navy Department in only five cases (the Navy was an interested party in thirty-six others), despite its ability to

[251] Gabriel Kolko, *The Roots of American Foreign Policy* (Boston: Beacon Press, 1969), 14–26.

[252] A third important committee, the Joint Congressional Committee to Investigate the Pearl Harbor Attack, was concerned with the organization and administration of the Navy Department (and War Department) more generally. It did not handle procurement.

[253] See Albion on the genesis, organization, and proceedings of the Truman Committee as it affected the Navy (Albion, *Makers*, 482–95). The committee lasted until 1948.

unearth numerous other instances of waste, scandal, and featherbedding.[254] Among the findings of the Truman Committee was that the Navy's incompetent management of the Higgins amphibious landing craft cost the United States "five full years" and at least $7 million.[255] The Truman Committee also took the Navy to task for its "hush-hush" attitude on Nazi submarine sinkings of Allied shipping, and for its poor cost accounting.[256]

Most of the Navy's affairs were heard by the more favorably inclined Vinson Committee (which avoided duplication with the Truman Committee, since the committees had overlapping jurisdictions).[257] Under the provisions of a House Resolution of 2 April 1941 (subsequently renewed in 1943 and 1945), the Vinson Committee investigated waste, poor planning, and excess costs in the administration of procurement. In the "Investigations of the Progress of the War Effort," for example, the Committee scored the Navy Department's handling of the Brewster Aeronautical Corporation and made a systematic study of the differences in cost between Navy and commercial shipyards. It also investigated the justification for the fees charged the Navy by design and procurement agents, such as the engineering firm Gibbs & Cox.[258]

[254] Albion and Connery, Forrestal and the Navy, 149.

[255] Harry S. Truman, "Our Armed Forces Must Be Unified," Collier's, 26 August 1944, in Department of Armed Forces, Department of Military Security, Hearings before the Committee on Military Affairs, United States Senate, 79th Cong., 1st sess., on S. 84 and S. 1482; also see Albion, Makers, 490–93. Truman recounts the example of a missing hinge that grounded a Navy DC-3 aircraft for weeks at an airport in Kansas. A Douglas plant nearby, which was under Army contract, could not release the necessary hinge. A replacement had to be shipped in from Oakland, California.

[256] By all accounts, then-Senator Truman conducted his investigations fairly, conscientiously, and, in the best sense of the word, patriotically. Truman's committee was even able to detect the funding for the Manhattan Engineering District project (the Manhattan Project) hidden in the military budgets (Roger Beaumont, "Quantum Increase: The MIC in the Second World War," in Benjamin Franklin Cooling, ed., War, Business, and American Society [Port Washington, N.Y.: Kennikat Press, 1977], 129; David McCullough, Truman [New York: Simon & Schuster, 1992], 289–91). Also see Frank McNaughton's report to James McConaughy, 16 January 1943, "Truman Committee," 3–18, file "McNaughton Reports, January 1943," Box 3, Papers of Frank McNaughton.

[257] Albion finds that the Navy "certainly fared far better than the Army, the War Production Board, or the War Manpower Commission." Moreover, the Truman Committee pointed to the Navy as exemplary in its provisions for defense housing, hotel acquisition, and other matters (Albion, Makers, 494–95).

[258] Report of the Committee on Naval Affairs, Pursuant to H.R. 30, 11 December 1944, pp. 171–80, 217–21; Albion and Connery, Forrestal and the Navy, 145–48; Albion, Makers, 495–500. One explanation for the Navy's favorable wartime record of contractor relations (in comparison to that of the War Department) might be size: less than one-half the size (in terms of appropriations) of the War Department (including the AAF). The Navy had far less to coordinate and supervise than did the Army Service Corps, the logistical arm of the War Department. Another explanation may be the Navy's "advantage of antiquity" (author's phrase): the very age of the Navy's administration of procurement may have made it more amenable to

Other committees investigated "hot" subjects, such as contract renegotiation. Congress held four separate hearings on renegotiation: the Senate Committee on Finance hearings of September 1942 on the proposed amendments to the Revenue Act of 1942; the Subcommittee on Price Adjustment of the Senate Special Committee Investigating the Defense Program hearings of January 1943 on renegotiation; the House Naval Affairs Committee hearings of June 1943; and the House Ways and Means Committee hearings of September 1943. The various majority and minority reports of the committees recommended changes in procurement procedures and criticized the Navy and the Price Adjustment Board—even as they consistently praised the renegotiation process.

On other occasions, Navy officials worked with members of Congress to thwart pro-business legislation.[259] The Navy disapproved the passage of the Lucas Bill (S. 1477), for instance, which authorized relief for contractors claiming losses between 16 September 1940 and 14 August 1945. Acting Secretary Sullivan held that settled contracts would be reopened and that the Government would incur indeterminate obligations with unsettling effects: the departments and agencies concerned would be additionally burdened, and the bill would eviscerate the provisions of the Contract Settlement Act of 1944 and the Renegotiation Act. The determination of a loss would accordingly be "difficult if not impossible to ascertain, verify, or appraise." Finally, the bill would reverse existing wartime procurement policy on fixed-price contracting, "whereby the contractor sought the reward of profit in return for his assumption of the business risks involved. S. 1477 would now in effect insure fixed-price contractors retroactively against loss."[260]

Assistant Secretary Kenney communicated to the Senate Judiciary Committee the Navy's response to the proposed legislation:

> The Navy Department has consistently maintained the position that contractors who entered into contracts with the Government should be held to the terms of the contract in the absence of fault on the part of the government, and that any loss resulting from business risks assumed by the contractor must be borne by him. By submitting and contracting for a price which eventually turns out to have been too low, the contractor obtained business which otherwise might have gone to others, and there does not seem to be any obligation—legal, equitable, or moral—upon the government to reimburse the contractor for his losses.[261]

---

rational reorganization than the Army's already reorganized administration of procurement as effected by Elihu Root in the early 1900s (Skowronek, *Building a New American State*, 212–47).

[259] The following draws from "History of Navy Department Renegotiation," Vol. 1, 7(a).

[260] Enclosed veto message to letter of John L. Sullivan to Paul H. Appleby, Acting Director, Bureau of the Budget, 30 July 1946, in "History of Navy Department Renegotiation."

[261] Letter of John W. Kenney, Acting Secretary of the Navy, to Senator Pat McCarran, Chairman of the Committee on the Judiciary, United States Senate, 2 May 1946, file CD 16–2–

The Navy emphasized law and process, rather than recompense for business.[262]

The Armed Services Procurement Act of 1948 further indicates Congress's willingness to regulate Navy-industrial relations. The Procurement Act specified the distribution of contracts, assistance to small businesses, and standard contract procedures. But it was not in the interest of material producers. Rather, it made business with the government only more cumbersome.[263] In short, the evidence from congressional hearings and legislation makes it hard to argue that Congress acted in unison with the Navy and with private industry in their joint economic interests.

A second argument suggesting that the military operated hand-in-hand with private interests—illustrating, therefore, the *de facto* presence of the relational state—is that business, through the military's action, profited greatly during the war. One military historian concludes that business rose to the demands placed on it by the Second World War but that "the price was too high, the production organization too precarious, and wastage too great." Business triumphed at the expense of American society at large: "compared with the power wielded by the industrial community, the power of labor, agriculture, and the consumer was indeed weak."[264]

Yet the evidence does not confirm the presence of close, profitable relations between the Navy and its material suppliers. Navy contractors did not earn large profits. Between the negotiation and renegotiation of contracts, plant inspections, and the excess profits tax, American aircraft and ship com-

---

5, Box 51, Navy Secretary Records. Also see memorandum of Frank N. Nash to John L. Sullivan, 23 July 1946, and letter of Robert P. Patterson, Secretary of War, to Senator Pat McCarran, Chairman of the Committee on the Judiciary, United States Senate, 18 March 1946, file CD 16–2–5, Box 51, Navy Secretary Records. The Lucas Bill became law in August 1946, over the protests of the Navy and War Departments.

[262] Because of strict interpretations of the Lucas Act, contractors would make only two successful claims. Accordingly, Congress passed an amended bill, H.R. 3436, "To amend the War Contractors Relief Act," on 20 June 1950. Still, the Departments of Defense, Justice, and Commerce and the Reconstruction Finance Corporation and General Accounting Office recommended that the President veto the bill. Truman did so on 30 June 1950 (Letter of Assistant Director, Legislative Reference, the Bureau of the Budget, to William J. Hopkins, The White House, Bill File "June 30, 1950," Bill Files, Truman Papers).

[263] Neither, however, did the Procurement Act on its own create a web of red tape to raise prohibitive barriers to entry in bidding for military business. It took the later regulations for awarding contracts to areas of high unemployment, small business set-asides, Occupation, Safety and Health standards (OSHA), and Equal Employment Opportunity requirements (EEO) to do so.

[264] Koistinen, *The Hammer and the Sword*, 800, 804. See Chapter 3 for the strengthened position of labor resulting from the war. See John Mark Hansen's historical account of the American Farm Bureau Federation for evidence on the wartime success of agriculture (John Mark Hansen, *Gaining Access: Congress and the Farm Lobby, 1919–1981* [Chicago: University of Chicago Press, 1991]). Also see Vatter, *The U.S. Economy in World War II.*

TABLE 5.7
Percentages of After-Tax Profits: Shipbuilders and Aircraft Manufacturers

Year	Bath	N.Y.	CR	TD	B.St	G.M.	B.A.	C.V.	GR	U
1940	11	5.3	(NA)	4.8	8.1	10	2.8	15	16	1
1941	3.4	3.2	1.0	7.4	3.5	8.0	0.5	8.4	5.0	
1942	4.9	1.7	1.1	4.8	1.6	9.0	(2.3)	3.6	0.9	
1943	2.9	1.8	0.45	2.7	1.7	3.9	(NA)	2.4	1.2	
1944	3.0	2.5	0.64	1.8	2.1	4.0	1.6	1.3	1.5	
1945	3.2	3.2	—	1.1	2.6	6.0	(35)	1.0	2.4	
1946	7.2	3.9	—	1.5	5.3	4.5	—	(20)	0.9	
1947	(13)	2.7	—	1.3	4.9	7.6	—	(35)	9.5	
1948	2.8	4.5	—	4.8	6.9	9.3	—	(10)	5.8	
1949	3.1	3.1	—	2.4	7.8	12	—	1.9	5.4	
1950	4.2	(16)	—	(11)	8.5	11	—	4.0	6.1	

Source: Moody's Manual of Investments, 1941–51.
Notes: See Table 5.4. Figures in parentheses are after tax losses as a percentage of gross revenues. Cramp sold its operations to the government in 1945. Brewster went out of business on 19 December 1

panies made low after-tax returns on their sales to the Navy (and War) Department(s).[265] Table 5.7 shows the low returns made by a range of military contractors: those with Navy contracts exclusively (Bath, Cramp, Grumman), a producer of both Navy and Army Air Forces aircraft (United Aircraft), a producer of AAF aircraft exclusively (Consolidated Vultee), manufacturers of a variety of merchant and combatant vessels (Todd, New York Shipbuilding), and conglomerates with extensive military contracts (General Motors [Eastern Aircraft], Bethlehem Steel [Federal Shipbuilding and Drydock]). After-tax profits for aircraft manufacturers and shipbuilders mostly averaged between 2 and 4 percent during the early 1940s. And the double-digit profits made by Chance-Vought, Grumman, and North American in 1939 and 1940 resulted from foreign sales to the French, British, and Dutch, among others.

Government and industrial experts alike recognized the low returns on the manufacture of aircraft. A confidential study of the aircraft industry made in 1942 found that "the financial condition of the aircraft industry as a

---

[265] Profit rates declined for the aircraft industry as a whole, dropping from 18 percent profit in 1939 to 13.4 percent in 1940 and 8.8 percent in 1941. Grumman earned only 3.1 percent in 1941 (5 percent, according to Moody's Manual of Investments), but aircraft profits were significantly higher at Boeing (7.5 percent), Douglas (9.3 percent), Ryan (9.9 percent), and Consolidated (7.7 percent) ("Confidential Report to Hon. Artemus L. Gates," An Investigation of the Financial Condition and Recent Earnings of Aircraft Contractors, by S. J. Ziegler, Captain, USN, and John W. Meader, 14 May 1942, p. 17, file "Contract Terminations," Box 5, Gates Papers).

whole is unsatisfactory, and governmental assistance in some form will have to be continued." The report went on: "Earnings rates on the average are not excessive, are declining, and may be insufficient to insure a healthy industry. The current political agitation against 'excessive war profits' is unfortunate and unless skillfully handled may lead to legislation which will hamstring the aircraft industry."[266] The Aeronautical Chamber of Commerce agreed:

> The rate of net profits on sales volume in aircraft is the lowest of any industry engaged in war production. In 1943, the percentage of net income to sales for twenty-four major aircraft and parts manufacturers was 1.8%, according to a survey by the National City Bank of New York [later Citibank]. Other industries, such as non-ferrous metals, earned 9%; petroleum products 6.8%; automobiles 3.2%; and iron and steel 2.8%.[267]

The Aeronautical Chamber of Commerce denied the claim of the CIO that managers and shareholders were profiting at the expense of the workers:

> Aircraft stockholders have not profited from the war. In fact, they are not as well off now as they were a year or so before Pearl Harbor. . . . The stockholders of 6 of the largest airframe manufacturers have lost 26% in market value . . . their dividends have increased 13% since 1940. The net result is that the average stockholder lost $6.62 in market value and gained $0.54 in dividends in four years. Average weekly wages of aircraft workers, using the figures in the CIO report, increased 47% from 1940 to 1942.[268]

Despite the increase in industrial concentration during the war, wartime contracts did not disproportionately reward larger firms. Pre-tax profits for all companies doing business with the government in fact varied inversely with company size: "the smaller the company, the greater its war-induced profitability."[269] By 1942, small companies, with assets of less than $1 million, realized profit increases of 739 percent, and large companies, with

[266] "Confidential Report to Hon. Artemus L. Gates," 1.

[267] Press release of the Aeronautical Chamber of Commerce of America, Inc., 11 July 1944, file "Murray Subcommittee on Postwar Aviation," Box 20, Gates Papers.

[268] Press release of the Aeronautical Chamber of Commerce of America, Inc., 11 July 1944. The Aeronautical Chamber of Commerce's statement was somewhat disingenuous: had the profits paid to shareholders and executives been paid to workers, each worker would have earned $102.56 more per year—a non-trivial sum in the 1940s.

[269] The War Production Board reported that "at the beginning of our war program 175,000 companies were providing 70% of the nation's manufacturing output and 100 corporations were producing 30%. Today, two and one-half years later, this ratio has been reversed; now 100 corporations hold 70% of the war and essential civilian contracts, while 175,000 small companies hold 30%" (Carl H. Monsees, *Industry-Government Cooperation: A Study of the Participation of Advisory Committees in Public Administration* [Washington, D.C.: Public Affairs Press, 1944], 12).

TABLE 5.8

Pre-Tax and After-Tax Profits for Military Contractors
and Manufacturers (percentages)

Fiscal Year	Procurement Profits		Manufacturing Profits	
	Pre-Tax	Margin	Pre-Tax	Margin
1940	18.4	9.22	8.02	5.69
1941	14.5	4.58	11.25	5.92
1942	12.5	2.86	11.50	4.57
1943	9.05	2.13	11.36	4.15
1944	9.67	2.05	9.66	3.56
1945	5.35	(1.43)	7.26	2.94
1946	(2.44)	0.86	8.39	5.08
1947	(11.9)	(2.16)	9.24	5.74
1948	6.83	3.58	9.07	5.66
1949	8.51	5.01	7.64	4.70
1950	6.16	1.46	10.82	5.97

Sources: Figures for contractors are from *Moody's Manual of Investments.* Figures for manufacturers are from "Selected Corporate Asset,
Liability, Income and Tax Items, and Dividends Paid, by Industrial Division: 1926 to 1970," Series V 167–181, *Historical Statistics,* 928.

Notes: "Procurement Profits" are the unweighted averages of the ten
companies listed in Table 5.4. Manufacturing pre-tax profit percentages
are "Total receipts less total deductions" divided by "Total receipts."
After-tax profit margins are "Income taxes" subtracted from "Total receipts less total deductions" and then divided by "Total receipts." Although the manufacturing data include firms of all sizes, the small firms
made up a very low percentage of receipts. Companies with receipts
under $500,000 accounted for only 7% of corporate assets in 1952, for
instance.

assets of $100 million or more, raised their profit by 112 percent (both in
comparison to a 1936–39 average).[270]

Not only did the smaller companies make higher profits than the larger
ones, but military contractors made substantially lower profits than did manufacturing companies in general (with the exception of 1940 earnings). Taking a basket of ten military contractors as representative, material producers
earned lower pre-tax profits after 1942 and had consistently lower after-tax
profit margins from 1941 on, in comparison to manufacturing firms in general, including military contractors (see Table 5.8).

[270] Even after taxes, "the small companies still realized a profit gain of 234 per cent compared to the giants' increase of only 18 per cent" (comparing fiscal 1942 with a 1936–39 average). Memorandum for the Assistant Secretary of the Navy, from Ferol D. Oberfelt, Commander, USN, 30 June 1945, file CD 29–1–37, Box 62, Navy Secretary Records.

As production costs decreased over time, contractors passed on their lower costs to the Navy: "In January 1945, the Navy was paying approximately a million dollars less per destroyer than it had paid at the beginning of 1942. The cost of one fighter plane had been reduced from $66,000 to $32,000 per plane. Generally speaking, the Navy by 1945 was obtaining 'about 25% more war supplies for each dollar expended.'"[271] The cost for the FM-2, for example, fell from $32,175 each for the first 753 aircraft, declined to $23,695 per unit for the next 1,720, and then dropped to $21,365 for the next 900. The Navy's target price for all FM-2 contracts had originally been $34,000.[272]

Navy Secretary Forrestal wrote Representative Vinson that "I want to leave this job with the satisfaction that there was no profiteering out of Navy contracts. I have seen enough to be absolutely confident that there will be such profiteering *without* a renegotiation law."[273] Forrestal mostly got what he wanted. As two investigators of the aircraft industry commented, "no business man in his right mind, with a free choice, would make a career of aircraft manufacture. It has appealed to the very few which [sic] had the sporting instinct to wrestle with an outrageous fortune and pit their wits against insuperable obstacles. It is a sad commentary on human nature that their hard-won accomplishments should occasionally be a cause, not of congratulation, but of envy."[274] The profits were not there.[275]

The deterioration of defense-related industries after the war indicates the U.S. government's disregard for large sectors of American industry, notwith-

[271] Office of Procurement and Material, Price Analysis Section, "Pricing in Navy Procurement," 18 January 1945, in Albion and Connery, *Forrestal and the Navy*, 113.

[272] "Contract NOA(s)-227 for FM's," file "Naval Aircraft—General," Box 21, Gates Papers.

[273] Letter from Forrestal to Rep. Vinson, 13 February 1943, file "Renegotiation," Box 42, Forrestal Papers; emphasis in original.

[274] "Confidential Report to Hon. Artemus L. Gates," 25.

[275] There are other measures of corporate profitability. One is the return on net worth. Problems with using net worth are that the measure of net worth varies with respect to accounting procedures and the specifics of debt, equity, debt convertible into equity (debentures, warrants), subordinate debt (placed privately), the goodwill value of a company, and the different industrial ratios of debt to equity.

Another measure comes from an "event study" of the change in the rates of return for a select group of stocks in response to a shock or series of events. Brian E. Roberts and the author performed such a test of military-contractor stocks using the "CRSP" data set (University of Chicago) over an approximately 115-month period of published contracts (for about 100 months before the 15-month period of 1940–41, and then for 10–12 months afterwards). A sale to one of eight military contractors (those with stock-price histories going back to the mid-1930s) as recorded in the *Wall Street Journal* was used as the event variable (0 or 1), with an equally weighted market portfolio as the control. There were no significant results. On the second pass, a system of "seemingly unrelated regression" equations was defined for each of the sales events of the eight companies used, in order to determine a correlation between the movement in stock prices and sales. Using coefficients for both conglomerate (General Motors, Goodyear, and Bethlehem Steel) and non-conglomerate firms (Bendix, Douglas, North American, and New York Shipbuilding), there were again no significant or positive coefficients found.

standing the fact that both the Navy and its suppliers were interested in
maintaining vigorous shipbuilding and aircraft industries in the event of mobilization for war. The building of ships and the existence of shipyards would
"enhance the national welfare of the United States by making positive contributions to two of its important phases, namely (1) National Security [and]
(2) National Prosperity."[276] But as of 30 June 1950, the United States had
only 0.04 million tons of combatant vessels (and only 0.4 million deadweight
tons of merchant vessels) under construction or under contract, and of the
eighty-eight shipyards producing craft of 1,000 tons or larger in WWII, only
eight were in business by 1950. Whereas U.S. shipyards employed 62,000
workers in 1936, 366,000 persons in 1941, and 1,387,000 persons in 1943,
they employed only 55,000 persons in 1950.[277]

Most of the existing stock of vessels was either mothballed, discarded, or
sold once the war ended. The Navy disposed of more than 4,500 vessels
available for commercial use under the 1946 Merchant Ship Sales Act, and
the government sold some two thousand ships, including 843 to foreigners.
The Chief of Naval Operations, Admiral Forrest Sherman, warned that
"[t]he condition of the U.S. commercial shipbuilding industry is critical" and
that the industry would "cease to exist" if conditions did not change soon.[278]
Despite the efforts of CNO Sherman, Defense Secretary Forrestal, Navy
Secretary Sullivan and the Joint Chiefs of Staff, Congress, and the Truman
Administration allowed the shipbuilding industry to atrophy.[279]

Nor was the aircraft industry spared. The Truman Administration canceled $21 billion in Navy and AAF aircraft orders by the end of 1945, and
only sixteen out of sixty-six airframe plants were left in operation; industry
sales declined from $16.0 billion in 1944 to $1.2 billion in 1947—a drop of
more than 90 percent. Both North American Aviation and Douglas lost
money in 1947, and Boeing lost $5 million in 1946 (and had an operating
loss in every year from 1945 to 1949).[280] Employment in the aircraft industry plummeted from its November 1943 peak of 2,101,600 workers to just
138,700 persons in February 1946.[281] Although aircraft employment

---

[276] *The Use and Disposition of Ships and Shipyards at the End of World War II*, 5.

[277] *The Use and Disposition of Ships and Shipyards at the End of World War II*, 5.

[278] Memorandum of Admiral Forrest Sherman, CNO, to the Secretary of the Navy, 15
July 1950, file "Classified Correspondence of Secretary Francis Matthew 1949–1950"; emphasis added.

[279] Total subsidies to American shipbuilding and related operations amounted to almost
$18.4 billion for the years 1936 to 1972—this apart from the $15 million a year in government
and industrial overheads (James M. Morris, *Our Maritime Heritage: Maritime Developments
and Their Impact on American Lives* [Lanham, Md.: University Press of America, 1978], 232).

[280] John B. Rae, *Climb to Greatness: The American Aircraft Industry, 1920–1960* (Cambridge, Mass.: Massachusetts Institute of Technology Press, 1968), 173, 176–78.

[281] William Glenn Cunningham, "Postwar Developments and the Location of the Aircraft
Industry in 1950," in G. R. Simonson, ed., *The History of the American Aircraft Industry*
(Cambridge, Mass.: Massachusetts Institute of Technology Press, 1968), 182.

climbed back to 212,000 workers by January 1950, the aircraft industry of 1950 was only one-eighth its size of 1944. What had been the nation's largest industry fell to being the fifteenth largest.[282] Brewster Aeronautical and four other aircraft companies were out of business by the war's end, the Naval Aircraft Factory in Philadelphia was shut down, and three other major aircraft companies founded in the early 1940s were liquidated in short order.[283]

Unlike shipbuilding, however, the story of the aircraft industry was not entirely one of decline. Thanks to postwar studies by the Navy Department, by the Congress, and by an independent commission, the military spent most its available procurement funds on developing and buying new aircraft. The Bureau of Aeronautics and the AAF recommended that long range aircraft plans and long-term procurement schedules be initiated in order to achieve economies of contracting, production continuity, manufacturing efficiency, production design, engineering and tooling, and eventually lower costs.[284] And the President's Air Policy Commission (the Finletter Commission) determined that the aircraft industry could not get by on its own, with commercial orders only. Commercial producers needed military aviation, just as the military depended on a thriving commercial aircraft industry in the event of wartime mobilization.[285]

Although it might therefore seem that the government was acting in the interests of the aircraft industry—in this instance at least—two factors militate against this conclusion. One is that the aircraft industry was atypical: aircraft had priority over other material procurement.[286] Even with the glimmers of hope for the aircraft industry, the volume of aircraft sales were still at multiples below their WWII and subsequent postwar levels; most military contractors returned to civilian production after the war, whether voluntarily or involuntarily.[287] Another is that the postwar expansion in the aircraft industry (to the extent that there was one) was not initiated by aircraft manufacturers in search of profits, but appears to have been initiated by Administration officials acting in long-term national security interests.[288] The history of the production and profits of the shipbuilding and aircraft industries thus seems inconsistent with the notion of a military-industrial complex: defense-related industries fared poorly in comparison to other

[282] Cunningham, "Postwar Developments," 196–97; industry size according to employment.

[283] Cunningham, "Postwar Developments," 186–87, 190.

[284] "Report on Long Range Aircraft Procurement Program," 14 February 1948, file "Aircraft Procurement," Box 24, NME Records.

[285] Donald J. Mrozek, "The Truman Administration and the Enlistment of the Aviation Industry in Postwar Defense," *Business History Review* 47 (1974): 73–94.

[286] Gregory Hooks, "The Rise of the Pentagon and U.S. State Building: The Defense Program as Industrial Policy," *American Journal of Sociology* 96 No. 2 (September 1990): 375.

[287] Hooks, "The Rise of the Pentagon and U.S. State Building," 375–83.

[288] Mrozek, "The Truman Administration and the Enlistment of the Aviation Industry in Postwar Defense."

businesses during the war and fared still worse in relation to other businesses between 1945 and 1950 (refer to Table 5.4).

A third indicator of the military-industrial complex could be the presence of a set of actors common to both military and industrial organizations, as manifest in the career paths of top military officials entering government service from corporate boardrooms and prominent law offices, and then returning to lucrative private occupations. This set of circulating personnel could be said to constitute "a class with joint functions and assumptions and larger economic objectives that carry with it the power to rule."[289] The expected interorganizational bridging of the Navy and societal actors could happen, then, through the actual personnel—i.e., through shared executives. Assumed by this scenario of the same persons occupying top government positions and high places in the business world is that military service be attractive for the contacts and potential contracts it brings: government service as a professional investment.

Many procurement administrators and corporate executives of Navy contractors were in fact the same people.[290] Of the Naval Reserve officers serving in the Industrial Cooperation Division, for instance, 42 percent were business owners or executives, 39 percent were consulting, management, or sales engineers, 11 percent were lawyers, bankers, or accountants, and 8 percent were affiliated with other enterprises.[291] Consider that the Chief of the Procurement Legal Division, Hensel, had been a practicing lawyer for seventeen years

> and was a partner in the firm of Milbank, Tweed & Hope in New York City. The Assistant Chief is W. John Kenney, who has practiced law for the past 14 years and who prior to coming with the Navy Department had his own office in Los Angeles. The men acting as Counsel for the Bureaus were all partners of law firms with substantial reputations in various commercial cities such as Baltimore, San Francisco, Buffalo and New York.[292]

[289] Kolko, *The Roots of American Foreign Policy*, 30–34. Kolko disputes the idea that the common backgrounds and similar credentials of political and military leaders lead to their consensus (contra the arguments of C. Wright Mills and others). Kolko claims that government, business, and military leaders simply identify the welfare of government with the welfare of business; Mills and Koistinen take the position that businessmen and military officials are cut from the same cloth, essentially, and therefore have similar interests and dispositions (Koistinen, *The Hammer and the Sword*, 797, 817; C. Wright Mills, *The Power Elite* [New York: Oxford University Press, 1956]).

[290] Koistinen, *The Military-Industrial Complex*, 123.

[291] "History of the Industrial Cooperation Division," 3, Office of Procurement and Material, Industrial Cooperation Division History (Folder 2), OP&M Appendices 1–7, Naval Administration.

[292] Adlai E. Stevenson, "Memorandum for The Secretary," 26 February 1943, pp. 4–5, file CD 70–1–41, Box 47, Records of the Secretary of the Navy Henry Knox, General Navy Records.

Both Forrestal and Eberstadt had also highly successful backgrounds as Wall Street investment bankers, of course, with Eberstadt founding his own firm and Forrestal being the former head of Dillon, Read. Most of the Navy's civilian employees hired during the war had business backgrounds.

Yet the similar business backgrounds of the Navy's civilian executives did not necessarily mean that they were working to further their own interests or those of their colleagues or clients. Forrestal explained the Navy's recruitment policy:

> Prior to 1940, the procurement of the Navy was handled largely by the system of competitive bidding. This procedure was obligatory upon the Navy under the law determining the methods by which Naval ships, planes and supplies were procured. As you, of course, are fully aware, it was a procedure quite sharply defined and left comparatively little, except determinations as to quality of product, to the judgment of procurement officers. With the elimination of the competitive bidding system and transfer to negotiated contracts, it seems to me it is obvious that different machinery became necessary. Negotiation, by its very nature means an agreement upon a fair price to both buyer and seller. The Department did not have the personnel nor to some extent the training or experience necessary for this function.
>
> In order to meet conditions created by this transfer to negotiated contracts there should be close scrutiny of each transaction at its inception. It was quite clear in a very short time that any attempt on my part to scrutinize contracts after their completion and processing through the regular legal channels of the Department was a futile attempt if we were to conduct our business with any real attempt at economy and efficiency. We, therefore, adopted the general principle that only civilians with substantial background of business experience should participate in the negotiation of contracts; further, that the agreements reached between our suppliers and the various bureaus through such negotiations should be promptly expressed by lawyers working directly with negotiations. In other words, our purpose and effort was to apply maximum care and scrutiny in the making of contracts at their inception rather than to submit them for review upon completion. The great urgency of war seemed to make the latter undesirable.[293]

The Navy pitted ambition against ambition—and with some success if the low profit figures and the findings from congressional hearings are indicative. The fact that many of the Navy negotiators came from Wall Street or LaSalle Street may speak more of where the legal, financial, and management talent lay for a wartime government desperate for people of ability and experience than it does of a shared class bias.[294] Nor does the fact that

---

[293] Letter of Forrestal to Mr. Sheppard, 30 January 1943, "Procurement and Material Division," Box 42, Forrestal Papers; emphasis added.

[294] On the "Good Man" list employed by Eberstadt and Forrestal for hiring personnel, see

executives serving in the Navy Department returned quickly to their own companies once the war was over necessarily mean that they had served the Navy ill or had acted in their private interests while in office.[295]

Indicative of the distant relations between the military and private industry was the small number of business managers willing to work in the military after the war: "most [top executives] preferred higher salaries in business and industry. Once eleven executives in succession turned down [Secretary of Defense] Forrestal's offer of a job before someone accepted. . . . Eberstadt told Forrestal that he had to select available people. 'If you are going to wait for the best,' he warned, 'you may never get started.'"[296] We should not infer that these executives were acting irrationally in not anticipating the future benefits from working in the military.

A consideration of Navy-industrial personnel changes, corporate profitability, and congressional action does not, therefore, substantiate the presence of a class-based American state. The record instead suggests that the accountants, lawyers, inspectors, and administrators employed by the Navy placed greater importance on their professionalism. Furthermore, there is a critical *absence* of evidence implicating businessmen in the betrayal of the public trust—despite the repeated investigations by House and Senate committees in search of precisely such compromised ethics on the part of Navy officials. The ties of mutual dependence between industry trade associations, constituent groups, their congressional representatives, and Navy officials typical of "iron triangles" or "policy networks" had yet to emerge in the 1940s.[297]

In sum, the record of the state-building in Navy procurement does not conform to three possible indicators of a military-industrial complex. First, the wartime and postwar government—the executive and legislative branches—frequently acted in ways counter to business interests. Second, profits for military contractors were consistently lower than manufacturing profits in general (with the exception of 1940 and 1941), and military sales were hardly a stable or particularly lucrative business; indeed, the Navy had good reason to avoid its own production whenever possible. Third, despite the appearance of a common set of personnel circulating from the legal,

---

Dorwart, *Eberstadt and Forrestal*. Dorwart holds that it was the common background of the "good men" that accredited them in the eyes of Forrestal or Eberstadt.

[295] One of the recommendations of the 1944 Archer-Wolf Report (the management study headed by T. P. Archer, General Motors vice president, and G. W. Wolf, president of United States Steel Export) was the establishment of a fiscal control agency, resulting in the creation of a Fiscal Director of the Navy (later "Comptroller") under Wilfred McNeil. Again, business executives acted on behalf of the Navy Department.

[296] Eberstadt to Forrestal, 23 July, 6 and 18 August 1947, Eberstadt Papers, in Dorwart, *Eberstadt and Forrestal*, 151.

[297] Peck and Scherer, *The Weapons Acquisition Process*, 112–13; Mrozek, "The Truman Administration and the Enlistment of the Aviation Industry in Postwar Defense," 89–93. Also see Markusen et al., *The Rise of the Gunbelt*.

business, and financial worlds to the Navy's civilian offices and then back again to the private sector, the behavior of Navy personnel, the record of contractor profits, the success of renegotiation, and the absence of procurement scandals during the 1940s all conform better to a model of public service and professional integrity.

Conclusions

Marriner Eccles's account of President Franklin Roosevelt's experience with the Navy Department bears retelling:

> The Treasury, . . . [the President said,] is so large and far-flung and ingrained in its practices that I find it almost impossible to get the action and results I want—even with Henry [Morgenthau] there. But the Treasury is not to be compared with the State Department. You should go through the experience of trying to get any changes in the thinking, policy and action of the career diplomats and then you'd know what a real problem was. But the Treasury and the State Department put together are nothing compared with the Na-avy. The admirals are really something to cope with and I should know [as former Assistant Secretary of the Navy]. To change anything in the Na-a-vy is like punching a feather bed. You punch it with your right and you punch it with your left until you are finally exhausted, and then you find the damn bed just as it was before you started punching.[298]

Yet the transformations of the 1940s hardly square with this picture of bureaucratic stasis.

The Navy may have changed reluctantly after the shattering attack on Pearl Harbor and the realities of a global war, but change it did—and drastically at that. "From 1940 to June 1945 the fleet inventory grew from 1,099 vessels to 50,759 vessels; its ranks of officers and sailors increased from 160,997 to 3,383,196," Hoopes and Brinkley report. "There were 8 new battleships, 92 new aircraft carriers, 35 new cruisers, 148 new destroyers, 365 new destroyer escorts, 140 new submarines, and 43,255 new landing craft."[299] The Bureau of Ships had 168 contracts out for $24.6 billion worth of ships (including $3.6 billion worth of destroyers) as of 30 June 1943, and the Bureau of Aeronautics had $6.3 billion in contracts for tactical combat aircraft (including $1.9 billion in fighters). The Navy required 162 models of 53 types of aircraft in 17 different tactical classifications over the duration of the war, the Aircraft Industries Association of America reported.[300] The extraordinary mobilization of American industry was complemented and supported by a proliferation of agencies for the administration of material

---

[298] Eccles, *Beckoning Frontiers*, 336.

[299] Hoopes and Brinkley, *Driven Patriot*, 184.

[300] The Aircraft Industries Association of America, "Aircraft Manufacturing in the United States," in Simonson, ed., *The History of the American Aircraft Industry*.

procurement, by an explosion in Navy spending, and by the rapid growth of the Navy's civilian bureaucracy.

With the Navy Department's and the Roosevelt Administration's immediate and desperate need for material, the government *had* to greatly extend its purchasing, improve its means of dealing with business firms, and devise means by which resources of sufficient quality and quantity could be secured as quickly as possible. The Navy was forced to develop a variety of contract forms for purchasing its supplies under conditions when costs, material quality, and delivery schedules were uncertain. It had to develop the expertise to negotiate and renegotiate contracts; it had to create the mechanisms for supervising its contracts, given the uncertainties of the contractor's half of the bargain (i.e., the reasonable pricing and timely provision of material supplies); it had to find ways to finance contractors with insufficient capital; it had to institutionalize the termination of contracts; and it had to coordinate procurement among the military services and between the civilian and military sectors.

The President's words of 6 January 1943 were to the point: "The Procurement Program must achieve *maximum production with minimum waste* and with the speed essential in time of war. This is the controlling objective not only for the original negotiation of contracts but also for the renegotiation required by law" (emphasis added). So it went for supervising contracts, inspecting munitions producers, financing manufacturers, and encouraging subcontracts. The Navy further rationalized its operations when the mobilization for war started to decelerate.[301] The Navy thus reformed its administration of procurement in the face of the threat from the Axis powers and the later threat from the Soviet Union in a world of jet-propelled aircraft and fissionable atoms.

The resource dependence perspective captures much of this statebuilding. The executive branch created most of the new institutions connected with Navy procurement, as we expect from the shift in government authority in wartime (Hypothesis 1a). Knox and Forrestal were able to change Navy buying from competitive bidding to negotiated contracts, replace obsolete bureau practices, create the Office of Procurement and Material, establish a legal organization for letting contracts, and coordinate procurement among the Bureaus and between the Navy and the government's agencies.[302] With the exception of renegotiation and subcontracting,

---

[301] Secretary Forrestal entitled the 1944 *Annual Report* "Creating a Logistics Organization," for instance. The Navy had developed four new strategies in fiscal 1944: clarifying responsibility and lines of authority; establishing overall logistic reporting and connecting logistics to strategic need in the Organization Planning Unit; providing the Vice Chief of Naval Operations (Air) with a staff for aviation logistics; and establishing inventory control offices beginning on 23 May 1944.

[302] Letter of Forrestal to Eliot Janeway, 4 July 1944, in Eliot Janeway, *The Struggle For Survival*, Yale Chronicles of America Series (New Haven: Yale University Press, 1951), 301–5.

Congress mostly went along with the Roosevelt Administration. And even in renegotiation and subcontracting, the interests of the Navy Department prevailed. Congress was often presented with a *fait accompli*—giving the President and the Secretary of the Navy's Office additional powers—or with bills drafted by the Navy and War Departments. As Miller has it, "the objective of all these [contracting] arrangements was the same: to facilitate maximum and expeditious production of war materials by appropriate allocation of risks and the provision of effective incentives."[303]

Departing from resource dependence expectations with respect to the command of state-building is the history of unification. The Navy triumphed over President Truman's initial preferences, and the Congress eventually agreed to using the Eberstadt plan as a model for the 1947 National Security Act—despite the supposedly stronger position of Congress in the non-emergency, post-crisis years (Hypothesis 1c). Neither the Congress nor the new Department of Defense could take over the control of procurement from the individual Navy bureaus. In fact, the bureaucratic logrolling allowed for in the Newport Conference in 1948 (that with an abundance of resources, the services would simply divide military functions—including the delivery of atomic weapons—and would tolerate the duplication and overlap of functions) came to characterize military procurement among the Navy bureaus and among the separate services for decades since.[304]

As for the organizational form that state-building took, the Navy and the Roosevelt Administration established a number of interorganizational connections between the military and the private sector, as we have seen in the sections above (Hypothesis 2b). But rather than the executive branch forging interorganizational linkages through the nationalization of material production (i.e., merger or joint venture) or through the creation of an extensive and more effective War Production Board (an interorganizational agency), the Navy reduced the uncertainty of its external relations by overwhelmingly relying on contracting—contracting which it then supervised and monitored by creating agencies *internal* to the government.

The Office of Procurement and Material was especially important in this regard.[305] The Bureau of the Budget found that the OP&M "has proved its usefulness . . . [as] a logical step to tie together the vertical organization of Navy supply activities in somewhat autonomous bureaus." The report praised the OP&M for creating a comprehensive statement of Navy supply, for supervising contract negotiations, and for assisting the bureaus in the transition to wartime negotiations of "vast business deals" and in avoiding

[303] Miller, *Pricing of Military Procurements*, 121.

[304] Hoopes and Brinkley, *Driven Patriot*, 410–12.

[305] Connery, *Industrial Mobilization*, 430–31; Albion and Connery, *Forrestal and the Navy*, 226–33; Hammond, *Organizing for Defense*, 135–58; and Furer, *Administration of the Navy*, 838–46.

unsound business deals, setting up records, redistributing scarce materials, breaking up numerous bottlenecks, coordinating the activities of some 30,000 naval inspectors, and expediting programmatic change. The Bureau of the Budget "assumed . . . that the main lines of the present Navy Department organization will continue."[306] They did.

Although the OP&M did the sort of supervision and expediting that we expect from an interorganizational body, it did so by using former businessmen and civilian executives and then including them in the Navy Department, rather than by explicitly building bridges to private contractors (like the Treasury's bond-selling agencies or the tripartite labor boards). The resource dependence perspective does not, then, predict the extent to which Navy-industrial ties remained voluntary or the extent to which the actual agencies connecting the Navy Department to private industry—the OPM, the SPAB, the WPB, and the OWMR—did not do the actual procurement of material supplies.

There was, furthermore, a clear persistence of the bureaucracies and administrative procedures of procurement in the postwar era (Hypothesis 3a). Under the new conditions of the postwar world, the Navy continued to need large amounts of material and the administrative tools sufficient to deal with a rival Soviet Union. We thus see extensive ratcheting in the size of Navy administration, although far less ratcheting in the extent of Navy procurement given the seriousness of the emerging Cold War. And the organization and administrative practices of procurement used during the war were not only retained but were even supplemented and enhanced during the postwar years. To the extent that the Navy kept its interorganizational ties with its contractors after the war, the "iron triangles" do not appear to have emerged until after the 1940s—after the growth of governmental regulations, after the development of more research-intensive technologies, and after bottom-up constituent demands for military spending were expressed in Congress.

Departing from the expectations of ratcheted state-building was the history of the postwar military budgets. That the conservative 80th Congress achieved balanced budgets in the postwar years comes as no surprise in a post-crisis period, but that the White House opposed the Navy (and other services) and cooperated with the Republican Congress runs counter to expectations and to assumptions here of the executive branch working as a team (or at least without overt conflict). The relatively small postwar defense budgets also confound the expectations from the resource dependence perspective, since the changes in both the international environment of the new

---

[306] "Office of Procurement and Material," Bureau of the Budget, Division of Administrative Management, 15 April 1944, pp. 1–2, Unit 34, Box 16, Series 39.6a, "Navy," Budget Records.

bipolar world and the revitalization of the national economy, especially industries associated with defense spending, would suggest more of a continuation of wartime government-society relations than turned out to be the case.

Finally, there were comprehensive shifts in the agenda of national politics, as manifest in the accepted higher levels of defense spending, the acknowledged need for a unified military, and the widespread recognition of the new international obligations of the United States in the postwar world (Hypothesis 3c).

A brief history of the Navy Department's dealings with the Brewster Aeronautical Corporation captures the difficulty and complexity of the Navy's dependence on its material suppliers. The Navy placed hundreds of millions of dollars in contracts with Brewster in the early 1940s, even though Brewster had only $1,738,500 of its own capital at the time. Its production backlog stood at $107 million in 1940, while its gross revenues came to under a million dollars a year.[307] Worse, labor disputes caused Brewster's production schedules to fall behind still further. So by February 1942, Brewster had $279 million of business on the books, even as it was producing far less than specified in its contracts.[308]

The Assistant Secretary for Air, Artemus Gates, investigated the Brewster situation and found that not a single acceptable dive bomber had been produced under the Navy, Dutch, or British contracts, that Brewster was making no progress on turning out fighter aircraft (it was licensed to produce the Chance-Vought Corsair, but the first F3A-1 would not be delivered until 1943, although it had been promised ten months earlier), and that Brewster's financial situation was precarious—it had already received cash advances from the British and the Navy, but the Navy's funding could not be applied to the dive bombers being produced for export, and the production of dive bombers competed with the manufacture of Navy fighter aircraft. Gates also determined that the company's accounting practices were such that its financial records did not permit an evaluation of its financial condition. Finally, Gates realized that private management had failed to turn the company around despite its troubles, and the United Auto Workers local was not observing the no-strike pledge, in disregard of National War Labor

[307] "Statement by Under Secretary of the Navy October 12, 1943 on Brewster," p. 5, file "Brewster #3," Box 44, Gates Papers. Brewster had three plants, the main one in Long Island City, New York.

[308] Telephone conversation between James Work of Brewster and Merrill C. Miegs, 24 February 1942, file "A–Misc—Brewster Aircraft Corp.," Box 42, Gates Papers. By April 1942, the situation at Brewster had deteriorated further, and a deal for the U.S. Rubber Company to rescue Brewster had fallen through.

Board rulings.[309] "All in all, therefore, it appeared in April that Brewster was on the verge of collapse."[310]

The Navy took over the Brewster operation in late 1941 through an executive order, with the aim of establishing management able to maximize aircraft production. The takeover lasted a month, at which point the Navy agreed with Brewster owners on the selection of a new president. Even so, labor problems escalated so that the December 1942 slow-down alone was estimated to take up 335,000 man-hours.[311] The persistence of production problems forced the Navy to bring in shipbuilder Henry Kaiser to become chairman of the Board (without compensation) in March of 1943. Kaiser appointed yet another company president.

When the production, financial, and labor difficulties at Brewster came to light, the House Naval Affairs Committee severely criticized Navy management. It determined that the Navy had not thoroughly investigated the situation at Brewster, that it had failed to take accounting safeguards, that it had vacillated and demonstrated a lack of firmness, and that it had needlessly approved a payment of half a million dollars to Brewster owners.[312] The Navy Department responded by saying that the Vinson Committee, the Truman Committee, and the press all fundamentally misconceived its actual powers:

> it is a novel proposition that it is the function of a Government procurement agency, even in times of peace, to determine from whom it should buy on the basis of its analysis of the labor contracts of its possible vendors. But in late 1941 and early 1942 . . . it was not only imperative to make use of every facility experienced in the manufacture of aircraft, but strenuous efforts were being made to bring into the field companies with no aircraft experience—witness the automotive industry—so great and imperative was the need for aircraft. . . .

[309] "Statement of Mr. Artemus L. Gates," Assistant Secretary For Air, to Subcommittee of House Naval Affairs Committee, 12 October 1943, file "Brewster #3," Box 44, Gates Papers. On the inefficient management at Brewster, see "Statement on Brewster Aeronautical Corporation" by George P. Robinson, President of George P. Robinson and Co., Inc., 9 September 1943, file "Brewster #3," Box 44, Gates Papers; and Agnes Miller, "Chaos and Tyranny Compete Bitterly at Brewster Plant," Washington *Post*, Sunday, 3 October 1943, p. 3B.

[310] "Statement of Mr. Artemus L. Gates," Assistant Secretary For Air, to Subcommittee of House Naval Affairs Committee, 12 October 1943, file "Brewster #3," Box 44, Gates Papers.

[311] There was also trouble with unionized plant guards, and with UAW-CIO Local 365 in general. See Miller, "Chaos and Tyranny Compete Bitterly at Brewster Plant;" "Statement of Mr. Artemus L. Gates, Assistant Secretary For Air, to Subcommittee of House Naval Affairs Committee, 12 October 1943, file "Brewster #3," Box 44, Gates Papers; Statement by Under Secretary of the Navy," 5 October 1943, file "Brewster #3"; Committee on Naval Affairs, House of Representatives, "Report of the Subcommittee Appointed to Investigate the Causes of Failure of Production of Brewster Aeronautical Corporation Under Its Contracts with the Navy"; and Committee on Naval Affairs, "Investigations of the Progress of the War Effort," 78th Cong., 2nd sess., 11 December 1944, p. 170.

[312] Committee on Naval Affairs, "Report of the Subcommittee Appointed to Investigate the Causes of Failure of Production of Brewster Aeronautical Corporation Under Its Contracts with the Navy."

It is natural and probably inevitable to say that since the labor problem obstructed production the Navy should have done something about it. The Navy did do something. . . . It exhausted every means at its disposal for creating harmony, and failing that, for bringing the disputed issues before the body duly constituted for adjudicating them, the War Labor Board. It . . . had neither legal nor moral right to attempt by threats either to modify a collective bargaining agreement or to nullify the election by the union of its own official, when that agreement and that election were validated by laws which the Navy did not pass and which established a forum for the orderly settlement of labor disputes.

The Navy believes that, in a war at least, cancellation of airplane contracts is a remedy to be employed when the planes are no longer needed or when it is satisfied that the contractor can not produce them in sufficient quantities to justify continuing the project.

The obstacles to smooth mass production of aircraft which result from an unproven design, weak management, poor planning and mushrooming growth are difficult to appreciate. From May, 1940 . . . until April, 1942, when the Navy took over, these factors did tremendous harm. When it became clear that they would never be remedied under the then owner-management, the Navy took over, insisted on the removal of earlier managers from both management and voter control and sought the ablest management it could find available. . . . The Navy feels that it has gone as far as a Government procurement agency properly could in attempting to solve a most serious problem.[313]

Assistant Secretary Gates repeated that "*management, not the Navy*, was running the business. The Navy has a multitude of problems and they cannot and should not be stretched to cover the detailed running of the business of its contractors. Our efforts have been to secure a management which could solve its own difficulties—not to solve them for the management after it was installed."[314]

Forrestal similarly noted that "the Navy's interest in Brewster flows entirely from a desire to get planes for our fighting men. It has been, and it always is, reluctant to interfere with private management and has only done so when it was apparent that there was no other course available."[315] The Under Secretary told Congress that "[t]he Navy needs those planes . . . keep that single fact always in mind—the Navy needs the Brewster-built planes. We have always needed them, even though we did not get them." It was the need for the Brewster aircraft that caused the government to invest "more than $9 million in facilities at Brewster," that "guaranteed the company a

[313] "Navy Department Statement as to House Naval Affairs Committee Report on Brewster Aeronautical Corporation," Draft of 13 December 1943, file "Brewster #4," Box 44, Gates Papers.

[314] "Statement of Mr. Artemus L. Gates, Assistant Secretary For Air, to Subcommittee of House Naval Affairs Committee, 12 October 1943, file "Brewster #3," Box 44, Gates Papers; emphasis added.

[315] "Statement by Under Secretary of the Navy," 12 October 1943, 8, file "Brewster #3."

V-loan amounting to $55 million," and that made the Navy "deal with the company in the face of poor production, weak management, labor troubles and high costs."[316] But the Navy was unwilling to take over day-to-day plant management in the middle of the war, or to guarantee effective management and productive labor.

As the war progressed and the need for aircraft and ships became less pressing, the Navy was authorized to cancel its contracts. The Navy therefore proceeded to cancel its outstanding contracts with Brewster in early 1944, given that Brewster was the highest-cost producer of Corsairs, had the smallest output, and was in the weakest financial condition of any manufacturer of Navy fighter planes.[317]

But the Navy did not give the company adequate advance notice of the fighter cutbacks when it announced its decision on 16 May 1944,[318] and the sudden closing made national headlines. The ensuing furor prompted quick congressional reaction. Senator James Murray (D., Mont.) proclaimed, "The recent events at the Brewster Aeronautical Corporation have already provided a 'test tube' of what lies before us in the days of conversion from war to peace." The closing was "a solemn warning that war contracts can be terminated without adequate planning for other types of production."[319] On 1 July 1944, Murray was able to pass legislation for the establishment of an office of postwar adjustment.

---

[316] "Statement by Under Secretary of the Navy," 12 October 1943, 8; emphasis in original.

[317] "Brewster," file "Brewster #5," Box 44, Gates Papers. For mid-production planes, the F3A-1 (Brewster) cost $71,800 per plane, while the Goodyear plane sold for $56,800 each and the Vought plane went for $63,327. Illuminatingly, the "Direct, Indirect labor and Administrative Expenses" amounted to 43 percent of costs for the production of Brewster Corsairs, but only 30 percent of Goodyear FG-1s and 28 percent of Chance-Vought F4U-1s (Memorandum, N. S. Ludington, Lieut. Comdr., to Finance Section, Production Division, Bureau of Aeronautics, 27 May 1944, file "Brewster #5," Box 45, Gates Papers).

The Chief of the Bureau of Aeronautics explained to one member of Congress, "The first order for the Corsair fighter plane from Brewster was placed August 11, 1941, and contemplated initial deliveries in October 1942. Orders for the planes were increased and the final contract dated March 5, 1943, with a revised delivery schedule, called for a total of 1508 planes and spare parts at . . . $140,565,751.32 and fee of $8,057,166.36, or a total of $148,622,917.68. Actually, the first plane was not accepted from Brewster until June 1943 and only 136 planes had been accepted by the end of that year. The contract was terminated in May 1944, effective July of that year. 735 planes were delivered, plus approximately the equivalent of 125 planes in spare parts, or the equivalent of 860 airplanes . . . To make possible the Corsair production the Navy caused a plant to be built at Johnsville, Pennsylvania, at a cost of $8,233,128 and supplied additional machinery and equipment at Brewster's New York plants, costing $859,593."

[318] A proportional cutback across producers would have left all three Corsair manufacturers with insufficient business.

[319] "Statement of Senator James E. Murray, Chairman, Senate Military Affairs War Contracts Subcommittee, before the New York Congress of Industrial Organizations, Manhattan Center, New York, New York," 1 June 1944, file "Brewster #6," Box 45, Gates Papers.

The Navy was obliged to take over operations at Brewster's Johnsville (Pa.) plant as an adjunct to the Naval Air Material Center in Philadelphia, and its Naval Material Redistribution Administration took over Brewster's Ford Building in Long Island City.[320] Yet the Navy was still owed $24.45 million on its 1 July 1943 V-loan of $55 million. The Navy negotiated a settlement with Brewster for its claims against the Navy but still had to bail out Brewster's debts, paying banks $26.54 million for the principal and interest on the V-loans. The outcry on the closure of Brewster in the press and on Capitol Hill forced the Navy's hand where simple mismanagement could not.

The experience of the Navy's purchasing of aircraft from the Brewster Corporation underscores the Navy's problems in securing desperately needed supplies. The Navy was strangely helpless, unable to secure the production of needed planes, and forced to tolerate the divisive labor-management relations and the inefficient business management already in place at Brewster. The Navy took over the Brewster operations with reluctance (after settling with Brewster for three-quarters of what it asked for, $13 million instead of $17 million upon the contract cancellation), in response to the public outcry. But if the Navy failed, so also did private enterprise. At the end, Brewster was out of business and the Navy did not get the planes it needed. Instead, the Navy was embarrassed politically and had to take over unwanted facilities.

---

[320] "Memorandum For Mr. Gates," from J. A. Gifford, Lt. Comdr., USNR , 5 July 1944, file "Brewster #6," Box 45, Gates Papers. For a public response, see Drew Pearson, Washington *Post*, 24 May 1944, and others in file "Brewster #5," Box 44, Gates Papers.

6

Relative State-Building in the 1940s:
The Terms of Exchange

The well-known reciprocal relation between a
despotic orientation and the warlike tendencies
of a group rests on this formal basis: war needs
a centralistic intensification of the group form,
and this is guaranteed best by despotism. And
vice versa.
  —Georg Simmel

A state of conflict . . . pulls the members [of
the group] so tightly together and subjects
them to such a uniform impulse that they must
either completely get along with, or completely
repel, one another.
  —Georg Simmel

THE SECOND WORLD WAR had uneven effects on societal actors relative to
each other and to the government. Following the arguments of the first
chapter, the bargains struck between the government and societal actors (or
clienteles) during the war should depend upon the sets of alternatives available to the government and clienteles, and on the uncertainty of resource
supplies.

The labor unions, investors in government securities, and Navy contractors should all fare equivalently well. The unions wanted to work and had
little alternative to cooperating with the government during the war, just as
the government had no alternative but to work with the existing labor
unions. Nonetheless, the supply of labor was uncertain, since skilled and
semi-skilled union members could choose not to work. With the nation at
war, organized labor should prosper.

The sale of government securities to individuals and institutions was likewise uncertain; the government could not be sure of attracting sufficient
funds even with set interest rates or extensive advertising campaigns. But
both security investors and the government had alternatives to dealing with

each other: investors had alternative places to put their savings (unlike the choices available to organized labor and material producers) just as the federal government had choices as to where it was going to raise money (again, unlike the government's position vis-à-vis the unions and material producers).

Material producers were advantaged in that the Navy could never be sure that its supplies would be produced to its standards or in a timely fashion, and the Navy was dependent on a few technically proficient companies. Yet industry had no choice but to produce for the government, given the restrictions on civilian production and the possibility of government sanctions. The combination of the uncertainty of production and the fact that neither the government nor material suppliers had other alternatives meant that military contractors should have the upper hand in dealing with the government and that they should do as well as the unions and investors (assuming that the mutual possession of alternatives is equivalent to the mutual absence of alternatives).

Social security stakeholders should fare less well. Although they had choices on how to save their money, the federal government also had choices: the earnings of existing or potential social security stakeholders represented only one of its options for raising revenue. Furthermore, the collection of social security taxes from employees and employers did not have the uncertainty of the provision of skilled labor, the attraction of investment into U.S. securities, or the securance of material supplies.

But taxpayers (individual and corporate taxpayers both) should do worst of all: they had no alternatives to paying income taxes, while the government had other funding choices. And the government had little uncertainty about the receipt of income tax revenues (although the Bureau of Internal Revenue had to expend some effort on enforcing tax payments).

In the postwar period, the assumption is that the terms of exchange between the government and societal actors depend on the size of the clientele, since the sets of alternatives available to the government and societal actors and the uncertainty of supplies matter less with the end of the government's desperate need for resources: the more voters in a policy domain, then, the better the chances for elected officials to be reelected, and thus the better the terms of exchange (using ordinal rankings). The 85 million registered bondholders as of 1945 should receive the best terms of exchange with the government in the postwar years, and (individual) income taxpayers the next best (with 50 million persons filing tax returns in 1945). Social security stakeholders, having the next largest number of voters, should not do as well. The labor unions, with about 15 million members, should fare worse yet. Finally, material producers, representing relatively few voters, should do worst of all.

The Terms of Exchange: Social Security

Although social security stakeholders had several alternatives (social security
contributors being at once taxpayers, employees, members of unions, and
military personnel), the presence of alternatives appeared to have little effect on public policy. Congress and the Roosevelt Administration supported
the competing programs for war veterans and encouraged the spread of
private pension plans instead of reinforcing the social security system by
raising OASI taxes and increasing social security coverage and benefits.

In a meeting on social security on 11 September 1941, Treasury officials
voiced concern over the effects and future commitments of a vastly expanded social security program as envisioned by Federal Security Administrator McNutt and SSB Chairman Altmeyer. Was there to be a positive
inflow to the OASI trust fund over the next three years, and what about the
outflow later? Would Congress choose only the politically attractive bene-
ficiary part and undercut the more unpleasant taxation side?[1]

As early as June 1941 Treasury officials were worrying whether "[t]he net
effect of the expansion in the Social Security Program *as a whole* [would]
make the fiscal problem more difficult." The Treasury feared that an expansion of social security outlays and OASI taxes in the next four years would
"deplete the net revenue able to facilitate the financing of the war effort,
and the increased outpayments would presumably exceed the increased revenue." Treasury officials thought that "shifting of buying power from
workers and enterprises to individuals with deficient incomes" would
worsen inflationary pressures "at a time when defense expenditure results in
increased pressure on civilian expenditure." It was not clear to the Roosevelt
Administration "that the expanded program will make it easier to retain the
tax provisions of the present social security program. If it is going to be
difficult to retain the scheduled tax increase in 1943 with an insurance program that will take in $5.8 billion more than it pays out in a four-year period,
why will it be easier with an enlarged insurance program that takes in $7.5
billion more than it pays out?"[2]

Despite the alternatives potentially available to social security stakeholders, Congress delayed increasing OASI taxes and benefits until 1950.
Recall that average monthly benefits rose modestly between 1940 (at $22.60
per month) and 1949 (at $26.00 per month), and real per capita benefits fell
from $51 per month in 1940 to $33 per month in 1949 (1958 dollars). Mean-

---

[1] Morgenthau, Diaries, Vol. 440, 26.

[2] Memorandum of G. C. Means to J. Weldon Jones, "Fiscal Implications of Proposed Expansion of Social Security Program," 18 June 1941, file "Social Security," Box 14, Papers of
Gardiner Means, emphasis in original.

while, those paying a constant 1 percent of their income to the social security system up to 1950 had to double their cash contributions, from an average of $932 in 1940 to one of $1,812 in 1950. Even as the amount of money in the OASI trust fund rose from $2 billion in 1940 to almost $12 billion by 1949, workers were paying more and beneficiaries were receiving less.

That social security stakeholders had alternatives to relying on the social security system in their old age did not, however, appear to enhance the position of social security stakeholders or undermine the expansion of rival programs: the eventual reforms in the social security program were delayed for five years after the end of WWII; veterans' programs were expanded such that the government paid out over $10 billion in benefits by 1955; and the growth of private pension and health plans reduced the demand for and attractiveness of comprehensive federal social programs. As Roosevelt said in 1940, when blocking further initiatives for national health care, "the Nation today, I am certain, is better prepared to meet the public health problems than at any previous time in the history of this country."[3] Although Roosevelt would later refer to national medical care in his "economic bills of rights" of 1944 and 1945, it was left to President Truman to propose national health care.

The Regulation of Labor-Management Relations

Neither the government nor organized labor had a choice but to cooperate during the war years: workers depended on the government to protect them against business management and to guarantee their rights, and the government depended on organized labor to provide a reliable workforce in wartime. Despite the government's critical wartime needs, however, organized labor suffered a number of setbacks at the hands of the Roosevelt Administration.

With the "Little Steel" decision of 15 July 1942, the NLRB held that wage increases could match, but not exceed, cost-of-living increases (the benchmark was to be the cost-of-living figures of 1 January 1941)—and wages were still at a Depression-era levels in most industries as of January 1941. The "Little Steel" ruling thereby eliminated hopes for additional hourly wage increases for those unions that had improved their situation between the end of 1940 and mid-1942. (NWLB Chairman Davis himself

---

[3] *Public Papers and Addresses of President Franklin D. Roosevelt*, 31 October 1940, p. 526, cited in Monte M. Poen, *Harry Truman Versus the Medical Lobby: The Genesis of Medicare* (Columbia: University of Missouri Press, 1979), 27. One supporter of national health care described efforts for promulgating medical insurance as being buried by "an avalanche of defense legislation" (27, n. 68).

stated on 15 September 1942 that the Little Steel formula automatically disqualified 75 percent of wage earners from any further increases.)[4] Yet the President fully supported the NWLB's decision and soon thereafter, on 5 October 1942, froze wage levels at their 15 September level.[5]

Roosevelt's neglect of labor interests was further evident in his efforts to impose mandatory work rules. In his message vetoing the Smith-Connally Act, the President commented that "Section eight ignores completely labor's 'no-strike' pledge and provides in effect for strike notices and strike ballots. Far from discouraging strikes, these provisions would stimulate labor unrest and give Government sanction to strike agitations." In the same veto message, Roosevelt asked that the Selective Service Act be amended "so that persons may be inducted into noncombat military service up to the age of 65 years. This will enable us to induct into military service all persons who engage in strikes or stoppages or other interruptions of work in plants in the possession of the United States."[6] Roosevelt repeated the request for "work or fight" legislation—anathema to organized labor—in the 1944 and 1945 State of the Union messages.

The President's crackdown against organized labor contrasted with the Administration's mild treatment of company managers who violated NWLB rulings. On the first of four occasions when the chairman of the Montgomery Ward Company defied NWLB decisions, the incident drew headlines, but the NWLB, the Roosevelt Administration, and the press barely noted Montgomery Ward's continued noncompliance.[7] Nor did the federal government stop awarding contracts to firms in violation of the Wagner Act, as it was required to do.

Consider also that the White House rejected out of hand Walter Reuther's plan for General Motors and the UAW to build five hundred planes a day in 1941 and that it did not consult organized labor when deciding the location of munitions plants or when administering programs for dealing with manpower supply and employee turnover. Nor did the Roosevelt Administration strive to uphold the "equality of sacrifice" for labor and management alike, as was agreed in the labor-management conference of 1941: the $25,000 cap on salaries was never imposed, and business profits had an

---

[4] Preis, *Labor's Giant Step*, 164. Because of the 48-hour week and the provisions for automatic double time for the seventh day of work, and time-and-a-half for more than a 40-hour workweek, workers were effectively able to exceed the 15 percent increase allowable under the "Little Steel" standard.

[5] The CIO protested, of course. See letter of Philip Murray to the President, 18 January 1945, and attachment, "CIO Resolution No. 5," file "Wages March–April 1945," Box 2, OF 98, Official Files, Roosevelt Papers.

[6] 25 June 1943, *Public Papers and Addresses of President Franklin D. Roosevelt*, 270, 271.

[7] Preis, *Labor's Giant Step*, 219.

effective tax rate of about 70 percent (given the various exemptions, deferments, and refunds) rather than the official rate of 90 percent.[8]

Organized labor in fact fared considerably worse than other income earners. Whereas real income for directly employed labor rose by 34 percent between 1939 and 1946, the workforce as a whole had a 48 percent increase in income, and the self-employed in business and agriculture saw their earnings rise by 204 percent over the same period (with self-employment being "divided nearly equally between agriculture on the one hand and on the other small proprietorship and the professional occupations"). The economist Alexander Sachs found that *"the increment in 'real' income by the average member of the self-employed group was better than double of the comprehensive working force (as employed by others and self-employed), and better than treble the gain in 'real' income of those in direct employment by others in industry and agriculture."*[9]

President Truman supported postwar legislation that imposed further restrictions on organized labor—including many of the provisions of the Taft-Hartley Act. The President succeeded in securing an injunction against John L. Lewis, with Lewis and the UMW being fined about $13 million (the fine was later reduced). Although the tougher fate for organized labor after the war is as expected in view of the relatively small numbers of union members, the wartime outcomes are worse than expected.

Critical to the inability of organized labor to obtain a better exchange with the Roosevelt and Truman Administrations was, of course, the split in the labor movement. As noted in Chapter 3, labor was no single clientele: the split created a divided, even fratricidal union movement which not only permitted but encouraged government intervention. With each union federation vulnerable to attacks from the other, and with CIO President Murray facing threats from the AFL, on one side, and from the UMW and Lewis, on the other, the CIO was especially receptive to Roosevelt's overtures.[10] The reliance of the AFL and CIO on the U.S. government to keep the peace between them, in combination with the war's no-strike pledge, meant that

[8] On equality of sacrifice and the $25,000 income ceiling, see Leff, "The Politics of Sacrifice."

[9] Alexander Sachs, "The Altered Social Income Structure of This Postwar Compared with Changes following the First World War," Special Report, Mid-May 1950, file "Public Finance, National Income, National Debt," Box 140, Papers of Alexander Sachs, "Introduction," p. 14, Table Ib, II; emphasis in original.

[10] See Lichtenstein, *Labor's War at Home*, 157–77; Dubofsky and Van Tine, *John L. Lewis*, 1977. The division between Lewis and Murray itself had several causes. Among them were Lewis's failed endorsement of Wendell Willkie for President in 1940 and Lewis's subsequent resignation of the CIO presidency. Dubofsky and Van Tine, as well as Alinsky (*John L. Lewis*), note Lewis's personal resentment of Murray, and Murray's determination to prove himself independent of his former mentor, Lewis.

the AFL and CIO had little alternative but to work with the U.S. government.

The division of the labor movement is of key importance, for there were several unsuccessful attempts made to reunite organized labor, in 1937, 1939, 1942, and 1946. In fact, at one point the Roosevelt Administration intervened in order to prevent the AFL, CIO, and UMW from establishing a working agreement among themselves—cooperation that threatened to unify the labor unions.[11] The President consequently set up an advisory "Labor Victory Committee" composed of equal numbers of representatives from the AFL and CIO—with Lewis and the United Mine Workers conspicuously left out.[12]

Given the divided labor movement, the Roosevelt Administration could act with reduced fear of union reprisal and could achieve better bargains in its negotiations with labor than would have been possible otherwise. Moreover, when labor unions did challenge the White House with wildcat strikes, the Roosevelt Administration was able to marshal formidable opposition against the unions: a powerful military community (including testimony by generals and injured soldiers returning from the front lines), a hostile press, an upset public, and a revived business sector.[13]

In short, organized labor did not receive the benefits from its exchange with the wartime government that might be expected from its advantaged position. The absence of a unified labor movement prevented the emergence of a more powerful labor sector and foreclosed the possibility of cor-

[11] The Roosevelt Administration, as well as the CIO under Murray, perceived Lewis's offer of an "accouplement" between the CIO and AFL—potentially unifying organized labor—as a serious threat. President Roosevelt and Murray were thus at pains to keep Lewis off the NWLB (Memorandum to the President from Wayne Coy, Office for Emergency Management, 22 January 1942, "Combined Labor War Board," Box 2/1, OF 4747, Official File, Roosevelt Papers; Alinsky, *John L. Lewis*, 249–53; Dubofsky and Van Tine, *John L. Lewis*, 405–7; Walter Galenson, *The CIO Challenge to the AFL* (Cambridge, Mass.: Harvard University Press, 1960), 68–70; Koistinen, *The Hammer and the Sword*, 154–59; New York *Times* reporter A. M. Raskin, personal communication with the author, December 1989).

Also see "Memorandum for the President" from E.M.W. (Brigadier General Edwin M. Watson, Secretary to the President), 1–20–42; "Personal and Confidential" memorandum to the President from Gardner Jackson, Under Secretary, U.S. Department of Agriculture, 20 January 1942; letter of the President to Philip Murray, 22 January 1942; letter of Philip Murray to the President, 25 January 1942; and Memorandum for the President from Wayne Coy, Office for Emergency Management, Executive Office of the President, 22 January 1942, "Combined Labor War Board," 1942–44, Box 2/1, OF 4747, Official File, Roosevelt Papers.

[12] The President and his "labor cabinet" met at least once for more than an hour on 17 March 1942. They agreed that voluntary action was preferable to restrictive measures by Congress ("Combined Labor War Board," 1942–44, Box 2/1).

[13] While the success of John L. Lewis and the UMW indicated the possibility of flouting the federal government's authority, Lewis and the UMW received nationwide vilification for the wartime strikes. The singular conditions of mining coal made strike-breaking uniquely difficult.

poratist government.[14] Yet the very possibility of a unified labor movement contradicts the view that organized labor in the United States was necessarily weak and suggests that more attention might be paid to the persons and events of the 1930s and 1940s that succeeded in keeping the labor movement divided. At the same time, however, the prominent industrial and craft unions could make their separate peace with management: the UMW, at once the most anti-government and the most traditional of unions, pushed for higher wages, better hours, safer conditions, and non-governmental health care and pension plans. Similarly, the United Auto Workers union exploited its position to get higher wages, as did the United Steel Workers and other large industrial unions.[15]

Public Finance

With regard to the terms of exchange between the income taxpayers and the investors in U.S. public debt, investors in U.S. securities did better during WWII in their relations with the government than did taxpayers. After the war, the reverse held true.

With the Federal Reserve Banks propping up bond prices, and with the Treasury's War Finance Division doing virtually all it could to ensure the success of the war loan campaigns, individual investors were guaranteed real returns on their savings, and individual companies made large profits by "quota riding" and security "switching." Although the government had other sources of funding available, financial institutions and individual savers had billions of dollars needed by the government—billions that could be invested in other ways and that the government could not be assured of getting. After the war, investors saw their bond values stay above par, even as inflation eroded the purchasing power of their savings and even as the opportunities of the war years were no longer present (see Chapter 4).

Conversely, taxpayers fared poorly from the cumulative effects of the Revenue Acts of 1940, 1941, and 1942. Taxpayers had no choice but to pay their taxes and were targets of opportunity for a resource-needy government, given the little uncertainty of the government's tax collection (with income withholding and legal sanctions against tax avoidance). After the war, taxpayers did better with the tax reductions of 1945 and 1948, and with the postwar decline in per capita tax receipts. Inconsistent with expectations for the postwar years is that the taxpayers did better in their

[14] See Quadagno, *The Transformation of Old Age Security*. Quadagno notes the postwar depoliticization of the unions and recognizes the importance of the split in the labor movement.

[15] See Harris, *Labor's Civil War*; E. Young, "The Split in the Labor Movement"; and Galenson, *Rival Unionism in the United States*.

terms of exchange than did the more numerous holders of U.S. government securities.

Navy Procurement

The Navy was able to limit the advantage accruing to its ship and aircraft contractors under emergency conditions. Despite the irreplaceable expertise and indispensable production facilities possessed by Navy suppliers, the Navy was able to revise its administration of procurement and thereby restrict its contractors to low after-tax profits. In fact, Assistant Secretary Kenney noted that many companies voluntarily limited profits in order to stay out of newspaper headlines and avoid charges of war profiteering (see Chapter 5).[16]

The immediate postwar years revealed an even poorer record. Business dried up, and so too, for most companies, did profits: Bath Iron Works, Todd Shipyards, and Consolidated Vultee operated at a loss for at least one of the years between 1945 and 1950, and most of the shipbuilding business and much of the aircraft industry collapsed in the postwar years (the exceptions were Grumman and United Aircraft: Grumman had average profits of over 6.5 percent in 1947 through 1950, and United Aircraft had annual profits averaging over 4.5 percent in the same period). Navy contractors underperformed manufacturing firms in general, and contractors with a larger portion of non-government contracts (e.g., Bethlehem Steel and General Motors) did better than firms selling more exclusively to the military. The Navy Department, fearful of adverse publicity and checked by Congress, was careful to monitor profits and supervise contracts.

The Relative Terms of Exchange Among Clienteles

Although we should expect organized labor to fare as well as investors and material producers during the early 1940s, investors in U.S. government securities did better than either Navy contractors or the labor unions. The bargains obtained by social security stakeholders and income taxpayers come closer to expectations: the significant increases in the personal and corporate income tax and the slowly deteriorating conditions for social secu-

---

[16] Voluntary price reductions by the Pratt & Whitney Aircraft (engines) and Hamilton Standard Propellers Divisions of United Aircraft amounted to approximately $4,000,000 on uncompleted Navy contracts (Letter from United Aircraft [no author] to the Secretary of the Navy, 13 May 1941, L4–3[1] Vol. 17, Aeronautics, 1925–42). General Motors' voluntary price reductions on FM-2s amounted to about $5,060,000, with another $1,500,000 refunded to the Navy at the end of 1944 ("Contract NOA[s]-227 for FM's," file "Naval Aircraft—General," Box 21, Gates Papers).

rity stakeholders show social security stakeholders and income taxpayers faring worse than other clienteles during the war. Moreover, social security stakeholders were better off than taxpayers: even as real benefit levels were declining, more were qualifying for future benefits; they would at least get individual benefits in return for their sacrifices. Meanwhile, individual income taxpayers paid three times as much in taxes in 1945 as they did in 1940, and spending on domestic programs fell. In short, labor unions benefited from the expanding employment in unionized industries, and military contractors were making money producing up to and even beyond capacity, only their gains were smaller and less one-sided than expected. The buyers of U.S. government debt did better than expected, and social security stakeholders and taxpayers fared about as predicted under a greatly expanded federal government in wartime.

After the war, material producers, with the fewest voters, did fare the worst. Labor unions, with only 15 million members, also fared poorly, with the repeal of the Norris-LaGuardia Act banning injunctions against labor and the passage of the Taft-Hartley Act. Taxpayers, the second largest clientele, fared best of all. Postwar tax legislation allowed for tax deductions for spouses and dependents, exempted up to $600 from tax liabilities, lowered income tax rates, and for the first time permitted married couples to split their income on joint returns. But federal bondholders experienced a slight worsening of their terms of exchange: real returns on government securities fell with inflation between 1946 and 1948, and institutions could no longer make large, quick profits from manipulating the war loan campaigns. Unexpected, however, were the delays and the compromises in the reform of the social security system, given the higher numbers of active social security contributors, and with additional retirees drawing from the OASI trust fund.

What, then, do we learn from this comparison of state-building across policy domains? One finding might be that a determination of the relative bargains obtained by societal actors in relation to each other and to the government in crisis and non-crisis periods is worth further exploration. Even if the hypotheses regarding the terms of exchange were not all borne out, the resource dependence perspective provides us with some leverage in understanding the alteration of government-society relations and how some societal actors might be advantaged vis-à-vis others in a critical period. Further exploration of relative state-building could come from additional measurement and evaluation of the terms of exchange, given that the terms of exchange for the various societal actors discussed here cannot always be compared fluently. How *do* the terms of exchange for union members (who were making the most money ever, even if not as much as other clienteles) match up against those of material producers (who were receiving huge gross incomes but small net profits)?

A second conclusion is more speculative. It may be that military contractors and organized labor did worse than expected because the Roosevelt Administration and the Congress—and perhaps the public as well—realized the advantages that material producers and labor unions could have as monopoly suppliers. The government may have tried to escape its disadvantaged terms of exchange by mobilizing support for measures to counteract the possible monopoly powers of organized labor and material producers. Consistent with this hypothesis are the Roosevelt Administration's condemnation of work stoppages, the President's personal intervention to break up the unification of the unions in 1942, and the concern over contractor profits exhibited by the Roosevelt Administration, Congress, and the public. For all of the beneficial terms of exchange enjoyed by the investors in U.S. government securities, they were themselves a congeries of corporate, governmental, and private actors which never had a monopoly over funding sources: the government could, after all, have raised more in taxes, forced loans, or penalized consumer spending. The assumption that the mutual presence of alternatives is equivalent to the mutual absence of alternatives may need to be rethought.

7

A Resource-Dependent American State

Our concern with grand plans for the social
and economic system and with the state arises
not because we have any interest in the "state"
or the "system" as such. For us, these
institutions are but means to an end, and that
end is the welfare, dignity, growth and freedom
of the individual human being. This putting the
individual first, is the genius of democracy and
of Christianity, and is the chief factor that
makes us reject and oppose the whole
totalitarian system with its inevitable dictators,
cruelty and slavery. For us the state is the
responsible agent, not the master of man.
  —Frederick Delano to President Franklin D.
     Roosevelt

No doubt, legend will confuse coincidence with
cause and Roosevelt will be credited with
having established Government as the
dominant entity in American life.
  —Eliot Janeway

THE SECOND WORLD WAR and its aftermath had a profound impact on the American state. The war transformed the bureaucracies of the federal government; it reconfigured the pattern of government-society relations; and it altered the means of public administration with respect to social welfare programs, the regulation of labor-management relations, public finance, and material procurement by the Navy Department. Nor were these effects experienced evenly or equally across policy domains.

But are these findings, gleaned from testing each of the hypotheses of the resource dependence perspective, generalizable beyond the policy histories studied here? What is the role of hegemonic war in a broader account of American state-building? What of other explanations of American political development? In order to address these issues, this chapter looks briefly at other evidence from the 1940s to see if it is consistent with the above findings, compares the state-building of 1915–25 with that of 1940–50, and discusses alternative explanations of American state-building.

The Resource Dependence Perspective

A look at the larger history of the 1940s does, in fact, offer more general support for a resource dependence explanation of American state-building.

Command of State-Building Recall that under the constitutional authority accruing to the executive branch in times of emergency (supplemented by the two War Powers Acts), the executive branch largely directed the regulation of labor-management relations, managed the public debt, and administered Navy procurement (Hypothesis 1a). Congress, however, played critical roles in policy domains where it retained its legislative authority, such as social security and taxation (Hypothesis 1b). After the war, there was a partial reversion to congressional control of labor policy but less change with respect to public borrowing and Navy procurement; Congress did continue to set social security and tax policies (Hypothesis 1c).

In order to see if the switch in authority from the presidential command of wartime policymaking and Congress's greater direction of policymaking in non-crisis periods was part of a broader phenomenon, we may compare the number of executive orders issued for each year of the 1940s to the annual number of enrolled bills (see Table 7.1). As the figures in the third column show, the highest proportion of executive orders to enrolled bills occurred in 1941 (0.74), during rearmament, and the lowest proportion in 1949, after reconversion and before the Korean War (0.16).[1] But because Congress consistently passes more bills in its second session than in the first (given that legislation not completed at the end of each congressional session has to be reintroduced), a further comparison between the annual number of executive orders and the yearly average of enrolled bills per Congress achieves a more precise reading of the change in presidential-congressional authority. We see that the ratio of executive orders to enrolled bills rose from 0.48 in the latter half of 1939 to 0.67 in 1941, declined to 0.34 in 1944, and then climbed back to 0.43 in 1945 (see the fifth column of

[1] The fact that the year of the war's climax, 1944, has a relatively low ratio of executive orders issued to bills passed (0.28), while 1945 has a relatively high proportion (0.55), suggests that it may be not only war *qua* war but the transitions of mobilizing for war and then demobilizing from war that prompt an increased proportion of executive orders to bills passed.

A comparison of the number of executive orders issued to bills passed per two-year Congress (not shown) indicates about one executive order being issued for every two bills enrolled for the 76th Congress (a ratio of 0.47), about three executive orders for every five enrolled bills for the 77th Congress (0.61), and then about only one executive order for every five enrolled bills for the 81st Congress (0.19).

TABLE 7.1
Executive Orders and Legislation

Year	Exec. Orders	Bills	E.O.s/Bills	Bills/Cong.	E.O.s/Cong.
1939	101	174 [348/2]	0.62	(76th, 1939–40)	0.48
1940	211	490	0.43	664	0.50
1941	279	375	0.74	(77th)	0.67
1942	227	455	0.50	830	0.55
1943	115	219	0.52	(78th)	0.40
1944	97	350	0.28	569	0.34
1945	162	292	0.55	(79th)	0.43
1946	142	443	0.32	735	0.38
1947	102	395	0.26	(80th)	0.22
1948	111	521	0.21	916	0.24
1949	71	440	0.16	(81st)	0.15
1950	105	481	0.22	921	0.23

Source: Compiled from the *Federal Register.*

Notes: Excludes military orders, administrative orders, and proclamations. Identical executive orders issued to different states are counted as a single executive order. "Bills" equals public laws passed. Reorganization plans are not counted (executive orders that came into effect after a certain date unless Congress voted against the orders). "E.O.s/Bills" is the ratio of executive orders to bills passed. "Bills/Cong." is the total number of bills passed per two-year Congress. "E.O.s/Cong." is the ratio of executive orders to bills passed, controlled for the Congress (the total of the two years is divided in half).

Figures are truncated for the 76th Congress, since the first half of 1939 was discarded. Laws signed over the two-year session (1939–40) totaled 838.

Table 7.1). After 1946, President Truman issued less than one executive order for every four bills that were presented for his signature.

These data corroborate the existence of a shift in the balance of presidential and congressional command of policymaking during and after World War II. In fact, eighty-seven executive orders were based either wholly or partially on the First War Powers Act.[2]

This record and the policy histories studied above thus confirm the presence of the president's extraordinary authority in wartime. President Truman's well-known prediction that President Eisenhower would say "'Do this! Do that!' *And nothing will happen.* Poor Ike—It won't be a bit like the Army" may be more a statement about the experience of a postwar presi-

---

[2] "Executive Orders Based in Whole or in Part upon Title I of the First War Powers Act, 1941," file "OF 161," Official File, Truman Papers. Much of the wartime and postwar legislation codified policies already in place because of executive orders. Table 7.1 suggests that for all of the new programs and anticommunist rhetoric of the late 1940s, the early Cold War was not much of a war in the sense of the president's exercise of exceptional authority.

dent, then, than a comment about the presidency as such.[3] Roosevelt's power in office *was* in large part the power of command—as opposed to persuasion—just as were Lincoln's, Wilson's, and even Truman's for a few short months.

Forms of Institutional Change Behind the seeming power of the president and the executive branch in a time of war was, however, the U.S. government's greater dependence on societal actors. The executive and legislative branches were forced to work with societal actors in order to secure needed resources. The Roosevelt Administration created tripartite labor boards consisting of representatives from management, organized labor, and the public at large; it formed a multitude of local, regional, and state organizations composed of both government and financial industry personnel for the purpose of selling government securities; and it set up a number of agencies that could coordinate military procurement with industrial producers (Hypothesis 2a). In policy domains with diffuse clienteles, the President and Congress expanded the Bureau of Internal Revenue and the Bureau of Public Debt, and agreed to smaller increases in the BOASI and the SSB/SSA (Hypothesis 2b).

In order to determine whether the lessons of the form of state-building held more generally, we may look at the form of state-building in other policy arenas: the petroleum industry and agriculture. In the case of oil, the Roosevelt Administration created the Petroleum Administration for War (PAW), which was charged with coordinating government and industry action for the purpose of maximizing production. The PAW was headed by Interior Secretary Ickes and staffed with "knowledgeable industry personnel." The administration also instituted "controls over prices and production, the allocation of supply, and the direction of refining, transportation, and distribution" in order to lessen the chance of oil shortages.[4]

With the establishment of the PAW as a bridge between the government and the oil companies, and with new economic controls in place, American oil production rose from 3.7 million barrels per day in 1940 to 4.7 million barrels per day in 1945—a 30 percent increase over the course of the war. Indeed, "between December 1941 and August 1945, the United States and its allies consumed almost 7 billion barrels of oil, of which 6 billion came from the United States."[5] This surge in productivity following from the new relationship forged between the government and the oil industry is analo-

---

[3] Neustadt, *Presidential Power*, 9; emphasis in original.

[4] G. John Ikenberry, *Reasons of State: Oil Politics and the Capacities of American Government* (Ithaca: Cornell University Press, 1988), 70. Note, however, that the WPB, the OPA, and the War Shipping Administration also had jurisdiction over allocation, pricing, and tanker shipments, respectively. Nor was the military very cooperative with Ickes and the PAW (Daniel Yergin, *The Prize* [New York: Simon & Schuster, 1991], 377–78).

[5] Yergin, *The Prize*, 379.

gous, then, to the successful collaboration of the labor unions with the government, and to the cooperation of company managers with the War Finance Division.

Departing from expectations, however, is the fact that the Roosevelt Administration tried to set up its *own* Petroleum Reserves Corporation for the purpose of acquiring and developing foreign reserves (especially those of Saudi Arabia). Despite the backing of the Joint Chiefs of Staff and the Army-Navy Petroleum Board, and despite Ickes's close relationship with the President, the plan was opposed by oil industry executives, members of the State Department, and members of Congress. It did not go through.[6]

The expansion of agricultural production was similarly indispensable to winning the war. The White House therefore established both the Food Production Administration and the Food Distribution Administration in December 1942 as part of the Department of Agriculture. (The WPB had previously controlled supplies for farm production and food processing.) The two agencies were combined into the War Food Administration (WFA) in the spring of 1943. The WFA, under Chester Davis, was to coordinate the entire food program, including the extensive purchasing for the Lend-Lease program.

Although the WFA ran into interference from the OPA over prices, from the Office of Defense Transportation over inland shipping, and from the Selective Service, the War Manpower Commission, and the NWLB over manpower and wages, the WFA was still a success—in large part because its "elaborate public management apparatus" built upon the preexisting administrative structures of the New Deal. The U.S. government already had much of the capacity to plan and direct "output and price planning of major products, soil conservation, subsidization, crop storage, marketing, and technological improvement."[7] Crop production rose from 66 in 1940 to 71 in 1943 and then 73 in 1945 (1967 = 100); livestock production rose from 60 in 1940 to 77 in 1943 and fell to 73 in 1945.[8]

An evaluation of the oil and agricultural policy domains points to uneven conformity with our expectations on the form of state-building: on the one hand, the Roosevelt Administration established new interorganizational agencies in both cases so as to handle the exigencies of war production, and the production of oil and agricultural products rose accordingly; on the

[6] Ikenberry, *Reasons of State*, 70–73. The fear was that Germany or Britain would dominate Persian Gulf supplies. It was proposed that the PRC acquire reserves directly by buying shares in the California Arabian Standard Oil Company.

[7] Vatter, *The U.S. Economy in World War II*, 48–50. The PAW also clashed with the OPA on prices.

[8] Vatter, *The U.S. Economy in World War II*, 52. The index of crop production came to 76 in 1942 and to 75 in 1944. But crop productivity per unit of land increased further still, with land being switched from farmland to pasture.

other hand, the administration tried (unsuccessfully) to establish its own oil production capacity in the early 1940s (rather than relying on or coordinating with societal actors on a program of expansion in the Middle East), and the control of farm prices and crop production, the agricultural extension services of the land grant universities, and research facilities such as the Bureau of Agricultural Economics had already been established through New Deal farm policies.

In short, the resource dependence perspective does not consistently predict the precise form of state-building during the war as noted in the above two cases, and with respect to the modest expansion of the BOASI and the shrinking of the SSB, the presence of mass-based, voluntary organizations for selling war bonds to individual citizens, and the fact that the agencies created to administer military procurement were in-house agencies of the Navy Department rather than agencies that spanned government organizations and industrial corporations. But the resource dependence perspective does predict that the government would set up tripartite, interorganizational labor boards, that the government's taxation of personal and corporate incomes would increase greatly, that it would rely on the resources of financial institutions and on material production by the most established industrial firms, and that it would create relatively small organizations to coordinate and supervise military-industrial relations, oil production, and agriculture.

Ratchet Effects With the shock of hegemonic war came lasting change in the state. But once the crisis ended, the organizations of government, government-society relations, and administrative changes did not revert to their previous conditions or reestablish their pre-crisis trajectories. Instead, the institutions of government adapted to the massive changes in their extranational and intranational environments—adaptations that entrenched much of the institutional change thought to be temporary (Hypothesis 3a). Consistent with this ratcheting were shifts in political agendas, with some policies becoming newly possible and others being removed from political consideration (Hypothesis 3b).

The direct effects of World War II on the social security system were limited. There was little expansion of the social security bureaucracy, no transition from a warfare state to a welfare state during the 1940s (as happened in Great Britain), and no introduction of a national health care program. The war had more obvious and more lasting effects on the regulation of labor-management relations: new labor boards were set up in 1940 and 1941, the USCS and the NLRB expanded in size, and the labor boards were hearing many more labor-dispute cases as the war went on. Meanwhile, labor leaders were appointed to government positions and met with President Roosevelt both publicly and privately; the Roosevelt Administration coopted those best positioned to upset its designs. Labor unions went from being risk-takers in the 1930s and early 1940s to becoming risk-averse actors in the mid- and late 1940s, anxious to protect the status quo.[9] The war caused the federal income tax to become the dominant source of federal revenue, as virtually all working Americans started to pay federal income taxes. And with the increase in public debt during the war, the assets of financial institutions and individuals became increasingly invested in the U.S. government. The finance bureaucracies expanded accordingly. Finally, the administration of Navy procurement was no less altered, with the thorough reorganization of the agencies and procedures that handled material procurement. The size of the postwar budgets and administration of the Navy would be on a scale unmatched in American history; the Second World War ushered out one era in U.S. national security and marked the start of another.[10]

Yet a number of wartime innovations did not last beyond 1945. The National War Labor Board and the Office of War Mobilization and Reconversion were dissolved once the war ended; the U.S. Employment Service

[9] Cooptation is the focus of Philip Selznick's study of the decentralization and delegation of government authority under the "grass roots" ideology of the Tennessee Valley Authority. *TVA and the Grass Roots: A Study of Politics and Organization* (Berkeley: University of California Press, 1949). *Formal cooptation* occurs when an organization needs to publicly absorb new elements, "signifying participation in the process of decision and administration." Formal cooptation is designed for legitimation and accessibility and is not intended as an actual transfer of power on the part of the coopting organization. *Informal cooptation* results from the necessity of an organization to come to terms with "the pressure of specific individuals or interest groups which are in a position to enforce demands." Informal cooptation is the adjustment of an organization to environmental constraints; the organization coopts the specific nucleuses of societal power that may threaten its operational survival. Cooptation "reflects a tension between formal authority and social power," and it not only results in a broadening of authority but has subsequent effect on the "character and role" of the coopting organization. The coopting organization now has new constraints on its policy choices (Selznick, 13–16, 260–61; italics in original). The U.S. government's two-sided cooptation (both formal and informal) resulted in localized interests being able to alter the administration of the TVA's programs and to defeat the New Deal goals as originally embodied in the TVA.

Selznick's organizational view of the federal government and its agencies coincides with the resource dependence perspective insofar as both approaches focus on the interorganizational field in which the government and its agencies administer policy. Indeed, the labor case reveals such cooptation: in terms of formal cooptation, President Roosevelt included labor leaders in the NDMB and NWLB, as well as in the SPAB and the WPB; in terms of informal cooptation, the White House made concessions to the AFL, the CIO, and other unions in the December 1941 Washington conference and in private meetings. But there is less evidence of a subsequent alteration of government organization as a result of the cooptation, to distinguish between the cooptation of the Roosevelt and Truman Administrations and that of the Democratic party.

I am grateful to Erwin Hargrove for suggesting a comparison with Selznick's work.

[10] See Peck and Scherer, *The Weapons Acquisition Process*, 112–13; Mrozek, "The Truman Administration and the Enlistment of the Aviation Industry in Postwar Defense," 89–93; and Samuel P. Huntington, *The Soldier and the State* (New York: Vintage Books, 1964).

devolved to the several states; the PAW and the WFA were disestablished; and food and fuel rationing, wage and price controls, and the military draft were all discontinued shortly after V-J Day.

Even so, the findings from the policy histories studied above were characteristic of more general changes in American government, politics, and society. Total U.S. government expenditures increased from 18.7 percent of GNP in 1940 to 23.0 percent of GNP in 1950, while civilian employment in the federal government (excluding emergency workers) rose from 7.6 percent to 9.7 percent of the civilian labor force over the same period.[11] Coincident with the growth in government was the growing affluence of Americans: national income rose from $99.7 billion in 1940 to $284.8 billion in 1950, and average per capita income increased from $754 in 1940 to $1,877 in 1950. Real national income also rose by more than 50 percent over the decade, from $227.2 billion to $355.3 billion, as economic productivity soared.[12]

The physical output of durable and non-durable manufactures and mining likewise rose from an index of 125 in 1940 to 200 in 1950 (to follow the Federal Reserve Board's Index of Industrial Production).[13] And the civilian workforce increased correspondingly, from 47.5 million persons in 1940 to 58.9 million persons in 1950—an increase of 11.4 million persons.[14] The war clearly transformed both the government and the economy of the United States.

The war had a further effect on political participation. The extraordinary changes of the 1940s in income and employment combined with the large demographic changes of workers leaving rural areas and the South to result in a drop in voter turnout.[15] Turnout in presidential elections fell from 49 million in 1940 (or 62.5 percent of eligible voters) to 48 million in 1944 (or 55.9 percent of eligible voters), and turnout in off-year elections fell from 36 million voters in 1938 to 28 million in 1942, and then increased slightly to 34 million voters in 1946. The low turnouts of the early 1940s had obvious

[11] Figures from "Indexes of the Size of the Government, 1900–1984," Table 2.1 in Higgs, *Crisis and Leviathan*, 22–23.

[12] Income statistics from "Gross National Product, Total and Per Capita, in Current and 1958 Prices: 1869 to 1970," Series F 1–5, *Historical Statistics*, 224. Federal expenditures came to 36 percent of GNP in 1980.

[13] Wartime production peaked at 239 in 1943 and declined to a postwar low of 170 in 1946. The figures for 1940, 1944, and 1946 are from *Labor Fact Book* 8 (New York: International Publishers, 1949), 9; 1950 figure from *Labor Fact Book* 10 (New York: International Publishers, 1951), 9.

[14] "Labor Force and Its Components: 1900 to 1947," Series D 1–10, and "Labor Force Status of the Population: 1870 to 1970," Series D 11–25, *Historical Statistics*, 126, 127. Civilian federal employment came to 15.2 percent of the labor force in 1980.

[15] Between 1940 and 1945 1.6 million persons left rural areas for the cities (Vatter, *The U.S. Economy in World War II*, 115).

and lasting repercussions on congressional representation and national policymaking.[16]

In short, the change in political participation, the surge in the economy, and the growth in government all point to the war's enduring impact on American political development. These changes were accompanied by shifts in political agendas. The political agenda of the late 1930s and early 1940s for expanding social security coverage and increasing contribution levels and retirement benefits was shunted aside for an agenda of limited adjustments to the social security system, generous provisions for war veterans and their survivors, private health and retirement programs, and national health insurance (albeit unsuccessfully).

The agenda in labor-management relations was also redirected. The war forced the delay of congressional counterattacks against organized labor and the alleged excesses of the Wagner Act, deradicalized the major labor unions, and resulted in the acceptance of collective bargaining for labor unions by government and business both.

The war made the personal income tax and income tax withholding acceptable (thanks to the unprecedented wealth of the 1940s), introduced the management of the public debt and interest rates as permanent issues of day-to-day politics, and caused fiscal policy to become a key instrument for the regulation of the national economy.

Finally, the Second World War revealed the failures of isolationism and the costs of uncoordinated administration of the military services and intelligence. The U.S. government had to have an assertive foreign policy and needed new organizations to support its altered position in the world. Economic and military assistance became staples of American foreign policy, and it became expected that the military establishment would lead research and development in a number of industries—nuclear power, jet aircraft, and, later, computer chips and digital sound, among other scientific and technological innovations, followed from defense work.

In order to determine if these changes were characteristic of more general shifts in the agenda of American politics, we may compare the Democratic party platforms of 1940 and 1948 as indicators of national political agendas (given that the Democratic party held the presidency from 1932 through 1952). The comparison both confirms the presence of widespread agenda shifts in the policy domains studied above and shows analogous shifts in other political agendas.[17]

---

[16] See Blum, V Was for Victory, 230–34. Blum also notes the effects of the war on voter turnout and on the domestic political climate.

[17] The fact that the politics of 1948 were unusual—there was a very weak incumbent (Truman) and a significant third-party campaign (the Dixiecrats), as well as the presence of a fourth party (the Progressives)—nonetheless allows for a comparison of party platforms. Democratic voters under President Truman still represented a broad swathe of American voters (farmers,

The 1940 platform treated social security briefly, and there was no mention of national health insurance,[18] whereas the 1948 platform called for "1. Increases in old-age and survivors' insurance benefits by at least 50 per cent, and reduction of the eligibility age for women from 65 to 60 years; 2. Extension of old-age and survivors' and unemployment insurance to all employees; 3. Insurance against loss of earnings on account of illness or disability; [and] 4. Improved public assistance for the needy." It also demanded "the enactment of a national health program, with adequate medical care for all prepaid by insurance," and "the establishment of a separate executive department to administer all federal functions relating to education, health, and security."[19]

In regard to "Labor Relations," the 1940 platform called for strengthened collective bargaining and continued efforts "to achieve equality of opportunity for men and women, without impairing social legislation which safeguards health, safety, and economic welfare of women workers."[20] But the 1948 program recommended the "repeal of the Taft-Hartley Act" and "the enactment of minimal legislation confined to prohibiting certain unexcusable secondary boycotts and to protecting the urgent demands of public health, safety or welfare against a tiny minority of irresponsible labor leaders who have demonstrated their disregard of such demands." It further called for "the extension of the coverage of the Fair Labor Standards Act and the substitution of the present obsolete and inadequate minimum of 40 cents an hour by a minimum of 85 cents an hour" and "restoring [to the Department of Labor] the functions, including mediation and conciliation, which properly belong to it and which the Republican 80th Congress recklessly took away."[21]

With respect to "Money, Jobs and Idle Money"—i.e., public finance and

---

union members, and blacks, among others), and the fact that Truman was threatened from both the left (the Progressives) and the right (the Dixiecrats) would appear to have a neutralizing effect. While the politics of 1948 were clearly not those of 1950—the Soviet Union had not exploded the bomb, NATO had not been established, and the national economy was still inflating in 1948—it seems hard to argue that the loss of two years in a comparison of political agendas (using 1948 instead of 1950) exaggerates the shifts in the political agendas over the course of the decade.

[18] It advocated that OASI benefits be extended and increased, that the permanently disabled be protected, and that unemployment compensation be strengthened ("Party Platforms, 1940," p. 2, file "Campaign Strategy—1940 Platform," Box 60, Personal Secretary File, Truman Papers).

[19] "Democratic Platform, 1948," pp. 11–12, Box 9, Papers of Samuel I. Rosenman, Truman Library.

[20] "Party Platforms, 1940," 2–3.

[21] It further urged "that the U.S. Employment Service be returned to the Department of Labor," that its facilities be expanded, and that an extension service for encouraging and aiding the education of workers be created ("Democratic Platform, 1948," 10–11).

the political economy—the 1940 platform noted that the incumbent administration had "provided important new outlets for private capital by stimulating home building and low-rent housing projects" and called for the removal
of tax-exempt privileges on future federal, state, and local bonds in order to
"encourage investment in productive enterprise."[22] The 1948 platform focused on inflation and economic controls instead:

> We obligate ourselves to act to curb inflation . . . and we whole-heartedly reaffirm
> President Truman's recommendation to the Congress that it: 1. Restore consumer
> credit controls and restraints to the creation of inflationary bank credit; 2. Autho
> rize the regulation of speculative trading on the commodity exchanges; 3. Autho
> rize machinery to induce the marketing of livestock and poultry at weights and
> grades which represent the most efficient use of grain; [and] 4. Authorize alloca
> tion and inventory control of scarce commodities which basically affect the cost of
> living or of industrial production.[23]

With respect to government-business relations in general, the 1940 platform boasted of the administration's attacks on "banking which exploits
America," "gambling in securities," "utility holding companies, which use
consumers' and investors' money to bludgeon legislatures, and control elections," and other "monopolies." A reelected Roosevelt Administration promised to "continue to oppose barriers which impede interstate commerce," to
"strengthen home markets, and to this end favor adjustment of freight
rates," and to "encourage investment in local productive enterprise."[24] The
1948 Democratic platform noted merely that the Truman Administration
opposed "monopolistic concentration of economic power" and that it deplored "the action of the Republican 80th Congress in exempting from the
antitrust laws the fixing of rates by railroads."[25]

As for "National Defense," the 1940 Democratic platform said that the
United States would not participate in foreign wars, that U.S. armed forces
would not be sent to fight in foreign lands except if America were attacked,

[22] "Party Platforms, 1940," 6–7.

[23] "Democratic Platform, 1948," 3–4. The 1948 platform also obligated the party to "5.
Extend and strengthen rent control, eliminating those provisions enacted by the Republican
80th Congress which have deprived many tenants of important protection and permitted profiteering exploitation; [and] 6. Authorize consumer rationing of products in short supply which
basically affect the cost of living."

[24] The platform boasted that the Democrats "[h]ave restored banking and financial system;
have insured bank accounts and protected small investors in security and commodity markets.
Have made low interest loans to the small business man, unfastening the yoke of money monopoly." The Democrats would "continue to attack exploitation of investor and consumer," in
view of how they had "enforced antitrust laws more vigorously than at any other time" ("Party
Platforms, 1940," 9–10).

[25] It also pledged to vigorously enforce laws "to prevent cartels, monopolies and restraints of
trade" ("Democratic Platform, 1948," 17).

that it would "rigorously enforce and defend" the Monroe Doctrine, and that it would "strengthen democracy by increasing economic efficiency."[26] By 1948, the isolationist tenor of 1940 had disappeared:

> To assure a world of peace and justice we pledge:
> To continue to reject isolationism and to continue to lead the way to a full partnership in world affairs.
> To give full and unstinting support for the United Nations, and to bring to maximum effectiveness the participation and leadership of the United States in the perfection of this great instrument of peace.
> To lead the way, in order that the United Nations may realize fully its potentialities as a means through which world order and justice may be achieved, toward curtailment of the use of the veto in the Security Council.
> To continue support of the use of regional arrangements within the framework of the World Charter. To continue to support the principle of international control of atomic energy under safeguards to assure all nations against the misuse of this terrible weapon which may otherwise destroy civilization.[27]

The new positions taken by the Democratic party on social policy, labor policy, inflation and business monopoly, and national security were consistent with the case histories studied above. But other platform planks also showed changes consistent with a large shift in the political agenda. With respect to civil rights, for instance, the 1940 platform said that the administration would "strive for complete legislative safeguards against discrimination in Government service and in defense forces." It noted that the "Negro has participated actively in economic and social advances launched by administration."[28] The program of 1948 was much more forceful:

> We assert our conviction that no nation can survive which condemns any of its peoples to second class citizenship or which tolerates distinctions on the basis of race, religion, color or national origin. We favor legislation by which the Federal Government will exercise its full constitutional power to assure that due process, the right to vote, the right to live and the right to work shall not turn on any considerations of race, religion, color or national origin.
> We favor immediate abolition of segregation in the armed forces to the full extent that the imperative demands of national defense permit, and a long term program of education to permit ultimate abolition of any vestige of such segregation.[29]

As for the fight against communism, the Democratic party of 1940 would "do all in power to destroy treasonable activities of disguised anti-

[26] "Party Platforms, 1940," 1.
[27] "Democratic Platform, 1948," 3–6. "United Nations" was the name originally adopted by the Allied powers in the Second World War, of course.
[28] "Party Platforms, 1940," 7–8.
[29] "Democratic Platform, 1948," 12.

democratic and un-American groups which sap from within and would destroy unity by inciting groups," whereas that of 1948 would "fight communism at home by attacking the breeding grounds of communism—injustice, poverty, hunger and social evils" and also "continue vigorously to enforce all laws against subversive activities."[30]

Further indicative of the changing agenda of national politics was the different order in which the planks appeared: "Social Security" fell from page 2 of the 1940 platform to page 11 of the 1948 document; "Government and Business, Monopoly" dropped from page 9 in 1940 to page 17 in 1948; and "Agriculture" went from page 3 in 1940 to page 15 in 1948. Conversely, "Money, Jobs and Idle Money" moved up from page 6 in 1940 to page 3 in 1948 (rephrased as "Taxation, Public Credit, and Public Spending").[31] The evidence from the 1940 and 1948 Democratic party platforms is, then, fully congruent with the earlier evidence on the presence of massive shifts in political agendas before and after critical periods.

Relative Terms of Exchange A fourth issue addressed above was the relative fate of clienteles under the new conditions of exchange in periods of war and then peace. We saw that investors, especially large investors, fared significantly better than the labor unions or military contractors; that shipbuilders and aircraft manufacturers averaged only 2–3 percent in after-tax profits during the peak war years despite the uncertainty of the Navy's material supplies; that social security stakeholders actually did worse in their terms of exchange with the government than did organized clienteles; and that income taxpayers did still worse (Hypothesis 4a). After the war, while it was expected that the size of clienteles would be the major determinant of terms of exchange, investors in U.S. securities (the largest clientele) did not do as well as taxpayers (the second largest clientele), although the smallest clientele, Navy producers, did in fact fare the worst. Meanwhile, the position of organized labor was damaged by the Taft-Hartley Act and the postwar inflation, and workers in non-unionized industries, especially in the South, would find it harder to organize (Hypothesis 4b).

Do the expectations of the relative terms of exchange according to the resource dependence perspective hold more generally? The records of the oil industry and the agricultural sector confirm the arguments offered here. We may expect the oil companies to enjoy favorable terms of exchange on

[30] "Party Platforms, 1940," 7–8. The Democrats of 1948 would, however, remain "free of hysteria" and "at all times observe the great guarantees of our constitutional freedoms" so that "all persons, no matter how distasteful their ideas, shall be free to engage in peaceful domestic political activities" ("Democratic Platform, 1948," 14).

[31] The 1948 platform did not begin to list the individual planks until page 3. Omitted from this comparison are the planks on agriculture, the real estate lobby, reemployment, tariff and reciprocal trade, immigration, American Indians, and U.S. territories. The 1948 platform also had planks on atomic energy, the European Recovery Program, China, and Israel—planks that had no precedent in the 1940 platform.

an order unmatched by investors in the public debt or military contractors: not only was there uncertainty about the supply of oil (given the vicissitudes of oil exploration, recovery, and transatlantic shipping), but the government had no option but to use kerosene, gasoline, and diesel fuel for its planes, motor vehicles, and ships. And a case could be made that the oil companies had their own alternatives, at least in theory: they could stockpile oil, sell to civilians, or change the proportion of domestic and overseas sales, even if they had fewer options in practice.

The profit records of major oil companies (Standard Oil of California [later Chevron], Socony-Vacuum [Mobil], Shell, Gulf, Texaco, and Standard Oil [Exxon]) indicate their favorable terms of exchange. The six internationals' net profits *after* taxes averaged 9.8 percent of gross income in 1940, 11 percent in 1941, 8 percent in 1942, 7.8 percent in 1943, 9 percent in 1944, and 9.2 percent in 1945—more than double the average net annual profits of manufacturing firms in general (see Table 5.8, above).[32]

The evidence from agriculture is further consistent with expectations. We may expect farmers to enjoy beneficial terms of exchange, since there was uncertainty on the part of the government: farmers could leave home to work in factories, and the war put a premium on the equipment and hired workers needed for crop and livestock production.[33] The government had no alternatives as to their sourcing of agricultural products. Nor, however, did farmers have real alternatives but to sell to the government, given the numbers of Americans now working for the federal government and the depressed conditions of the 1930s.

Not surprisingly, farm prices soared after 1940. The price index of farm production ("prices received") went from an index of 30 in 1940 (1967=100) to an index of 49 in 1941, 63 in 1942, 76 in 1943, 78 in 1944, and 81 in 1945. Correspondingly, the personal income of the farm population—from farm sources only—rose from $4.8 billion in 1940 ($158 per capita) to $12.8 billion in 1945 ($524 per capita); the share of a "typical market basket of farm food products" received by the farmers "jumped from 40 percent in 1940 to 53 percent in 1945"; the "proportion of farm personal income from nonfarm sources to income from farm sources declined notably during the war . . . contrary to the long-run pattern"; and "the number of

[32] Figures compiled from *Moody's Manual of Investments*. Profits at the oil majors ranged from 6 to 15 percent in 1940, from 6 to 15 percent in 1941, from 5 to 13 percent in 1942, from 6 to 12 percent in 1943, from 6 to 13 percent in 1944, and from 5 to 16 percent in 1945. Standard Oil of California averaged the highest returns; Shell Oil, the lowest. (Royal Dutch Shell is, of course, principally a British and Dutch company, not American.) Gross operating incomes for the six majors almost doubled in the course of the war, from 1940 to 1945. This of course omits the study of the smaller U.S. oil companies. Brian Falbo helped compile these data.

[33] Indeed, the WPB and the War Manpower Commission were set up precisely to deal with the allocation of scarce human and material resources.

mortgaged farms fell 27 percent [while] the total value of farm real estate jumped 79 percent."[34]

The evidence from the oil industry and agriculture is thus consistent with the contention that more than supply and demand was at work: the demand for virtually all raw materials and finished products used in the war effort greatly exceeded the available supply, given the government's requirements and competing civilian demands. Yet some societal actors (e.g., major oil companies, investors in government securities) happened to benefit much more from their wartime relations with the government than did other clienteles (e.g., social security stakeholders, taxpayers).

After the war, the resource dependence expectations hold less well. Oil companies enjoyed very favorable returns (with average net profits of 10.8 percent in 1946, 12.5 percent in 1947, 14.2 percent in 1948, 11.2 percent in 1949, and 12 percent in 1950 for the same companies discussed above), despite the small numbers of voters represented. But farm incomes rose only modestly, from $12.8 million in 1945 ($705 per capita) to $14.1 million in 1950 ($884 per capita), despite the presence (and voting strength) of 24.4 million farmers in 1945 and 23.0 million farmers in 1950 (operators and hired workers).[35]

The record on the relative terms of exchange thus leaves gaps. The evidence from the labor and Navy procurement cases suggests that the assumption that the mutual possession of alternatives is equivalent to the mutual absence of alternatives may need to be rethought, as noted in Chapter 6. It may well be that the government and the public alike sought to limit the ability of monopoly suppliers (i.e., organized labor and military contractors) to exploit their positions vis-à-vis the government and were successful in doing so. Another factor explaining the relative terms of exchange that the resource dependence perspective does not take into account is the relative distribution of resources among clienteles in a non-war period: tax liabilities were distributed far more evenly among the populace than were the holdings of U.S. securities (since a few investors held large amounts of government debt while the vast majority of bondholders had little at stake). The average taxpayer thus paid much more in (coerced) taxes than he or she had (voluntarily) invested in U.S. government securities. The asymmetry between the amount of taxes owed by individuals and the amount of government securities owned by investors—irrespective of the numbers of taxpayers and bondholders involved—may account for the unexpected re-

[34] "Farm Income and Expenses: 1910 to 1970," Series K 256–285, *Historical Statistics*, 483; Vatter, *The U.S. Economy in World War II*, 54–55. Vatter calls this a new "golden age" for farmers.

[35] "Farm Income and Expenses: 1910 to 1970," *Historical Statistics*. But farmers earned much more in the first few years after the war, thanks to the food and meat shortages. Personal farm income rose to $15.5 billion in 1946, to $15.8 billion in 1947, and to $18.0 billion in 1948.

versal in the terms of exchange that taxpayers and investors had with the U.S. government in the immediate postwar years.

In sum, the resource dependence perspective's attention to organizational environment allows for the tailoring of hypotheses to U.S. policy domains of the 1940s, where the impact of hegemonic war affected both the extranational and intranational environments. Testable propositions could be generated on the command of state-building, the form of institutional change, the reasons for the persistence of the state-building resulting from crisis, and the relative fates of societal actors vis-à-vis the government in a crisis and post-crisis period. While not all the hypotheses derived from the resource dependence perspective are confirmed, enough of them are upheld by the record to merit, it seems, further application of the resource dependence perspective to national government and its component organizations.

Even on the occasions where the hypotheses are not borne out, however, the falsifiability of the resource dependence perspective may offer insights into American political development. Consider four such examples: the behavior of President Truman during the late 1940s; the low profits earned by Navy contractors; the non-expansion of the social security system; and the absence of new forms of revenue collection.

President Harry Truman appears as an ideologue in comparison to the political flexibility of President Franklin Roosevelt. Consider that Roosevelt went against his earlier resistance to bonus payments for World War I veterans and his support for a comprehensive social security system, to push for a large expansion in veterans' benefits. Nor would Roosevelt establish a "procurement czar," despite the need for centralized leadership in the coordination of government procurement during the rearmament and mobilization periods. Nor would Roosevelt support labor consistently; instead, he rode the labor bandwagon from the mid-1930s through the early 1940s, and then jumped off.[36] Roosevelt acted in a risk-averse manner, adapting to the times.

But if Roosevelt's political expediency is exactly as we might expect, Truman's behavior seems odd. Despite the end of the wartime emergency and the renewed power accruing to Congress, Truman pushed for the politically unpopular expansion of the social security system and for a national health care program. This advocacy came at the expense of Truman's own political standing as well as that of the Democratic party.[37] Sam Rosenman, counsel

[36] President Roosevelt left out the Wagner Act when reciting his New Deal accomplishments in his 1944 State of the Union address. Richard Hofstadter, for one, has remarked upon Roosevelt's political flexibility (*The American Political Tradition and the Men Who Made It* [New York: Vintage Books, 1974 [1948], 410–59]).

[37] See Neustadt, "Congress and the Fair Deal," and Poen, *Truman Versus the Medical Lobby*.

and speechwriter for both presidents, observed that Truman "paid much less attention to what his actions were doing towards his chances for reelection. . . . Truman did a great many things that Roosevelt, because he knew the effect it would have, never would have done."[38]

A second anomaly was the low profits being earned by military contractors during the war, despite the Navy's almost complete dependence on large industrial producers and its uncertainty over the timeliness, quality, and cost of its purchases. Navy contractors fared poorly relative to manufacturers in general and to the major oil companies in particular, because of the high excess profits taxes, the laws on the negotiation and renegotiation of contracts, the legacy of war profiteering from World War I, and the professionalism of Navy administrators. Money did not rule, and corruption did not run rampant—a procurement record that contrasts with that of more recent decades. High levels of defense spending were exceptional in the early 1940s; they became unexceptional after 1950.

A third departure from expectations was the separation of efforts to expand the social security system from attempts to raise additional revenue, despite the logic of such action; a fourth anomaly was the absence of innovative tax legislation during the early 1940s, despite the government's desperate need for funds. Both events—or, rather, non-events of no change in OASI rates and no new kinds of taxes—suggest the fiscal conservativeness and anti-state sentiments of Congress and the American electorate. Yet the record of the social security and tax policies cases contrasts markedly with the *pro*-stateness of the increased government intervention in labor-management relations, the expansion of veterans' programs, and the scope of international aid after the Second World War.

The implication of these differences is that Congress and the electorate were not so much anti-state as they were anti-redistributive: veterans' benefits and social insurance have both been framed as entitlements of individual desert, whereas federal taxation and social provisions have been typically framed as collectivist programs and features of "big government." The further regulation of labor-management relations has been similarly viewed as providing for domestic stability and "law and order," and not as a program of

[38] Oral History of Sam Rosenman, in McCullough, *Truman*, 476. Another example of Roosevelt's plasticity was the loud silence of the White House during the Dies Committee hearings in 1943 (Blum, *V Was for Victory*, 234–54; Stone, *The War Years*, 147–49). Compare also the civil rights records of the two: Truman desegregated the military and insisted that a civil rights plank be included in the 1948 Democratic Party Platform, whereas Roosevelt backed off from policies that would threaten his support from southern Democrats. David McCullough writes that when Strom Thurmond was asked why he was breaking off from the Democratic party in 1948, given that Roosevelt had earlier made exactly the same promise to promote civil rights, Thurmond replied, "But Truman really means it" (McCullough, *Truman*, 645). See Ferrell, *Harry S. Truman*, 292–99.

bigger, more interventionist government—just as the large defense sector has been seen as indispensable to U.S. national security and separate from concerns over collectivism or big government. Anti-statism in the United States has hardly been constant or uniform across policy domains.

But the reluctant and delayed expansion of the social security system also touches on the matter of race: agricultural workers, domestic servants, and government employees, who were among those prominently excluded from the 1935 and 1939 legislation on social security and included only in part in the 1950 reforms, were disproportionately African American. The extension of social security coverage or the introduction of a health insurance program would have shifted tax dollars from whites to blacks. Consistent with race-based policymaking, the Southern-dominated Democratic Congress blocked the expansion of the social security system. And the social security system remains scarcely redistributive.[39]

World War II and World War I

If it is fair to say that the war had comprehensive effects on the domestic programs of the 1940s, what, then, are the effects of major wars more generally on state-building? In order to ascertain the effects of hegemonic war on American state-building, we may compare the effects of the First World War with those of the Second World War in the policy domains studied above: the initiatives for public health care (there being no social security system in the 1910s, of course), the federal regulation of labor-management relations (in terms of the USCS only, since the Wagner Act was not passed until 1935), public finance (both income taxation and public borrowing), and military procurement. World War I, like World War II, should exert a profound impact on these public policies thought to be typical of American exceptionalism.[40]

Given the different scales of World Wars II and I and the different do-

[39] Several of the essays in Weir, Orloff, and Skocpol, eds., *The Politics of Social Policy in the United States* also suggest this point.

[40] There are a number of studies of the effects of war on government institutions. See Karen A. Rasler and William R. Thompson, "War Making and State Making: Government Expenditures, Tax Revenues, and Global Wars," *American Political Science Review* 79 No. 2 (March 1985): 491–507; Rasler and Thompson, "Global War, Public Debts, and the Long Cycle," *World Politics* 35 (1983): 489–516; Alan T. Peacock and Jack Wiseman, *The Growth of Public Expenditures* (Princeton: Princeton University Press, 1961); and Peacock and Wiseman, "Approaches to the Analysis of Government Expenditure Growth," *Public Finance Quarterly* 7 No. 1 (January 1979), 3–23. On European state-building, see Charles Tilly, "Reflections on the History of European State-making," in Tilly, ed., *The Formation of National States in Western Europe*; Hintze, *Historical Essays*; and Samuel E. Finer, "State- and Nation-Building in Europe" in Tilly, ed., *The Formation of National States in Western Europe*.

mestic situations, however, we should expect less institutional change occurring as a result of the earlier war and less ratcheting of the wartime state-building.[41] Consider that World War II was about nine times as expensive as WWI (and a dollar could buy more in the 1940s than it could during the 1920s), and that U.S. government spending came to one-quarter of GNP at the height of World War I, but to almost one-half the level of national income in 1944.[42] Real per capita income rose from $1,267 in 1914 and $1,315 by 1920 (1958 dollars), but it rose from $1,720 in 1940 to $2,538 by 1945—over eight times the earlier increase. Whereas U.S. GNP rose at an annual average of 0.9 percent between 1914 and 1920, it rose at an annual average of 9.4 percent between 1940 and 1945—ten times the earlier rate. Finally, the United States was engaged in the First World War for only 18 months, in contrast to the 44 months of World War II. Yet as a hegemonic war being waged by a democratic government, World War I should affect American state-building in ways equivalent to those of the later war, the differences in size and duration notwithstanding.

Public Health Care While proposals for public health care failed in both periods, the histories of the two non-outcomes differed considerably: the effect of the First World War was to quash efforts at promulgating public health care; in contrast, the later war had the effect of reviving health care initiatives and at once laying the foundation for sustained political opposition to government health care programs.

Sixteen states introduced legislation for health insurance from 1915 to 1918, as the American Association for Labor Legislation (AALL) moved from its success in workmen's compensation laws to a new realm.[43] Led by Isaac Rubinow, John Commons, Henry Seager, and others, AALL progressives and former president Theodore R. Roosevelt pushed for state legislation that included medical aid, sick pay at two-thirds wages, and maternity benefits for insured women and the wives of insured men. Reformers believed that the provision of public health care would break the vicious cycle of poverty and would stabilize income levels through risk-pooling public insurance.

In 1916, the American Medical Association joined with the AALL to set

---

[41] This section concentrates on the first two dimensions of the state: the bureaucracies and the institutionalized relations between the government and societal actors.

[42] Whereas the Bureau of Labor Statistics' Consumer Price Index (1967=100) came to 32.7 in 1916, it stood at 60.0 by 1920. Whereas the CPI stood at 42 in 1940, it came to only 54 in 1945 ("Consumer Price Indexes" Series E 135–166, *Historical Statistics*, 210–11). Steel billets were 40 percent more expensive in 1920 than 1945, crude oil 35 percent more expensive, cotton over 50 percent dearer, and copper more than twice as expensive (*Treasury Annual Report, 1945*, 4).

[43] Odin Anderson, *Health Care: Can There Be Equity? The United States, Sweden, and England* (New York: Wiley, 1972), 65.

up a committee (chaired by Alexander Lambert, Theodore Roosevelt's personal physician) to study the recent British legislation of 1911. The Commission of Industrial Relations, founded by President Woodrow Wilson in the wake of labor violence, also recommended health insurance in its final report.[44] Legislation for comprehensive medical care appeared probable in New York, California, and other states.

Then came the war. Physicians went into the services; the American Medical Association dissolved its committee; and politicians and journalists linked German belligerence with social insurance: the "Prussian menace" was "inconsistent with American values."[45] In California, the League for the Conservation of Public Health joined with Christian Scientists to declare that a program of government health insurance "is a dangerous device, invented in Germany, announced by the German Emperor from the throne the same year he started plotting and preparing to conquer the world."[46] The war "diverted attention from social reform," according to the sociologist Paul Starr, "channeled the enthusiasm for doing good into a crusade abroad, and divided the old nationalist progressives like Roosevelt from the more pacifist and isolationist elements of the movement." It "proved to be the graveyard of an already faltering Progressive movement."[47]

After the war, the strident anti-Bolshevism on the part of business and much of the press routed the remaining advocates of government health insurance (mostly Progressives). By 1920 the Atlanta AMA passed a resolution opposing "the institution of any plan embodying the system of compulsory contributory insurance which provides for medical service to be rendered contributors or other dependents, provided, controlled, or regulated by any state or the Federal Government."[48]

Whereas Starr and the historian Monte Poen give the war direct credit for derailing the Progressive-era momentum towards public health care, the health services researcher Odin Anderson does so indirectly: Anderson talks of the support for public health insurance as late as 1916 and then discusses the successful countermobilization of 1920 without reference to any political activity between the years 1916 and 1920.[49] But the opposition of AMA officials, business executives, and labor leaders to public health care dating

[44] Paul Starr, *The Social Transformation of American Medicine* (New York: Basic Books, 1982), 248.

[45] Poen, *Truman Versus the Medical Lobby*, 3–15.

[46] Starr, *The Social Transformation of American Medicine*, 253.

[47] Starr, *The Social Transformation of American Medicine*, 254.

[48] Anderson, *Health Care: Can There Be Equity?*, 66.

[49] Anderson does say that after the war, social welfare programs would be spearheaded by the corporate efforts towards "welfare capitalism." Also see Berkowitz and McQuaid, *Creating the American Welfare State*; and Skocpol and Ikenberry, "The Political Formation of the American Welfare State." Nor do Skocpol and Ikenberry discuss health insurance initiatives in the years between 1916 and 1920.

from before the war makes it difficult to establish a direct causal relationship between the incidence of the war and the fate of public health care initiatives.

One important setback for government-provided medical insurance came early on, when two prominent New York county societies of AMA physicians withdrew their support. Illinois medical professionals also actively opposed government-sponsored health insurance.[50] Even the most liberal business group, the National Civic Federation, opposed compulsory health insurance. In fact, neither business—especially insurance industry giants such as Prudential or Metropolitan—nor organized labor sought what they saw as competition coming from state governments. AFL President Gompers opposed government-sponsored health insurance for the reason that health coverage would undermine the selective appeal of union membership.

With the Progressive movement "already faltering" before the war, it is difficult to gauge the independent effect of the war. Yet the war's effects on the national economy, the labor force, and the unity of the Progressives, make it nonetheless possible to argue that the First World War *was* instrumental in the failure of the AALL's efforts.[51]

Public health care failed in quite another way in the 1940s: rather than eliminating public health care from consideration, World War II caused the reemergence of public health care as a political issue. As the poor condition of the nation's health became more apparent as the war went on, the Roosevelt and Truman Administrations paid renewed attention to a national program of health care (both the 1943 and 1945 Wagner-Murray-Dingell bills contained provisions for national health insurance, for instance). Once the war ended, President Truman proclaimed national health insurance to be part of the economic security that every citizen deserved, integral to "freedom from want."[52] It would be the keystone of Truman's five-part health program, and the President would repeat his request for universal medical coverage in every annual message to Congress from 1945 through 1950.

But the countermobilization against national health insurance came quickly. Appeals for a national medical program were repeatedly connected to Marxism-Leninism, and national health insurance became tagged as "socialized medicine." Even as the Second World War brought public health care back to the political agenda, the new world order, divided into Soviet and American spheres of influence, provided fertile ground for anticommu-

[50] Starr, *The Social Transformation of American Medicine*, 253.

[51] See Richard Hofstadter, *The Age of Reform* (New York: Vintage Books, 1955), 274–82, and Christopher Lasch, *The New Radicalism in America* (New York: Norton, 1965).

[52] In a cabinet meeting on 7 September 1945, President Truman called for a national medical program, containing "a redistribution of medical facilities for the benefit of the average man." The situation in the country was "alarming" (file "Notes on Cabinet Meetings—White House File [Set 1] 1945—September 7, 21 and 28," Box 1, Connelly Papers).

nist and anti-collectivist appeals. Poen describes the 1946 hearings on national health insurance:

> Interrupting Chairman [James] Murray's opening statement in which the Montana senator urged that witnesses refrain from using the terms *communistic* or *socialistic* when referring to the national health bill, [Senator Robert] Taft exclaimed, "I consider it socialism. It is to my mind the most socialistic measure that this Congress has ever had before it." Murray's full-employment bill had come straight out of the Soviet constitution, continued Taft, and so, too, he hinted, had the national health bill. Flustered, red-faced, Murray refused to allow Taft to continue.[53]

Taft subsequently walked out of the committee hearings and thereby ensured that the Wagner-Murray-Dingell Bill would get little Republican support. Lining up against the President's program were the American Medical Association, the American Hospital Association, the American Protestant Hospital Association, the Catholic Hospital Association, the American Bar Association, the National Grange, the U.S. Chamber of Commerce, and the Woman's Auxiliary of the American Farm Bureau Federation.[54]

In 1947 the Harness Subcommittee on Government Publicity and Propaganda of the House Committee on Expenditures in the Executive Departments (Forest A. Harness, R., Ind.) would further associate public health care with communism. Its final report read that "American communism holds this [health] program as a cardinal point in its objectives; and that, in some instances, known Communists and fellow travelers within the Federal Agencies are at work diligently with Federal funds in furtherance of the Moscow party line in this regard."[55]

Upon the convening of the 81st Congress, the AMA turned up the heat further still. In a pamphlet entitled "The Voluntary Way Is the American Way," the AMA asked, "Would socialized medicine lead to the socialization of other phases of American life?" and answered, "Lenin thought so. He declared: 'Socialized medicine is the key-stone to the arch of the socialist state.'"[56] If the anticommunist rhetoric and hysteria was one thing, the indictments against Alger Hiss, Gerhart Eisler, and Judith Coplon were another; they gave the label "socialized medicine" an immediacy that savaged

---

[53] U.S. Senate, *Hearings on S. 1606*, 47, in Poen, *Truman Versus the Medical Lobby*, 88.

[54] Poen, *Truman Versus the Medical Lobby*, 89.

[55] U.S. Senate, *Hearings on S. 545 and S. 1320*, 1200, in Poen, *Truman Versus the Medical Lobby*, 127.

[56] Poen, *Truman Versus the Medical Lobby*, 148. Senator Murray responded to this oft-repeated quotation by releasing a letter that noted that researchers from the Library of Congress's Legislative Reference Service were unable to find such a statement in Lenin's speeches or writings (148–49). Poen provides ample documentation of the connection between the opposition to national health insurance and the appeal to anticommunist sentiment, especially from 1947 through 1949.

the chances for a national health care program. The Omnibus Health Bill, introduced 25 April 1949, never made it out of committee, despite the Democratic majorities in both houses of the 81st Congress, and efforts towards a national health care program were exhausted by 1950.[57] President Truman's efforts would result only in the Hill-Burton Hospital Construction Act of 1946. Medicare (health coverage for the elderly) and Medicaid (health coverage for the poor) would not come until the 1960s.[58]

The history of the 1940s thus suggests that the war played a role in the reemergence of public health care on the political agenda: national health insurance was a natural successor to the war programs; it was consistent with New Deal objectives; and it was necessary for the health of American soldiers as well as for social justice. Insofar as collectivist policies could be linked to communism in the new postwar world, however, the changes effected by World War II worked against government health care initiatives.

Common to the failures of health care initiatives in the two periods of war was the fact that neither presidential administration directly linked public health care to the war effort; it was not portrayed as being necessary to national security or as the necessary reward for wartime service. If anything, the opposite: the public policies of Germany and the Soviet Union—both more collectivist than the United States—were precisely the wrong models to follow. When the Great War ended, then, there was no influential constituency present to insist on a government health program, just as after World War II there was no established constituency ready to force the postwar government to change its health policy; American servicemen and their dependents were being cared for separately.[59]

The Regulation of Labor-Management Relations The First World War caused the establishment of temporary labor-management boards and provoked greater intervention in labor-management relations on the part of the federal government, as during the 1940s. Government-labor ties expanded both formally, with the creation of temporary boards to handle labor-management disputes in wartime, and informally, with the Wilson Administration working closely with the American Federation of Labor so as to minimize the risk of work stoppages. But the formal and informal collaboration between labor and the government did not persist after World War I to the degree it did after the later war.

[57] Also see Rimlinger on the AMA's negative campaign (*Welfare Policy and Industrialization*, 240–42).

[58] President Lyndon B. Johnson signed the 1965 Medicare Bill into law at a ceremony at the Harry S. Truman Library in Independence, Missouri. Former President Truman was at his side.

[59] The 1943 visit of Lord Beveridge to the United States and the parallel with the British case—the belief that the nation's workers should be rewarded for their wartime sacrifices by increases in social benefits—appeared to have little effect.

Faced with lumber disputes in the Pacific Northwest and the deteriorating conditions in the copper mines of Arizona (a result in part of the greater economic activity spurred on by the war in Europe), Wilson formed the President's Mediation Commission in the summer of 1917. After the entry of the United States into the war, the National Industrial Conference Board recommended that the Council of National Defense set up a unified administration of labor. Accordingly, the Secretary of Labor (newly appointed as War Labor Administrator) formed the War Labor Conference Board in January 1918. The Board recommended that a wartime board be established for the settlement of labor-management disputes, and on 8 April 1918 President Wilson created the National War Labor Board, made up of equal numbers of employer representatives from the National Industrial Conference Board and employee representatives from the AFL.

The governing principles of the (first) NWLB read remarkably like the later Wagner Act, with an introductory no-strike pledge:

1. There should be no strikes or lockouts during the war.
2. The right of organizations of workers and collective bargaining is affirmed.
3. The right of employers to bargain collectively is affirmed.
4. Employers shall not discriminate against union members.
5. Workers shall not use coercive measures against non-union members or employees.
6. Union standards shall be maintained in union shops.
7. Established safeguards and regulations for the protection of health and safety of workers shall not be relaxed.
8. Women shall be allowed equal pay for equal work and shall not be allotted tasks disproportionate to their strength.
9. The basic 8-hour day is recognized as applying in all cases where law requires it. . . .
13. The right of all workers to a living wage is declared.
14. In fixing wages, minimum pay shall be established which will insure the subsistence of the workers and his family in health and reasonable comfort.[60]

The NWLB received 1,125 cases, all of them referred to it by the USCS. The cases involved more than 1,100 establishments and 711,500 persons. More than half the disputes concerned wages, and a hundred cases pertained to employee rights. Sixty-four cases concerned the employment of women, and eighteen of these concerned demands for equal pay with equal work. The board disbanded several months after Armistice Day.

[60] The NWLB was not to interfere with the USCS; it had a maximum of about 250 employees and was composed of six departments. See Valerie Jean Conner, *The National War Labor Board: Stability, Social Justice and the Voluntary State in World War I* (Chapel Hill: University of North Carolina Press, 1986).

As soon as the war ended, the Wilson Administration convened a labor-management conference in order to secure organized labor's continued cooperation. But little came of the conference, which met at the height of the steel strike in October 1919. The U.S. government subsequently used the Lever Act against the unions (the original purpose of which was to facilitate the provisioning of food and fuel in wartime) and employed federal troops in the suppression of labor-management disputes.[61] Businesses, too, cracked down on organized labor after the war, helped by the severe economic recession and the cooperation of state and local governments.[62] Indeed, the immediate post-WWI history of the postwar recession and crackdown against labor unions points to a virtual return to the prewar voluntarism of the labor movement.[63]

Labor policy during and after World War I paralleled that of World War II. The AFL's Gompers cooperated with the Wilson Administration during WWI so as to weaken the rival International Workers of the World and competing socialist unions, just as CIO President Murray and AFL President Green cooperated with the Roosevelt Administration in cracking down on wildcat strikes and condemning Lewis's United Mine Workers. AFL membership rose by about 50 percent during the war period, from 2.3 million members in January 1917 to 3.2 million members by January 1919—analogous to the increase in union membership from about 10 million persons in 1940 (or 27 percent of the nonagricultural workforce) to 14.75 million workers by war's end (35.5 percent of the nonagricultural workforce).[64]

The expenditures of the U.S. Conciliation Service increased from $44,800 in 1915 to $173,800 in 1919, and then never fell below $117,400 a year in the early 1920s. The increase in USCS expenditures during the 1940s

[61] Ellis W. Hawley, *The Great War and the Search for a Modern Order: A History of the American Peoples and Their Institutions, 1917–1933* (New York: St. Martin's, 1979), 49; Edward Berman, "Labor Disputes and the President of the United States," Ph.D. diss., Columbia University, 1924.

[62] The nativist, conservative backlash after World War I hit immigrants especially hard. See Robert Morlan, "The Reign of Terror in the Middle West," and Stanley Coben, "Postwar Upheaval: The Red Scare," in Arthur S. Link, ed., *The Impact of World War I* (New York: Harper & Row, 1969).

[63] Berman, "Labor Disputes and the President," and Conner, *The National War Labor Board.*

The effects from the Second World War were more lasting, of course, helped by the absence of a postwar recession, the establishment of the fact-finding boards, and the continuation of private White House meetings between labor leaders and administration officials (during the postwar strike wave).

This is not to contrast the activity of the U.S. government with the passivity of labor unions or business: no doubt both labor and management believed it to be in their interest to use federal mediation. Yet the intervention amounted to state-building nonetheless.

[64] Philip S. Foner, *History of the Labor Movement in the United States*, Vol. 7: *Labor and World War I, 1914–1918* (New York: International Publishers, 1987), 338.

TABLE 7.2
Change in the USCS Bureaucracy (expenditures in thousands)

Fiscal Year	Expend.	Personnel	Fiscal Year	Expend.	Personnel
1915	$ 44.8	13	1940	$ 316	107
1916	70.4	14	1941	382	160
1917	68.1	12	1942	832	274
1918	164.8	60	1943	1,847	385
1919	173.8	79	1944	2,173	300
1920	176.9	23	1945	2,214	444
1921	130.9	49	1946	2,476	495
1922	117.4	54	1947	2,582	381
1923	147.4	74	1948	2,680	442
1924	182.1	82	1949	3,840	388
1925	176.9	62	1950	2,725	336

Source: Department of Labor *Annual Reports.*

Notes: "Expend." is the expenditures reported by Department of Labor. "Personnel" are full-time USCS conciliators under employ as of the end of the fiscal year (30 June).

echoed that of the earlier period, rising from $316,000 in 1940 to $2.2 million in 1945, and then leveling off. There were equivalent percentage changes in USCS personnel (see Table 7.2).

The number of USCS cases being heard annually and the ratio of the number of cases heard to the number of work stoppages—independent of those being heard by the several war boards—also indicate the parallel increases in government intervention. The government heard 227 cases in 1916, 1,780 cases in 1919, and 559 cases in 1925, whereas it heard 3,751 cases in 1940, 25,907 cases in 1945, and 16,956 cases in 1950.

Meanwhile, the proportion of USCS cases to work stoppages never rose higher than about one USCS case for every two work stoppages in the years between 1915 and 1925, whereas the USCS heard between one and five cases for each work stoppage during the 1940s (see Table 7.3). Again, we see a similar pattern of ratcheted indicators of dispute mediation with respect to the number of cases being heard and the ratio of USCS cases being heard to work stoppages. Despite the decline in the number of union members after World War I (by half a million persons, to 3.56 million in 1925), the number of USCS personnel, number of USCS cases being heard, size of USCS expenditures, and ratio of USCS cases to work stoppages were all ratcheted upwards.[65]

[65] In contrast, after an increase during the 1940s, union membership remained at around wartime levels in the immediate postwar period (with 14.27 million union members in 1950),

TABLE 7.3
Industrial Seizures, USCS Cases, and Work Stoppages

Year	Szrs.	Cases	Strikes	Ratio	Year	Szrs.	Cases	Strikes	Ratio
1915	—	41	1,593	0.026	1940	—	3,751	2,508	1.49
1916	—	227	3,789	0.060	1941	5	5,599	4,288	1.30
1917	2	378	4,450	0.085	1942	6	8,511	2,968	2.86
1918	7	1,217	3,353	0.363	1943	8	17,559	3,752	4.68
1919	1	1,780	3,630	0.493	1944	23	24,797	4,956	5.00
1920	—	802	3,411	0.235	1945	29	25,907	4,750	5.45
1921	—	457	2,385	0.192	1946	9	18,840	4,985	3.78
1922	—	370	1,112	0.333	1947	—	16,711	3,693	4.52
1923	—	534	1,553	0.344	1948	1	12,208	3,419	3.57
1924	—	544	1,249	0.436	1949	—	18,882	3,606	5.22
1925	—	559	1,301	0.430	1950	2	16,956	4,843	3.50

Sources: Department of Labor *Annual Reports;* Federal Mediation and Conciliation Service *Annual Reports;* Blackman, *Presidential Seizure in Labor Disputes,* Appendix A; "Work Stoppages . . . " Series D 970–975, *Historical Statistics,* 179.

Notes: "Cases" is the total number of received cases disposed. For 1915–25, cases are total numbers of cases minus those pending for the next year and plus those "pending" from the preceding year. "Strikes" are "work stoppages." "Ratio" is the proportion of cases heard by the USCS to the number of work stoppages. After 1947, USCS figures are those of the Federal Mediation and Conciliation Service (FMCS). Provisions under the Taft-Hartley Act (the 1947 Labor Management Relations Act) made the FMCS independent of the Department of Labor.

The history of the regulation of labor-management relations during and after World War I is consistent, then, with what we know of the effects of hegemonic war during the 1940s.

Financing the Wars: Taxes The extension of income taxation during the late 1910s also indicates the impact of hegemonic war. Congress passed two major tax initiatives before the actual declaration of war. In September 1916 it doubled the normal income tax from 2 to 4 percent, doubled corporate taxes from 1 to 2 percent, increased the maximum surtax from 6 to 13 percent, and made munitions manufacturers pay a 12.5 percent tax on earn-

---

consistent with the post-WWII ratcheting in the USCS bureaucracy, in the number of USCS cases heard, and in the change in the case-to-strike ratio. By 1950 there were four times as many union members in the nonagricultural workforce as there were in 1925, and there was almost triple the percentage of union members in the nonagricultural workforce (Department of Labor, Bureau of Labor Statistics, in "Labor Union Membership, by Affiliation: 1897 to 1934," Series D 940–945, *Historical Statistics,* 177; Goldfield, *The Decline of Organized Labor in the United States,* 10, Table 1, "National Union Membership as a Proportion of Labor Force and Nonagricultural Employment, Selected Years, 1930–1978"). (Although I use Bureau of Labor Statistics numbers throughout, the Wolman figures are virtually identical to the BLS figures for the 1915 to 1925 period.)

ings.[66] In March 1917 it levied an 8 percent excess profits tax on all business income over $5,000 (among other measures).

The first wartime tax legislation came in October 1917. Lengthy and controversial, the bill "overwhelmed any previous financial action by the government in terms of both the amount of revenue eventually collected and the distribution of the tax burden. It also marked the shift of the finances of the United States from a base of customs and excises to one of income taxes."[67] The bill lowered exemptions to $1,000 for single persons and $2,000 for married couples, set the normal tax on individual incomes at 2–4 percent (a 4 percent tax rate on incomes over $3,000 [over $4,000 for married couples]), increased maximum surtaxes from 13 to 63 percent, and started the surtax at $3,000 (at $6,000 for partnerships) instead of $20,000.[68]

The Revenue Act of 1918 then raised the normal tax to 6–12 percent on 1918 incomes and to 4–6 percent on 1919 incomes. Although Congress passed the bill after the Armistice, the Revenue Act of 1918 nonetheless called for higher surtaxes (up to a maximum 65 percent), for increases in the corporate income tax (to 12 percent in 1918 and to 10 percent thereafter for incomes over $2,000), and for harsher excess profits taxes on net income (up to 30–65 percent for 1918).[69]

As soon as the war ended, Congress passed the Revenue Act of 1921 at the behest of Treasury Secretary Andrew Mellon. The Act repealed the excess profits tax and reduced the minimum surtax rates to 50 percent (among other provisions). The government had a budget surplus of $2.3 billion from 1920 to 1923.[70] The 1924 Revenue Act further reduced normal rates and surcharges, and cut taxes for "earned income." In 1926 Congress cut taxes even further, following Secretary Mellon's proposals. The U.S. government was nonetheless able to lower the public debt to $16 billion, or $10 billion less than the debt level of 1920.

Meanwhile, employment at the Bureau of Internal Revenue rose from 4,730 persons in 1915 to about 20,000 persons in the early 1920s, and Internal Revenue spending rose from about $7 million in the mid-1910s to $29 million by 1920, and then climbed to above $40 million after World War I (see Table 7.4). The total expenditures of the Department of the Treasury rose even faster, from $71 million in 1915 to $290 million by 1919, and to $317 million by 1925. Again, the history of the First World War fore-

---

[66] Studenski and Krooss, *Financial History*, 285.

[67] Witte, *Federal Income Tax*, 84.

[68] Witte, *Federal Income Tax*, 84. The bill also raised the corporate income tax from 2 to 6 percent, established a new, progressive excess profits tax at rates ranging from 8 to 60 percent, and reduced to 10 percent the munitions tax levied on profits in excess of 7–9 percent of the average net earnings from 1911 to 1913 (p. 84; Studenski and Krooss, *Financial History*, 296).

[69] Studenski and Krooss, *Financial History*, 297–98; Witte, *Federal Income Tax*, 85.

[70] Witte, *Federal Income Tax*, 92.

ABLE 7.4

ureaucracies of Public Finance (expenditures in millions)

scal ar	Internal Revenue Employm't	Internal Revenue Expend.	Treasury Expend.	Fiscal Year	Internal Revenue Employm't	Internal Revenue Expend.	Treasury Expend.
)15	4,730	$ 6.805	$ 71.107	1940	22,423	$ 59.106	$177.221
)16	4,618	7.199	73.737	1941	28,563	66.902	204.623
)17	5,053	7.699	84.902	1942	29,065	74.162	159.496
)18	8,854	12.003	181.848	1943	36,338	95.149	224.600
)19	14,055	20.573	289.914	1944	46,171	130.069	285.181
)20	18,440	29.647	260.451	1945	49,814	138.437	300.016
)21	19,593	40.204	492.253	1946	59,693	170.827	342.645
)22	21,388	41.577	263.407	1947	52,830	200.704	401.292
)23	20,995	45.316	287.203	1948	52,143	183.731	380.093
)24	19,203	42.896	277.659	1949	52,266	209.206	395.717
)25	19,333	47.631	317.984	1950	55,551	230.408	362.372

Source: Treasury Annual Reports.

Notes: Figures represent "disbursements" or "expenditures." "Internal Revenue" is the Bureau of Internal evenue, Department of the Treasury. Personnel figures for 1915–17 are combined Bureau of Internal Reve- e field and Washington figures. The "Treasury" budget is the Treasury Department total administrative penses. The Treasury total in 1921 includes over $100 million earmarked for the Bureau of War Risk surance—in 1922, expenditures for the Bureau of War Risk Insurance were divested from the Treasury epartment and allotted to the newly formed U.S. Veterans Bureau. The Bureau of Public Debt did not exist ior to 1940.

shadowed the increases in the employment and expenditures of the Bureau of Internal Revenue and the Treasury Department during the 1940s. In both cases, these increases were ratcheted into place afterwards, equal to or exceeding their wartime levels.

The number of tax returns filed, amount of income tax receipts, and pro- portion of the workforce paying income taxes each provide further evidence of the permanent state-building induced by World War I. Whereas only 337,000 Americans filed tax returns in 1915, 3.4 million persons—ten times as many—did so by 1917, and over seven million persons filed income tax returns in 1920. After the war, about seven million Americans filed tax re- turns annually during the early 1920s, up until 1925 (see Table 7.5).

Income tax receipts similarly rose from $68 million in 1915 to $691 mil- lion in 1917, and to $1.27 billion in 1919. Income tax receipts then dropped to $735 million by 1925. Income taxpayers as a proportion of the workforce rose in parallel, from less than 1 percent of the workforce in 1915 to over 17 percent of the workforce by 1920, and then back to approximately 9 percent by 1925 (see Table 7.5). And income and profits taxes on individuals and

TABLE 7.5

Income Tax Returns (individual returns in thousands)

Fiscal Year	No. of Returns	% of Workforce	Inc. Tax/ Revenue	Fiscal Year	No. of Returns	% of Workforce	Inc. Tax/ Revenue
1915	337	0.8	(NA)	1940	14,578	25.9	16.1%
1916	437	1.1	8.9%	1941	25,770	44.8	17.2
1917	3,473	8.5	16.4	1942	36,456	60.4	21.4
1918	4,425	10.5	(NA)	1943	43,507	67.4	25.8
1919	5,333	12.9	(NA)	1944	47,111	71.3	42.2
1920	7,260	17.4	(NA)	1945	49,933	76.4	36.7
1921	6,662	15.7	(NA)	1946	52,817	86.6	37.0
1922	6,787	15.9	(NA)	1947	55,099	89.2	41.2
1923	7,698	17.6	(NA)	1948	52,072	83.9	42.6
1924	7,370	16.6	(NA)	1949	51,814	82.4	37.4
1925	4,171	9.2	23.2	1950	53,060	83.1	38.5

Sources: "Individual Income Tax Returns: 1944 to 1970" and "1913 to 1943," Series Y 393–401 and 402–411, *Historical Statistics*, 1110.

Notes: "% of Workforce" is the percentage of the total labor force paying income taxes. "Inc. Tax/Revenue" is the percentage of the federal government's revenue constituted by the individual income tax. Total government revenue includes receipts from government land sales and social security revenues.

corporations accounted for 87 percent of the increase in revenue from $0.8 billion in 1917 to $3.7 billion in 1918. These developments once more foreshadow the greater changes in income taxation occurring in the 1940s.[71] The Wilson Administration paid for 30 percent of WWI spending out of income tax revenues; the Roosevelt Administration financed 46 percent of WWII expenditures through taxes.[72]

Financing the Wars: Public Debt. As during World War II, the U.S. government had to borrow heavily to pay for the First World War. But the public debt declined much more immediately after World War I than in the late 1940s.

[71] Witte, *Federal Income Tax*, 85. The wartime inflation also contributed to revenue increases.

[72] Blough, *The Federal Taxing Process*, 85. Annual income tax receipts after World War I would never be less than five times their prewar levels, and income tax revenues after the war would never be less than seven times prewar averages (David Kennedy, *Over Here* [New York: Oxford University Press, 1980], 112–13).

The lessening importance of the personal income tax after 1920, and especially from 1925 through 1931, belies John F. Witte's statement that the First World War marked the shifting of sources of federal revenue to the income tax (Witte, *Federal Income Tax*, 124,126). It took the later war to make that shift permanent.

Despite the fact that financial experts in the Wilson Administration and Treasury Department viewed higher taxes as a solution to the inflationary pressures of wartime spending, Treasury Secretary William McAdoo decided that financing more than one-third of the war through taxes would be excessive and potentially destructive.[73] The Treasury therefore relied heavily on short-term obligations (such as certificates of indebtedness) "in order to encourage a wide-spread participation of banks in new Government issues and prevent unusual disturbances of the money market by withdrawing funds prior to their need by the Government."[74] The Treasury also depended on the sale of Liberty Bonds, but it did nothing to discourage individuals from buying bonds with bank-borrowed money. In consequence, the "commercial holdings of government obligations increased, demand deposits rose, consumer spending increased, and an upward pressure was exerted on prices."[75]

The money supply rose from $11.6 billion on 30 June 1914 to $23.7 billion on 30 June 1920—a total increase of 104 percent, or an average of 12.9 percent annually. With the rise in the money supply came an even greater increase in wholesale prices, rising at an annual rate of 15.3 percent on average.[76] Interest rates rose as well. On 30 June 1914 the average return on interest-bearing government debt stood at 2.35 percent, and the public debt came to $1 billion; six years later, on 30 June 1920, the rate of interest on government debt stood at 4.22 percent, and the U.S. public debt came to $24 billion. With the higher interest rates and without federally guaranteed price levels on U.S. government securities, the Treasury had to pay out more in interest to attract investment, and the value of the bonds outstanding fell accordingly.

The Treasury and the Federal Reserve set up committees and built up extensive networks for facilitating the sale of War Savings Stamps, Liberty Bonds, and certificates of indebtedness to farmers, the self-employed, union members, and government and corporate employees.[77] "Banks, bankers, trust companies, business men, associations and societies, and thousands of men and women throughout the country patriotically cooperated with the Treasury and the War Loan Organization" to sell government securities and savings stamps during the war loan drives.[78]

The War Loan Organization, responsible for the publicity and sale of the

[73] Witte, *Federal Income Tax*, 83; Studenski and Krooss, *Financial History*, 288. The Wilson Administration had originally planned to finance fully half of the war through taxes.

[74] 12 February 1947, file "Fiscal—Financing 1946–52, folder 2," Box 15, Snyder Papers.

[75] Studenski and Krooss, *Financial History*, 292.

[76] Friedman and Schwartz, *Monetary History*, 546.

[77] See Kennedy (*Over Here*, 105–6) on Secretary McAdoo's promotion of the war loan drives.

[78] *Treasury Annual Report, 1919*, 71.

war loans, had branches in the twelve Federal Reserve Banks which coordi-nated the efforts of about two million persons for the war loan drives.[79] But the War Loan Organization was dissolved after the Fifth War Loan drive, whereas the War Finance Division was retained after 1945 in the form of the Savings Bonds Division of the Treasury Department.[80]

Spending on national security rose from $300 million in 1915 to more than twice the prewar mark in the early 1920s (with a peak of $17 billion in military spending in 1919). As in the 1940s, the postwar government had to keep its funding sources—especially ones as effective as the income tax and the marketing and sale of government securities—given its new interna-tional responsibilities (see Table 7.6). Not surprisingly, per capita public debt soared over the late 1910s and declined moderately afterwards. Per capita debt rose from under $12 a person in 1915 to $29 in 1917 and $243 in 1919, and declined to $221 a person in 1921, $200 in 1923, and $177 in 1925. Per capita public debt amounted to just $131.04 in 1930. Similarly, per capita public debt climbed from $326 a person in 1940 to $1,853 in 1945, and then steadied at $1,721 in 1948 and $1,697 in 1950.

The Wilson Administration made mistakes when financing World War I, however, resulting in pressures on interest rates and on prices. The Liberty Bonds paid interest currently, thus adding to the money supply, whereas the WWII E bonds paid the interest and the principal upon the maturity or redemption of the bond (the bonds had a fixed schedule of redemption values printed on them). The Liberty Bonds also happened to be negotiable; they could be cashed in by the finders, and the losers were unable to get replacements. The E bonds, in contrast, were issued in the name of the purchaser and thus could be easily replaced. In addition, the Liberty Bonds were tax-exempt and benefited wealthy investors, whereas the investors of the 1940s had to pay taxes on the interest earned from their government securities. Furthermore, the Treasury also offered a narrow range of securi-ties in the late 1910s, in contrast to a much wider variety of securities avail-able in the war loan campaigns of the 1940s.[81] Because of the more attractive offerings of U.S. securities, the set pattern of interest rates estab-lished in the early 1940s (supported by the Federal Reserve's purchase of

---

[79] *Treasury Annual Report, 1918*, 62; *Treasury Annual Report, 1919*, 69.
[80] *Treasury Annual Report, 1950*, 130.
[81] By tailoring securities to different investors in the 1940s—offering assorted classes of marketable and nonmarketable securities in a range of maturities—Treasury officials were able to claim after the war that "there has been a sellers' market in Government securities. Marketa-ble securities have generally been 'scarce' and in demand. It has been a privilege to buy them. This, more than anything else, has fundamentally distinguished government finance in World War II from that in World War I" ("The Federal Reserve Ratio and Money Market Manage-ment during Fiscal Year 1945," pp. 1–2, file "Financing Problems over the Next Few Months," Box 4, Subject Files, WFD).

TABLE 7.6
Spending on National Security (billions)

Year	Domestic	Security	% USG	Year	Domestic	Security	% USG
1915	$0.245	$ 0.302	40	1940	$ 4.024	$ 1.556	16
1916	.208	0.311	44	1941	4.318	6.208	44
1917	.265	1.493	76	1942	4.764	25.811	75
1918	.371	11.858	94	1943	3.790	66.532	84
1919	.460	17.048	92	1944	4.262	80.516	86
1920	.569	4.432	70	1945	4.112	84.897	89
1921	.749	2.664	52	1946	3.898	47.470	77
1922	.669	0.939	28	1947	5.043	17.611	48
1923	.640	0.694	22	1948	5.871	17.666	48
1924	.611	0.662	23	1949	8.919	19.218	47
1925	.652	0.606	21	1950	10.666	17.894	41

Source: "Outlays of the Federal Government, by Major Function: 1900 to 1934" and "1940 to 1970," Series Y 460–471 and 472–487, *Historical Statistics*, 1115 and 1116.

Notes: "Domestic" is gross federal expenditures minus national security, international affairs and finance, interest, and veterans' services and benefits for 1915–25; for 1940–50, "Domestic" equals health, income security, education, national resources and environment, and community development and housing expenditures. "Security" equals Navy and War Department spending for 1915–25 and equals Navy, War, and Defense Department spending in addition to "international affairs and finance" for the 1940s. "% USG" is the amount of spending for national security as a percentage of total federal expenditures.

securities), and the higher tax rates (and lower tax exemption levels), whole-sale prices rose by an average of only 8.7 percent a year between 30 June 1939 and 26 May 1948—at the same time that the money supply increased from $33.4 billion to $108.6 billion, or an average yearly increase of 12.1 percent.[82]

In short, the programs of income taxation and deficit financing introduced during the two world wars were strikingly parallel. They were marked by large increases in the numbers paying and amounts collected in income taxes, by large increases in the expenditures by and numbers of personnel employed in the finance bureaucracies, and by large increases in the num-

[82] "Highlights of Recent Business Developments and Comparison of 1920 and Present," 28 July 1948, file "Highlights," Box 82, Snyder Papers. Other factors behind the great expansion of credit in the late 1910s were a relaxation of reserve requirements, the expansion of the supply of currency, and the increase of bank loans. The gold stock also grew at a faster rate in the earlier war, rising 61 percent over the years of World War I versus an increase of 46 percent during the later war. Finally, member banks of the Federal Reserve System were borrowing $2.7 billion from the Fed by mid-1920, as opposed to only $54 million in mid-1948 ("Raising the Funds for Victory," A Report by the Secretary of the Treasury, 17 July 1945 [Washington, D.C.: U.S. GPO, 1945]).

bers and amounts of the (much bigger) federal debt owned by the American public. Most of the changes in public finance experienced during the First World War remained in place afterwards.

Navy Procurement The indicators of state-building in Navy procurement also show significant ratcheting during the earlier war period. In 1916 President Wilson and the U.S. Congress became convinced that the United States fleet should be "second to none." The government therefore approved a vast shipbuilding effort for battleships, cruisers, destroyers, and smaller vessels, and the individual bureaus had contractors make competitive bids for building ships at fixed prices, as they had in the past.[83] But with the wartime demand vastly exceeding the available supply, the Navy had no way to readily determine its material needs, solicit bids, or assess the bids it received. Accordingly, the Navy had to award contracts by other means, such as cost-plus-fixed-fee contracts or cost-plus-percentage-of-cost contracts. This was especially the case for big-ticket items such as destroyers or battleships.[84]

Aircraft, however, were just starting to become tactical weapons in the 1910s. Only late in the war did the United States start to purchase standardized pursuit and bomber aircraft from American producers; at the outset, the U.S. government relied on foreign producers. Congress therefore established the National Advisory Committee for Aeronautics to "supervise and direct the scientific study of flight."[85] The United States had an infant industry.[86]

While the Navy's procurement and total budgets fell after the war, they did not return to their prewar levels.[87] Nor, however, did the United States attempt to challenge or outspend Great Britain at the 1919 peace negotiations in Paris.[88] Then, at the Washington Conference, the British managed to get Secretary of State Charles Evans Hughes and the Harding Adminis-

[83] The bill called for 156 vessels, including 10 battleships, 50 destroyers, and 68 submarines (Albion, *Makers*, 222).

[84] Furer, *Administration of the Navy*, 814–15.

[85] Irving Britain Holley, *Ideas and Weapons* (Washington, D.C.: Office of Air Force History, 1983 [1953]), 107.

[86] On WWI aeronautics, see Holley, *Ideas and Weapons*; John B. Rae, *Climb to Greatness*; Simonson, ed., *The History of the American Aircraft Industry*; and Vander Meulen, *The Politics of Aircraft*.

[87] The actual amounts spent on procurement by the Navy were not available for the two periods in question. I have therefore used two other indicators: Navy budgets and civilian employment in defense (the Navy and War Departments and, after 1949, the Department of Defense). The use of the Navy budget figures assumes that spending on procurement co-varies with absolute budget size, and the use of the numbers of civilian employees assumes that the number of personnel administering material procurement (lawyers, inspectors, negotiators, etc.) vary in proportion to overall defense employment.

[88] Navy plans included a scenario for naval warfare against Great Britain (Albion, *Makers*, 226).

tration to agree to scrap thirty U.S. capital ships, despite the fact that many were still under construction at the time. The total tonnage of dreadnoughts was not to exceed 500,000 tons, and the United States was to keep a 5:5:3 ratio of naval tonnage to that of Great Britain (5) and Japan (3).[89]

The Navy budgets and personnel figures indicate the impact of World War I. Navy budgets more than doubled, rising from $141 million in 1915 to a plateau of more than $300 million a year after the war (with a wartime peak of $2.0 billion), and defense employment rose by half from fewer than 60,000 employees in 1915 to a postwar plateau of over 90,000 workers (with a wartime peak of 237,000 employees). Once more, this paralleled the later (and larger) increases in the Navy budgets (from less than $1 billion in 1940 to a postwar plateau of a little over $4 billion), and defense employment (from 256,000 persons in 1940 to over 850,000 employees in 1947, 1948, and 1949). See Table 7.7.

The history of military-industry relations from 1915 to 1925 also fore-shadowed the later experience of wartime boom in shipbuilding and aircraft production, followed by a postwar collapse. The Navy bought few destroyers in the mid-1910s, 104 destroyers in 1919, and then none from 1923 through 1925; it purchased 20 destroyers in 1940, 130 destroyers in 1943, and none from 1947 through 1950. The fate of the merchant marine is further illustrative of the parallels between the two war eras: American shipyards launched an average of 605 ships a year from 1915 through 1920, but launched an average of only 99 annually from 1921 through 1925; similarly, 167 vessels were launched in 1940, 880 in 1945, and only 51 in 1950.[90]

Aircraft purchases also surged during the wars and settled at higher levels afterwards, although almost no aircraft had been purchased before World War I. The production of military aircraft rose from 26 in 1915 to 14,000 in 1918, only to fall to 447 planes by 1925. Similarly, production rose from

[89] Albion, *Makers*, 226–33. See Albion on the Washington Conference for disarmament and especially for a discussion of the politics involved and the role of Theodore Roosevelt. The ratio on naval tonnage applied to capital ships and did not include cruisers or smaller vessels.

[90] "Merchant Vessels Launched and Owned—World and United States: 1895 to 1970," Series Q 473–480, *Historical Statistics*, 755. An average of 74 merchant ships per year were launched between 1925 and 1930. Nor were the profits from the First World War very impressive. Gross corporate profits rose by 49 percent between 1914 and 1920; they rose by 301 percent between 1939 and 1947. After-tax profits rose by 8.9 percent between 1914 and 1920; they rose by 215 percent between 1939 and 1947 (Bureau of Internal Revenue and Office of the Technical Staff of the Office of the Secretary of the Treasury, "Corporate Profits," in "Highlights of Recent Business Developments and Comparison of 1920 and Present," 28 July 1948).

In comparison, industrial stock prices were 55 percent above their 1914 average in 1920, and 43 percent above their 1939 average on 21 July 1948 ("Highlights of Recent Business Developments"). Yet there were no vindictive congressional hearings following the Second World War, and the Navy and private industry were both praised widely for their achievements and restraint.

TABLE 7.7
Navy Budgets and Defense Employment (budgets in millions)

Fiscal Year	Navy Dept. Expend.	Defense Employment	Fiscal Year	Navy Dept. Expend.	Defense Employment
1915	$ 141	58,286	1940	$ 891	256,025
1916	153	63,395	1941	2,313	556,073
1917	239	91,982	1942	8,579	1,291,093
1918	1,279	(NA)	1943	20,888	2,200,064
1919	2,002	(NA)	1944	26,537	2,246,454
1920	736	237,212	1945	30,047	2,634,575
1921	650	138,293	1946	15,164	1,416,225
1922	476	107,126	1947	5,597	859,142
1923	333	94,001	1948	4,284	870,962
1924	332	92,331	1949	4,434	879,875
1925	346	94,772	1950	4,129	753,149

Sources: "Paid Civilian Employment of the Federal Government: 1816 to 1970," Series Y 308–317, *Historical Statistics,* 1102; "Outlays of the Federal Government: 1789 to 1970," Series 457–465, *Historical Statistics,* 1114.

6,028 aircraft in 1940 to 95,272 planes in 1945, and then subsided to 2,773 aircraft in 1950 (see Table 7.8).[91]

Another feature common to both periods was the absence of formal organizations that connected the Navy with its material suppliers. Although the War Industries Board combined representatives from the government, business, and labor in the assignment of priorities, coordination of production, and facilitation of deliveries, the Navy bureaus did their business with private contractors independently of WIB—unlike the bond-selling by the War Loan Organization and the mediation of labor-management disputes by the (first) National War Labor Board, but similar to the later experience of the WPB.

The First World War did not wholly foreshadow the later war, however. Not only was there the problem of scale, with Navy expenditures coming to $3.5 billion between fiscal years 1916 and 1919, and $100 billion between fiscal years 1941 and 1945, but airplanes were barely incorporated into military plans in the earlier war (and they were built out of spruce rather than aluminum). Moreover, the ships of the 1910s were almost devoid of the electronic equipment that by itself constituted a major purchasing item during the later war (costing the Navy about $2.5 billion over the course of

[91] "Aircraft Production and Exports: 1913 to 1970," Series Q 565–576, *Historical Statistics,* 768.

TABLE 7.8

Procurement of Naval Destroyers and Military Aircraft (Deliveries)

Year	Destroyers	Aircraft	Year	Destroyers	Aircraft
1915	7	—	1940	20	
1916	9	—	1941	16	
1917	5	9,742	1942	81	300,317
1918	44	(April 1917 to	1943	130	(July 1940 to
1919	104	Nov. 1919)	1944	76	Sept. 1945)
1920	79	256	1945	74	
1921	28	389	1946	15	1,417
1922	3	226	1947	1	2,122
1923	0	687	1948	0	2,536
1924	0	317	1949	0	2,592
1925	0	447	1950	0	2,680

Sources: Destroyer figures are from Smith and Brown, "Shipyard Statistics," in Fassett, *The Shipbuilding Business,* 119–20, Table 43 and 44; aircraft figures are from Rae, *Climb to Greatness.*

Note: Aircraft figures encompass War Department and Navy Department aircraft.

World War II).[92] Neither did research and development—and thus obsolescence—play the role it would in the 1940s. Nor did the Navy overhaul its administration of procurement during the First World War, in contrast to Elihu Root's reorganization of the War Department in the 1910s and the Navy's experience of the 1940s.

A comparison of the two world wars with respect to Navy procurement reveals less of a parallel than in the preceding cases. Not only were there the obvious differences in scale and technology, but the Navy did not undergo administrative changes during and after WWI analogous to those that typified the later era. Despite these discrepancies there was parallel ratcheting in the budgets and personnel of the Navy Department and a similar postwar atrophying of the shipbuilding and (to a lesser degree) aircraft industries.

In sum, the First World War had pervasive effects on political institutions that are considered the results of American exceptionalism: the direct and indirect effects of World War I helped to squelch initiatives for public health care coming out of the Progressive era; the war helped to suppress labor radicalism by virtue of the new government-labor cooperation and greater intervention by the government in labor-management relations; it entrenched the positions of Gompers's American Federation of Labor against socialist unions and the IWW; it demonstrated the efficacy of the individual

[92] Furer, *Administration of the Navy,* 813.

(and corporate) income tax and of public borrowing (and thereby obviated the emergence of other means of revenues collection); and the Great War manifestly altered the balance between domestic and military spending in the late 1910s and early 1920s.[93]

Alternative Explanations

It could be argued, however, that the extraordinary effects of World War II on the American state—and of the two world wars in general—are the artifacts of preceding policies and preexisting institutions. That is to say that the impact of the Second World War on the American state may be better explained as the consequence of the legacies of the 1930s and the interwar years—the unemployment, unused industrial capacity, and policy innovations of the 1930s. This emphasis on the historical continuities of American politics and the U.S. system of political representation may be termed a "structuralist" argument, to follow the work of Theda Skocpol and co-authors on the American state.[94]

The absence of public health care may thus be explained as the outcome of factors endogenous to the United States, such as the existing array of corporate and other interests, the absence of historical precedents, the decentralized and federated system of government, and the alignment of political partisanship. Accordingly, we should expect neither President Wilson nor President Roosevelt—politicians sensitive to the balance of political forces and the realm of the possible—to advocate public health care. And, in fact, Wilson made no special effort to push for public health care either

[93] The data from the two periods suggest two patterns of ratcheting. One is the different scale of the ratchets. From 1915 to 1925 there were large *percentage* increases in the indicators of bureaucracy and government-society ties, whereas there were smaller percentage increases in the 1940s but greater *absolute* changes. Compare the postwar ratcheting of USCS personnel, cases heard, and case-to-strike ratios (Tables 7.2 and 7.3), Internal Revenue employment and Internal Revenue and Treasury expenditures (Table 7.4), the number of individual taxpayers and the percentage of the workforce filing tax returns, income tax revenues as a percentage of U.S. government revenues (Table 7.5), and the level of U.S. public debt.

The exception to this pattern, and the second finding suggested by these data, is that this difference between percentage and absolute increases does not hold for national security: defense expenditures (Table 7.6), Navy budgets, and defense employment (Table 7.7) were bigger after 1945 on both a percentage and an absolute basis than those obtaining after the First World War.

[94] See Skocpol, "Society Without a State"; Weir and Skocpol, "State Structures and the Possibilities for 'Keynesian' Responses to the Great Depression in Sweden, Great Britain, and the United States"; Skocpol and Ikenberry, "The Political Formation of the American Welfare State"; and Amenta and Skocpol, "Taking Exception." Given that there are other structuralist explanations of political development, I make no claims about structuralism *per se*. See, for instance, Jill Quadagno, *The Transformation of Old Age Security*.

during or after World War I, while Franklin Roosevelt eliminated any mention of a program for national health insurance from the 1935 Social Security Bill—contrary to the recommendations of the Committee on Economic Security—and discouraged the promulgation of public health care during the 1940s. President Truman's efforts, being sown on such barren ground, were bound to fail.

With respect to the regulation of labor-management relations, the establishment of the Department of Labor and the U.S. Conciliation Service in 1913 prepared the way for the measures taken during the First World War for the stabilization of labor-management relations and the improvement of industrial production. And the initiatives of the 1910s laid the groundwork for the National Labor Act and the National Labor Relations Board of 1933, and for the Wagner Act and the second NLRB of 1935. The presence of these institutions were obvious and necessary precursors to the developments of the 1940s.[95]

Attending to historical continuities also captures the adoption of the federal income tax as the workhorse of the U.S. government's revenue collection (possible after the 16th amendment of 1913) and explains the increase of over ten million in the number of tax returns filed in the interim period (going from 4 million receipts in 1925 to 14.5 million receipts in 1940), the jump from 9 percent to almost 26 percent of the workforce paying income taxes over these same years, and the increase in the gross public debt per capita from $177 to $325. Recall that the only innovative tax policy of the 1940s was the introduction of current withholding; even the bond sales of the war years built on the precedents of the First World War and security issues of the 1930s. Consistent with a focus on endogenous political factors, spending on domestic programs rose from $650 million in 1925 to $4.0 billion by 1940.

Finally, a critical part of the military procurement record of the 1940s was the prevailing suspicions on the part of members of Congress and the public with respect to material producers, as manifested in the attacks on war profiteering and business management prevalent during the interwar years and in the passage of the Vinson-Trammel Act. Hence the Navy's creation of extensive supervisory bodies for administering procurement, the absence of joint ventures or collaborative efforts between the military and industry, and, of course, the high excess profits taxes on U.S. businesses.

In short, a structuralist explanation has much to recommend it. At the same time, however, the historical record also points to important independent effects of World War II on American political development. The stagnation and then delayed reform in the social security system, the redirection

---

[95] The historian William E. Leuchtenburg makes a similar argument ("The Impact of the War on the American Political Economy," in Link, ed., *The Impact of World War I*, 59).

of social provisions away from redistributive and universal principles, and the expansion of veterans' and private-sector health and retirement programs are cases in point. The increases in the size of the USCS bureaucracy and in the number of labor-dispute cases heard by government boards further indicate the independent impact of World War II on labor policy, as does the altered character of the labor movement resulting from the employment, industrialization, and government-labor cooperation brought on by the war.

Other parts of the tax and public debt records suggest the limited impact of the New Deal on the American state, relative to that of World War II. Internal Revenue employment rose from 19,000 persons in 1925 to 22,000 in 1940 and then to 55,500 by 1950. Similarly, Internal Revenue budgets increased from $47 million in 1925 to $60 million in 1940, and then to $230 million by 1950. Meanwhile, the Treasury's budget fell from $318 million in 1925 to $177 million in 1940, and then increased to $362 million by 1950. The proportion of federal revenues received from federal income taxes *declined* from 23.2 percent of revenues in 1925 to 16.1 percent in 1940 and then more than doubled, to 38.5 percent, by 1950; and the principal on the public debt stood at $20.5 billion in 1925 and at $43 billion in 1940, and then took off, rising to $257 billion in 1950—a sixfold increase in ten years.[96]

Finally, the independent effects of the world war(s) are manifestly apparent in the massive increases in the Navy budgets, defense personnel, and the quantity of ships and planes being purchased, as well as in the administrative reform of the Navy's procurement practices. Indicatively, domestic spending increased hardly at all over the course of the 1940s (except at the very end of the decade), while spending on national security rose from $1.5 billion in 1940 to around $18 billion a year in the late 1940s (refer to Table 7.6). The fact that the United States could no longer maintain its isolationism had widespread repercussions on American government and society.

In sum, a structuralist explanation of American state-building as presented here has mixed results. It is consistent with the growth in the numbers of income tax returns, the greater spending on domestic programs, the increase in the public debt, and the larger percentage of the workforce paying income taxes in the years from 1925 to 1940. It is further consistent with the lack of change in the *form* of state-building as noted with respect to the absence of corporatist government, the limited change in federal tax policy, and the reliance on government controls over Navy procurement.

But a structuralist argument understates the more general effects of World War II on social provisions, the regulation of labor-management rela-

---

[96] "Public Debt of the Federal Government: 1791 to 1979," Series Y 493–504, *Historical Statistics*, 1117.

tions, and public finance. The record of the 1920s and 1930s scarcely hints at the U.S. government's later reliance on the personal income tax, the soaring government spending, or the changes in the administration and scale of military procurement. World War II was more than mediated by the existing organizations of government. Rather, the war caused the creation and expansion of government organizations, redefined government-society relations, and refined the instruments of administration.[97] The changes in American government and society made for a new world of the late 1940s that was a far cry from that of the 1930s. The Second World War affected twentieth-century American government and government-society relations at least as much as did the New Deal.[98]

A second alternative explanation is ideological: that the state-building of the 1930s and 1940s resulted from changes in popular ideas about government. Robert Higgs, for one, finds that "[n]othing had a greater effect on the twentieth century economy, polity, and society of the United States" than the ideological revolution of the New Deal.[99] The "most important legacy of the New Deal" was "the now-dominant ideology of the mixed economy, which holds that the government is an immensely useful means for achieving one's private aspirations and that one's resort to this reservoir of potentially appropriable benefits is perfectly legitimate."[100] The new ideology of the 1930s, promulgated by the "propaganda" of American "elites," was reinforced by the incidence of the Second World War and the presence of so many influential dollar-a-year businessmen serving in Washington.[101] The

[97] See Michael Goldfield, "Worker Insurgency, Radical Organization, and New Deal Labor Legislation," *American Political Science Review* 83 No. 4 (December 1989): 1257–82, on the point that the NLRA was itself a compromise on the part of organized labor and undergirded the subsequent decline of U.S. labor unionization.

[98] Theda Skocpol's earlier work highlights the impact of transnational forces on political development. See *States and Social Revolutions*.

[99] Higgs, *Crisis and Leviathan*, 189.

[100] Higgs, *Crisis and Leviathan*, 195. Higgs's explanation of the ratcheted growth of the U.S. government is that government responds to crisis (and to an "ill-defined" public wish that something be done) by hiding costs rather than by using market-driven and cost-revealing measures. The combination in a crisis period of the rhetoric of public officials with the new demands of voters produces ideological change that causes a permanent growth in government beyond the ratcheting possible from (more empowered) public officials simply acting in their own interests.

[101] Higgs, *Crisis and Leviathan*, 233, 236. Selznick's analysis of the TVA also contains the element of betrayal: the TVA's appeal to the grass-roots approach obscured the conservative practices of its actual operation, and thus the public interest was betrayed by the TVA's cooptation of the extension services. Parallels might also be made with the pro-war publicity used to encourage the cooperation of industrial workers, and with the bond-marketing and savings-stamps campaigns: the ostensible objectives of U.S. government were, no doubt, misleading. Only the risk-averse behavior of the TVA, illuminated by Selznick, is exactly what we should

business community and the American public would continue to tolerate government intervention after the war, where they had not previously.

Although an ideological explanation is consistent with the changes noted above in ideas and political agendas, to argue that the change in ideology was the *primary* cause of the state-building of the 1940s seems mistaken. Not only were the early postwar efforts to expand the social security system and to introduce national health insurance undermined by the war (despite the purported change in ideology), but the institutional changes of the 1930s and 1940s happened inconsistently across policy areas, as noted in the contrast between the postwar changes in the extent and intensity of the ownership of the public debt, on the one hand, and in the extent and intensity of income taxation, on the other.[102]

In fact, the ideological changes of the 1940s were at each instance accompanied by tangible changes in the U.S. government, government-society relations, and the national economy. Only after the economic success of the war was the right to collective action by industrial unions widely accepted, for instance, and only after the revealed success of the financing of the war would proactive fiscal policy be recognized as a legitimate function of the U.S. government for the reduction of unemployment and the stabilization of the national economy. Ideology cannot be viewed apart from what the government was able to offer individual citizens and corporate actors, and from what societal actors were in turn able to expect from the government.

Nor does the history of the 1940s show ideological change to be the result of promotional efforts by self-serving political officials or clever company men benefiting from government largesse; the record shows instead that executive branch officials scrambled to come up with programs that at once responded to the crisis at hand and were acceptable to societal actors in possession of resources needed by the government. Take public finance. The Roosevelt Administration attempted to raise as much in taxes as possible in order to prevent the inflation of the First World War, to fund with low fixed interest rates, and to supervise producer costs; the tax burden was obvious for all to see. Although Congress did not raise taxes as much as the Roosevelt and Truman Administrations wanted, both Administrations relied on raising funds through the voluntary (and extremely visible) sales of government securities, despite the low return on the sale of U.S. securities to medium- and low-income Americans, rather than resorting to hidden taxes

---

expect from government organizations. But my interest is on resources rather than ideology, and Selznick does not focus on state-building (though he does mention democratic planning and the "age of control").

[102] Higgs allows that aggregate quantitative indicators are insufficient, but uses aggregate figures of the government's share of GNP or national employment nonetheless. He does not explore the implications of the fact that aggregate figures may be misleading (*Crisis and Leviathan*, 20–34).

or more regressive forms of financing. The Treasury Department, the Federal Reserve, and the Congress made sure that the necessary funds would be available while at the same time trying to minimize inflation, as noted, with the support of the pattern of low interest rates used during the war years, the use of wage and price controls, rationing, and the imposition of higher taxes. Although it is conceivable that, given the international and domestic demands, the government could have continued its wartime deficit spending into the late 1940s, the Roosevelt and Truman Administrations embraced policies that made present costs explicit—contra Higgs—with the former calling for more progressive taxation and the latter insisting on balanced budgets.

The state-building of the war years did not lead to the government becoming a near-tyrannical force in American society, then, as Higgs and others claim: the greater presence of the U.S. government in the economy and in individual lives was consistent with the necessary expansion of national government and extension of government-society ties during a world war. That the U.S. government became the new locus of exchange as a result of the war did not mean that the government, by itself, necessarily had greater authority. The jointness of the wartime state-building implicated nominally private actors in the expansion of the government and at once constrained the scope of federal authority. The private became public, and the public included the private; both built the state.

A third explanation of American state-building in the twentieth century emphasizes the sectional divisions in the United States. The political scientist Richard Bensel follows and extends the work of Immanuel Wallerstein to show the consistent sectional stresses of national policymaking. Through an analysis of "high-stress" roll call votes in the House of Representatives, Bensel finds the root cause of the major and enduring sectional differences— the "massive fact" of sectional conflict—to be the economic geography that divides the United States into a set of core and peripheral markets (roughly, the Northeast and Midwest on the one hand and the South on the other, although the exact boundaries shift over time).[103]

[103] Richard Franklin Bensel, *Sectionalism and American Political Development 1880–1980* (Madison: University of Wisconsin Press, 1984).

In one sense Bensel's sectional explanation is incommensurable with the one here: Bensel does a longitudinal analysis of American political development from 1880 to 1980, whereas the present study looks only at the period from mid-year 1940 to mid-year 1950. Indeed, the ten-year period between Bensel's high-stress roll calls is too long to pick up the impact of World War II, and his research does not for the most part cover the policy domains discussed here.

Although Bensel documents the divisions in the 79th Congress over the extension of wartime controls and examines the 1942 Civil Rights vote, we know nothing of the sectional conflict surrounding the passage of the Revenue Act of 1943, the regional debates over the Case Bill or the Taft-Hartley Act, the clashes over the reforms in the Social Security Act, or the

Indeed, a regional focus poses a direct challenge to the very notion of the state: if the American polity is distinguished by its divided character and not by its union, then political authority at the national level would seem to be secondary or even epiphenomenal to the politics of sectional differences. Yet Bensel himself suggests the centrality of the state. He observes that the inevitable political competition between regions had two major results: the first effect, lasting through the "early twentieth century," was "tribute gathering" (the siphoning of money from the periphery to the core); the second, manifest "in more recent federal policies," was the promulgation of "redistributive" policies. But if an "ostensibly neutral national state" is able to conduct redistributive policies on behalf of peripheral regions (a practice which Bensel says favors the interests of the core regions), this suggests that policymaking on the national level is more than the mere artifact of regional preferences.[104]

Indeed, the period between the "early twentieth century" and the "more recent decades" that made for the fundamental change in the American polity, according to Bensel, was precisely the period of the 1930s and 1940s. Consider the widespread effects of the Second World War on government spending on military equipment and raw materials, food and textiles, personnel salaries, and veterans' benefits. The redistribution of national income during the mid- and late twentieth century, the doubling of per capita income between 1940 and 1944, the industrialization of the South, and the alteration of American demographics that occurred as a result of that oldest of public works: preparation for war.[105] The very persistence of sectionalism as a factor in American politics suggests that it cannot account for the short-lived bursts of state-building during critical periods—especially the state-building resulting from hegemonic war.

It cannot be claimed, then, that regional conflict dominates any other explanation of American political development.[106] Indeed, the preceding chapters show that World War II "decisively shaped the *institutional structures, political parties,* and *ideological belief systems* of American political life" every bit as much as regional competition did.[107] Surely the Second World War and the beginning of the Cold War had profound effects, both

controversy behind the National Security Act (even if the sectional aspect of these cases could be demonstrated). Bensel's research on the 79th Congress is preceded by a study of high-stress roll call votes on a variety of New Deal issues dating between 1933 and 1939, and followed by a discussion of the agricultural supports of 1955–56.

[104] Bensel, *Sectionalism*, 8, 51–52. Bensel generally refers to "the American political system," "the American nation," or "American politics."

[105] Bensel does at one point allow that World War II brought about significant intervention by the U.S. government in the national economy (Bensel, *Sectionalism*, 175–79).

[106] Bensel, *Sectionalism*, 411.

[107] Bensel, *Sectionalism*, 411; emphasis added. When discussing policymaking during World War I, however, Bensel does show the sectional splits in congressional voting (*Sectionalism*, 104–28).

direct and indirect, on the *institutional structures* of the policies and players in social issues, labor-management relations, public finance, and national defense. Surely the 1940s marked a transformation of *political parties*, with the Democrats broadening their base to include more black, elderly, and working-class voters, and with the Republicans returning to power in Congress (1946) and then the White House (1952) because of the resurgence of business, the increase in personal incomes, the rise in consumer and investor confidence, and the lower voter turnout.[108] And surely there was a sea change in *ideological belief systems* during the 1940s, with the acceptance of social insurance as a (minimal) safety net for elderly workers, the acknowledgement of the rightful presence of labor unions in American industries, the recognition of the federal government's responsibility for the nation's economy, and the realization that the United States was indubitably integrated into the international system of states.[109]

[108] Gourevitch also refers to the "historic compromise" in national politics that emerged from the traumas of the Depression and the Second World War (Gourevitch, *Politics in Hard Times*, 18).

[109] Another explanation of the more permanent government change after World War II is wealth. As Wagner's Law has it, the wealthier a society, the larger the percentage of national income that can be devoted to government goods and services, since the consumption of public goods is more elastic than that of private goods. The higher incomes and greater productivity resulting from the war should therefore allow for a commensurately larger state.

The data are persuasive. Real per capita discretionary income increased 37 percent from 1913 to 1925, according to one expert, but rose 80 per cent between 1939 and 1949. The residual of aggregate social income increased by 49 percent from 1913 to 1925, and by 127 percent between 1939 and 1949—or by 139 percent and 300 percent, respectively, to use current rather than constant dollars (Sachs, "The Altered Social Income Structure of This Postwar Compared with Changes following the First World War," 9; also see "Highlights of Recent Business Developments"). The United States was clearly a much wealthier country by the mid-1940s, hence the greater spending on government organizaitons and the larger capacity needed to finance a more munificent government.

Wagner's law has its problems, however. The increases of national income and discretionary incomes in the 1940s was partly the result of the depressed conditions of the 1930s, just as the unexpectedly high savings rates during and after World War II (coincident with the low rate of bond redemptions) was partly caused by the Depression-induced change in individual preferences for liquid assets rather than equity or real estate investments (Friedman and Schwartz, *Monetary History*, 558). Consider that in 1940 national income (GNP) was only 12 percent higher than the level of 1937, that the value of the gross stock of business and plant in 1940 was below that of 1926, and that there was 14.6 percent unemployment in 1940 (Vatter, *The U.S. Economy in World War II*, 7).

Moreover, the increase in wealth had uneven effects. The increases in government spending and in national income had little effect on social provisions, particularly social security and public health care, and they could not prevent the later controversy over the expansion of social benefits. Nor was a wealthier United States able to resolve the controversies over the role of the government in the regulation of labor-management relations; nor was a richer and older United States of the 1940s more willing to pay off its public debt than had been a poorer and younger United States of the 1920s. And the great increase in discretionary income did not enable the postwar military budgets to match the military services' requests or smoothly resolve the unification issue.

Revisiting the American State

The increased attention to the "state" by political scientists, political sociologists, and historians points to a new perspective on the American polity that calls into question the dominant pluralist theories of political authority and offers a different answer to Robert Dahl's query "Who Governs?"[110] Pluralists such as Arthur Bentley and David Truman answered "a balance of veto groups," and Dahl himself answered that nobody ruled—or that almost anybody ruled—at least in New Haven.[111] The answer that the wealthy govern is echoed in various forms by Ralph Miliband, James O'Connor, William Domhoff, and Fred Block. And C. Wright Mills responded that a three-part "power elite" ruled, composed of military, business, and political leaders.[112]

Only recently, however, has the state returned to being the focus of political science research. Given this renewed attention, the aim here has been to explore the effects of hegemonic war on the state as specified here and as represented in several policy domains.[113] The redirection of the provision of social benefits in the United States, the altered regulation of labor-management relations, the revolutions in the institutions of U.S. public finance, and the transformation of military procurement—all policy outcomes identified with American exceptionalism—were the product of the necessary creation, expansion, intensification, and improvement of institutions of American government because of the Second World War.[114]

---

[110] For historians writing on the state, see Ellis W. Hawley, "Social Policy and the Liberal State in Twentieth Century America"; Barry D. Karl, *The Uneasy State: The United States from 1915 to 1945* (Chicago: University of Chicago Press, 1983); and William E. Leuchtenburg, "The Pertinence of Political and Historical Reflections on the Significance of the State in America," *Journal of American History* 73 No. 3 (December 1986).

[111] Robert Dahl, *Who Governs?* (New Haven: Yale University Press, 1961); Arthur Bentley, *The Process of Government: A Study of Social Pressures* (Chicago: University of Chicago Press, 1908); and David B. Truman, *The Governmental Process* (New York: Knopf, 1951). Also see Krasner ("Approaches to the State") and Nordlinger ("The Return to the State: Critiques") for discussions of pluralism, the state, and the work of Dahl.

[112] Miliband, *The State in Capitalist Society*; O'Connor, *The Fiscal Crisis of the State*; Domhoff, *Who Rules America?* (New York: Touchstone, 1967), and *Who Rules America Now?* (New York: Touchstone, 1983); Block, "The Ruling Class Does Not Rule"; Mills, *The Power Elite*.

[113] Daniel Bell acknowledges the international component of American exceptionalism but denies the argument being made here: "Significantly, the external foreign policy pressures and the internal domestic factors were *not* intertwined" (Bell, "The 'Hegelian Secret': Civil Society and American Exceptionalism," in Shafer, *Is America Different?*, 67; emphasis in original).

[114] This omits a consideration of changes in individual state and local governments, demography, or popular culture—all greatly affected by the two world wars, of course. Nor is it clear what difference "winning" or "losing" might have made for the United States following the two wars. Consider the difference between a Japan and Germany versus a United States and Great Britain, and, among winners, between Great Britain and the United States—where Great Britain experienced larger losses of military and civilian lives, especially in proportion to its size, and had much of its infrastructure destroyed.

Defining the state as the bureaucracies of government, government-society ties, and the instruments of administration has allowed for an exploration of state-building and may also be consistent with the work of Max Weber. The measuring of state-building across policy domains has thereby made it possible to see the differentiated quality of state-building: changes in the size of government organizations did not necessarily coincide with the greater extent or greater intensity of government-society relations within a policy domain, just as the alteration of government-society ties did not necessarily coincide with adaptations in the means of administering policies.[115]

The project has offered an organizational model of state-building—the resource dependence perspective—in order to explain the process of state-building. Although the resource dependence perspective might suggest a top-down view of state-building, accounting for the behavior of government organizations and that of their individual executives as they respond to changes in their environments has allowed for a micro-level explanation of state-building that transcends the president and the White House to include a large number of public officials coordinating with and responding to individual and corporate societal actors.

This is not to deny the role of political parties, congressional politics, or electoral campaigns in an explanation of political development; but these were neither what I sought to explain—my dependent variables—nor what I took to be the primary determinants of how government organizations were able to maintain themselves—my independent variables.[116] Elections, congressional institutions, and political parties are possibly more useful in explaining politics-as-usual. But this was a study of politics during and immediately following a critical period, politics-as-*unusual*.

To the extent that the resource dependence perspective is able to explain how the institutions of U.S. government were matter-of-factly affected and altered by the Second World War as a hegemonic war, it becomes apparent to what a degree state-building was *non*-exceptionalist. American political development may not have to be understood differently from that of other states.[117]

[115] The stagnation in social security policymaking and the decline in real social security benefits, for instance, were at odds with the administrative improvements in the social security system. Similarly, the postwar developments in the Navy's administration of procurement were inconsistent with the deterioration of military-industrial ties.

[116] Almond's arguments in "The Return to the State" slight the interorganizational and perspectival advantages of state-centered research. Although the propositions here concerning the direction of crisis policymaking, the form that government takes, the permanence of government change, and how various clienteles fare vis-à-vis the government may be rephrased and reanalyzed in terms of presidential-congressional relations, interest groups, policy networks, and administrative studies, such a reworking would miss the point: that the actions of national government can be viewed in terms of organizations and those individuals within a complex of organizations which and who respond to changes in their environments.

[117] This follows the wording of Byron Shafer (Shafer, "Preface," in *Is America Different?*, v).

Select Bibliography ────────────────────────

Archives

U.S. National Archives, Washington, D.C.

Actuarial Records of the Social Security Administration,
Informal Minutes of the Social Security Administration
Central Files of the Social Security Board
Minutes of Social Security Commissioner
Department of Labor, Records of the Office of the Secretary
Records of the Bureau of the Budget
Records of the Secretary of the Treasury, War Finance Division and U.S. Savings
    Bonds Division
Records of the National Defense Advisory Commission
Records of the Office of the Secretary of the Navy
Records of the Assistant Secretary for Air, Artemus Gates
Records of the National Military Establishment
Records of the Office of the Secretary of Defense
Records of the Joint Chiefs of Staff

Washington National Record Center, Suitland, Md.

Records of the Executive Director of the Social Security Board
Records of the Commisioner of the Social Security Administration
Records of the Federal Mediation and Conciliation Service
Records of the National War Labor Board
Records of the Bureau of Ships
Records of the Bureau of Aeronautics

Franklin D. Roosevelt Library, Hyde Park, N.Y.

President Franklin D. Roosevelt Official Files, Subject Files, and Confidential Files
Papers of Mary Dewson
Papers of Harry L. Hopkins
Papers of Gardiner C. Means
Papers and Correspondences of Henry Morgenthau, Jr.
Henry Morgenthau, Jr., Diaries.
Papers of Samuel I. Rosenman
Papers of Alexander Sachs

Harry S. Truman Library, Independence, Mo.

President Harry S. Truman, Official Files, Subject Files, and Confidential Files.
Papers of Eben A. Ayers
Papers of John D. Clark

Papers of Clark M. Clifford
Papers of Matthew Connelly
Papers of Robert L. Dennison
Papers of George M. Elsey
Papers of Oscar A. Ewing
Papers of W. John Kenney
Papers of Leon H. Keyserling
Papers of Dan A. Kimball
Papers of Frederick Lawton
Papers of Francis Matthews
Papers of Frank McNaughton
Papers of Richard E. Neustadt
Papers of Edwin G. Nourse
Papers of Frank Pace
Papers of Samuel I. Rosenman
Papers of Harold Smith
Papers of John Snyder
Papers of John L. Sullivan
Papers of Stuart A. Symington
Papers of James E. Webb

Miscellaneous

Administrative History of the United States Navy in World War II, Office of Naval History, Washington Navy Yard, Washington, D.C.
Papers of Frederic Vinson, University of Kentucky Library, Lexington, Kentucky (microfilm).
Papers of Ferdinand Eberstadt, Seeley G. Mudd Manuscript Library, Princeton University, Princeton, New Jersey.
Papers and Diaries of James V. Forrestal, Mudd Manuscript Library, Princeton University.
Wilbur J. Cohen Papers, State Historical Society of Wisconsin, Madison, Wisconsin.

Published Works and Dissertations

Abbott, Charles Cortez. *The Federal Debt*. New York: Twentieth Century Fund, 1953.
Acheson, Dean. *Present at the Creation*. New York: Norton, 1987 [1969].
Adams, Gordon. *The Politics of Defense Contracting*. New Brunswick, N.J.: Transaction Books, 1982.
Albion, Robert Greenhalgh. *Makers of Naval Policy 1798–1947*. Rowena Reed, ed. Annapolis, Md.: Naval Institute Press, 1980.
Albion, Robert Greenhalgh, and Robert Howe Connery. *Forrestal and the Navy*. With the collaboration of Jennie Barnes Pope. New York: Columbia University Press, 1962.
Albion, Robert Greenhalgh, and Samuel H. P. Read, Jr. *The Navy at Sea and Ashore*. Washington, D.C.: U.S. Department of the Navy, 1947.
Alford, Robert R., and Roger Friedland. *Powers of Theory: Capitalism, the State, and Democracy*. Cambridge: Cambridge University Press, 1985.

Alinsky, Saul. *John L. Lewis: An Unauthorized Biography*. New York: G. P. Putnam's Sons, 1949.

Almond, Gabriel A. "The Return to the State." *American Political Science Review* 82 No. 3 (September 1988): 853–74.

Altmeyer, Arthur J. *The Formative Years of Social Security*. Madison: University of Wisconsin Press, 1966.

Amenta, Edwin, and Theda Skocpol. "Taking Exception: Explaining the Distinctiveness of American Public Policies in the Last Century." In Francis G. Castles, ed. *The Comparative History of Public Policies*. London: Polity Press, 1989.

———. "Redefining the New Deal: World War II and the Development of Social Provision in the United States." In Margaret Weir, Ann Shola Orloff, and Theda Skocpol, eds. *The Politics of Social Policy in the United States*. Princeton: Princeton University Press, 1988.

Anderson, Odin. *Health Care: Can There Be Equity? The United States, Sweden, and England*. New York: Wiley, 1972.

Anderson, Perry. *Lineages of the Absolutist State*. London: New Left Books, 1974.

Annual Reports of the Secretary of the Navy. Fiscal Years 1945–1948. Washington, D.C.: U.S. Department of the Navy.

Annual Reports of the Secretary of Treasury on the State of the Finances. Washington, D.C.: U.S. GPO.

Ashford, Douglas E. *The Emergence of the Welfare States*. London: Basil Blackwell, 1986.

———. "The Whig Interpretation of the Welfare State." *Journal of Policy History* 1 No. 1 (1989): 24–43.

Axelrod, Robert. *The Evolution of Cooperation*. New York: Basic Books, 1984.

Bailey, Stephen Kemp. *Congress Makes a Law*. New York: Columbia University Press, 1950.

Ballard, Jack Stokes. *The Shock of Peace: Military and Economic Mobilization After World War II*. Lanham, Md.: University Press of America, 1984.

Balogh, Brian. "Securing Support: The Emergence of the Social Security Board as a Political Actor, 1935–1939." In Donald T. Critchlow and Ellis W. Hawley, eds. *Federal Social Policy: The Historical Dimension*. University Park: Pennsylvania State University Press, 1988.

Barber, James David. *The Presidential Character*. Englewood Cliffs, N.J.: Prentice-Hall, 1977.

Bendix, Reinhard. *Max Weber: An Intellectual Portrait*. Berkeley: University of California Press, 1977 [1960].

Bensel, Richard Franklin. *Sectionalism and American Political Development 1880–1980*. Madison: University of Wisconsin Press, 1984.

Bentley, Arthur. *The Process of Government: A Study of Social Pressures*. Chicago: University of Chicago Press, 1908.

Berkowitz, Edward D. *America's Welfare State: From Roosevelt to Reagan*. Baltimore: Johns Hopkins University Press, 1991.

———. "Growth of the U.S. Social Welfare System in the Post-World War II Era: The UMW, Rehabilitation, and the Federal Government." *Research in Economic History* 5 (1980): 233–47.

———. ed. *Social Security after Fifty Years*. New York: Greenwood Press, 1987.

Berkowitz, Edward D., and Kim McQuaid. *Creating the Welfare State*. Second Edition. New York: Praeger, 1990.

Berman, Edward. "Labor Disputes and the President of the United States." Ph.D. diss., Columbia University, 1924.

Bernstein, Barton J. "The Truman Administration and the Politics of Inflation." Ph.D. diss., Harvard University, 1963.

———. "The Removal of War Production Board Controls on Business." *Business History Review* 39 No. 2 (Summer 1965): 243–60.

———. "The Truman Administration and Its Recoversion Wage Policy." *Labor History* 6 No. 3 (Fall 1965): 214–31.

———. "The Debate on Industrial Reconversion." *American Journal of Economics and Sociology* 26 No. 2 (April 1967): 159–72.

———. "Economic Policies." In Richard S. Kirkendall, ed. *The Truman Period as a Research Field*. Columbia: University of Missouri Press, 1967.

Bernstein, Barton J., and Allen Matusow, eds. *The Truman Administration: A Documentary History*. New York: Harper Colophon Books, 1966.

Bernstein, Irving. *A History of the American Worker*, Vol. 1: *The Lean Years, 1930–1933*. Baltimore: Penguin Books, 1966 [1960].

———. *A History of the American Worker*, Vol. 2: *The Turbulent Years, 1933–1941*. Boston: Houghton Mifflin, 1971.

Blackman, John L., Jr. *Presidential Seizure in Labor Disputes*. Cambridge, Mass.: Harvard University Press, 1967.

Blaug, Mark. *Economic Theory in Retrospective*. Fourth Edition. Cambridge: Cambridge University Press, 1985.

Block, Fred. "The Ruling Class Does Not Rule: Notes on the Marxist Theory of the State." *Socialist Revolution* 33 (May–June 1977): 6–28.

Blough, Roy. *The Federal Taxing Process*. New York: Prentice-Hall, 1952.

Bluestone, Barry Peter Jordan, and Mark Sullivan. *Aircraft Industry Dynamics*. Boston: Auburn House, 1981.

Blum, John Morton. *From the Morgenthau Diaries*, Vol. 3: *Years of War, 1941–1945*. Boston: Houghton Mifflin, 1967.

———. ed. *The Price of Visions: The Diary of Henry A. Wallace 1942–1946*. Boston: Houghton Mifflin, 1973.

———. *V Was for Victory: Politics and American Culture during World War II*. New York: Harcourt Brace Jovanovich, 1976.

Braeman, John, Robert H. Bremner, and David Brody, eds. *The New Deal*, Vol. 1: *The National Level*. Columbus: Ohio State University Press, 1975.

Brinkley, Alan. "The New Deal and the Idea of the State." In Steve Fraser and Gary Gerstle, eds. *The Rise and Fall of the New Deal Order, 1930–1980*. Princeton: Princeton University Press, 1989.

Brinkley, David. *Washington Goes to War*. New York: Knopf, 1988.

Brody, David. *Change and Continuity in Twentieth-Century America*. Columbus: Ohio State University Press, 1964.

———. *Workers in Industrial America*. New York: Oxford University Press, 1980.

Brown, J. Douglas. *An American Philosophy of Social Security: Evolution and Issues*. Princeton: Princeton University Press, 1972.

Burawoy, Michael. "Two Methods in Search of Science." *Theory and Society* 18 (May 1989): 759–805.

Burkhead, Jesse. *Government Budgeting*. New York: John Wiley & Sons, 1956.

Burns, James MacGregor. *Roosevelt: The Lion and the Fox*. New York: Harcourt Brace Jovanovich, 1984 [1956].

———. *Roosevelt: The Soldier of Freedom*. New York: Harcourt Brace Jovanovich, 1970.

Carnoy, Martin. *The State & Political Theory*. Princeton: Princeton University Press, 1984.

Carroll, Glenn R., Jacques Delacroix, and Jerry Goodstein. "The Political Environment of Organizations: An Ecological View." In Barry M. Staw and L. L. Cummings, eds. *The Evolution and Adaptation of Organizations*. Greenwich, Conn.: JAI Press, 1990.

Cates, Jerry R. *Insuring Inequality: Administrative Leadership in Social Security, 1935–54*. Ann Arbor: University of Michigan Press, 1983.

Catton, Bruce. *The War Lords of Washington*. New York: Harcourt Brace, 1948.

Clayton, James L. *The Economic Impact of the Cold War*. The Forces in American Economic Growth Series. New York: Harcourt Brace & World, 1970.

Cohen, Wilbur J., ed. *The Roosevelt New Deal: A Program Assessment Fifty Years After*. Austin: Lyndon Baines Johnson Library, Lyndon B. Johnson School of Public Affairs, 1986.

Coletta, Paolo. *The United States Navy and Defense Unification, 1947–1953*. Newark: University of Delaware Press. 1981.

Collins, Robert M. *The Business Response to Keynes, 1929–1964*. Contemporary American History Series. New York: Columbia University Press, 1981.

Conner, Valerie Jean. *The National War Labor Board: Stability, Social Justice and the Voluntary State in World War I*. Supplementary Volumes to The Papers of Woodrow Wilson. Chapel Hill: University of North Carolina Press, 1983.

Connery, Robert Howe. *The Navy and the Industrial Mobilization in World War II*. Princeton: Princeton University Press, 1951.

Cook, Fred J. *The Warfare State*. New York: Macmillan, 1962.

Cook, Karen S. "Exchange and Power in Networks of Interorganizational Relations." *Sociological Quarterly* 18 (1977): 62–82.

———. ed. *Social Exchange Theory*. Newbury Park, Calif.: Sage, 1987.

Cook, Karen S., R. M. Emerson, M. R. Gillmore, and T. Yamagishi, "The Distribution of Power in Exchange Networks: Theory and Experimental Results." *American Journal of Sociology* 89 (1983): 275–305.

Cooling, Benjamin Franklin, ed. *War, Business, and American Society*. Port Washington, N.Y.: Kennikat Press, 1977.

Cornell, Cecilia Stiles. "James V. Forrestal and American National Security Policy, 1940–1949." Ph.D. diss., Vanderbilt University, 1987.

Corwin, Edward S. *The President: Office and Powers 1787–1984*. Fifth Revised Edition, with Randall W. Bland, Theodore T. Hindson, and Jack W. Peltason. New York: New York University Press, 1984.

Cronin, Thomas E. *The State of the Presidency*. Second Edition. Boston: Little, Brown, 1980.

Crum, William L., John F. Fennelly, and Lawrence H. Seltzer. *Fiscal Planning for Total War*. New York: National Bureau of Economic Research, 1942.

Cuff, Robert D. *The War Industries Board*. Baltimore: Johns Hopkins University Press, 1973.

———. "Herbert Hoover, The Ideology of Voluntarism and War Organization during the Great War." *Journal of American History* 64 No. 2 (September 1977): 358–72.

Cyert, Richard, and James G. March. *A Behavioral Theory of the Firm*. Englewood Cliffs, N.J.: Prentice-Hall, 1963.

Dahl, Robert. *Who Governs?* New Haven: Yale University Press, 1961.

———. *Dilemmas of Pluralist Democracy*. New Haven: Yale University Press, 1982.

Derber, Milton, and Edwin Young, eds. *Labor and the New Deal*. Madison: University of Wisconsin Press, 1957.

Derthick, Martha. *Policymaking for Social Security*. Washington, D.C.: Brookings Institution, 1979.

de Tocqueville, Alexis. *Democracy in America*. J. P. Mayer, ed. New York: Anchor Books, 1969.

DiMaggio, Paul. "Interest and Agency in Institutional Theory." In Lynn G. Zucker, ed. *Institutional Patterns and Organizations: Culture and Environment*. Cambridge, Mass.: Ballinger, 1988.

Domhoff, William G. *Who Rules America?* New York: Touchstone, 1967.

———. *Who Rules America Now?* New York: Touchstone, 1983.

Donovan, Robert J. *Conflict and Crisis: The Presidency of Harry S Truman, 1945– 1948*. New York: Norton, 1977.

———. *Tumultuous Years: The Presidency of Harry S Truman, 1949–1953*. New York: Norton, 1982.

Dorwart, Jeffrey M. *Eberstadt and Forrestal: A National Security Partnership, 1909–1949*. College Station: Texas A&M University Press, 1991.

Dubofsky, Melvyn, and Warren Van Tine. *John L. Lewis*. New York: Quadrangle, 1977.

Eatwell, John, and Murray Milgate, eds. *Keynes's Economics and the Theory of Value and Distribution*. Oxford: Oxford University Press, 1983.

Eccles, Marriner. *Beckoning Frontiers*. New York: Knopf, 1951.

Economic Concentration and World War II. Report of the Smaller War Plants Corporation to the Special Committee to Study Problems of American Small Business, United States Senate. Washington, D.C.: U.S. GPO, 1946.

Emerson, Richard M. "Power-Dependence Relations." *American Sociological Review* 27 No. 1 (1962): 31–40.

———. "Exchange Theory, Part II: Exchange Relations and Networks." In J. Berger, M. Zelditch, and B. Anderson, eds. *Sociological Theories in Progress*, 2. Boston: Houghton Mifflin, 1972.

Evans, Peter B., Dietrich Rueschemeyer, and Theda Skocpol, eds. *Bringing the State Back In*. Cambridge: Cambridge University Press, 1985.

Fassett, F. G., Jr., ed. *The Shipbuilding Business in the United States of America*. 2 vols. New York: Society of Naval Architects and Marine Engineers, 1948.

———. *Woodrow Wilson and World War I, 1917–1921*. New York: Harper & Row, 1985.

Ferrell, Robert H. *Harry S. Truman: A Life*. Columbia: University of Missouri Press, 1994.

Finegold, Kenneth, and Theda Skocpol. "State, Party and Industry: From Business Recovery to the Wagner Act in America's New Deal." In Charles C. Bright and Susan Harding, eds. *Statemaking and Social Movements: Essays in History and Theory*. Ann Arbor: University of Michigan Press, 1983.

Foner, Philip S. *History of the Labor Movement in the United States*, Vol. 7: *Labor and World War I, 1914–1918*. New York: International Publishers, 1987.

Forrestal, James V. *The Forrestal Diaries*. Edited by Walter Millis, with the collaboration of E. S. Duffield. New York: Viking Press, 1951.

Fraser, Steven. *Labor Will Rule: Sidney Hillman and the Rise of American Labor*. New York: Free Press, 1991.

Freeman, Gary P. "Voters, Bureaucrats, and the State: On the Autonomy of Social Security Policymaking." In Gerald Nash, Noel Pugach, and Richard F. Tomasson, eds. *Social Security, The First Half-Century*. Albuquerque: University of New Mexico Press, 1988.

Freeman, Joshua. "Delivering the Goods: Industrial Unionism during World War II." *Labor History* 19 (1978): 570–93.

Freeman, Richard B., and James L. Medoff. *What Do Unions Do?* New York: Basic Books, 1984.

Friedberg, Aaron L. "Why Didn't the United States Become a Garrison State?" *International Security* 16 No. 4 (Spring 1992): 109–42.

Friedman, Milton, and Anna Jacobson Schwartz. *A Monetary History of the United States*. New York: National Bureau of Economic Research, 1963.

Furer, Julius Augustus. *Administration of the Navy Department in World War II*. Washington, D.C.: U.S. Department of the Navy, 1959.

Gaddis, John Lewis. *The United States and the Origins of the Cold War, 1941–1947*. Contemporary American History Series, William E. Leuchtenburg, general ed. New York: Columbia University Press, 1972.

Galambos, Louis, ed. *The New American State: Bureaucracies and Policies since World War II*. Baltimore: Johns Hopkins University Press, 1987.

Galenson, Walter. *The CIO Challenge to the AFL*. Cambridge, Mass.: Harvard University Press, 1960.

———. *Rival Unionism in the United States*. New York: Russell & Russell, 1966.

Gansler, Jacques S. *The Defense Industry*. Cambridge, Mass.: Massachusetts Institute of Technology Press, 1980.

Gaventa, John. *Power and Powerlessness: Quiescence and Rebellion in an Appalachian Valley*. Urbana: University of Illinois Press, 1980.

Gilbert, Charles. *American Financing of World War I*. Contributions in Economics and Economic History, 1. Westport, Conn.: Greenwood, 1970.

Gilpin, Robert. *War and Change in World Politics*. New York: Cambridge University Press, 1981.

Glaberman, Martin. *Wartime Strikes: The Struggle against the No-Strike Pledge in the UAW during World War II*. Detroit: Bewick Editions, 1980.

Goldfield, Michael. "Recent Historiography of the Communist Party U.S.A." In M. Davis, F. Pfeil, and M. Sprinker, eds. *The Year Left: An American Socialist Yearbook*. New York: Verso, 1985.

———. *The Decline of Organized Labor in the United States*. Chicago: University of Chicago Press, 1987.

———. "Worker Insurgency, Radical Organization, and New Deal Labor Legislation." *American Political Science Review* 83 No. 4 (December 1989): 1257–82.

Goodwin, Doris Kearns. *No Ordinary Time: Franklin and Eleanor Roosevelt: The Home Front in World War II*. New York: Simon & Schuster, 1994.

Goulden, Joseph. *The Best Years 1945–1950*. New York: Atheneum, 1976.

Gourevitch, Peter. "The Second Image Reversed: The International Sources of Domestic Politics." *International Organization* 32 No. 4 (Autumn 1978): 881–911.

———. *Politics in Hard Times: Comparative Responses to International Economic Crises*. Ithaca: Cornell University Press, 1986.

Graebner, William. *A History of Retirement*. New Haven: Yale University Press, 1980.

Greenstone, J. David. "Group Theories." In Fred Greenstein and Nelson Polsby, eds. *Handbook of Political Science*, Vol. 2. Reading, Mass.: Addison-Wesley, 1975.

———. *Labor in American Politics*. New York: Knopf, 1969.

Gross, James A. *The Reshaping of the National Labor Relations Board: National Policy in Transition 1937–1947*. Albany: State University of New York Press, 1981.

Hall, Peter A., ed. *The Political Power of Economic Ideas: Keynesianism Across Nations*. Princeton: Princeton University Press, 1989.

Halperin, Morton H. *Bureaucratic Politics and Foreign Policy*. Washington, D.C.: Brookings Institution, 1974.

Hammond, Paul Y. *Organizing for Defense*. Princeton: Princeton University Press, 1961.

———. "The Political Order and the Burden of External Relations." *World Politics* 19 (April 1967): 443–64.

Hansen, John Mark. *Gaining Access: Congress and the Farm Lobby, 1919–1981*. Chicago: University of Chicago Press, 1991.

Hargrove, Erwin C. *Presidential Leadership*. New York: Macmillan, 1966.

———. *The Power of the Modern President*. Philadelphia: Temple University Press, 1974.

Hargrove, Erwin C., and Michael Nelson. *Presidents, Politics, and Policy*. New York: Knopf, 1984.

Harris, Herbert. *Labor's Civil War*. New York: Knopf, 1940.

Harris, Howell John. *The Right to Manage: Industrial Relations Policies of American Business in the 1940s*. Madison: University of Wisconsin Press, 1982.

Harvard University, Graduate School of Business Administration. *The Use and Disposition of Ships and Shipyards at the End of World War II*. A Report Prepared for the United States Navy Department and the United States Maritime Commission, No. 48. Washington, D.C.: U.S. GPO, 1945.

Hassler, Warren W. *The President as Commander in Chief*. Reading, Mass.: Addison-Wesley, 1971.

Hawley, Ellis W. *The Great War and the Search for a Modern Order: A History of the American Peoples and Their Institutions, 1917–1933*. New York: St. Martin's, 1979.

———. "Social Policy and the Liberal State in Twentieth Century America." In Donald T. Critchlow and Ellis W. Hawley, eds. *Federal Social Policy: The Historical Dimension*. University Park: Pennsylvania State University Press, 1988.

Heclo, Hugh. "General Welfare and Two American Political Traditions." *Political Science Quarterly* 101 No. 2 (1986): 179–220.

Hess, Stephen. *Organizing the Presidency*. Washington, D.C.: Brookings Institution, 1976.

Higgs, Robert. *Crisis and Leviathan: Critical Episodes in the Growth of American Government*. New York: Oxford University Press, 1987.

Higley, John, and Gwen Moore. "Elite Integration in the United States and Australia." *American Political Science Review* 75 No. 3 (September 1981): 581–97.

Hintze, Otto. *The Historical Essays of Otto Hintze*. Felix Gilbert, ed. New York: Oxford University Press, 1975 [1902].

Hofstadter, Richard. *The American Political Tradition and the Men Who Made It*. New York: Vintage Books, 1974 [1948].

Holley, I. B., Jr. *Ideas and Weapons*. Special Studies. Washington, D.C.: Office of Air Force History, 1983 [1953].

———. *Buying Aircraft: Materiel Procurement for the Army Air Forces*. Special Studies, United States Army in World War II Series. Washington, D.C.: Office of the Chief of Military History, Department of the Army, 1964.

———. "A Detroit Dream of Mass-Produced Fighter Aircraft: The XP-75 Fiasco." *Technology and Culture* 28 No. 3 (1987): 578–93.

Holtzman, Abraham. *The Townsend Movement: A Political Study*. New York: Bookman, 1963.

Homans, G. *Social Behavior: Its Elementary Forms*. Revised edition. New York: Dorsey Press, 1974 [1961].

Hooks, Gregory. "The Rise of the Pentagon and U.S. State Building: The Defense Program as Industrial Policy." *American Journal of Sociology* 96 No. 2 (September 1990): 358–404.

———. *Forging the Military-Industrial Complex: World War II's Battle of the Potomac*. Urbana: University of Illinois Press, 1991.

Hoopes, Townsend, and Douglas Brinkley. *Driven Patriot: The Life and Times of James Forrestal*. New York: Knopf, 1992.

Horowitz, David. *The Free World Colossus*. Revised Edition. New York: Hill and Wang, 1965.

Huntington, Samuel P. *The Common Defense*. New York: Columbia University Press, 1961.

———. *The Soldier and the State*. New York: Vintage Books, 1964.

———. *American Politics: The Promise of Disharmony*. Cambridge, Mass.: Belknap Press of Harvard University Press, 1981.

Huzar, Elias. *The Purse and the Sword: Control of the Army by Congress through Military Appropriations, 1933–1950*. Ithaca: Cornell University Press, 1950.

Ikenberry, G. John. *Reasons of State: Oil Politics and the Capacities of American Government*. Ithaca: Cornell University Press, 1988.

Ikenberry, G. John, and Theda Skocpol. "Expanding Social Benefits: The Role of Social Security." *Political Science Quarterly* 102 No. 3 (1987): 389–416.

Industrial Relations Research Association. *Emergency Disputes and National Policy*. Irving Bernstein, Harold Enarson, and R. W. Fleming, eds. New York: Harper & Brothers, 1955.

Isaacson, Walter, and Evan Thomas. *The Wise Men*. New York: Simon & Schuster, 1986.

Jacoby, Sanford. *Employing Bureaucracy*. New York: Columbia University Press, 1985.

Janeway, Eliot. *The Struggle for Survival*. Yale Chronicles of America Series. New Haven: Yale University Press, 1951.

Karl, Barry D. *The Uneasy State: The United States from 1915 to 1945*. Chicago: University of Chicago Press, 1983.

Katzenstein, Peter J., ed. *Between Power and Plenty: Foreign Economic Policies of Advanced Industrial States*. Madison: University of Wisconsin Press, 1978.

Katznelson, Ira. *City Trenches*. Chicago: University of Chicago Press, 1981.

―――. "Rethinking the Silences of Social and Economic Policy." *Political Science Quarterly* 101 No. 2 (1986): 307–25.

―――. "The Welfare State as a Contested Institutional Idea." *Politics & Society* 16 No. 4 (1988): 517–31.

―――. "Was the Great Society a Lost Opportunity?" In Steve Fraser and Gary Gerstle, eds. *The Rise and Fall of the New Deal Order, 1930–1980*. Princeton: Princeton University Press, 1989.

Katznelson, Ira, and Bruce Pietrykowski. "Rebuilding the American State: Evidence from the 1940s." *Studies in American Political Development* 5 No. 2 (Fall 1991): 301–39.

Katznelson, Ira, and Kenneth Prewitt. "Constitutionalism, Class and the Limits to Choice in American Foreign Policy." In Richard R. Fagen, ed. *Capitalism and the State in U.S.-Latin American Relations*. Stanford: Stanford University Press, 1979.

Kennedy, David M. *Over Here*. New York: Oxford University Press, 1980.

Keohane, Robert. *Neorealism and Its Critics*. New York: Columbia University Press, 1986.

Keynes, John Maynard. *How to Pay for War*. London: Macmillan, 1940.

―――. "The General Theory of Employment." *Quarterly Journal of Economics* 51 (1937): 209–23.

―――. *The General Theory of Employment, Interest and Money*. London: Macmillan, 1936.

Kilmarx, Robert A., ed. *America's Maritime Legacy: A History of the U.S. Merchant Marine and Shipbuilding Industry Since Colonial Times*. Boulder, Co.: Westview Press, 1979.

Koistinen, Paul A. C. "Mobilizing the World War II Economy: Labor and the Industrial-Military Alliance." *Pacific Historical Review* 42 No. 4 (November 1973): 443–78.

―――. *The Hammer and the Sword*. New York: Arno Press, 1979.

―――. *The Military-Industrial Complex*. New York: Praeger, 1980.

Kolko, Gabriel. *The Roots of American Foreign Policy*. Boston: Beacon Press, 1969.

Krasner, Stephen D. *Defending the National Interest*. Princeton: Princeton University Press, 1978.

―――. "Approaches to the State: Alternative Conceptions and Historical Dynamics." *Comparative Politics* 23 (January 1984): 223–46.

Kuhn, Thomas S. *The Structure of Scientific Revolutions*. Second Edition. Chicago: University of Chicago Press, 1970 [1962].

Lafeber, Walter. *The United States, Russia, and the Cold War, 1945–1984*. Fifth Edition. New York: Knopf, 1985.

Lacey, Michael J., ed. *The Truman Presidency*. Woodrow Wilson International Center for Scholars. New York: Cambridge University Press, 1989.

Lasch, Christopher. *The New Radicalism in America*. New York: Norton, 1965.

Laumann, Edward O., and David Knoke. *The Organizational State*. Madison: University of Wisconsin Press, 1987.

Lee, R. Alton. *Truman and Taft-Hartley*. Lexington: University of Kentucky Press, 1966.

Leff, Mark H. "Taxing the 'Forgotten Man': The Politics of Social Security Finance in the New Deal." *Journal of American History* 70 No. 2 (September 1983): 359–81.

———. "Speculating in Social Security Futures: The Perils of Payroll Tax Financing, 1939–1950." In Gerald D. Nash, Noel H. Pugach, and Richard F. Tomasson, eds. *Social Security: The First Half Century*. Albuquerque: University of New Mexico Press, 1988.

———. "The Politics of Sacrifice on the American Home Front in World War II." *Journal of American History* 77 No. 4 (March 1991): 1296–1318.

Leffler, Melvyn P. *A Preponderance of Power: National Security, the Truman Administration, and the Cold War*. Stanford: Stanford University Press, 1992.

Lekachman, Robert. *The Age of Keynes*. New York: McGraw-Hill, 1966.

Leontief, Wassily. "The Fundamental Assumption of Mr. Keynes' Monetary Theory of Unemployment." *Quarterly Journal of Economics* 51 (1937): 192–97.

Leuchtenburg, William E. *Franklin D. Roosevelt and the New Deal*. The New American Nation Series. New York: Harper & Row, 1963.

———. "The Pertinence of Political and Historical Reflections on the Significance of the State in America." *Journal of American History* 73 No. 3 (December 1986): 585–600.

Levine, Daniel. *Poverty and Society: The Growth of the American Welfare State in International Comparison*. New Brunswick, N.J.: Rutgers University Press, 1988.

Lichtenstein, Nelson. "Auto Worker Militancy and the Structure of Factory Life, 1937–1955." *Journal of American History* 67 No. 2 (September 1980): 335–53.

———. "Industrial Democracy, Contract Unionism, and the National War Labor Board." *Labor Law Journal* (August 1982): 524–31.

———. *Labor's War at Home: The CIO in World War II*. Cambridge: Cambridge University Press, 1982.

———. "From Corporatism to Collective Bargaining: Organized Labor and the Eclipse of Social Democracy in the Postwar Era." In Steve Fraser and Gary Gerstle, eds. *The Rise and Fall of the New Deal Order, 1930–1980*. Princeton: Princeton University Press, 1989.

Link, Arthur S., ed. *The Impact of World War I*. Interpretations of American History. John Higham and Bradford Perkins, eds. New York: Harper & Row, 1969.

———. *Woodrow Wilson and the Progressive Era, 1910–1917*. New York: Harper & Row, 1954.

Lowi, Theodore J. "American Business, Public Policy, Case Studies, and Political Theory." *World Politics* 16 No. 4 (July 1964): 677–715.

———. *The End of Liberalism: Ideology, Policy, and the Crisis of Public Authority*. New York: Norton, 1969.

———. *The Personal President: Power Invested, Promise Unfulfilled*. Ithaca: Cornell University Press, 1985.

Lukes, Stephen. *Power: A Radical View*. New York: Macmillan, 1974.

———. ed. *Power*. New York: New York University Press, 1986.

Maier, Charles S. "The Two Postwar Eras and the Conditions for Stability in Twentieth-Century Western Europe." *American Historical Review* 86 No. 2 (1981): 327–52.

March, James G., and Johan P. Olsen. "The New Institutionalism: Organizational Factors in Political Life." *American Political Science Review* 78 No. 4 (1984): 734–49.

Markowitz, Norman D. *The Rise and Fall of the People's Century: Henry A. Wallace and American Liberalism, 1941–1948.* New York: Free Press, 1973.

Markusen, Ann, Peter Hall, Scott Campbell, and Sabina Deitrick. *The Rise of the Gunbelt.* New York: Oxford University Press, 1991.

Mayhew, David. *Congress: The Electoral Connection.* New Haven: Yale University Press, 1974.

McClure, Arthur F. *The Truman Administration and the Problems of Postwar Labor, 1945–1948.* Rutherford, N.J.: Fairleigh Dickinson University Press, 1969.

McConnell, Grant. *Private Power and American Democracy.* New York: Knopf, 1966.

McCullough, David. *Truman.* New York: Simon & Schuster, 1992.

Milgate, Murray. *Capital and Employment.* New York: Academic Press, 1982.

Miliband, Ralph. *The State in Capitalist Society.* New York: Basic Books, 1969.

Miller, Gary J., and Terry M. Moe. "Bureaucrats, Legislators and the Size of Government." *American Political Science Review* 77 No. 2 (June 1983): 297–322.

Miller, Glenn W. *American Labor and the Government.* New York: Prentice-Hall, 1948.

Miller, John Perry. *Pricing of Military Procurements.* Studies in National Policy. New Haven: Yale University Press, 1949.

Millis, Harry A., and Emily Clark Brown. *From the Wagner Act to Taft-Hartley.* Chicago: University of Chicago Press, 1950.

Millis, Walter. *Arms and the State: Civil-Military Elements in National Policy.* With Harvey Mansfield and Harold Stein. New York: Twentieth Century Fund, 1958.

Millett, John D. "The Direction of Supply Activities in the War Department; An Administrative Survey, I." *American Political Science Review* 38 No. 2 (1944): 249–65.

———. "The Direction of Supply Activities in the War Department; An Administrative Survey, II." *American Political Science Review* 38 No. 3 (1944): 475–98.

Mills, C. Wright. *The Power Elite.* New York: Oxford University Press, 1956.

Milward, Alan S. *War, Economy and Society, 1939–1945.* Berkeley: University of California Press, 1979 [1977].

Mingos, Howard. "The Rise of the Aircraft Industry." In G. R. Simonson, ed. *The History of the American Aircraft Industry.* Cambridge, Mass.: Massachusetts Institute of Technology Press, 1968.

Moe, Terry M. "The New Economics of Organization." *American Journal of Political Science* 28 (1984): 739–77.

———. "Control and Feedback in Economic Regulation: The Case of the NLRB." *American Political Science Review* 79 No. 4 (1985): 1094–1116.

———. "Interests, Institutions, and Positive Theory: The Politics of the NLRB." In *Studies in American Political Development*, 2. Karen Orren and Stephen Skowronek, eds. New Haven: Yale University Press, 1987.

Monsees, Carl H. *Industry-Government Cooperation: A Study of the Participation of Advisory Committees in Public Administration.* Washington, D.C.: Public Affairs Press, 1944.

Moody's Manual of Investments: American and Foreign. New York, 1928–1954.

Morris, James M. *Our Maritime Heritage: Marine Developments and Their Impact on American Lives.* Lanham, Md.: University Press of America, 1978.

Morriss, Peter. *Power: A Philosophic Analysis.* New York: St. Martin's, 1987.

Mrozek, Donald J. "The Truman Administration and the Enlistment of the Aviation Industry in Postwar Defense." *Business History Review* 47 No. 1 (1974): 73–94.

Murphy, Henry C. *National Debt in War and Transition.* New York: McGraw-Hill, 1950.

Musgrave, Richard A., and Peggy B. Musgrave. *Public Finance in Theory and Practice.* Fourth Edition. New York: McGraw-Hill, 1984.

Myers, Robert J. *Social Insurance and Allied Government Programs.* Homewood, Ill.: Irwin, 1965.

Nelson, Donald M. *Arsenal of Democracy: The Story of American War Production.* New York: Harcourt Brace, 1946.

Nettl, J. P. "The State as a Conceptual Variable." *World Politics* 20 (July 1968): 559–92.

Neustadt, Richard E. *Presidential Power.* New York: Wiley, 1980 [1960].

———. "Congress and the Fair Deal: A Legislative Balance Sheet." In Richard M. Abrams and Lawrence Levine, eds. *The Shaping of Twentieth Century America.* Boston: Little, Brown, 1965.

Nordlinger, Eric A. *On the Autonomy of the Democratic State.* Cambridge, Mass.: Harvard University Press, 1981.

———. "Taking the State Seriously." In Myron Weiner and Samuel P. Huntington, eds. *Understanding Political Development.* Boston: Little, Brown, 1987.

Nordlinger, Eric A., Theodore J. Lowi, and Sergio Fabbrini. "The Return to the State: Critiques." *American Political Science Review* 82 No. 3 (September 1988): 875–901.

Nye, Joseph. "Neorealism and Neoliberalism." *World Politics* 40 No. 2 (1988): 235–51.

O'Brian, John Lord, and Manly Fleishmann. "The War Production Board and Adminstrative Policies and Procedures." *The George Washington Law Review* 13 No. 1 (1944): 1–60.

O'Connor, James. *The Fiscal Crisis of the State.* New York: St. Martin's, 1973.

Offe, Claus. "Structural Problems of the Capitalist State." In Claus von Beyme, ed. *German Political Studies* 1 (1974): 31–55.

Offe, Claus, and Volker Runge. "Theses on the Theory of the State." *New German Critique* 6 (1975): 137–48.

Olson, Mancur. *The Logic of Collective Action.* Cambridge, Mass.: Harvard University Press, 1965.

Orloff, Ann Shola, and Theda Skocpol. "Why Not Equal Protection? Explaining the Politics of Public Social Spending in Britain, 1900–1911, and the United States, 1880s–1920." *American Sociological Review* 49 (December 1984): 726–50.

Orren, Karen. "Liberalism, Money and the Situation of Organized Labor." In J. David Greenstone, ed. *Public Values & Private Power in American Politics.* Chicago: University of Chicago Press, 1982.

Orren, Karen. "Union Politics and Postwar Liberalism in the United States, 1946–

1979." In *Studies in American Political Development*, 1. Karen Orren and Stephen Skowronek, eds. New Haven: Yale University Press, 1986.

Padgett, John F. "Bounded Rationality in Budget Research." *American Political Science Review* 74 No. 2 (March 1980): 354–72.

———. "Hierarchy and Ecological Control in Federal Budgetary Decision Making." *American Journal of Sociology* 87 No. 1 (1981): 75–129.

———. "The Alchemist of Contingency Theory." *American Journal of Sociology* 99 No. 5 (March 1992): 1462–71.

Page, Benjamin I., and Mark P. Petracca. *The American Presidency*. New York: McGraw-Hill, 1983.

Patterson, Bradley H., Jr. *The Ring of Power*. New York: Basic Books, 1988.

Peacock, Alan T., and Jack Wiseman. *The Growth of Public Expenditures*. Princeton: Princeton University Press, 1961.

———. "Approaches to the Analysis of Government Expenditure Growth." *Public Finance Quarterly* 7 No. 1 (January 1979): 3–23.

Peck, Merton J., and Frederic M. Scherer. *The Weapons Acquisition Process*. Boston: Division of Research, Graduate School of Business Administration, Harvard University, 1962.

Perrett, Geoffrey. *Days of Sadness, Years of Triumph: The American People 1939–1945*. New York: Coward, McCann & Geoghegan, 1973.

———. *A Country Made by War*. New York: Random House, 1989.

Perrow, Charles. *Complex Organizations: A Critical Essay*. Third Edition. New York: Random House, 1986.

Pfeffer, Jeffrey. "A Resource Dependence Perspective on Intercorporate Relations." In Mark Mizruchi and Michael Schwartz, eds. *Intercorporate Relations*. Cambridge: Cambridge University Press, 1987.

Pfeffer, Jeffrey, and Gerald Salancik. *The External Control of Organizations: A Resource Dependence Perspective*. New York: Harper & Row, 1978.

Pious, Richard M. *The American Presidency*. New York: Basic Books, 1979.

Poen, Monte M. *Harry S. Truman Versus the Medical Lobby: The Genesis of Medicare*. Columbia: University of Missouri Press, 1979.

Polenberg, Richard. *War and Society: The United States, 1941–1945*. Philadelphia: Lippincott, 1972.

Pomper, Gerald. "Labor and Congress: The Repeal of Taft-Hartley." *Labor History* 2 (Fall 1961): 323–43.

Poulantzas, Nicos. *Political Power and Social Classes*. New York: Verso, 1987.

Preis, Art. *Labor's Giant Step*. New York: Pioneer Press, 1964.

Quadagno, Jill. "Welfare Capitalism and the Social Security Act of 1935." *American Sociological Review* 49 No. 4 (October 1984): 632–47.

———. "Two Models of Welfare State Development: Reply to Skocpol and Amenta." *American Sociological Review* 50 No. 3 (1985): 575–78.

———. *The Transformation of Old Age Security: Class and Politics in the American Welfare State*. Chicago: University of Chicago Press, 1988.

Rae, John B. *Climb to Greatness: The American Aircraft Industry, 1920–1960*. Cambridge, Mass.: Massachusetts Institute of Technology Press, 1968.

Rasler, Karen A., and William R. Thompson. "Global War, Public Debts, and the Long Cycle." *World Politics* 35 (1983): 489–516.

————. "War Making and State Making: Government Expenditures, Tax Revenues, and Global Wars." *American Political Science Review* 79 No. 2 (March 1985): 491–507.

Rearden, Steven L. *History of the Office of the Secretary of Defense*, Vol. 1: *The Formative Years 1947–1950*. Alfred Goldberg, general ed. Washington, D.C.: Historical Office of the Office of the Secretary of Defense, 1984.

Reedy, George E. *The Twilight of the Presidency*. New York: New American Library, 1970.

Rimlinger, Gaston V. *Welfare Policy and Industrialization in Europe, America and Russia*. New York: Wiley, 1971.

Robertson, David Brian. "The Bias of American Federalism: The Limits of Welfare-State Development in the Progressive Era." *Journal of Policy History* 1 No. 3 (1989): 262–91.

Robertson, Dennis H. "Some Notes on Mr. Keynes' General Theory of Employment." *Quarterly Journal of Economics* 51 (1937): 168–91.

Rockoff, Hugh. "The Response of the Giant Corporations to Wage and Price Controls in World War II." *Journal of Economic History* 41 No. 1 (1981): 123–28.

Rogers, Joel. "Divide and Conquer: The Legal Foundations of Postwar U.S. Labor Policy." Ph.D. diss., Princeton University, 1984.

Roosevelt, Franklin D. *The Public Papers and Addresses of Franklin D. Roosevelt*. Samuel I. Rosenman, comp. New York: Harper & Brothers, 1950.

Rosen, Steve, ed. *Testing the Theory of the Military-Industrial Complex*. Lexington, Mass.: Lexington Books, 1973.

Rosenberg, Gerald N. *The Hollow Hope: Can Courts Bring About Social Change?* Chicago: University of Chicago Press, 1991.

Rosenman, Samuel I. *Working with Roosevelt*. New York: Da Capo Press, 1972 [1952].

Ross, Davis B. *Preparing for Ulysses: Politics and Veterans during World War II*. New York: Columbia University Press, 1969.

Rossiter, Clinton. *The Supreme Court and the Commander in Chief*. Ithaca: Cornell University Press, 1951.

Russett, Bruce M. *What Price Vigilance?* New Haven: Yale University Press, 1970.

Samuelson, Paul A. "Fiscal Policy and Income Determination." *Quarterly Journal of Economics* 56 (1942): 575–605.

Schattschneider, E. E. *The Semi-Sovereign People*. Hinsdale, Ill.: Dryden Press, 1975 [1960].

Scher, Seymour S. "The National Labor Relations Board and Congress—A Study of Legislative Control of Regulatory Activity." Ph.D. diss., University of Chicago, 1956.

Schlesinger, Arthur Meier. *The Rise of Modern America*. New York: Macmillan, 1951.

Schlesinger, Arthur M., Jr. *The Imperial Presidency*. Boston: Houghton Mifflin, 1973.

Seidman, Joel. *American Labor from Defense to Reconversion*. Chicago: University of Chicago Press, 1953.

Selznick, Philip. *TVA and the Grass Roots: A Study of Politics and Organization*. Berkeley: University of California Press, 1949.

Shafer, Byron E., ed. *Is America Different?* Oxford: Clarendon Press, 1991.

Sherry, Michael S. *The Rise of American Air Power*. New Haven: Yale University Press, 1987.

Sherwood, Robert E. *The White House Papers of Harry L. Hopkins*, Vol. 1: *September 1939 – January 1942*. London: Eyre & Spottiswoode, 1948.

———. *The White House Papers of Harry L. Hopkins*, Vol. 2: *January 1942 – July 1945*. London: Eyre & Spottiswoode, 1948.

Silverstone, Paul H. *U.S. Warships of World War II*. Garden City, N.Y.: Doubleday, 1965.

Simmel, Georg. *Conflict & the Web of Group Affiliations*. Translated by Kurt H. Wolff and Reinhard Bendix. New York: Free Press, 1955.

Simonson, G. R., ed. *The History of the American Aircraft Industry*. Cambridge, Mass.: Massachusetts Institute of Technology Press, 1968.

Singer, J. David. "The Level-of-Analysis Problem in International Relations." In Klaus Knorr and Sidney Verba, eds. *The International System: Theoretic Essays*. Princeton: Princeton University Press, 1961.

Skocpol, Theda. *States and Social Revolutions*. Cambridge: Cambridge University Press, 1979.

———. "Political Responses to the Capitalist Crisis: Neo-marxist Theories of the State and the Case of the New Deal." *Politics & Society* 10 No. 2 (1980): 155–201.

———. "A Society Without a 'State'? Political Organization, Social Conflict, and Welfare Provision in the United States." Manuscript. Harvard University, 1988.

Skocpol, Theda, and Edwin Amenta. "Did Capitalists Shape Social Security?" (Comment on Quadagno, *ASR*, October 1984). *American Sociological Review* 50 No. 3 (1985): 572–75.

———. "States and Social Policies." *Annual Review of Sociology* 12 (1986): 131–57.

Skocpol, Theda, and Kenneth Finegold. "State Capacity and Economic Intervention in the Early New Deal." *Political Science Quarterly* 97 No. 2 (1982): 255–78.

Skocpol, Theda, and G. John Ikenberry. "The Political Formation of the American Welfare State in Historical and Comparative Perspective." *Comparative Social Research* 6 (1983): 87–148.

Skocpol, Theda, and Margaret Somers. "The Uses of Comparative History in Macrosocial Inquiry." *Comparative Studies in Society and History* 22 (1980): 174–97.

Skowronek, Stephen L. *Building a New American State: The Expansion of National Administrative Capacities, 1877–1920*. Cambridge: Cambridge University Press, 1982.

Smith, J. Malcolm, and Stephen Jurika. *The President and National Security*. Dubuque, Iowa: Kendall/Hunt, 1972.

Somers, Herman Miles. *Presidential Agency: OWMR, the Office of War Mobilization and Reconversion*. Cambridge, Mass.: Harvard University Press, 1950.

Sparrow, Bartholomew H. "From the Outside In: The Effects of World War II on the American State." Ph.D. diss., University of Chicago, 1991.

Starr, Paul. *The Social Transformation of American Medicine*. New York: Basic Books, 1982.

Stein, Arthur A. *The Nation at War*. Baltimore: Johns Hopkins University Press, 1975.

Stein, Herbert. *The Fiscal Revolution in America*. Chicago: University of Chicago Press, 1969.

Stepan, Alfred. *The State and Society*. Princeton: Princeton University Press, 1978.

Stevens, Beth. "Labor Unions, Employee Benefits, and the Privatization of the American Welfare State." *Journal of Policy History* 2 No. 3 (1990): 233–60.

Stimson, Henry L., and McGeorge Bundy. *On Active Service in Peace and War*. New York: Harper & Brothers, 1948.

Stinchcombe, Arthur L. *Information and Organizations*. Berkeley: University of California Press, 1990.

Stone, I. F. *The War Years 1939–1945*. A Non-Conformist History of Our Times. Boston: Little, Brown, 1988.

———. *The Truman Era 1945–1952*. A Non-Conformist History of Our Times. Boston: Little, Brown, 1972 [1953].

Strayer, Paul J. *Fiscal Policy and Politics*. New York: Harper & Brothers, 1958.

Studenski, Paul, and Herman E. Krooss. *The Financial History of the United States*. New York: McGraw-Hill, 1952.

Swanborough, Gordon, and Peter M. Bowers. *United States Navy Aircraft Since 1911*. Second Edition. Annapolis, Md.: Naval Institute Press, 1968.

Taft, Philip. *Organized Labor in American History*. New York: Harper & Row, 1964.

Tatalovich, Raymond, and Byron W. Daynes. *Presidential Power in the United States*. Belmont, Calif.: Wadsworth, 1984.

Taussig, F. W. "Employment and the National Dividend." *Quarterly Journal of Economics* 51 (1937): 198–203.

Thompson, James D. *Organizations in Action*. New York: McGraw-Hill, 1967.

Tilly, Charles, ed. *The Formation of National States in Western Europe*. Princeton: Princeton University Press, 1975.

———. *Coercion, Capital, and European States AD 990–1990*. Cambridge, Mass.: Basil Blackwell, 1990.

Timberlake, Richard H. *Monetary Policy in the United States: An Intellectual and Institutional History*. Chicago: University of Chicago Press, 1978.

Tomlins, Christopher L. *The State and the Unions*. Cambridge: Cambridge University Press, 1985.

Trimble, William F. "The Naval Aircraft Factory, the American Aviation Industry, and Government Competition, 1919–1928." *Business History Review* 60 No. 2 (1986): 175–98.

Truman, David B. *The Governmental Process*. New York: Knopf, 1962.

Truman, Harry S. *Memoirs of Harry S. Truman*, Vol. 1: *Years of Decisions*. New York: Da Capo Press, 1955.

———. *Memoirs of Harry S. Truman*, Vol. 2: *Years of Trial and Hope*. New York: Da Capo Press, 1956.

———. *Off the Record: The Private Papers of Harry S. Truman*. Robert H. Ferrell, ed. New York: Penguin, 1980.

Tulis, Jeffrey K. *The Rhetorical Presidency*. Princeton: Princeton University Press, 1987.

Tushman, Michael L., and Elaine Romanelli. "Organizational Evolution: A Metamorphosis Model of Convergence and Reorientation." In Barry M. Staw and L. L. Cummings, eds. *The Evolution and Adaptation of Organizations*. Greenwich, Conn.: JAI Press, 1990.

U.S. Bureau of the Budget. *The United States at War*. Washington, D.C.: U.S. GPO, 1946.

U.S. Department of Labor. *The National Wage Stabilization Board*. Washington, D.C.: U.S. GPO, n.d.

U.S. National War Labor Board. *The Termination Report of the U.S. National War Labor Board*. Washington, D.C.: U.S. GPO, n.d.

Vander Meulen, Jacob. *The Politics of Aircraft*. Lawrence: University of Kansas Press, 1991.

Vatter, Harold G. *The U.S. Economy in World War II*. Columbia Studies in Business, Government, and Society. Eli Noam, ed. New York: Columbia University Press, 1985.

Viner, Jacob. "Mr. Keynes on the Causes of Unemployment." *Quarterly Journal of Economics* 51 (1937): 147–67.

———. "The United States as a Welfare State." In S. W. Higginbotham, ed. *Man, Science, Learning and Education*. Semicentennial Lectures at Rice University. Rice University Studies, Supplement 2 to Vol. 49. Houston: William Marsh Rice University, 1963.

Waltz, Kenneth. *Man, the State and War*. New York: Columbia University Press, 1959.

———. *Theory of International Politics*. New York: Random House, 1979.

Warne, Colston, ed. *Labor in Postwar America*. Brooklyn: Remsen Press, 1949.

Weaver, Carolyn L. "The Social Security Bureaucracy in Triumph and in Crisis." In Louis Galambos, ed. *The New American State: Bureaucracies and Policies since World War II*. Baltimore: Johns Hopkins University Press, 1987.

Weaver, R. Kent. "The Politics of Blame Avoidance." *Journal of Public Policy* 6 No. 4 (1986): 371–98.

Weber, Max. *Economy and Society*. Guenther Roth and Claus Wittich, eds. Berkeley: University of California Press, 1978.

———. *From Max Weber: Essays in Sociology*. H. H. Gerth and C. Wright Mills, trans. and eds. New York: Oxford University Press, 1946.

Weir, Margaret. "Ideas and Politics: The Acceptance of Keynesianism in Britain and the United States." In Peter A. Hall, ed. *The Political Power of Economic Ideas*. Princeton: Princeton University Press, 1989.

Weir, Margaret, Ann Shola Orloff, and Theda Skocpol, eds. *The Politics of Social Policy in the United States*. Princeton: Princeton University Press, 1988.

Weir, Margaret, and Theda Skocpol. "State Structures and the Possibilities for 'Keynesian' Responses to the Great Depression in Sweden, Britain, and the United States." In Evans, Rueschemeyer, and Skocpol, eds. *Bringing the State Back In*. Cambridge: Cambridge University Press, 1985.

Wildavsky, Aaron. "The Two Presidencies." In Aaron Wildavsky, ed. *Perspectives on the Presidency*. Boston: Little, Brown, 1975.

Williamson, Oliver E. *Markets and Hierarchies: Analysis and Antitrust Implications*. New York: Free Press, 1975.

Witney, Fred. *Wartime Experiences of the National Labor Relations Board*. Urbana: University of Illinois Press, 1949.

Witte, John F. *The Politics and Development of the Federal Income Tax*. Madison: University of Wisconsin Press, 1985.

Woods, Randall B., and Howard Jones. *Dawning of the Cold War: The United States' Quest for Order*. Athens: University of Georgia Press, 1991.

Woytinsky, W. S. "What Was Wrong In Forecasts of Postwar Depression." *Journal of Political Economy* 55 No. 2 (April 1947): 142–51.

Young, Edwin. "The Split in the Labor Movement." In Milton Derber and Edwin Young, eds. *Labor and the New Deal*. Madison: University of Wisconsin Press, 1957.

Young, Roland. *Congressional Politics in the Second World War*. New York: Da Capo Press, 1972.

Index

About the Author

BARTHOLOMEW H. SPARROW is Assistant Professor of Government at the University of Texas at Austin. The work on which this book is based received both the Leonard D. White Award and the Franklin L. Burdette Pi Sigma Alpha Award of the American Political Science Association.